D1516228

WITHDRAWN

IDENTITY PAPERS

IDENTITY PAPERS

Contested Nationhood in Twentieth-Century France

Steven Ungar and Tom Conley, editors

University of Minnesota Press
Minneapolis
London

Copyright 1996 by the Regents of the University of Minnesota
A different version of Rosemarie Scullion, "Family Fictions and Reproductive Realities
in Vichy France: Claude Chabrol's *Une Affaire de femmes*," appeared in *L'Esprit Créateur*
33.1 (Spring 1993), used by permission.

All rights reserved. No part of this publication may be reproduced, stored in a
retrieval system, or transmitted, in any form or by any means, electronic, mechanical,
photocopying, recording, or otherwise, without the prior written permission of
the publisher.

Published by the University of Minnesota Press
111 Third Avenue South, Suite 290, Minneapolis, MN 55401-2520
Printed in the United States of America on acid-free paper

Library of Congress Cataloging-in-Publication Data

Identity papers : contested nationhood in twentieth-century France /
    Steven Ungar and Tom Conley, editors.
        p.   cm.
    Includes bibliographical references and index.
    ISBN 0-8166-2694-4. — ISBN 0-8166-2695-2 (pbk.)
    1. National characteristics, French.   2. Multiculturalism—France.
3. France—Civilization—20th century.   4. Nationalism in
literature.   5. Ethnicity—France.   I. Ungar, Steven, 1945-
II. Conley, Tom.
DC34.I34   1996
944.08—dc20   95-26623

The University of Minnesota is an equal-opportunity educator and employer.

DC
34
.I34
1996

030497-2760R

For Robin, Verena, and Powerhouse

Contents

Acknowledgments

The origins of this book go back to 1966–68, when graduate work at the University of Wisconsin-Madison with Germaine Brée, Elaine Marks, and Alfred Glauser introduced us to the full range of French studies that built on an interplay of language, literature, ideas, and history. Beyond the facts, concepts, and skills that they conveyed, each in her and his own way, these three challenged us to read with intelligence and to write with clarity. In so doing, they also conveyed a respect for intellectual generosity that we have sought to emulate in our teaching and writing. *Aime bien qui critique bien.*

For their work on proofreading and the index, we thank Janette Bayles and Kathryn Karczewska.

This project has been supported by The University of Iowa Obermann Center for Advanced Studies. Thanks, once again, to Jay Semel and Lorna Olson.

Introduction: Questioning Identity

Steven Ungar

Acculturation is the rule. One is not born French (in this sense of the word);
one becomes French.   *Tzvetan Todorov*

The title of this collection explores a slippage in meaning among those in twentieth-century France for whom the category of citizenship has increasingly separated from identity, understood in both individual and collective expressions.
This slippage has been heightened among naturalized foreigners for whom acquired citizenship has increased the feelings of difference and exclusion it was
once expected to alleviate or even end. From the start, the English terms *alien*
and *foreigner* that translate the French *étranger* convey an ambivalence linking
the assertion of national identity to attitudes concerning race and ethnicity.
Strong and persistent, these links are most often denied or "forgotten" through
silence and omission. Tzvetan Todorov has argued that the common grounding
of nationalism and racism in affect is tempered by significant differences.
Whereas nationalism leads naturally to xenophobia by asserting from within
the priority or privilege of citizens against foreigners, racism casts difference in
the individual man or woman: "One can change one's nation, not one's race
(the first notion is moral, the second physical). The nationalist operates on a
single plane, even if he changes sector; he attaches moral judgments to differences in political status and cultural membership. The racist, for his part, establishes a relationship between two different planes, by assimilating the moral

1

to the physical."[1] As Todorov concludes, these conceptual differences remain important despite the fact that nationalism and racism often coexist.

Todorov's remarks corroborate my sense that some of the intensity in recent debate surrounding national identity in France originates in a displacement of affect from the general attitudes concerning race and ethnicity to localized debate surrounding immigration. Returning to Frenchness and identity in light of the latter, one might wonder to what extent it is natural for someone born in Berlin, Saigon, Bamako, or Fez to become French when such naturalization imposes norms, values, and conventions that are anything but natural. The point is enhanced by the expression *Français par acquisition*, as though a commodified Frenchness equated with citizenship were essentially distinct from its native—that is, "natural" or biological and presumably authentic—strain. Immigration remains an integral—and, for some, even a predominant—aspect of debate surrounding the idea of nation in twentieth-century France. Whether one asserts the primacy/priority of citizenship over identity or vice versa, consensus all along the political spectrum holds that naturalization "no longer performs as it once had."[2] What gives the current breakdown singular urgency is the equation of naturalization and assimilation. If citizenship coincides less and less with identity on a lived basis—and it remains unclear to what extent they ever coincided in a strict sense—noncoincidence measures the fact that citizenship no longer entails an absolute commitment on the part of the would-be *Français(es) par acquisition* to reject aspects of their culture by conforming to the norms of a Frenchness they might well consider alien and unacceptable. Where tradition has cast American society as a melting pot of multiple cultures and subcultures, French immigration policies since the Third Republic have tended to assimilate difference in the name of a single nation and a single culture.

Long after France's colonies and protectorates attained self-rule, the equation of citizenship and assimilation has extended practices linked to colonial sensibilities by imposing acculturation that appropriates rather than integrates difference.[3] Resistance to assimilation on the part of resident minorities in France derives at least in part from the fact that the acculturation to which, for some, any would-be citizens ought to aspire is often perceived from the side of the potential *Français(es) par acquisition* as a deculturation that would leave them decidedly between cultures. If the terms are shifted from citizenship, naturalization, and immigration in order to consider instead the place of foreigners in France, much of what is at stake in current debate can be conveyed by asserting that the place of foreigners in France is in France. Along the lines of a slogan adapted from the rhetoric of contemporary gay and lesbian activism, one might assert that foreigners are here (or "there") to stay. Such an assertion measures the extent to which a prevalent model of citizenship grounded in assimilation breaks down in ways that are perceived as threats to the future of France as a nation, society, and state.

Because many North African and sub-Saharan Muslims living in France consider religion the prime point of reference of their identity over and above concurrent citizenship, there is reason to believe that whether or not these Muslims become French in the strict sense of acquiring citizenship, their devotion to Islam is likely to make them unassimilable. If members of these Islamic minorities become citizens, they will inevitably transform French identity in its present expression. If they do not, they will continue to constitute a threat as an unassimilated minority.[4] Either way, the impact of their presence on the future of France is undeniable. Strict curbs on immigration such as those proposed in June 1993 by Edouard Balladur do little to alleviate the force of a resident minority—whether naturalized, temporary, or illegal—whose presence is increasingly militant.

The guarantee afforded by identity equated with citizenship is often taken for granted. Among those who carry and display passports for purposes of travel across international borders, the force of this guarantee is experienced negatively in the form of a challenge, as when mobility assumed to have been granted is questioned and revoked. This challenge is all the more daunting when it occurs not at a designated point of passage across borders, but unexpectedly as a claim to rightful presence. Random checks—"un petit contrôle, s'il vous plaît"—on the métro or on the train are anything but simple or innocent. These interpellations operate as minor elements within networks of surveillance whose demand to show cause for rightful presence—"Vos papiers! [Your papers!]"—is enhanced by the absence of a verb. The primal scene evoked has the force of a nightmare recalling any number of films embedded with the image of a Nazi soldier barking his command to a foreigner or maybe even a Jew—yet exactly how might foreignness or Jewishness be visible?—in a Vichy France reduced to submission.

Sad to say, it is all too easy to imagine the previous scene restaged today—fifty years after the Liberation—in a presumably "open" France. This time, however, the principals might be a member of the police or CRS and a nonwhite whose physical appearance marks an identity presumably in need of checking. Slippage in this case would obtain between identification understood as evidence of acceptable and/or legitimated identity and the set of rights that this identity validates. To determine identity through identification in this instance—"Vos papiers!" or the paternalist variant, "Tes papiers!"—asserts a power over those for whom rightful presence would appear—once again, one wonders exactly why—open to ongoing challenge. As a contributor to this collection notes through a recent quote from *Le Monde*, the demand to require the Algerian or the Senegalese to produce on demand proof of identity is also to seek reassurance about Frenchness ("about who we are").[5] The irony sharpens when the "other" turns out to hold French citizenship. Nonwhite adolescents and especially *Beurs* are routinely picked up and asked for their papers. A sixteen-year-old student born in France of Moroccan parents complains that even when he presents credentials showing that he is French, the police assume the papers are false. A government immigration expert, Jean-Claude Barreau, asserts that the French are not racists, before adding that what they want is for foreigners to become French, to be discreet about religion, to become integrated at schools as individuals: "Now, for the first time, we have people born in France who are not French."[6]

My remarks on the *petit contrôle* respond to what I have come to see on a larger scale in post-World War II France as a progressive loss of faith in identity linked to collective categories such as society and nation. This loss is discernible among both those it oppresses on a daily basis and others such as myself who experience it infrequently and in large part from outside. Not claiming to be French through birth, acquired citizenship, or an acculturation that allows me to emit unquestionable signs of Frenchness, my identity as an American who may (or may not) pass at times for French is something I have come to accept less as a liability or deviation from a perceived norm than as a condition of in-betweenness or hybridity (*métissage*) that I have learned to assert to my advantage.[7] Frequent visits to and extended residence in France over the past thirty years have confirmed another slippage of identity associated in formal logic with a condition of necessary sameness. If France is no longer what it was five, ten, or fifty years ago, who is better qualified than an informed and presumably sympathetic outsider to chart differences that daily exposure might fail to reveal? Images of France in the decade of its current *fin de siècle* range from Euro-Disney and fast food outlets on the Champs-Elysées to les Halles as a multi-level underground shopping center with its own *vidéothèque* and the TGV (*train à grande vitesse*) that reduces rail travel between Paris and Marseille to four hours. Even more daunting is the new Bibliothèque de France, often referred to as the TGB (*très grande bibliothèque*) in ironic parallel with the TGV. What, then, would it mean—both practically and symbolically—for the venerable BN (Bibliothèque Nationale) to get up to technological speed on a global *autoroute de l'informatique*?

This volume is concerned with little scenes instead of big pictures. The essays in this collection are meant to inform further debate surrounding national identity in France by providing case studies in a variety of contexts and media. The immediate origin of this collection is a series of special sessions organized in conjunction with the ninth and tenth International Colloquia on Twentieth-Century French Studies, held at the University of Pennsylvania (March 1992) and the University of Colorado (March 1993).

The late Fernand Braudel noted at the start of his last book, *The Identity of France*, that the profession of historian had changed so utterly in the previous half century that the images and problems of the past had taken on a completely new complexion. These images and problems, he continued, "still unavoidably confronted us, but in different terms."[8] The change attributed by Braudel to a difference in terms was set against a more constant (durable?) element in the form of an "us." Perhaps Braudel never clarified this usage because the referent of the first-person plural was the tacit and seemingly all-inclusive "we French" (*nous autres Français*). Alternatively, Braudel's failure to clarify the designation may have subtended his entire inquiry so that the status of collective identity remained a basic problem with which his study was meant to contend.

Readers of Braudel's earlier studies on the Mediterranean world in the Age of Philip II and on capitalism and material life from 1400 to 1800 know the importance he placed on long duration (*la longue durée*) of up to several centuries at a time. Long duration was the grounding element of a model of temporality that also included the shorter durations of the conjuncture (eras and ages ranging from decades to centuries) and the discrete event. Braudel mixed not only durations, but disciplines. Following the example of his mentors, Marc Bloch and Lucien Febvre, he drew freely from geography, economics, and demography. The result was a writing of history that subsumed the shorter durations of event and conjuncture within the permanence of a *longue durée* that remained for Braudel the significant level of understanding. Yet when, in *The Identity of France*, Braudel reasserted his ambition to write a total history of France, he was also responding to Marc Bloch's view that there is no French history apart from European history. In this sense, Braudel believed that although the autonomy of national history is neither expropriated nor obliterated by a dialogue with the outside world, the obligatory dialogue is nonetheless burdensome: "The *longue durée* then (first and indeed foremost), the hexagon [*sic*], Europe, the world—these are the dimensions of space and time for which I will be working."[9]

Such caveats show that Braudel understood what was at stake in his making such introductory statements at a moment when the transition from a Gaullist vision of postwar France to François Mitterrand's France of the 1980s cast those statements as conservative and perhaps even retrograde. Braudel's reader may wonder all the more today to what extent the position he took at the start of the 1980s has shown itself in the interim as prophetic or untimely. Especially troubling is Braudel's assertion of a permanence grounded in terms of space and geography (primacy of the "Hexagone") as well as his apparent reluctance to engage the emergent aspects of difference in a France undergoing vast economic, demographic, and cultural shifts. In the words of Perry Anderson, the double force of the term *identity* in the title of Braudel's last book denotes both what subsists and what distinguishes: "The premise of Braudel's multi-disciplinary enquiry is that the particular and the permanent in France have been one."[10] Even Braudel's meditation at the end of *The Identity of France* on the future of North African populations within a society resistant to a growing Islamic minority only began to engage the deep impact that France under Mitterrand had begun to undergo.

In his monumental *France 1848–1945*, published about a decade before Braudel's *Identity of France*, Theodore Zeldin had argued that the exaggeration of difference and diversity in nineteenth-century France was offset not just by attempts to unite politics throughout—and even beyond—the Hexagone, but also by a school system whose fabled uniformity promoted a common heritage linked to the singularity of a civilization that was irreducibly national:

> To be a Frenchman, in the fullest sense, meant to be civilised, which required that one accepted the models of thought, behaviour, and expression held to esteem in Paris. At one level, to accept civilisation meant to accept cultural uniformity and centralisation. By this definition, to be a Frenchman meant more than being born in France, or to be a mere peasant; it involved adherence to a set of values, but in return one could hope to benefit from all the rewards that the state showered on those who adopted those values.[11]

When, a few pages later, Zeldin notes that civilization is, to some extent, a war cry preaching peace, the intended irony played on the implicit links between this strong sense of France's civilizing mission and a concomitant emphasis on race cast along the lines of a cultural crusade. Herman Lebovics has taken Zeldin one step further by analyzing conflicts surrounding divergence and assimilation viewed as wars over cultural identity staged in the name of a "true France." Lebovics traces the rise and fall of this essentialist idea of Frenchness constructed by a discontented right that laid claim to exclusive control over a French identity grounded in a cultural universalism inherited from Gallican Catholicism. Grounding his demonstration on the notion of anthropology embodied in the figure of Louis Marin, staged at the 1931 Colonial Exposition, and cast in the discourse of traditional popular arts under Vichy, Lebovics argues for the disastrous effects of a conservative vision of French identity grounded on the values of "a small-town, traditional, Catholic, imperial society."[12] The result is a compelling series of insights into how the notorious mission to civilize associated with colonial rule was brought home to France through attempts to implement a conservative vision of national culture that was profoundly static and antihistorical.

By exploring how debate surrounding identity was recast in terms of culture from the Dreyfus affair to the 1944–45 Liberation, Lebovics traces the extent of ongoing irresolution that surrounded the nature of France's national heritage (*patrimoine*) as well as the matter of who was authorized to speak for it. By focusing on various claims to speak for a "true France," Lebovics seeks to determine not simply the content of the claims themselves, but the evolving sites and ambitions of culture identified with what Benedict Anderson has referred to as feelings of "nationness."[13] This same focus allows Lebovics to direct each of his individual analyses toward wider assessments of the essentialist identity that proponents of a conservative cultural politics sought to implement between 1900 and 1945. In a typical passage combining historical specificity and a more critical objective, Lebovics asks whether the values of Saint Louis or Joan of Arc still "inspired the contemporary nation" or whether French civilization is instead a "cosmopolitan, multicultural, syncretic and ever-changing product of the lives of diverse populations" and thus irreducible to a single identity or essence.[14] The latter alternative is especially pertinent to this volume because it suggests that inscribed within the struggle ("wars") over exclusivity to speak in the name of France is a more fundamental question of why one needs to speak in terms of a French identity or essence at all. It is by contextualizing the incidence of "true France" as a discursive and historical phenomenon that Lebovics inscribes it within evolving practices of cultural chauvinism and exclusion the study of which might enhance our ways of overcoming them.[15]

The shifting of debate surrounding national identity in France from politics to culture is no longer the exclusive strategy of a discontented right. Since François Mitterrand's 1981 election as French president, it has remained a vital component of state practices grounded in progressive reform. The first three chapters in this volume address an antecedent of debate under Mitterrand by focusing on the 1937 International Exposition of Arts and Technology in Modern Life, held in Paris. In chapter 1, Shanny Peer analyzes how creators of the Rural Center sought to represent the farm and the farmer as symbols of tradition integral to France's future prosperity. Along these lines, Peer notes that the model *village-synthèse* at the Porte Maillot, which many saw as a tribute to the inhabitants of France's countryside, also expressed an attempt by the Popular Front government under Léon Blum to promote the ongoing economic importance of agriculture. This refashioning of the peasant at the 1937 Expo was anything but innocent. Its potential usefulness to agendas all along France's political spectrum appealed to groups and lobbies ranging from proponents of a nostalgic regional diversity to advocates of modernized agriculture.

The silhouette of a silo on the horizon of the Avenue Maréchal Pétain was so striking in its own right that at least one recent chronicler has wondered whether the radiant farm (*ferme radieuse*) modeled on Le Corbusier's *village radieux* did not detract from the rural center by insisting too much on aesthetics at the expense of politics.[16] In chapter 2, Elizabeth Ezra explores a similar tension between aesthetics and politics in her study of the Miss France d'Outre-mer beauty contest held at the Centre des Colonies. Ezra argues that the event held on the Ile des Cygnes and referred to as the Concours du Meilleur Mariage Colonial (Best colonial marriage contest) was itself a hybrid of colonialism and nationalism under the guise of eugenics. Components of prejudice concerning race and gender are likewise discernible in the expectation that whenever possible, each female contestant would be the product of a union between a French male and a native female from the colonies.

Eugenics served in the mid-1930s to revive a declining birthrate (*dénatalité*), presumably in preparation for future combat against Germany. The contest also staged a more abstract conflict between assimilation and association that enhanced ironies surrounding the central term of "union" that grounded the contest in a colonialist mentality of racial difference. As Ezra argues, the Miss France d'Outre-mer contest illustrated that in order to be intelligible, difference had to be domesticated (neither too white nor too nonwhite) under the normalizing gaze of the viewing audience. Only when it was transformed into lack was difference no longer seen as threatening.

Philip Solomon's essay on Louis-Ferdinand Céline's *Bagatelles pour un massacre* (Trifles for a massacre) examines the extent to which one writer perceived the display of difference at the 1937 exposition as threatening. Solomon asserts that the anti-Semitic theses set forth by Céline in *Bagatelles* went beyond allegations concerning a specific Jewish presence at the 1937 Expo toward disclosing the full range of an "implacable, conquering Jewish megalomania."[17] Contrary to Céline's denials, the catalyst for the prejudicial remarks in the pamphlet was less the exposition itself than the symbolic significance that he attributed to it. Solomon argues that statements in *Bagatelles* show a clear affinity with the chimerical assertions typical of anti-Semitic literature distributed in

France through various centers of documentation and propaganda. By showing how Céline constructed his figure of the Negro-Jew, Solomon helps to explain how a conflation of anti-Semitism and xenophobia grew from Céline's reaction to a perceived insult by the arts committee of the exposition, which had rejected the scenario of a ballet he had submitted for consideration. For Céline, this rejection was not simply a personal affront, but an assault by an irrevocably foreign group on the French, whom he portrayed as "children of the native soil."[18]

In chapter 4, Lynn Higgins traces the evolving forms of a matrix or core fable from Marcel Pagnol's 1931–40 Marseilles trilogy—*Marius*, *Fanny*, and *La Fille du puisatier* (The well-digger's daughter)—to a 1953 version of *Manon des sources* and Claude Berri's highly acclaimed 1986 remakes, *Jean de Florette* and *Manon des sources*. The fable mobilizes key elements of melodrama toward a belated disclosure of paternity that undermines the ideals of stable identity and lineage it might otherwise have reinforced. Higgins works outward from the two-volume novel of *L'Eau des collines* by relating variants of the core fable to successive crises of collective identity. She does this first by showing how the tension between nation and region on which Pagnol grounds the singular *esprit méridional* of his plays, novels, and films is supplemented by narrower oppositions such as those of the rural versus the urban, superstition and popular knowledge versus reason and technology, and—tellingly—the oral versus the written. Higgins sets these elements of form and structure against the capability to resolve contradiction that Claude Lévi-Strauss argues is a prime virtue of mythic activity. In so doing, she seemingly pits Lévi-Strauss against Jacques Derrida by arguing that if *L'Eau des collines* repeatedly fails to resolve all its contradictions, it is because these contradictions are integral to the conditions of Provençal identity that Pagnol portrays.

Each of the successive versions of Pagnol's core fable illustrates in its own way that the search for identity—whether individual or collective—yields only difference, because the heart or essence of identity, is elsewhere (*ailleurs*) and never where one expects to find it. What displaces paternity within and across the versions of Pagnol's core fable is a recurrent commitment to colonial empire and foreign military service linked to chauvinist support of the fatherland. It is a cruel irony (and only somewhat accurate) when César Soubeyran asserts belatedly that his fate was "all the fault of Africa." Even after he learns the truth concerning a paternity to which he had remained blind for years, Soubeyran still displaces the desire for displacement invoked in the phrase "J'ai envie d'ailleurs [I long for elsewhere]" at the origin of his blindness.

Jacques Feyder's and Georg Pabst's adaptations for film of Pierre Benoit's

L'Atlantide are the points of departure for David Slavin's study of the national-ist sentiment and Christian faith that, under the guise of a civilizing mission, were invoked to justify France's colonial presence in North Africa. Slavin ex-amines differences between the two adaptations of Benoit's 1918 novel before looking more closely at Charles de Foucauld, the real-life priest who inspired Benoit's Morhange. In analyzing Foucauld's cult status, Slavin asserts that the novel and its film adaptations were enhanced by popular fascination with a Berber myth of exotic otherness fueled by tourism, postcards, expositions, and ethnography.

Only in the past twenty years has access to new or discovered—often termed "forgotten"—materials documented the practices and policies of France under Vichy in ways that have questioned and often revised received understanding of the period. A major issue raised by Richard Golsan in chapter 6 is the extent to which reconsiderations of the Occupation are subject to the pitfalls of distor-tion and tendentiousness evoked by reference to revisionary practices. Golsan focuses on the reception of Louis Malle's 1974 feature film *Lacombe Lucien* as a case study of the revisionary practices in literature, film, and the popular press known as *la mode rétro*. Assessing the range of responses to Malle's film, Golsan argues that its evolving reception can be instructive about the impact of post-war views of the Occupation on French perceptions of national identity in the decade following 1968. Even more polemically, Golsan contends against the views of some critics that *Lacombe Lucien* is less a symptom than a victim of what Henry Rousso and others have called the "Vichy syndrome." Compar-isons of Malle's 1974 film with his 1987 *Au Revoir les enfants* support Golsan's remarks on the pivotal role of ambiguity around which a number of interpreta-tions and judgments have extended not only toward the accounts of the Occu-pation in his two films, but also toward recent debate surrounding judicial pro-ceedings against Klaus Barbie, Paul Touvier, and René Bousquet.

Where Golsan traces the evolving debate surrounding collaboration and re-sistance in *Lacombe Lucien*, Rosemarie Scullion analyzes the story of a female abortionist portrayed in Claude Chabrol's 1989 film, *Une Affaire de femmes*. Casting her remarks against the relative invisibility surrounding gender con-cerns in existing studies of the Occupation, Scullion explores the impact of Vichy policies concerning birthrates and the family on the daily lives of women who often provided sole support for their children. Of particular relevance in conjunction with Golsan's remarks on Malle and the Vichy syndrome are Scul-lion's remarks on the blind spots in a film that ostensibly foregrounds the plight of women under Pétain's paternalist regime. Despite reservations concerning much of what she sees as dubious in Chabrol's male-centered pathos, Scullion recognizes the success with which Chabrol portrays Marie Latour's refusal to allow her selfhood to be forgotten or her desires to be effaced.

Scullion's conclusion that Marie Latour's execution was necessary to uphold the interests of a paternalist regime complements Florianne Wild's remarks on Jewishness and scapegoating in Julien Duvivier's 1946 feature film *Panique*. Less explicit as a historical account than either *Lacombe Lucien* or *Une Affaire de femmes*, *Panique* stages an allegory of crime and punishment. Wild argues that the progression from a criminal act perpetrated by one individual on another precipitates a collective hysteria whose purging leads to violence. As in *Une Affaire de femmes*, this violence evolves toward necessity. Yet, unlike Chabrol's tendentious depiction of Vichy as a repressive order, *Panique* portrays a violence from which references to interwar or wartime France are doubled and unstable. The effect is that of a historiographic project that is skewed and puzzling. Historical elements abound, but they are dispersed into words, names, and symbols whose accumulation promotes what Wild (following René Girard) refers to as "sacrificial crisis." Allusions to the *ancien régime* and to the Revolution are unmistakable. Is it merely a coincidence that the murder victim is a certain Mademoiselle Noblet—a variant of *noble*—or that the surname of the detective investigating the case is the same as that of the nineteenth-century author of the *Histoire de la Révolution Française*, (Jules) Michelet? Wild assesses these markers of a graphic unconscious around which the film constructs the central character of Désirée Hire (played by Michel Simon) as a *victime émissaire*. Allusions to the historical past are also set against references to films of crime and mass behavior such as Fritz Lang's *M*.

T. Jefferson Kline begins his analysis of François Truffaut's 1975 *L'Histoire d'Adèle H.* by noting that it and *L'Enfant sauvage* are Truffaut's only two films explicitly anchored in a historical intent. Approaching *Adèle H.* as a film on Victor Hugo's "other" daughter, Kline links a double displacement—from Adèle to the sister, Léopoldine, who drowned at Villequier, and from Léopoldine to the father, Victor Hugo—to the attempt on the part of Truffaut to reconfigure memory by imbricating past and present. Kline asserts that the motivation for this gesture points to Truffaut's engagement with identity in terms of family and culture linked to role models such as André Bazin and—especially—Alfred Hitchcock. He also sees Truffaut's ambition to engage his own patrimony through filmmaking as tied to his desire following May 1968 to convert the story of Victor Hugo's other daughter into his (own) story.

Adèle H. illustrates the extent to which film rewrites the past as meaningful within the present. Kline concludes that Truffaut constructs memory as a dream screen of intertexts mixing the personal and the collective. What he terms, following Michel de Certeau, the experience of "autobiocinematography" contends not only with subject or content of identity within the Freudian family romance, but with reference related to films that have remained in the life of filmmaker and/or spectator through memory as a cultural datum highly charged with personal value. If Truffaut's cultural father is Alfred Hitchcock, the key film datum is Hitchcock's *Rear Window* and the key action (shades of *Panique* and *Monsieur Hire*) that of voyeurism. For Kline, the progression in *Adèle H.* from biography to autobiography mobilizes a subversive slant on Victor Hugo, the figure of paternalism at the level of both family and nation. In so doing, it posits a set of multiple displacements in which Truffaut identifies with the daughter against the father, with femaleness against maleness, with the New World (Halifax) against Europe (France, the Channel Islands), and finally, with film against poetry.

Truffaut's choice to film the *Histoire* (both story and history) *d'Adèle H.* and to make it his own suggests that the choice of subject was supplemented by something more personal and forceful. In chapter 10, Anne Donadey explores a similar force in a compulsion among contemporary Francophone Algerian writers to contend with the 1954–62 conflict leading to self-rule. More than thirty years after the Evian agreements that ended French colonial rule in Algeria, the complexity of "coming to terms" with this period of conflict is evident in the multiple expressions—such as *events, conflict, pacification,* and *police operation*—that refer euphemistically to a war whose place in France's recent past remains unresolved. Donadey assesses this irresolution among a generation of young Algerians living in France by setting Leïla Sebbar's 1984 novel *Le Chinois vert d'Afrique* against an institutional silence surrounding the 1954–62 events in Algeria that did not appear in the official curricula of French schools until the early 1980s. Donadey approaches Sebbar's novel as a prod to memory and corrective to a silence and forgetting she interprets in conjunction with what Henry Rousso has analyzed concerning the Occupation as a Vichy syndrome.

Donadey extends Rousso's hypothesis by questioning the extent to which the belated coming to terms with Vichy displaces a similar need to contend with the more recent conflict surrounding self-determination in Algeria. Sebbar's novel recounts the price of this displacement among immigrants, who are portrayed as victims of an ongoing racism among military veterans resentful of France's ouster from the former colonies of Vietnam and Algeria. As it appears in *Le Chinois vert d'Afrique*, racism fuels the affect surrounding irresolution over the place of the Algerian conflict and a colonial past in current debate surrounding French national identity. Along similar lines, in chapter 11 Panivong Norindr approaches current debate surrounding identity through architecture understood as a nation-space. Norindr's hypothesis involves the extent to which architecture in projects ranging from the 1931 Exposition Coloniale in Paris to the proposed Bibliothèque de France is by necessity an ambivalent practice of nation building that problematizes the relation of art and politics. Across this range of examples, Norindr sees in François Mitterrand's *grands travaux* (literally, large or even major projects) elements of the cultural precedent of a colonialism that imposes integration and assimilation onto difference. Along such lines, he considers the "historical axis" connecting the Carousel du Louvre, the Arc de Triomphe, and the Grande Arche as extending the ambitions of urban designers from the Second Empire to the present.

What, then, are Mitterrand's politics of architecture, and what conception of France as nation do they assert? Norindr asserts that the links between architecture and politics are neither direct nor simple. Architecture is not a mimetic practice that reflects or expresses a specific reality, but a set of evolving practices and discourses whose convergence elaborates—literally "reworks"—reality in a specific time and place. Where Mitterrand asserts his belief in a true pluralism and heterogeneity of images, Norindr sees instead an updated form of the 1931 Exposition Coloniale, at which the grounding principle of Greater France (*la plus grande France*) served as a catchall for a politics of expansionism that imposed assimilation to a predominant value of Frenchness over the cultural and political difference of the colonized nations. Commenting, for example, on the new Institut du Monde Arabe, Norindr notes that those who see it as a monument to "dialogue between cultures" fail to recognize that the dialogue in question is transnational and that the term *culture* serves in this instance to mask more urgent relations involving trade. Whose interests, then, does the new building serve? Not those of the alienated Maghrebi or *Beur* youth of the suburbs.

The final chapter is my attempt to explore a convergence of collective identity and deep-seated attitudes toward race and ethnicity at a specific moment in post-de Gaulle France when immigration from former colonies and protectorates in North Africa had begun to be perceived among "normal" French as threatening. I examine perceptions of such normality in terms of satirical sketches performed on stage and screen in the mid-1970s by Michel Colucci, a.k.a. Coluche. The wide appeal of these sketches and the growing cult surrounding Coluche since his 1986 death suggest the extent to which resentment toward difference at the level of race and ethnicity persists not simply within a lower-middle-class minority, but also among more educated *Français moyens* (average Frenchmen), for whom such prejudice has often been an object of denial. My illustration compares two sketches from the mid-1970s—"Histoire d'un mec sur le Pont de l'Alma" (Story of a guy on the Pont de l'Alma) and "Je me marre" (It really cracks me up)—and a scene with Coluche and Richard Anconina from Claude Berri's 1983 feature film *Tchao Pantin*.

Notes

1. Tzvetan Todorov, *Of Human Diversity: Nationalism, Racism, and Exoticism in French Thought*, trans. Catherine Porter (Cambridge: Harvard University Press, 1993), 248. The title of this translation differs significantly from the title of the French original, *Nous et les autres: La Réflexion française sur la diversité humaine* (Paris: Seuil, 1989).

2. Stanley Hoffmann, "Thoughts on the French Nation Today," *Daedalus* 122, no. 3 (1993): 66.

3. On the distinction between assimilation and integration, see the introduction and first chapter in Maxim Silverman, *Deconstructing the Nation: Immigration, Racism and Citizenship in Modern France* (New York: Routledge, 1992), as well as Etienne Balibar and Immanuel Wallerstein, *Race, Nation, Class: Ambiguous Identities* (New York: Verso, 1991).

4. See Hoffmann, "Thoughts on the French Nation," 65.

5. Bertrand le Gendre, *Le Monde* (16 August 1993), cited by Lynn Higgins in chapter 4 of this volume.

6. Quoted in Alan Riding, "France, Reversing Course, Fights Immigrants' Refusal to Be French," *New York Times*, 5 December 1993, 6.

7. Alice Kaplan's *French Lessons: A Memoir* (Chicago: University of Chicago Press, 1993) provides a number of superb insights concerning the dynamics of such marginality among Americans for whom exposure to the subtleties of the French language serves as a ritual of passage staged by constructing (or even inventing) a complex identity that is often cast against appearances. See also Robert Young, *Colonial Desire: Hybridity in Race, Culture, and Theory* (New York: Routledge, 1995).

8. Fernand Braudel, *The Identity of France*, vol. 1, *History and Environment*, trans. Siân Reynolds (New York: Harper Perennial, 1990), 17. The book appeared in France in 1986, shortly before Braudel's death and before he had completed a full draft of the three volumes he had projected for his study.

9. Ibid., 21.

10. Perry Anderson, "Fernand Braudel," in *Zone of Engagement* (New York: Verso, 1993), 252. Braudel set forth his model of the three durations in "History and the Social Sciences: The *Longue Durée*," in *On History*, trans. Sarah Matthews (Chicago: University of Chicago Press, 1980), 25–54.

11. Theodore Zeldin, *France 1848–1945*, vol. 2 (New York: Oxford University Press, 1977), 6.

12. Herman Lebovics, *True France: The Wars over Cultural Identity, 1900–1945* (Ithaca, N.Y.: Cornell University Press, 1992), 50.

13. See Benedict Anderson, *Imagined Communities: Reflections on the Origin and Spread of Nationalism*, rev. ed. (New York: Verso, 1991).

14. Lebovics, *True France*, 140.

15. Ibid., xi.

16. Jean-Claude Vigato, "Le Centre régional, le centre artisanal, et le centre rural," in *Paris 1937: Cinquantenaire de l'Exposition Internationale des Arts et des Techniques dans la Vie Moderne* (Paris: Institut Français d'Architecture/ Paris-Musée, 1987), 277.

17. Louis-Ferdinand Céline, *Bagatelles pour un massacre* (Paris: Denoël, 1937), 124.

18. Ibid., 40.

Part I

The Nation Exposed between the Wars

1 / Peasants in Paris: Representations of Rural France in the 1937 International Exposition

Shanny Peer

The dispute between France and the United States over agricultural subsidies, resurgent in late 1992 and 1993 in connection with the GATT trade talks, stirred French politicians and journalists of different political persuasions to revive a long-standing defense of French farmers in the name of national interest and cultural identity. Socialist Prime Minister Pierre Bérégovoy proclaimed in November 1992, "We are dealing with the defense of France's interests, our agriculture, our economy, our rural way of life."[1] Just as important as the economic stakes were the social structures and cultural values—the "rural way of life"—considered to be embodied in the family farm and protected by the French state. One observant French journalist offered a potential explanation for the widespread public support shown for French farming with regard to the GATT talks and similar decisions affecting farmers: "With the disappearance of the peasants, our society has the impression that it is losing part of its identity. France, after all, remains attached to a peasantry which no longer exists and which was allowed to die."[2]

The "peasant" has long been—and continues to be—a "potent and highly manipulable (and manipulated) symbol of French culture, one on which a variety of ideas is projected and legitimized."[3] Notably, images of the peasant have often been used to express attitudes toward modernization in a country that, up until the Second World War, resisted full-scale industrialization and maintained a large, and largely inefficient, agricultural sector: more than a third of the French working population remained in farming until the war.

During *les trentes glorieuses*, the thirty years of rapid growth following the war, French agriculture modernized rapidly along with the rest of the French economy, and the proportion of the active population working in agriculture would drop to around 10 percent by 1975; it stands at approximately 5 percent today.

Just before this watershed, described by Henri Mendras as the end of the peasantry, rural France was showcased in the 1937 International Exposition, the sixth and last French world's fair to be held in Paris.[4] During the profoundly troubled decade before the war, when many believed that France and Europe were undergoing a "crisis of civilization," the peasant, along with other key cultural symbols, was to some extent "reinvented" as a constitutive element of French national identity through the 1937 Exposition.[5] This was all the more significant in an exposition inaugurated by the leftist Popular Front, usually depicted as favoring urban workers at the expense of the peasantry, and held just three years before Vichy would reappropriate the peasant in its reactionary ideological arsenal.[6] Through a close examination of the politics behind, and discourse surrounding, rural exhibits in the 1937 exposition, I will analyze in this essay why and how images of the peasant and of rural France were refashioned through the exposition.

The representation of rural France in 1937 was not merely a short-lived attraction made for passive contemplation by fair visitors. Indeed, as Dean MacCannell has argued, expositions and other "cultural productions" "contribute to the progress of modernity by presenting new combinations of cultural elements and working out the logic of their relationship." Cultural productions "are not merely repositories of models for social life; they organize the attitudes we have towards the models and life."[7] The 1937 Rural Center gave shape to an emerging model of the modern family farmer, and helped mold receptive attitudes toward that model. Certain agricultural policies tested under Vichy or adopted later under the Fifth Republic would carry out the rural vision first projected on a national stage in the 1937 Exposition. However, even though this vision earned broad sectoral consensus among agricultural organizations and state officials, political forces on the left and right would compete to invest it with their own particular social and ideological vision.

Because rural, provincial France was largely neglected in previous expositions, it is important to consider the reasons for the newfound status accorded rural life in the 1937 Exposition, construed by politicians and fair officials as a showcase for refurbishing the national image. Since peasants constituted a potent cultural symbol upon which different meanings could be projected, but also a social category and increasingly organized interest group in the interwar years, the role played by different social and political forces in bringing French farmers to the fair provides an interesting case study of the strategies of social representation.

Peasants in Paris

Beginning with the first world's fair held in London's Crystal Palace in 1851, international expositions had celebrated and disseminated the values of urban, industrial, capitalist society. Accordingly, the French expositions, held in 1855, 1867, 1878, 1889, and 1900, had largely neglected the provinces and their rural inhabitants, treating them condescendingly on the rare occasions when they were represented.

By contrast, the 1937 Rural Center represented an idealized modern French village, complete with working model houses, cooperatives, administrative buildings, and even a silo. The *village-synthèse*, conceived for fifteen hundred to two thousand inhabitants, was brought to life with product displays, contests, demonstrations of farming innovations and artisanal crafts, and picturesque "peasant festivals." General Commissioner Edmond Labbé characterized it as the "tribute we owe to our dear inhabitants in the French countryside."[8] Agrarians praised the exhibit, which, "for the first time in France, places rural France on almost the same level as that reserved for the rest of the country."[9]

This tribute to rural France was indeed unprecedented. The nineteenth-century expositions had regularly featured agriculture as a theme, typically displaying agricultural goods, as well as the tools, machines, and methods used to work the land and process its yield.[10] But the farmers themselves, and the social and economic conditions shaping the lives of their rural communities, were doubly ignored. On the one hand, Parisians would certainly have considered the presence of the backward, "uncivilized" peasant unseemly at world's fairs intended to demonstrate France's status as an industrial power, producer of luxury goods, and "mother of the arts." On the other hand, fair exhibits addressing workers' conditions in urban, industrial society also tended to overlook the peasantry. Nineteenth-century exhibits on "social economy," like those on urbanism, public health, and housing (complete with models of "healthy" and "unhealthy" houses), focused on urban problems. The social reformists responsible for planning these exhibits overlooked rural living conditions, which they presumably considered relatively innocuous in comparison with the urban slums where workers congregated.

Peasants may also have been excluded from such exhibits because the ruling elite in Third Republic France did not categorize them as members of the working class. Conservatives generally portrayed the peasantry as healthy and stable, in opposition to the "dangerous classes" of urban workers, who had again manifested their terrifying revolutionary potential in the Paris Commune of 1871 and began organizing trade unions and political parties in the late nineteenth century. Starting in the early decades of the Third Republic, agrarians joined the parliamentary majority and the Radical-dominated Agriculture Ministry in idealizing the small farmer as "the bulwark against socialism, the source of a healthy and growing population, and the ballast against economic and social instability."[11] The peasant became an image-symbol in an oppositional paradigm that praised the peasant and countryside in order to vilify the *ouvrier* and city. Idealized portraits of the healthy, hardworking, moral peasant were reproduced not only in political discourse, but in novels, schoolbooks, paintings, and movies. Pierre Bourdieu has noted how such images objectified the peasant class:

> The peasant class . . . is the perfect example of the class-object, forced to form its own subjective identity out of its objectification. . . . It is certain that peasants are almost never thought of in and of themselves, and that the very words used to exalt their virtues and those of the countryside are only euphemisms for speaking about the vices of urban workers and of the city.[12]

Widely produced after 1870, romanticized images of the peasantry often glossed over the actual conditions and needs of rural society; these remained largely invisible in world's fairs and in other representations of rural France produced by and for the urban bourgeoisie. Because the ruling elite had political and ideological reasons for portraying peasants as the nation's wholesome, stabilizing force and country living as simple and healthy, they failed to perceive—or at least to address adequately—the serious deficiencies of rural society. Even the Socialists, who, unlike the conservatives, emphasized the similarities between peasants and workers, seemed as a consequence unable to articulate a clear agrarian vision that took into account the specificities of the rural world.

At the inauguration of the 1937 "Exhibit on Rural Living Conditions in Europe," the secretary general of the League of Nations explicitly stated that research on rural socioeconomic conditions had needed first to overcome myths about clean country living:

> In recent years the League of Nations' Hygiene Committee has become preoccupied with rural hygiene. It has had the courage to fight against pernicious illusions. Isn't country living healthy living par excellence? Before improving the conditions of urban existence, was it necessary to worry about those living in pure clean air? Alas, statistics and surveys have shown that sanitary conditions in the country are not superior to those in the city.[13]

Pastoral myths needed to be debunked before social reformers could begin to focus their attention on the squalid, uncomfortable dwellings in which most peasants lived and worked.

The Politics of Bringing the Farm to the Fair

Given the virtual exclusion of rural society from earlier Parisian expositions, and its absence in the original 1934 mandate for the 1937 fair, what can explain the decision to incorporate a model French village in the exposition? Three factors converged to bring farmers onto the national stage. Rural exodus in the 1920s, combined with the social and economic crisis during the Depression, generated renewed concern about the hazards of "overindustrialization" and focused national attention on the inadequate working and living conditions of French farmers. Agricultural organizations were able to channel these concerns and pressure fair organizers into adding a rural exhibit. However, agrarian leaders might not have succeeded without a third factor: the active support and sponsorship of the state administration and, ultimately, the Popular Front government.

In the years following the First World War, which was itself a veritable hemorrhage for the French peasantry, many of the more marginal peasant smallholders and hired farm laborers abandoned the countryside and moved to cities in search of work. As a result of this new wave of *exode rural*, the urban population surpassed the rural one by 1931, and the proportion of the active population working in agriculture declined from 42 percent to 36 percent between 1921 and 1936.[14] Although this movement would slow during the Great Depression, migration to the cities accelerated again sharply after 1936, due in part to the enticing forty-hour workweek and two-week paid vacations Blum's government instituted for wage earners. Almost 300,000 farmers, mostly under thirty years of age, were lured to the city between 1936 and 1939.[15]

This rural out-migration raised alarms about the potentially devastating effects of upsetting the "healthy" equilibrium deliberately maintained in France between agriculture and industry, and between large and small producers, while Britain, Germany, and the United States industrialized more rapidly. The Depression appeared to confirm the value of France's "dual economy," as family farms had often adapted relatively easily to the economic downturn and were able to reabsorb temporarily those family members who lost their jobs in industry. Unemployment and labor unrest in the 1930s—and especially the hundreds of thousands of striking workers in 1936 after the Popular Front victory—pointedly underlined the dangers of a large industrial workforce and certainly convinced conservatives of the need to stem the rural-to-urban migration.

But an inaugural speech and exhibit catalog written by the Socialist Henri Sellier, Popular Front minister of public health, for the 1937 exhibit on rural housing in Europe suggests there was a broader political consensus about the desirability of maintaining an equilibrium between country and city. Sellier construed this exhibit as a response to the progressive abandonment of the countryside, and warned that the acceleration of this process threatened to create a "serious economic and social disequilibrium." Whereas industry and agriculture had continued to coexist in relative harmony until recently, now, Sellier explained, "we're on the verge of upsetting the balance," and "the city is threatening to kill the earth which nourishes it."[16] One solution to this problem was to offer an attractive, optimistic image of country life in order to slow the flight to the city. In the words of Sellier:

> At the present time, when the agricultural population in every country has been reduced to the minimum necessary to ensure agricultural viability, the problem of finding ways to keep rural inhabitants in the countryside, and to improve living conditions so that the population can be stabilized, becomes all the more urgent.[17]

In 1932, when the French Parliament began considering plans for an exposition, a Socialist deputy, Fiancette, succeeded in imposing an "exhibit on workers' and peasants' lives" as part of the fair program. His proposal, signed by 130 fellow deputies (mostly Socialists and Radicals) attested to the new level of national concern about the living and working conditions of farmers. However, conservatives undoubtedly disapproved of grouping farmers together with workers in an exhibit addressing explicitly social questions, and the conservative Doumergue government eliminated Fiancette's project in 1934, when it imposed the more limited theme of "arts and techniques in modern life." When Edmond Labbé was appointed as general commissioner in 1934, he was given neither the mandate nor the budget to include a rural exhibit (much less one on industrial workers).[18]

As plans for the fair proceeded, agricultural organizations objected to their exclusion, but Labbé retorted that agriculture did not conform to the exposition's designated theme of "modern arts and techniques." This exclusion fueled rural resentments against international expositions past and present, which were decried as extravagant expenditures that profited Paris while draining the provinces of money and business, and even "uprooting new waves of rural inhabitants."[19] Led by the Assemblée permanente des présidents de chambres d'agriculture, agricultural organizations launched a national campaign to pressure fair planners into including a rural village in the exposition. If this were to be a truly national exposition, they argued, it should take into account the importance of agriculture in the national economy and recognize the vital place of rural citizens in French society. When Labbé resisted their continued demands, he became, "throughout all of France, the target of a press campaign that went so far as to recommend that the agricultural population boycott the Exposition."[20]

In March 1936, under Sarraut's Radical-dominated cabinet, as the state began to assume a greater role in planning the exposition, the Ministry of Agriculture stepped into the impasse, allocating 2 million francs for a rural exhibit (tenuously approved in January) and pressuring Labbé to add 1.2 million francs from the fair budget. However, agrarian leaders continued to doubt Labbé's commitment to the project and maintained considerable pressure on the fair administration, even rallying supporters in Parliament to appeal before the Senate and Chamber of Deputies. In the end, it was Georges Monnet's Ministry of Agriculture, under the Popular Front, that committed itself to sponsoring the project fully, allocating an additional 6 million francs in June 1936.[21]

In leading a successful campaign for "fair" representation, French agricultural organizations demonstrated their newfound effectiveness in the 1930s. As Gordon Wright has argued, before the Great Depression, the French peasantry had been largely atomized, passive, and inarticulate. He quotes Marcel Faure as saying the Depression marked a watershed, when farmers as a group reached a turning point: "That stage can be described as the arrival of the peasant mass at an awareness of its collective needs."[22] New peasantist movements such as the Parti agraire et paysan français, Dorgerès's Comités de défense paysanne, and the Jeunesse agricole paysanne mobilized French farmers and gave them a greater collective visibility in French society. The interwar years also witnessed the creation of national agricultural organizations: the Confédération nationale des associations agricoles (CNAA) and the Association permanente des présidents de chambres d'agriculture, formed in 1935 to represent the chambers of agriculture legalized since 1924, provided vehicles for the defense of farming interests on a national level.[23] The leaders of these organizations, along with those of the established syndical federations, the right-wing Union centrale des syndicats agricoles de France (revitalized by new leadership and renamed the Union nationale des syndicats agricoles in 1934) and the center-left Fédération nationale de la mutualité et de la coopération agricole, would all participate in creating the Rural Center. Although these agrarian leaders were typically notables who represented primarily the interests of large growers, and should not therefore be equated with the real "masses" of peasants for whom they claimed to speak, they did constitute a powerful national lobby for agriculture. As such, their role in the Rural Center certainly influenced the manner in which the peasant and rural France were refashioned through the 1937 Exposition, for, in the "poetics and politics" of cultural display, "the struggle is not only over what is to be represented, but over who will control the means of representing."[24]

In the end, however, the agricultural lobby could not have won its cause in 1937 without the timely support of the state and, ultimately, of Georges Monnet's Ministry of Agriculture. Just as the fear of being upstaged by foreign exhibitors had pushed the French state to become more directly involved in a fair it continued to reshape and expand, so was the addition of the Rural Center justified to the French Parliament in terms of national *amour-propre*. Joseph Faure argued before the Senate in March 1936:

> Our country is in a state of inferiority compared to other nations with regards to the aesthetics, comfort and especially the hygiene of its farmers' houses and farm buildings; it is therefore advisable to construct a model village to serve as an example.[25]

The state's decision to subsidize the Rural Center also coincided with the more interventionist role it was beginning to assume in agriculture in response to the Depression, even before the Popular Front came to power.[26]

Thus, the Popular Front shares credit with the agricultural organizations for bringing farmers into the national limelight in 1937. Several factors help explain the Popular Front's decision to subsidize and oversee plans for the Rural Center. These included the Left's desire to attract and retain a growing rural constituency and to reassure farmers of its commitment to their particular needs. The Socialist and Communist parties both sought to increase their influence among farmers during the interwar period through the creation of syndical organizations and peasantist party organs. The Communist Party's agricultural specialist, Renaud Jean, formed the Confédération générale des paysans travailleurs in 1929. In 1936, the Party created an official weekly newspaper for farmers, *La Terre*, replacing Jean's semiofficial *La Voix paysanne*. Communist agrarians affirmed their commitment "to be wherever the masses are, in the cooperative, in the mutual society, at the credit office, in farmers' and hunters' syndicates. . . . Let's not remain isolated in any case, for any reason!"[27] In 1933, Henri Calvayrac formed the Socialist-oriented Confédération nationale paysanne and began to publish a weekly organ for farmers, *La Volonté paysanne*. Although the Confédération nationale paysanne denied any official link to the SFIO (the Section française de l'internationale ouvrière—the French Socialist

Party), its leadership shared strong personal and ideological ties with Socialist leaders, and Calvayrac's organization emerged more clearly as an agency of the SFIO under the Popular Front. Calvayrac's movement reinvigorated the Socialist agricultural program, and its grassroots activism enlarged the Socialist audience among farmers.[28]

If the impact of these left-wing syndical organizations remained quite limited, and the syndical movement, as well as the new agrarian parties, remained strongly dominated by the Right, the 1936 elections nevertheless showed significant gains for the Left in rural areas. Of the parties in the Popular Front coalition, the Radicals historically depended most heavily on rural voters. In 1936, however, the SFIO also gained ground in some rural areas, compensating for the votes lost to the Communist Party in many traditionally Socialist urban strongholds, particularly around Paris.[29] The Communists also attracted more rural voters, particularly in areas of the Massif Central and southwest.

The Rural Center can be understood as part of a leftist strategy to buttress this rural support. By highlighting farmers in the Parisian exposition, the Popular Front appealed to a constituency and a cause long championed more successfully by the Right. Popular Front sponsorship of the Rural Center also repudiated fears that it would attend solely to the interests of urban industrial workers. Many agrarian critics of the Popular Front agreed with Breton deputy Caziot, who lamented, "They say that, in every society, there must be slaves to ensure the wealthiness of others. The Popular Front has chosen its slaves: the peasants."[30] The acceleration of rural out-migration under the Popular Front appeared to confirm fears that the new social legislation (forty-hour workweek, paid vacations, and wage hikes) benefited the urban working class at the expense of farmers. Even leftist agrarians warned against the potentially negative effects of Popular Front policies on farmers. Calvayrac's Socialist-oriented weekly urged Blum's government to enact quickly the agricultural policies promised in its platform: "It's a question of dignity, of affirming that [farmers] no longer accept being considered as second-class citizens."[31]

Although the Popular Front was unable to enact most of its proposed agricultural policies (mostly because of resistance from the Senate), the Rural Center testified to its commitment to a comprehensive, modernist vision of economic progress and social order in rural France.[32] Whereas, before the 1930s, the Socialists and Communists had been less able than the Right to articulate an agricultural program that took into account the specificities of the rural world, in 1937 the leftist coalition could lay claim to a well-conceived and widely approved plan for the future of French agriculture.

Planning the Rural Center

The Popular Front, however, was neither the author nor the sole promoter of the prescriptive rural scenario played out on the exposition's stage. The Rural Center was originally conceived by Michel Augé-Laribé and Joseph Faure, with Georges Monnet stepping in to oversee its final production. A renowned rural economist and active agrarian lobbyist, Augé-Laribé was an ardent critic of the agricultural policies instituted under the Third Republic, beginning with the Méline tariff in 1892.[33] He was just as critical of Socialist and Communist agricultural programs as he was of other party policies, characterizing all of them as "demagoguery."[34] In the plans he originated for the Rural Center, Augé-Laribé promoted agricultural modernization and mechanization, as well as farmers' cooperatives and mutual benefit societies, and he advocated agricultural education and social legislation for farmers (which lagged behind that for industrial workers).

In January 1936, the Assemblée permanente des présidents de chambres d'agriculture endorsed Augé-Laribé's proposal, and Senator Joseph Faure was named president of the exposition's Agriculture Committee. Faure, a conservative senator from the Corrèze region, had been a member of the bicameral parliamentary Agriculture Commission for some seventeen years, was active in the Confédération nationale des associations agricoles, and had led the successful campaign for the creation of chambers of agriculture legalized in 1924. Like Augé-Laribé, Faure stressed the importance of innovation and modernization in agriculture and promoted farmers' syndicates, mutual aid societies, and similar associative organizations.

Faure presided over the exposition's Agriculture Committee, whose other members represented the Ministry of Agriculture and Génie rural, the principal syndical federations and national agricultural organizations, and especially the new specialized associations, such as the beet growers' association, formed in the 1920s to speak for the growers of particular crops. Thus, the committee was composed of representatives of national *professional* agricultural organizations, but excluded the more explicitly political agrarian parties of either the Right or the Left.[35] The diverse members of this committee collaborated to create a prescriptive vision, which ultimately expressed a fairly broad sectoral consensus about the direction French agriculture should take to regain its health and ensure future vitality. Thus, the Rural Center constituted a significant symbolic exercise both in "peasant unity" and in group-state *concertation* before Vichy's experimentation with the "Corporation paysanne" and the neocorporatist agricultural policies pursued under the Fifth Republic.[36] However, because the Popular Front sponsored this project, and because Right and Left differed in their fundamental conceptions of the rural social order and of the role the state should play in agriculture, the Rural Center was ultimately interpreted in a more partisan spirit than the united one that brought it into being. Polemical reactions to the model village illustrate how the bitterly divisive mood of the 1930s, accentuated under Blum's government, cast political shadows over all projects and attest to the contest between Left and Right for the authority to reshape social order and identity in rural France.

The Rural Center

In the official brochure on Le Centre rural, Georges Monnet warned visitors that "the aim is not to evoke, for the enjoyment of amateurs of the picturesque, the charms of a conventional little village." Instead, the exemplary village would demonstrate "the technical and social efforts that must be pursued across our countryside so that its inhabitants might benefit from a sense of well-being, security, spiritual life and relaxation, no less valuable than the advantages enjoyed by inhabitants in the most modern cities."[37] Thus, the explicit objective was to replace anachronistic and romanticized images of quaint country life—such as those in Jean Giono's *Regain* or in Marcel Pagnol's *Angèle* and *La Femme du boulanger* dating from the same period—with a vision of rural progress, comfort, and "well-being," meant to elevate the social status of farmers and to encourage them to adopt these improvements in their farms and villages.[38] An important subtext, detectable in Monnet's preface, ran throughout the official discourse on tractors, electricity, and mechanized farm machinery: these improvements alone—or the hope of them—would prevent farmers from fleeing to the cities, and so maintain the "healthy equilibrium" between industry and agriculture, seen as fundamental to French national health. However, as we shall see, the "picturesque" element was not altogether eradicated in this modernist vision. "Peasant festivals," folk singers and dancers, and women lace makers dressed in regional costume animated the town square and community center, reassuring visitors that progress would not eliminate tradition in rural France.

Like the romanticized image it replaced, this new, modernizing vision retained the status of representation: it did not correspond to actual conditions prevalent throughout most of rural France, projecting instead an idealized picture intended, in this case, to alter the manner in which a particular social group perceived itself and was viewed by members of the dominant culture. Indeed, the planners of the Rural Center consciously shaped their exhibit for audiences from both city and country. They sought simultaneously to refashion the image of the modern *agriculteur* for an urban bourgeois audience and to educate and persuade the rural audience into imitating its idealized image on display in the fair.

The Rural Center occupied a five-acre area in the exposition's Porte Maillot annex, which it shared with the Artisan Palace, Le Corbusier's Modern Times Pavilion, the League of Nations rural exhibit, and several smaller pavilions. The buildings grouped around the town square or single road in this model village fell mostly into three categories. Administrative services included a town hall, a school, a post office, a health clinic (which doubled as first-aid station for fair visitors), public baths, a fire station, and water and electric utilities. Professional services were represented in a second group of buildings, including a *Maison des agriculteurs* housing various professional farmers' organizations, a community center, a union meeting hall, and numerous working cooperatives. A third set of structures evoked a "medium-size farm" and model home for a hired farmhand. Additionally, the covered marketplace, inn, and sampling hall served as display areas for product exhibits held throughout the fair. Notably absent from this village was a church; this omission provoked such an outcry that it became the focal point in right-wing criticism of the Rural Center.

As an ensemble, these pavilions exemplified modernization, both of the working methods and living conditions of farmers and of communal rural services. They demonstrated or documented the material improvements then making slow inroads into rural France, such as better roadways, electricity, water and sewage systems, mechanical irrigation and drainage methods, and telephones. Electrification of the countryside progressed spectacularly between the wars, and by the late 1930s the vast majority of communes had access to electricity; most rural homes made only minimal use of this new luxury, however, typically using it only to illuminate one dim light bulb hung over the kitchen table. During a time when less than 20 percent of rural dwellings had running water, and even fewer had indoor toilet facilities or modern sewage systems,[39] visitors must have been impressed by this well-lit, mechanized village graced with its own electrical generator, modern plumbing, and telephones. In addition to indoor toilets and running water, the farmhouse displayed an enviable collection of electrical appliances for the modern farmer's wife, including an electric iron, water heater, sewing machine, and radio.

The Rural Center also displayed the technical innovations that could help farmers enhance their productivity and improve the quality of their agricultural production. Whereas only about thirty-five thousand tractors were actually being used in all of France by the 1930s, tractors and other mechanized field equipment figured prominently in the rural exhibit, and documentary materials suggested how farmers could collectively purchase and exploit them. Six cooperatives, each an "ideal model equipped with the latest techniques," demonstrated methods for processing, packaging, and storing agricultural products.[40] The grain cooperative, for example, used mechanized conveyor belts, elevators, ventilators, and vacuums to clean, separate, and weigh seeds and grains before storing them in the silo.

Whereas many smaller farmers, especially those in more remote rural areas, continued in the 1930s to practice barely productive subsistence agriculture, or to produce almost exclusively for local consumption, the Rural Center also implicitly promoted a more complete integration of French agriculture into national and international markets. By organizing product and livestock displays around regional themes in the "weekly regional festivals" held throughout the exposition, the Agriculture Committee demonstrated how regional specialization could be used to manage and market this wider integration. Thus, the Rural Center promoted the production and marketing—indeed in some cases even the "invention"—of "regional" specialties for a national and international clientele.

The utopian "Village '37" also highlighted the social amenities gradually improving the lives of rural inhabitants. Education received particular attention: the village school displayed several model classrooms, including a "domestic science class" for girls and a "manual skills class" for boys, while a communal library and traveling *bibliobus* attested to the goal, shared by members of the Agriculture Committee and the Ministry of Agriculture, to spread instruction, and particularly to "popularize" modern farming methods, among adults. Other modern amenities such as the health clinic, public baths, fire station, cinema, and community center demonstrated the ideal modern community's concern for the physical, social, and psychological well-being of its members.

If the creators of this rural utopia championed the "modern evolution of agriculture" and emphasized the material, technical, and social improvements gradually making their way into French farms and villages, they did not, however, advocate the larger-scale concentration of French agriculture favored by "neophysiocrats" as a means to attain even higher levels of efficiency and productivity. The Rural Center promoted instead the family farm as the linchpin of its balanced modernist formula. Its four-bedroom farmhouse (three children, please!) was designed for a twenty-hectare farm (just under fifty acres), classified in France as a "medium-size farm." This was characterized as "a farm which is neither too small nor too big, in a word, one which corresponds to the formula of the future, exploited by the family alone, without outside help."[41]

Although the self-sufficient family farm was embraced as the ideal model, the Rural Center also exhibited a farmworker's home, showing the more modest comforts available to the hired hand.

The Rural Center reflected the general trend between the wars (and indeed since the late 1890s) toward the consolidation of medium-size family farms (between ten and fifty hectares), as more marginal farms were abandoned, and as larger landholdings (more than one hundred hectares) also decreased in number, but this trend implied, of course, a further reduction of the agricultural population. Despite the widespread condemnation of *exode rural* by spokespersons for the exposition and many of their contemporaries in the 1930s, the spotlight on the "medium-size" farm in the 1937 rural exhibit suggests its producers recognized that French agriculture, to ensure its long-term viability, would ultimately need to consolidate more sizable farms. They proposed a viable compromise solution for French agriculture: maintain family farms while making them large enough to be productive and efficient.[42]

The Popular Front's promotion of the family farm in 1937 was also significant in that it advanced the leftist strategy of convincing family farmers their interests would be defended by the Left. Of the three parties in the leftist coalition, the Radicals' continuing defense of the independent farmer was not surprising. Socialists and Communists, however, were portrayed by their opponents as threats to landowning farmers. In fact, French Socialists had repudiated Marxist orthodoxy regarding the inevitable collectivization of agriculture as early as the 1890s, when Jean Jaurès began defending the interests of the small independent farmer, and the unified SFIO continued after 1905 to defend smallholders.[43] But, even though the SFIO promised "not to take the tools away from the artisan or agricultural worker, even if they owned some property,"[44] conservatives insisted the Socialists were hiding ulterior plans to collectivize French agriculture once in power.

Right-wingers portrayed the Communist Party as even more threatening to smallholders. Even if the Party accepted some private ownership as an interim measure, it still subscribed to the eventual necessity of collectivization and applauded the "successful" adoption of collectivized farming in the Soviet Union. However, under the Popular Front, the Communists publicly changed their tune. A 1938 "booklet of the rural propagandist" outlined two essential Party principles, which coincide exactly with the Rural Center's vision: "1. Guarantee and ensure for farmers working conditions and a well-being equivalent to those enjoyed by the urban population; 2. Defend small landowning farmers."[45] Of course, critics found the second point especially disingenuous, and the Communist propaganda booklet did not evoke the long-term evolution of agriculture. Nonetheless, this rural platform situates the Popular Front's promotion of the family farm as part of a strategy to attract and reassure independent farmers within a growing leftist rural constituency.

How did the Rural Center propose to reconcile the preservation of the traditionally independent family farm with the recognized need for greater modernization in agriculture? For planners of the rural exhibit, the answer lay in the development of professional farmers' organizations, including syndicates, cooperatives, mutual insurance companies, credit bureaus, and other mutual aid societies. Six working cooperatives demonstrated how farmers could join forces to purchase expensive new machinery and cooperatively process and market their produce in a more rationalized, cost-effective manner, while still preserving the benefits of independence.

Cooperatives and other associative farmers' organizations had grown rapidly in France since the late nineteenth century, as part of the growing syndical movement in the French countryside. By 1937, as many as two million farmers, out of more than four million men working in agriculture, belonged to at least one of the syndicates, cooperatives, or mutual aid societies grouped under one of the two national syndical organizations, the right-wing Union nationale des syndicats agricoles or the Radical-oriented Fédération nationale de la mutualité et de la coopération agricole.[46] Agrarians of both the Right and the Left promoted these kinds of organizations, and so should have agreed in principle with their representation in the exposition. However, they held differing views about the long-term objectives such organizations might advance. Radicals viewed cooperatives and other mutual aid societies as a means of collective self-help for independent farmers, and Socialists and Communists hoped they would prepare peasants for socialism, whereas many conservatives conceptualized *syndicats* (the term preferred by the Right, with *coopérative* more often used by the Left) as building blocks for corporatism. This difference explains right-wing wariness about the "cooperative spirit" espoused so enthusiastically by the Popular Front sponsors of this project, especially since Georges Monnet used the Rural Center to suggest how the state could enhance this "cooperation" by assuming a greater regulatory role in agriculture. Many conservatives, too, had begun to recognize the need for more regulation in agriculture, but they promoted a greater regulatory role for the profession itself, and vehemently rejected statism.

Village or Kolkhoz?

Thus, although the Rural Center translated a broad political and sectoral agreement about the need to modernize agriculture, maintain medium-size family

farms, and develop professional farmers' organizations (particularly cooperatives or syndicates), consensus between Right and Left foundered over deeper
social and ideological issues. Disagreement over the respective roles of the
church and state in rural society and right-wing fears of the Left's supposed
plans to collectivize agriculture would fuel the only substantive criticisms
launched by Popular Front critics against the Rural Center, which they otherwise approved or ignored. The most virulent right-wing attacks concerned the
absence of a church in the model village. As it turns out, this oversight dated
from plans made before Monnet's arrival. Nonetheless, the conservative agrarian press broadly denounced the Rural Center's leftist sponsor for its "narrow
sectarianism [which] has voluntarily omitted the steeple, the spiritual axis of
our rural villages."[47] A National Committee for the Erection of a Church in the
Exposition Village was even formed, and the conservative Paris Municipal
Council joined the tide of protest, passing a resolution—on Christmas Eve—
to demand that the church be "restored" to the village, because its exclusion of-
fended not only Catholics, but also "the immense mass of occasional worship-
pers [*tièdes*] who . . . on solemn occasions . . . spontaneously find their way
back to the sanctuary."[48] This polemic, which emblematized the perceived
struggle between the church and secular state for the souls of French villagers,
apparently roused considerable public reaction. Visitors revived this "irritating
question" on "every page" of the Rural Center's *Livre d'or* (where guests were
invited to record their impressions), "sometimes to protest the missing church,
other times to applaud its absence."[49]

The silo became the secular centerpiece in this churchless village; fittingly,
the exhibits it housed informed visitors about the Popular Front's Wheat
Office, symbol of the greater regulatory role the leftist coalition advocated for
the state in agriculture. Conservative critics warned against the "statism" promoted by the Popular Front, and hinted that the Rural Center's cooperative
theme had a collectivist taint: "Cooperatives here, cooperatives there; a silo instead of a church. Hum! This smells very much like a kolkhoz!"[50] Another
critic sarcastically identified the name Le Centre rural as a euphemism for the
Soviet-style collectivized farm: "In correct French, one could translate this simply with an essentially French word of French origin: 'kolkhoz.'"[51] Directed at
French farmers who followed—often with great trepidation—the collectivization of Soviet agriculture, *kolkhoz* served as a potent epithet to decry the Popular Front's supposedly collectivist agenda.

Ironically, the Catholic press adopted a more conciliatory tone in its assessment of the Rural Center, pointing out that many of the accusations against

Monnet were unjustified. An article in *Le Foyer rural,* published by the Jeunesse agricole catholique, cautioned:

> It is unfair, in particular, to accuse the minister of agriculture of having wanted to present a kolkhoz to the French people. The Rural Center is presenting dairy, fruit and wine cooperatives which have existed for years in France. But an important part of the Rural Center is devoted to the small French farm . . . and the whole plan dates back to January 1936![52]

Many of the criticisms launched against Monnet were indeed unfounded, and certain features of the Rural Center attributed to him were in fact first proposed by Augé-Laribé and developed by members of the Agriculture Committee working in collaboration with the Ministry of Agriculture. Given the broad consensus on the essential features of this 1937 "formula for the future of French agriculture," the polemical press coverage attests less to substantive disagreement about the contents of the Rural Center than to the struggle between Right and Left to lay claim to this image of a modernizing rural France and to adapt it to their differing visions of social order. The contest between Left and Right for the authority to reshape the social structures and identity of modern rural society intensified in the 1930s, as the Rural Center was planned and presented, and would continue in earnest after the Second World War.

Planners called the Rural Center "a look into the future, with its improvements, its advantages and its possibilities,"[53] and indeed their time machine predicted quite accurately—or prescribed successfully—the general direction French agriculture would take in the coming decades. It anticipated certain policies to be instituted by Vichy, including legislation to facilitate *remembrement* (the regrouping of scattered land parcels) and to prevent, in some cases, the division of farms among inheritors, both measures aimed at encouraging the consolidation of medium-size family farms.[54] The Rural Center also foreshadowed the more enduring agricultural policies to be pursued under the Fifth Republic. Beginning in the early 1960s, state policies would encourage the consolidation, rationalization, and mechanization of medium-size family farms in order to stimulate industrial growth, increase agricultural productivity, and facilitate the integration of French agriculture into European and international markets.[55]

Picturesque Modernity

The formal features of this utopian village prescribed a harmonious synthesis of the modern and the traditional. In a significant departure from the European expositions of the late nineteenth century, where national exhibits (mostly non-French) often featured pastiches, reconstitutions or derivations of rural architecture, the fair's Agriculture Committee decided in 1937 not to reproduce an existing village or create an anachronistic *village-pastiche* as a "tourist attraction."[56] Instead, they proposed to show visitors a model of a modern *village-synthèse*, an idealized image of "what could be."[57]

The Rural Center's design exemplified a new approach to rural planning, coined as "ruralism" in articles about the model village. Designed by architects Leconte and Metz, this village seamlessly blended modern practicality and comfort with provincial "rusticity." Eschewing shockingly modern lines, it offered instead comforting images of updated rural architecture. The architects deliberately combined modern construction methods and materials such as cement with forms and materials that had long been used in different vernacular architectures and that remained readily available in many rural areas, including wood, bricks, tiles, rubble stone, and limestone. Thus, for example, the covered market presented a stunning example of traditional craftsmanship in its wooden roof and exposed wooden ceiling, whereas the cement silo followed a strictly utilitarian conception. Most structures harmoniously blended cement with brick, crowning these with steep tile roofs. Interiors were conceived rationally and simply, incorporating "the latest comforts and conveniences" such as modern bath and kitchen facilities, and refrigerated storage spaces in the cooperatives. Except for the enlarged windows (which met hygienists' prescriptions for more air and light in rural dwellings), these structures evoked a generic rural aesthetic. The architectural director underlined that the village was not intended as a "regionalist work," but as a "national exhibit" and a "state presentation," and consequently planners deliberately avoided imitation of any particular regional style.[58]

Thus, rurality was defined in the 1937 fair in contradistinction to both urban and regionalist architecture. This oppositional function served to confirm what rural architecture was *not* and what it was reacting against. The decidedly rural character denoted a negation of the urban aesthetic as a potential model for rural villages in France. This oppositional stance allowed a reformulation of "rurality" in which elements of rural architecture could be manipulated and recombined in a new syncretistic form as self-conscious signs of the rural. The "Village '37" was also presented as a "national" exhibit in that it ignored regional styles. This choice dissociated rural France from its provincial context for the purposes of the exposition, positing the existence of a national French ruralism. As a reviewer for *L'Architecture* observed, the modern architecture exemplified in the Rural Center combined a "thoroughly national" and a "peasant" character.[59] Sponsored by a leftist government, this image can be interpreted in part as a Jacobin strategy to represent rural France, within the symbolic national space of the fairgrounds, as a coherent, national whole, in contrast with traditionally right-wing regionalist sympathies. The "nationalizing" strategy deployed in the Rural Center echoes the one used in 1937 with regard to folklore.[60]

At the same time, if the image represented in 1937 was that of a generic "national" village, its buildings were not proposed as "ideal types" or "standardized models" meant to be imitated throughout rural France. They were offered instead as examples that could be adopted according to local styles, climate, and availability of materials; it was hoped that they would inspire new efforts to reconcile vernacular forms with current standards of practicality, comfort, and hygiene.[61] In this way, traditional styles, instead of either resisting renewal or ceding to a standardized modern aesthetic, could be harmoniously refashioned. As the journal *L'Architecture* pointed out, in applauding the 1937 village:

> It is not by vainly attempting to preserve archaisms that we remain faithful to tradition, but rather by shaping life according to the conditions of the surrounding environment and the experiences of the past, without neglecting to incorporate the comforts, conveniences, and improvements made possible by recent discoveries.[62]

Planners did not wish for this village to appear like a drab pedagogical lesson. Against an architectural backdrop that was "deliberately anonymous and technical," a series of week-long festivals brought the village to life. Each festival featured a different region, displaying its agricultural products in the market, sampling hall, cooperatives, and tavern. The "spiritual and traditionalist character" of these regional weeks was provided by "peasant festivals." Costumed galas created an "artistic and picturesque" ambiance and evoked the eternal peasant soul. After witnessing one such festival, a journalist for *L'Oeuvre* reminisced, "We heard forgotten songs that bring tears to the eyes, evoking the grape harvest combined with apple picking in fraternal spirit."[63] Ironically, most of these spectacles were performed by costumed groups from Paris rather than by folk groups from the provinces.

In one such spectacle, the "Harvest Festival," hundreds of costumed participants paraded across Paris and through the fairgrounds to the Rural Center. Gleaners in provincial costumes from the Beauce region sat atop tractor-pulled wagons singing regional tunes, while old-fashioned peasants bearing scythes and sickles led mechanized harvesters; thus was celebrated the happy marriage of eternal peasant and machine. The staging of traditional rural artisans at work added to the picturesque atmosphere. For instance, the week devoted to

Quercy, Rouergue, and Haut-Languedoc featured a live display of women lace makers from Le Puy. The official newspaper, *Le Centre rural,* showed the lace makers wearing picturesque costumes and headdresses as they created "very pretty models with modern designs."[64]

This display was typical of the Rural Center's representations of peasant women, who were depicted almost exclusively as picturesque, old-fashioned peasants in the Rural Center's village museum and in official documentation and press releases. Aside from images of lace makers and a short article about the winner of the "Valiant Farmer's Wife" contest, the Rural Center's newspaper depicted women only as participants in folk festivals and dressed in traditional provincial costumes. Elsewhere, the town hall's village museum displayed photographs of women in Romenay hand-spinning hemp and plucking chickens by hand, and a panel about "the stages of life" showed younger and older women wearing traditional Bressan bonnets considered appropriate for their ages. Even if captions informed visitors that these photographs showed practices that were either outdated ("In the days when women wore bonnets, the number of rows of flutes was proportionate to the size of the young woman's dowry") or reconstructions ("Former spinners re-create the movements of their craft"), the obsolete images illustrating these commentaries provided virtually the only visual representations of women.[65] Rural Center guidebooks and other documentation did not describe or depict women doing anything modern or at variance with their traditionally assigned gender role; they were never shown attending conferences, giving speeches, handling machinery, presenting animals or agricultural products in competitions, or even wearing modern attire.

Women were instead assigned a key role as keepers of tradition in the Rural Center's image of harmonious synthesis between old and new. Representations of traditional women peasants (along with artisans and folk groups) apparently sought to reassure visitors that modernization would not change the traditional spirit and character of French villages. One journalist conveyed the intended message: "[In the Rural Center], many city dwellers will rediscover their rustic soul, many peasants will understand that it is not necessary to standardize the countryside in order to modernize it."[66] Another journalist reminisced nostalgically about the simpler village life left behind:

> Nothing offers as much charm and spice as a visit to the Rural Center. . . . There you feel at home, close to yourself, in the atmosphere of your native village . . . you feel reconciled with what you ran away from. The families you miss and friends who have died reappear secretly in your heart which has been eaten away by cities without memory or sweet pleasures.[67]

Some visitors were less enticed by the old-fashioned cultural traditions staged in the Rural Center. A journalist writing in *La Belle France* quoted farmers overheard as they departed from the rural exhibit: "The little folklore festivals, of course they're very nice, but aren't there other more up-to-date festivals to celebrate?"[68] These farmers perceived the quaint depiction of village life as harmless, but curiously incongruent with their real lives. Although the Rural Center aimed to debunk certain myths historically associated with peasants, it still invited individual farmers to appropriate an image of themselves as defined and objectified by others, in this case by national agricultural leaders and the state.

Le Corbusier's Modern Times Pavilion and Other Rural Exhibits

If the Rural Center constituted the primary rural exhibit in the 1937 Exposition, several additional exhibits also spotlighted rural society, confirming that it had indeed become a "universal preoccupation" in interwar France. Rural questions were addressed in exhibits on European and French rural houses, and in the 1937 Folklore Conference, as well as in Le Corbusier's Modern Times Pavilion. And, for the first time in a French world's fair, the section usually devoted to urbanism added rural planning (*ruralisme*) to its agenda, signifying that urban planners had begun to recognize that rural spaces, previously thought to obey a kind of self-regulating organic order, also required rational planning.

Henri Sellier presented the League of Nations "Exhibit on Rural Living Conditions in Europe" as a recognition of the threatened disequilibrium between city and country, explaining, "The problem we face everywhere now is to try to establish conditions which will allow us to maintain the rural population in the countryside, and to stabilize the proportion of the population living in the city and in the country."[69] This discourse was both reminiscent of Jules Méline, who had advocated a "return to the earth" in 1905, and premonitory of Petain.[70] The Vichy government would in fact offer a subsidy to returning farmers, although this and other agricultural policies it instituted were largely ineffectual and fell far short of Vichy's official peasantist discourse.[71]

Architects at the International Folklore Conference expressed another set of concerns about the growing modern "anomie" in provincial France[72] and denounced the Le Corbusian approach to "houses built like machines, with standardized parts."[73] Echoing many of their contemporaries in France, these architects warned that French regions could easily lose their cultural identity in an increasingly standardized world. But the solution they embraced was a conciliatory one. Echoing the Rural Center's efforts to synthesize old and new elements in its model country village, architects at the Folklore Conference debated ways to combine vernacular traditions with modern materials and techniques. All of these exhibits and speeches on rural France in 1937 expressed a common concern about the radical transformation of traditionalist rural France and proposed similar solutions to ensure its adaptation and survival.

Le Corbusier endorsed some aspects of this shared vision in his Modern Times Pavilion, but he also dissented in important ways. Le Corbusier's pavilion promoted his notorious urban schemes, but it also presented for the first time his novel ideas for the restructuring of rural spaces. Like his fellow planners who added "ruralism" to the urbanism exhibit in 1937, the master urbanist asserted the need to extend planning and development schemes to the countryside as well as the city. Le Corbusier borrowed terms and concepts from his "radiant city" in these proposals for a "radiant farm" (*ferme radieuse*) with its *logis du paysan* and *unités agraires*. His approach to rural planning shared certain precepts seen elsewhere in the exposition. Most important, he maintained the family farm as the basic unit in this rural utopia. As in the other rural exhibits, Le Corbusier's *logis du paysan* came equipped with the same modern comforts and commodities as its urban equivalent (the *logis citadin*): "air, water, sun, electricity, heat, and all the domestic conveniences to liberate the farmer's wife."[74] Administrative, social, and economic services were centralized in a small "cooperative village." As in the Rural Center, cooperatives were to play a key role in the agricultural economy, and a cooperative silo—"stomach of the village, insurance against speculation"—provided the focal point of the village. Le Corbusier, too, omitted the church from his modern rural utopia, but his other town features were hardly revolutionary: they included a town hall, post office, club, school, mechanic's garage, cooperatives, lodging, and a swimming pool and sports stadium (showing that he too recognized the need for modern leisure facilities).

Le Corbusier parted company with the other rural visionaries, however, in his architectural aesthetic. Whereas they sought to maintain to some extent the traditional character of rural France, he called for an architectural revolution in city and country: "The house is cluttered with garbage. We must clean, sweep, throw into the trash. Wake up societies in torpor. Shake off the torpor. Act."[75] Le Corbusier conceptualized farmhouses and other rural structures primarily as tools. Modern functionalism dictated their layout, design, and choice of materials and building methods. The farmer's *logis* constituted perhaps the most radical design: set on cement pillars (*pilotis*), its long rectangular facade and flat roof created an unbroken plane of cement and glass panels. Inside, the entrance opened into a vast, minimally furnished "communal room," serving also as a panoptic "command post": the entire farm was visible from its large, second-floor windows. Here, as in Le Corbusier's urban housing designs, the pure, clean lines of a minimalist interior flooded with air and light provided their own aesthetic pleasure.

Although he shared the common concern about rural society, Le Corbusier's recommendation to make a tabula rasa of the French rural landscape, erasing traces of its local and regional history to clear the ground for a modern functionalism, contradicted the exposition's dominant rural message, which called for a moderate degree of modernization to be harmonized with vernacular traditions. The marginalization of his modernist vision in 1937 further suggests that the interwar debate between regionalist and modernist architects had definitely shifted in favor of regionalism by 1937.[76] In contrast with Le Corbusier's rural aesthetic, the prescriptive vision espoused throughout the other rural exhibits was encapsulated in the Rural Center's village museum, created by Georges-Henri Rivière, director of the National Museum of Popular Arts and Traditions.

The Ideal French Village: Romenay-en-Bresse

Mounted in the Rural Center's town hall, Rivière's prototypical "village museum" (*musée de terroir*) featured the small French village of Romenay-en-Bresse, located in the Saone-et-Loire region. The minister of agriculture initially justified his selection of Romenay-en-Bresse for the Rural Center exhibit because it already possessed a local museum, founded several years earlier. Georges Monnet wanted to acknowledge this effort at local cultural preservation and encourage the founding of similar village museums throughout France.

But the designation of this particular village, and the manner of its representation, also served larger purposes. The village museum vividly underlined the exposition's omnipresent message: progress could be integrated without extinguishing tradition, and only the successful synthesis of old and new could guarantee a continued vitality and sense of identity in rural France. Rivière's museum presented a series of documentary panels (combining photographs with text) and material artifacts emphasizing Romenay's deep historical roots and illustrating its evolution from pre-Roman times to the present. Indeed, even its name asserts a formative Roman influence. By emphasizing this historical grounding, the exhibit suggested that Romenay had followed on a microcosmic scale all the stages of French history. But despite its long past and exposure to diverse cultural influences, Romenay was represented as having maintained its cohesion and identity. Located precariously on the border between the *pays d'oc* and the *pays d'oïl*, "the miracle of Bresse was that it had preserved, despite all sorts of divisions to which it had been subjected, a profound unity," explained folklorist Louis Cheronnet in an article on the Romenay museum. Furthermore, Romenay's ramparts (*gouilla*) "had protected it for a long time from all the attacks of Parisian progress and centralization."[77]

In other words, Romenay had successfully resisted the effects of centralization and of cultural "homogenization" that many viewed as threats to traditional local cultures. Indeed, as Cheronnet explained, Romenay's inhabitants demonstrated that they had not abandoned their inherited ways: "They showed us that clothing styles from Paris had not destroyed their taste for the costumes worn by their grandmothers."[78] The Rural Center's museum displayed photographs and material artifacts—costumes, tools, and artisanal creations—attesting to Romenay's thriving traditional culture. For instance, a panel titled "Tools" showed photographs of spinners, wheelwrights, woodcutters, and blacksmiths using time-honored artisanal techniques to perform their work. Another panel showing women dressed in Bressan costumes and bonnets informed visitors that the folkloric "Romenay group" was reviving interest in the traditional local costume.[79]

Such attempts to preserve traditional ways also help account for the choice of Romenay for the Rural Center's museum: in addition to founding a local museum, its inhabitants had organized a folklore group and resurrected the local costume. The mayor of Romenay explained that such efforts had helped "provide our community with a new feeling of cohesion and greater sense of dignity."[80] In spotlighting Romenay, the agriculture minister applauded its efforts at cultural preservation and its "newfound cohesion" secured during a time of profound cultural transformation. "On the other hand," Romenay's mayor further explained, "this respect [for the past] has not prevented us from adopting the most modern forms of agriculture and social progress." As demonstrated by the photographs, documents, and textual narrative in the Rural Center's museum, Romenay had managed to increase agricultural production and gradually introduce forms of progress—including electricity, a new school, a fire engine, and a municipal band—allowing it to modernize without sacrificing its unique character.[81]

The village museum thus reinforced the idealized image evoked in the Rural Center and throughout the other 1937 rural exhibits. It represented Romenay-en-Bresse as a harmonious synthesis of old and new that maintained its cultural integrity and "profound unity" while simultaneously adapting to the modern world. Georges Monnet hoped the Rural Center as a whole would convey this same message:

[It is] a sort of living prefiguration of what our French countryside [*notre terre de France*] will soon become, drawing from its age-old traditions the inspiration to proceed courageously, patiently and methodically toward the construction of a new world. . . . in the words of Jean Jaurès, "The river is faithful to its source when it goes toward the sea."[82]

Conclusions

As French farmers continued in the 1930s to migrate to cities plagued by unemployment and labor unrest, policy makers across the political spectrum affirmed the need to stem the "rural exodus" and agreed on the desirability of maintaining a balance between industry and agriculture, then still occupying one-third of the French working population. To meet these goals and also ensure the long-term viability of French agriculture, the planners of the Rural Center adopted a balanced modernist formula: support independent landowning farmers, encourage them to rationalize their production and increase their productivity, and develop the existing network of cooperatives and other farmers' associations. Just as perceptions in the late nineteenth century of the small French farmer as guarantor of social stability (and of agriculture as a necessary counterbalance to industrialization) underlay the protectionist 1892 Méline tariff, which had very real and lasting effects on French agricultural development, so the newfangled image of the modern *agriculteur*, projected in the 1937 Exposition, helped give shape to a new vision of the efficient, medium-size family farmer that would inspire policy makers under the Fifth Republic.

However, the 1937 village was not merely the staging of a socioeconomic blueprint for rural France. It also recast the image of the French peasant, debunking both the romanticized notions of country living that had glossed over deficient conditions plaguing real rural communities and the negative counter-model of the backward, uncivilized peasant. Like those it replaced, the refashioned image of the modern *agriculteur* invited French farmers to appropriate an externally defined image, fashioned by agricultural leaders working in neo-corporatist collaboration with the state and tailored to suit a national social and economic agenda.

Images of rural France and the French peasantry further suggest that cultural policies and symbols long identified with the Vichy regime were in fact rooted in republican France. Three years before Pétain's National Revolution adopted a ruralist rhetoric with the motto "The earth does not lie" and championed the peasant as virtuous guardian of the French race, these themes were showcased in the 1937 Exposition. Such continuity is all the more significant in an exhibit sponsored by the Popular Front government, often portrayed by its opponents as an antagonist of the French peasantry. Popular Front involvement in the Rural Center attests instead to the considerable attention it gave to defining and promoting the well-being of the countryside. The championing by the Left of images previously exploited more effectively by the Right demonstrates how cultural symbols like the "peasant" and "rural France" were—and continue to be—refashioned and reinterpreted as constitutive elements of a French collective identity. However, the history of the Rural Center also suggests that the Popular Front did not simply adopt a hegemonic "essentialist discourse" elaborated by the conservative Right around a "true France" of peasants and provincials. Rather, Right and Left competed to articulate a prescriptive social vision for farmers and made different uses of the polysemic "peasant" image that carried such potency in France during the unsettling decade of the 1930s.[83]

Even today, images of peasants and provincial France remain key emblems of French national identity, and continue to serve as vehicles to express concerns about such issues as the social and cultural costs of unbridled "progress" or the impact of centralization and cultural hegemony. As such, their use and the meanings they are made to bear may be contested and "reinvented" by different social or political groups. Thus, to cite but one example, whereas ruralism carried a Vichyist taint for some time after the Occupation, leftists began to champion a return to the land and a progressive form of rural communitarianism in the post-1968 reaction against the dominant values of modern consumer society.[84]

The success of books such as *Le Cheval d'orgeuil* (1975), Pierre Jakez-Helias's memoirs of his childhood on a farm in Britanny, and movies like *Jean de Florette* and *Manon des sources*, 1980s adaptations of Marcel Pagnol stories about a citified son of peasant parents who "returns to the earth" with his own wife and daughter, and the more recent movies about Pagnol's own Provençal childhood at the turn of the century (*La Gloire de mon père* and *Le Château de ma mère*) attest to a continued public interest in France's rural and provincial identity. However, this interest is variable, affected today, as in 1937, by historical circumstances shaping public receptivity to such images—rural nostalgia seems to be strongest in times of economic difficulty and social malaise—and by the meanings invested in these images by those producing and receiving them.

Notes

I would like to thank Susan Carol Rogers, John Keeler, and Michel Beaujour, as well as Steven Ungar and Tom Conley, for their helpful comments on this essay. For a fuller discussion of the questions raised here, see Shanny Peer, "Modern Representations of

Tradition in the 1937 International Exposition: Regions, Peasants and Folklore," Ph.D. dissertation, New York University, 1992. Unless otherwise noted, all translations in this chapter are my own.

1. "France Criticizes Farm Trade Pact as 'Unacceptable,'" *New York Times*, 21 November 1992.

2. "Paysans: Pour en finir avec les idées fausses," *Nouvel observateur*, 10–16 December 1992, 46–47.

3. Susan Carol Rogers, "Good to Think: The 'Peasant' in Contemporary France," *Anthropological Quarterly* 60 (April 1987): 56. For a discussion of rural imagery in British literature, see Raymond Williams, *The Country and the City* (New York: Oxford University Press, 1973).

4. Henri Mendras, *La Fin des paysans: Changements et innovations dans les sociétés rurales françaises* (Paris: SEDEIS, 1967).

5. Among the numerous articles analyzing representations of peasants in France, see Rogers, "Good to Think"; Jean-Claude Chamboredon, "Peinture des rapports sociaux et invention de l'éternel paysan: Les deux manières de Jean-François Millet," *Actes de la recherche en sciences sociales* 17–18 (November 1977): 6–28; Richard Brettell and Caroline Brettell, *Painters and Peasants in the Nineteenth Century* (New York: Rizzoli, 1983); Yves Lequin, ed., *Histoire des Français XIXe–XXe siècles: La Société* (Paris: Armand Colin, 1984), 121–51.

6. See Christian Faure, *Le Projet culturel de Vichy: Folklore et Révolution nationale 1940–1944* (Paris/Lyon: CNRS/Presses universitaires de Lyon, 1989).

7. Dean MacCannell, *The Tourist: A New Theory of the Leisure Class* (New York: Schocken, 1976), 26–27.

8. Edmond Labbé, *Exposition internationale des arts et techniques dans la vie moderne, Paris 1937: Rapport général*, 11 vols. (Paris: Imprimerie nationale, 1938–40), 4:623.

9. "Exposition 1937: Vue d'ensemble," *La Voix de la terre*, 9 July 1937, 1.

10. See Isabelle Collet, "Le Monde rural aux expositions universelles de 1900 et 1937," in *Muséologie et ethnologie: Notes et documents du Musée national des arts et traditions populaires* (Paris: Editions de la Réunion des musées nationaux, 1988).

11. Richard Kuisel, *Capitalism and the State in Modern France: Renovation and Economic Management in the Twentieth Century* (Cambridge: Cambridge University Press, 1981), 17. In this chapter, I use the term *agrarian* in keeping with Pierre Barral's broad definition: "farmers [or their representatives] fighting to defend their place in industrial society." It bears no value judgment, may refer to large landowners or small farmers, and is not associated with any particular political orientation; agrarians may be politically conservative or progressive. Pierre Barral, *Les Agrariens français de Méline à Pisani* (Paris: Presses de la Fondation nationale des sciences politiques, 1968), 13.

12. Pierre Bourdieu, "Une Classe objet," *Actes de la recherche en sciences sociales* 17–18 (November 1977): 4.

13. Mr. Avenol, inaugural speech given at the "Exposition européenne de l'habitation rurale," 17 June 1937. Reproduced in Labbé, *Rapport général*, 4:627.

14. Annie Moulin, *Les Paysans dans la société française de la Révolution à nos jours* (Paris: Seuil, 1988), 180.

15. Gordon Wright, *Rural Revolution in France: The Peasantry in the Twentieth Century* (Stanford, Calif.: Stanford University Press, 1964), 69.

16. Henri Sellier, introduction to *L'Exposition européenne de l'habitation rurale: Catalogue officiel* (Paris: n.p., 1937).

17. Henri Sellier, inaugural speech given at the Exposition européenne de l'habitation rurale, 4 June 1937. Reproduced in Labbé, *Rapport général*, 4:631.

18. The Popular Front would later add a Maison du Travail pavilion devoted to the working classes.

19. "L'Exposition à faire," *Le Progrès agricole*, 7 November 1937, 1.

20. Minutes of the Exposition's Permanent Commission, 26 June 1936, File F12 230 (temporary classification), French National Archives.

21. Labbé, *Rapport général*, 4:133–34.

22. Marcel Faure, cited in Wright, *Rural Revolution*, 40.

23. Founded in 1919 by agrarian syndicalist leaders, the Confédération nationale des associations agricoles was intended to act as a coordinating body to represent farmers' interests on a national level and inspire peasantist unity. However, political and professional rivalries soon prevented the CNAA from fulfilling its aspirations. See Augé-Laribé, *La Politique agricole de la France de 1880 à 1940* (Paris: Presses universitaires de France, 1950), 441–43; Barral, *Agrariens*, 206.

24. Ivan Karp, "Culture and Representation," in *Exhibiting Cultures: The Poetics and Politics of Museum Display*, ed. Ivan Karp and Steven Lavine (Washington, D.C.: Smithsonian Institution Press, 1991), 15.

25. In *Journal officiel, Débats du Sénat*, 19 March 1936, 355.

26. For a discussion of the state's role, see Wright, *Rural Revolution*, 40–46, 58–74; Moulin, *Les Paysans*, 179–92.

27. Quoted in Barral, *Agrariens*, 248.

28. Wright, *Rural Revolution*, 55–56.

29. The 1932 and 1936 elections showed rising support for the SFIO in some rural districts, particularly in the Centre and the Midi. In 1936, an increase in rural votes for the SFIO compensated for losses in urban areas. However, rightists still outnumbered leftists in rural areas by two to one.

30. In *Journal officiel, Débats de la Chambre*, 19 February 1937, 643.

31. "Les Partis du Front populaire vont-ils tenir les engagements qu'ils ont pris vis-à-vis de la paysannerie?" *La Volonté paysanne*, 5 December 1937, 1.

32. The demand-side economics of the Popular Front essentially relied on wage hikes for salaried workers to increase demand, thereby theoretically raising prices for agricultural and other goods. This approach failed; prices remained low, and many farmers remained destitute. See Augé-Laribé, *Politique*, 422, or Wright, *Rural Revolution*, 59, for more information on the Popular Front's agricultural platform.

33. Augé-Laribé served for much of the interwar period as general secretary of the Confédération nationale des associations agricoles and represented France at the Institut international d'agriculture in Rome.

34. Augé-Laribé subscribed to the common perception that the CGT and SFIO favored urban workers over farmers (*Politique*, 380). Although he approved of certain measures taken by Georges Monnet, he held that Monnet's accomplishments were in fact realizations of "previously planned projects" (387).

35. Thus, the committee included representatives of the Union nationale des syndicats agricoles, the Fédération nationale de la mutualité et de la coopération agricole, the Assemblée permanente des présidents de chambres d'agriculture, and the Confédération nationale des associations agricoles. The right-wing agrarian movements, including Dorgerès's Peasant Defense Committees and the Agrarian Party, were not represented, nor was the JAC, but neither were the Socialist CNP or the Communist CGTP.

36. John Keeler, *The Politics of Neocorporatism in France: Farmers, the State, and Agricultural Policy-Making in the Fifth Republic* (New York: Oxford University Press, 1987).

37. Georges Monnet, "Preface," in *Exposition internationale des arts et techniques, Paris 1937: Le Centre rural* (Paris: n.p., 1937).

38. For an excellent study on regionalist literature in France, see Anne-Marie Thiesse, *Ecrire la France: Le Mouvement littéraire régionaliste de langue française entre la Belle Epoque et la Libération* (Paris: Presses universitaires de France, 1991).

39. Moulin, *Paysans*, 207.

40. *Le Centre rural*, n.p.

41. "Le Centre rural à l'Exposition 1937," printed document published by the exposition, on file at the Bibliothèque Historique de la Ville de Paris.

42. This formula, inspired by the Danish and Dutch models, corresponded to one of the three schools of thought popular among French agrarians between the wars, the other two being inspired by the "neophysiocrat" and corporatist models. See Wright, *Rural Revolution*, 46–49.

43. On the Socialist agricultural policies elaborated by Compère-Morel and Jaurès, see Barral, *Agrariens*, 152–64, 243–47.

44. Compère-Morel, speaking in 1919, cited in Barral, *Agrariens*, 195.

45. Barral, *Agrariens*, 249.

46. Estimates on these numbers vary. See Augé-Laribé, *Politique*, 477–78; Barral, *Agrariens*, 233, 341; Moulin, *Paysans*, 189.

47. "Un Beau Mirage: Le Centre rural de l'Exposition," *Le Petit Journal*, 16 July 1937.

48. *Bulletin municipal officiel: Procès-verbaux du Conseil municipal de Paris*, 24 December 1936, 681.

49. "Le Centre rural à l'Exposition," *La Croix*, 22 November 1937.

50. "Où en est l'Exposition?" *L'Effort paysan*, 5 June 1937, 1.

51. "L'Agriculture à l'Exposition: Le Village sans clocher," *Avenir du plateau central*, 27 March 1937.

52. "L'Eglise à l'Exposition," *Le Foyer rural*, 15 March 1937, 1.

53. "Le Centre rural à l'Exposition 1937."

54. See Barral, *Agrariens*, 256–282.

55. For a discussion of agricultural legislation adopted by the Fifth Republic, see Michel Gervais, Marcel Jollivet, and Yves Tavernier, *La Fin de la France paysanne de 1914 à nos jours*, vol. 4 of *Histoire de la France rurale*, ed. Georges Duby and Armand Wallon, 4 vols. (Paris: Seuil, 1976), 583–626.

56. The French were less likely than the Swiss, the Swedes, or the Hungarians—who lived in countries where folklore served to consolidate national identity—to use rural architecture to symbolize the nation. Catherine Bertho-Lavenir discusses national uses

of rural architecture in world's fairs in an unpublished paper titled "Naissance et développement de l'idée régionaliste: Essai de comparaison européenne."

57. Jean Lecronier, "L'Exposition de 1937 et l'agriculture," *Revue d'agriculture*, May 1937, 72–75.

58. Ibid., 72.

59. René Gobillot, "Le Centre rural à l'Exposition," *L'Architecture*, 15 August 1937, 284.

60. See Shanny Peer, "The French Uses of Folklore: The Reinvention of Folklore in the 1937 International Exposition," *Folklore Forum* 22, nos. 1/2 (1989): 62–77.

61. Lecronier, "L'Exposition de 1937," 75.

62. Gobillot, "Le Centre rural," 284.

63. "La Fête au village," *L'Oeuvre*, 19 July 1937.

64. "Les Dentellières du Puy au Centre rural," *Le Centre rural* (weekly newspaper published by the Agriculture Committee during the Exposition), 15 June 1937, 1.

65. Panels of the Romenay museum, held in the archives of the Musée national des arts et traditions populaires.

66. *Arts et métiers graphiques*, 15 March 1938, 58.

67. Léon-Paul Fargue, "Un Flâneur à l'Exposition: Le Centre rural," *Le Figaro*, 11 September 1937.

68. Cincinnatus, "Le Centre simili-rural à l'Exposition," *La Belle France*, July 1937, 38.

69. Sellier, introduction, iii–iv.

70. In 1905, Jules Méline wrote a book recommending a policy of "return to the land" to "protect us from the troubles which result from the too exclusive development of manufacture." Jules Méline, *Return to the Land*, trans. Justin McCarthy (New York: Dutton, 1907), 220–21.

71. See Barral, *Agrariens*, 256–82; Moulin, *Paysans*, 193–201.

72. Speakers in the section on "modern construction" included architects Henri Pacon, René Clozier, Henri-Jacques Le Même, and Charles Moreux, and sculptor Joël Martel. See *Travaux du Premier Congrès international de folklore: Tenu à Paris du 23 août au 28 août 1937 à l'Ecole du Louvre* (Tours: Arrault, 1938).

73. Henri Pacon, "Faut-il maintenir à la maison des caractères folkloriques?" in ibid., 365.

74. Charles-Edouard Jeanneret, *Des canons, des munitions? Merci! Des logis S.V.P. Le Pavillon des Temps Nouveaux* (Boulogne: L'Architecte d'aujourd'hui, 1938), 24.

75. Ibid., 51.

76. See Jean-Claude Vigato, "L'Architecture du régionalisme: Les origines du débat (1900–1950)," in *Dossiers et documents 4: Les Trois Reconstructions: 1919–1940–1945* (published by the Institut français d'architecture) (December 1983).

77. Louis Cheronnet, "Voyage folklorique en Bresse," *Marianne*, 7 April 1937.

78. Ibid.

79. "Le musée de terroir de Romenay," photographs in the archives of the Musée national des arts et traditions populaires, Paris.

80. "Les Bressans à Paris," *L'Indépendent* (Louhans), 1 September 1937.

81. For a detailed description of the Romenay museum, see Georges-Henri Rivière's article in *Chambres d'Agriculture: Faits et documents*, 30 March 1938, E11–E12.

82. Monnet, "Preface," n.p.

83. Herman Lebovics argues that the Right developed an essentialist discourse around the notion of "True France" that became a dominant cultural paradigm in France between 1900 and 1945. According to Lebovics, rural France, the provinces and folklore, constituted important tropes in this paradigm, and the Popular Front was simply adopting the Right's hegemonic discourse by taking up these themes and adding workers to the idea of a fixed national cultural heritage. See *True France: The Wars over Cultural Identity, 1900–1945* (Ithaca, N.Y.: Cornell University Press, 1992).

84. See Claude Karnoouh, "The Lost Paradise of Regionalism: The Crisis of Post-Modernity in France," *Telos* 67 (1986): 11–26.

2 / Colonialism Exposed:
Miss France D'Outre-mer, 1937

Elizabeth Ezra

In a coffee-table book published in conjunction with the 1937 Exposition universelle, there is an account of a beauty contest held on the Ile des Cygnes, the narrow strip of land in the middle of the Seine that housed a miniature replica of France's colonial empire:

> Les dix beautés concurrentes, qui postulent le titre envié de Miss France d'outre-mer, toutes élues dans leur pays d'origine, sont nées de l'alliance d'un Français avec une Indigène de nos colonies ou ce qui se présente assez rarement, d'une Française ou d'une Européenne avec un Indigène. Ce sont des métisses, à l'exception de l'une d'elles, admirable créole de race blanche de la Réunion, et qui, pour cette raison, se sait hors concours.[1]

> [The ten beauties competing for the coveted title of Miss Overseas France, all elected in their country of origin, are each the product of a union between a French man and a woman from the colonies, or, what's much less common, between a French woman and a male native. These are hybrids, with the exception of one of them, a splendid Creole of the white race from Reunion Island who, for this reason, knows that she is out of the running.]

Miss Reunion Island, by virtue of her white skin, has an unfair advantage over the other, less fortunate, contestants; she is disqualified in the interest of fairness, but put on display so that spectators can behold her "admirable" beauty. Ironically, she stands out from her peers precisely because she is not different enough—too much "France," not enough "Outre-mer." Yet the winner of the contest cannot be *too* different, as the same account suggests: "Le jury décerne le titre de Miss France d'outre-mer à la Guadeloupéenne, Mlle Casalan, à la chair d'une pâleur ivoirine [The jury bestows the title of Miss Overseas France upon the Guadeloupean, Miss Casalan, whose skin is as pale as ivory]."[2] The winner must be as white as possible, without being so white that she would be "hors concours." She must be white enough to conform to French standards of beauty, yet she must retain the mark of difference that makes her exotic.

What this event ultimately exhibits, besides flesh, is the tension between identity and difference that characterized French imperial rhetoric throughout the Third Republic. It is the literal embodiment, or representation through the body, of the assimilation debate that not only informed France's colonial relations, but also played a determining role in its relations with other world powers. The identity that France was perpetually constructing in relation to those countries it dominated culturally, politically, and militarily reinforced the aggressive image it sought to convey to countries that posed a military threat to France—particularly Germany. This dual position, which might be deemed at once offensive and defensive, can be read in our beauty contest's title, in which the word "Miss," which reflects the foreign origins of this cultural event, undermines the hegemonic pretensions of the expression "France d'Outre-mer."[3]

It is no accident that the close ties linking colonialism to nationalist posturing were most visible in the decades following the Franco-Prussian War and in those that separated the two world wars. Between 1880 and 1895, French colonial possessions increased in area from 1 to 9.5 million square kilometers, and the number of colonial subjects rose from five to fifty million.[4] Between the two world wars, territorial expansion gave way to promotional expansiveness, resulting in two major exhibitions devoted entirely to colonialism, including the 1922 Marseille exhibition and the enormously popular 1931 Exposition coloniale internationale, as well as lavish celebrations commemorating the one-hundredth anniversary of the conquest of Algeria. In the 1930s, a growing emphasis was placed on colonial issues in mass-circulation papers such as *L'Echo de Paris, Le Petit Parisien,* and *Le Figaro;* special supplements and even entire issues devoted to the empire were published by *Le Temps, les Annales,* and *l'Illustration.*[5] It is not without reason that this period is often referred to as the "apogee" of French imperialism.[6]

Colonialism and nationalism converged explicitly in the proposal for the Miss Overseas France contest, submitted to exhibition organizers in 1936, which pitted France against Germany in a battle of birthrates:

> Nous souffrons d'une déficience terrifiante de natalité (700,000 enfants par an contre 1,200,000 en Allemagne) et tous les remèdes essayés pour aveugler cette

hémorragie ont échoué. Notre empire colonial de 60 millions d'habitants nous offre peut-être le dernier, par l'amalgame de ces races prolifiques avec la nôtre?[7]

[We are suffering from a terrifying deficiency in birthrate (700,000 babies a year versus 1,200,000 in Germany) and all the remedies attempted in order to stop this hemorrhage have failed. Perhaps our colonial empire of 60 million inhabitants offers us the final remedy, through the amalgamation of these prolific races with ours.]

This was not the first time that France had appealed to its colonial empire for a solution to its manpower problem: the use of colonial subjects, particularly West Africans, as cannon fodder in World War I has been well documented.[8] Rather than soliciting bodies for the purpose of using them as human battle shields, however, this proposal envisages another function for them—as reproductive partners.

The emphasis on comparative birthrates in the contest proposal reflected a persistent French preoccupation with *dénatalité* (declining birthrate), the vestiges of which can be seen in France today in the discounts for *familles nombreuses* (large families) offered at movie theaters and zoos. This preoccupation resulted in the increasing rhetorical value placed on maternity through the first decades of the twentieth century.[9] The contestants vying for the title of Miss France d'Outre-mer represented motherhood doubly: first, by virtue of their status as products of *mariages coloniaux* (colonial marriages), and second—because, like most beauty contests, this one was designed to appeal to men—by virtue of their status as potential producers in future unions. The Miss France proposal reflects this double status, as well as the equation of beauty and racial compatibility that was to be the ultimate justification for the contest:

Mais cet amalgame faut-il l'encourager, et avec lesquelles? Faut-il le décourager avec de telles autres? Entre la doctrine coloniale espagnole, qui a pratiqué cet amalgame, et la doctrine anglaise qui l'abomine, la France pourrait faire des *Distinguos* suivant les races. Un jeune Français, fonctionnaire ou commerçant, qui va se fixer aux colonies, saurait les races qui se marient à la nôtre, en beauté, et celles qui avortent en laideur.[10]

[But should we encourage this amalgamation, and if so, with which races? Should we discourage mixtures with certain races? Between the Spanish colonial doctrine, which practiced this interbreeding, and the English doctrine, which abhors it, France could create *Distinguos* according to race. A young French bureaucrat or businessman who settles in the colonies would know which races to marry with ours by their beauty, and which abort in ugliness.]

The use of the verb *avorter* here to describe unsuitable marriage partners is extremely suggestive, especially coming just a few sentences after France's declining birthrate is described as a *hémorragie,* a term that stands out not only because of its illustrative force, but also because it is a poor metaphor: a hemorrhage is the loss of something that already exists, not the failure to create something that does not yet exist. This passage exemplifies what Alice Yaeger Kaplan has called the "abortion anxiety" that took hold of France between the wars.[11] Abortion and contraception had been illegal in France since 1920, the year in which, not uncoincidentally, a government decree had established a series of medals to be awarded to mothers of large families.[12]

Motherhood and the national obsession with race also converged at another display at the 1937 Exposition titled "La Famille, la Femme, l'Enfant," whose promotional claims were echoed in a popular women's magazine: "Nous vous demandons de considérer ici, d'un œil tendre et grave, le plus important problème de notre époque [Here we ask you to consider, compassionately and seriously, the most important problem of our era]," to which was added this parenthetical comment: "Le plus important, en effet, puisqu'il s'agit de l'avenir de notre race [The most important indeed, because it concerns the future of our race]."[13] A problem conceived in terms of the future of a "race," whose solution lay, as the organizer of the beauty contest claimed, in determining which were the right "amalgames," made perfect sense at an exhibition that included a section devoted to the triple theme of sports, physical education, and eugenics.[14] Here, improvement of the individual was linked in no uncertain terms to the improvement of the race.

In official documents, the Miss France d'Outre-mer contest was referred to as the Concours du Meilleur Mariage Colonial (best colonial marriage contest) and pitched as "une présentation relative à l'eugénisme [a presentation on eugenics]."[15] The desire to determine which were the "best" marriages was a logical extension of *puériculture,* a term used by eugenicists to denote "questions of heredity and selection in their application to the human species."[16] An outgrowth of the natalist organizations of the 1890s, which united conservatives concerned about the declining birthrate and Catholics opposed to birth control, the *puériculture* movement appealed to a wide variety of health professionals because it advocated prenatal care, breast-feeding, and premarital health examinations. Were it not for what William H. Schneider calls their "hereditarian underpinnings," such proposals would amount to little more than routine medical advice.[17] However, a preoccupation with "biological regeneration" blurred the boundaries between well-baby care and social engineering, resulting in the motto "Puericulture before procreation," which expanded prenatal care to include considerations of the moral as well as physical influence of ancestry. The physicians, statisticians, and public health officials who founded the French Eugenics Society in 1912 usually limited their recommendations for "social hygiene" to campaigns against alcoholism and disease, but there were also those who advocated restrictions on immigration and the sterilization of "undesirables."[18]

Proposals designed to increase the population thus coexisted with those intended to regulate it. Both perspectives ultimately converged in the concept of ethnic purity, the popularity of which coincided with the sharp rise in immigration after World War I. The eugenicists, bolstered by the writings of racial theorists such as Alexis Carrel and Joseph-Arthur de Gobineau (whose *Essai sur l'inégalité des races humaines* reached a wide audience only after the turn of the century, although it was first published in 1853), sought to reinforce the racial divisions they deemed natural by cloaking their theories of racial hierarchies in the positivistic language of the biological sciences. One such race-thinker was René Martial, a public health physician and lecturer at the Institut d'Hygiène de la Faculté de Médecine de Paris, who used the biochemical index of blood types devised by Ludwik and Hannah Hirszfeld to develop an influential theory of "interracial grafting." This index showed a higher proportion of type B blood among non-Europeans, which prompted Martial to recommend the following guidelines for immigration policy: "Keep the O's and the A's, eliminate the B's, and keep the AB's if the psychological and health examination is favorable."[19] Although it might seem that the separatist exhortations of the eugenicists contradicted the inclusive discourse of the advocates of *métissage,* the extent to which these discourses actually overlapped should become clear in the pages that follow.

Organized by the Institut International d'Anthropologie, the Premier Congrès Latin d'Eugénique (the very name of which indicates a predilection for dividing the world into neat categories) met on 1–3 August 1937 in conjunction with the world's fair.[20] One of the speakers at the conference, a Dr. Georges Schreiber, who held various leadership roles in the French Eugenics Society throughout his career, presented a paper titled "Allocations familiales et eugénique [*sic*]" (Familial and eugenic incentives) in which he advocated a system of financial subsidies designed to promote what he considered to be desirable marriages:

> Nous estimons . . . qu'il serait possible de tirer des Allocations familiales des effets eugéniques. Pour qu'elles exercent une influence sur la qualité de la population, il conviendrait d'une part d'élever notablement le taux de ces Allocations chaque fois que les parents, après enquête, seront considérés comme des procréateurs désirables et les enfants qu'ils mettent au monde comme des êtres sains, vigoureux et aucunement entachés d'une tare héréditaire.[21]

[We believe it possible to create eugenic results from the Familial Incentives. So that they influence the quality of the population, it would be best to raise appreciably the amounts of the incentives each time the parents, upon examination, are considered to be desirable procreators, and the children they bring into the world, healthy, vigorous, and unblemished by hereditary defect.]

Lest there be any confusion about the provenance of these ideas, René Martial, who also spoke at the conference, took pains to distinguish French eugenics from that practiced by the Germans—but he was equally anxious to distance himself from what he called the "laisser-aller" (free-for-all) of unions based solely on mutual attraction:

Les deux opinions les plus répandues aujourd'hui en matière de métissage sont les suivantes. Ou bien on en revient à la vieille idée de la pureté à jamais perdue et à l'exclusion formelle de certaines races. Exemples: le massacre des Peaux-Rouges par les Américains, l'expulsion des Marranes d'Espagne par Philippe II et celle des Juifs par Hitler; ou bien, on se contente du laisser-aller et de l'anarchie, on dit que le mélange des races est inoffensif et que l'on ne voit pas pourquoi le sentiment d'amour ne serait pas le seul guide entre un chinois [*sic*] et une française [*sic*] ou une américaine [*sic*]. Les deux théories, celle de l'exclusivisme comme celle du laisser-aller, sont également mauvaises, car, s'il y a de bons métissages, il y en a aussi de très mauvais.[22]

[The two most widely held opinions today concerning interbreeding are the following. Either we return to the old idea of some long-lost purity, to the formal exclusion of certain races. Examples: the massacre of the redskins by the Americans, the expulsion of the Marranes of Spain by Philip II and that of the Jews by Hitler. Or we settle for chaos and anarchy, we say the mixing of races is inoffensive and we fail to see why love cannot be the sole guide between a Chinese man and a French or American woman. Both theories, that of exclusivity as well as that of *laisser-aller,* are equally bad; because, if there are good mixtures, there are also very bad ones.]

French eugenics was to provide a happy medium between the equally abhorrent excesses of genocide and reproductive freedom. While the Miss France d'Outre-mer contest was busy crowning one of the "bons métissages"—indeed, the "meilleur"—scientists at the eugenics conference were warning against those deemed "très mauvais." In his paper, Martial invoked his expertise on the subject of blood type in order to provide examples illustrating the danger posed by certain combinations. These examples are worth citing at length:

1er Cas. Un homme créole épouse une française [*sic*] et en a trois filles. L'aînée a quatre enfants bien portants; la seconde a épousé un juif, un de ses deux enfants, le garçon, est un enfant fortement arriéré. Il y a eu métissage entre un sang déjà métissé et un sang d'origine asiatique.

2me Cas. Un juif épouse une anglaise. Sa fille épouse un français. De ce mariage naissent trois garçons, tous trois en bon état. Deux restent célibataires, un se marie et a cinq enfants, dont quatre garçons, solides et bien portants et une fille idiote. Métissage d'un sang asiatique avec un sang occidental.

3me Cas. Un français épouse une orientale. Ils ont quatre enfants. L'aîné est un mythomane avéré et presque dangereux. Métissage d'un français avec une asiatique.

4me Cas. Un français épouse une orientale dont il a un garçon et deux filles. L'aînée des deux filles paraît tout-à-fait normale mais épouse un chinois. Est-ce l'instinct des sangs B qui la pousse?[23]

[Case 1. A Creole man marries a French woman and they have three daughters. The eldest daughter herself has four healthy children; the second marries a Jew, and one of their two children, a boy, is severely retarded. This is a case of interbreeding between already mixed blood and blood of Asiatic origin.

Case 2. A Jew marries an English woman. Their daughter marries a Frenchman. This marriage produces three boys, all three healthy. Two of them remain single, and one marries and has five children: four solid, healthy boys, and a mentally impaired daughter. A case of intermingling of Asiatic blood and occidental blood.

Case 3. A Frenchman marries an Asian woman. They have four children. The eldest is a known mythomaniac and almost dangerous. A case of mixing French and Asiatic blood.

Case 4. A Frenchman marries an Asian woman with whom he has a son and two daughters. The eldest daughter appears normal, but marries a Chinese man. Was it the instinct of the B-type bloods that drove her to it?]

Martial's point is clear: unsavory unions such as these produce grotesquely abnormal offspring, ranging from a man known to embellish the truth to a woman who *appears* to be normal, but marries a Chinese. Using this logic, Martial advocates the institution of a "sélection sévère" (rigorous selection) in immigration policy.

It is apparent from the examples he cites that one of the groups targeted for exclusion by Martial is the Jews. Despite his condemnation of Hitler for putting into practice such a policy, his own suggestion that the union of Jews and non-Jews can only produce disastrous results amounts to implying that excluding the Jews from France would be an important part of the effort to improve the French "espèce." The long history of specifically French anti-Semitism notwithstanding, Martial's insinuations situate him closer to Hitler than his efforts to carve out a place for a national eugenics movement would suggest; indeed, this affinity would leave the realm of abstraction and innuendo some five years later, as the Vichy government rounded up thousands of French Jews and sent them to death camps.[24] Ironically, Martial is unable to differentiate himself from Hitler precisely to the extent that he insists upon differentiating among ethnic groups.

In his persistent quest to uncover difference in disguise, Martial also studied the family trees of certain monarchs who displayed signs of mental illness, tracing their ancestry back, in some cases five hundred years, until he found evidence of a "mixed" marriage by which to account for the future abnormality.[25] (His determination to locate difference at the root of all evil no doubt caused him to overlook the more obvious fact that, on the contrary, dull-witted royals are most often the products of an incestuous *lack* of difference.) This arbitrary imposition of difference—like Martial's attempt to differentiate himself from Hitler even while advocating Hitlerian policies and his exclusionary attribution of difference to certain ethnic groups—is the flip side of the equally contrived imposition of homogeneity implicit in the eugenicists' claims to French racial unity.

At first glance, the attempts by one branch of the scientific community to maintain barriers between ethnic groups may seem strangely at odds with the collapse of such barriers promoted at the Best Colonial Marriage Contest. Yet the dichotomy between the separatism advocated by the physicians and anthropologists at the eugenics conference and the *métissage* promoted by the beauty contest is a false one. These positions in fact constituted complementary aspects of the same discourse—a discourse that informed the debate over two seemingly divergent, but actually inseparable, components of French colonial administrative policy.

Assimilation and Association

The complicity between the equally arbitrary categories of sameness and difference exhibited at the 1937 Exposition found its reflection in the ostensibly conflicting strategies of "assimilation" and "association." Inspired by the egalitarian rhetoric of the French Revolution, the goal of assimilation was to make model French citizens of colonial subjects, who were taught the intricacies of French language and culture in a centralized educational system. The distance between rhetoric and reality, however, was great. In most colonial possessions, there were separate governing bodies for indigenous people and French colonists. Citizenship was granted only in the *anciennes colonies* (former colonies—the Antilles, Guyana, Reunion Island, and the four "communes" of Senegal)—and even then, it was often far from automatic.[26] A case in point is West Africa, about which Michael Crowder has noted that "the African had no policy-making role, not even at the level of local government as the chief had in the Native Authority system in British West Africa. . . . Only if he managed to gain a good French education, become Christian, and prove his loyalty to France through service could he become 'assimilated' and gain the rights of a French citizen. Before 1945 less than 500 Africans had become assimilated in this way."[27] The hypocrisy of a policy that barred access to the very equality it preached is underscored by Albert Memmi in his *Portrait du colonisé:* "Le colonialiste n'a jamais décidé de transformer la colonie à son image. *Il ne peut admettre une telle adéquation, qui détruirait le principe de ses privilèges* [The colonialist has never sought to transform the colony in his image. *He cannot allow such equality, which would destroy the justification for his privileges*]."[28]

"Association," which had replaced "assimilation" as the fashionable term early in this century, claimed to respect indigenous customs; it was presented, according to Martin Deming Lewis, as "a kind of partnership of the colonial peoples with the metropolitan power, for mutual benefit."[29] Association, as it was promoted, would have amounted to a recognition of the cultural, if not political, autonomy of the countries under colonial rule. But, like assimilation, the notion of association glossed over the contradiction inherent in the notion of a partnership between colonizer and colonized. As Georges Balandier has noted, "Le rapport colonial est par essence inauthentique, il ne peut à la fois instituer la domination et reconnaître l'Autre [The colonial relationship is by definition inauthentic; it cannot at once institute domination and recognize the Other]."[30] Although both assimilation and association were featured components of colonial rhetoric, the context of subjugation that gave rise to them precluded their enactment in practice. One official in the ministry for the colonies called the alternatives "unrealisable assimilation or hypocritical association, two systems in equally flagrant contradiction of *the facts*."[31] Each discourse merely reflected a different form of spin control, a different way of serving up colonialism to the general public.[32]

Because colonial rhetoric had so little to do with colonial practice, there was ample room for ambiguity. A striking example of this can be seen in a promotional statement written in 1937 by Henry Béranger, who served the empire in a triple capacity as senator of Guadeloupe, president of the Commission des Affaires étrangères of the French Senate, and president of the Commission de la France d'Outre-mer at the world's fair. Béranger begins his preface to *L'Empire colonial français à l'Ile des Cygnes* by emphasizing the cohesion between colony and *métropole:* "Provinces d'au-delà des mers, nos possessions des cinq continents complètent, par un prolongement naturel, le tableau artistique et technique de nos provinces métropolitaines [Overseas provinces, our possessions on the five continents complete, by a natural extension, the artistic and technological tableau of our native provinces]."[33] Yet, only three paragraphs after having asserted this assimilationist view of the colonies as an extension of France, Béranger uses the word "association," which, although in this context it applies to the relationship between France and other world powers, necessarily evokes the connotation specific to early twentieth-century colonial discourse: "Dans l'évolution contemporaine qui a porté tant de grandes nations à n'être plus les provinces de tel ou tel continent, mais de véritables systèmes intercontinentaux, irradiant toute la planète, la France a marqué sa place comme créatrice d'un idéal d'association des races [In the light of modern evolution, which has impelled so many great nations to be no longer the provinces of a given continent, but instead, veritable intercontinental systems reaching across the globe, France has staked out its place as the creator of an ideal comprising an association of races]."[34] The word "province" changes meaning from one paragraph to the next: France's overseas "provinces" would enable it to outgrow the boundaries that would otherwise limit its status to that of a European province. By effacing differences between itself and its colonies, "la plus grande France" would be able to differentiate itself from the rest of Europe. The altered meaning assigned to the word "province" in the second quote also makes it necessary to take the word "association" to refer to cultural *assimilation,* a concept to which it would normally be opposed in colonial discourse. The ambiguity of the phrase "idéal d'association des races," which can refer either to relations between France and its colonial possessions or to relations between France and other world powers, results in the seemingly contradictory assertions that the colonies were both assimilated and associated, at once a part of and separate from France—much like the Ile des Cygnes itself, site of a miniature French colonial empire, in relation to the other attractions at the world's fair. Colonial administrators were unable to choose between asserting the assimilability of the colonial possessions and proclaiming their absolute alterity because they needed to do both: the politics of inclusion, which appealed to nationalist concerns about military strength, was inseparable from the politics of exclusion, which appealed to xenophobic impulses.

A Colonial Aesthetic

The tension between identity and difference in colonial discourse was made visible at the Miss France d'Outre-mer contest, which promoted an ideal that consisted of equal parts exoticism and familiarity. In order to be intelligible, difference had to be brought home to the viewing audience; it had, in other words, to be domesticated.

The domestication of difference played a major role in representations of gender as well as race. By billing contestants as the offspring of *French men* and *colonial women,* the Miss France d'Outre-mer pageant evoked the age-old allegory of the feminized colony offering herself up for the enjoyment of a masculine empire. The colonized partner in the "best" colonial marriage could only be female, just as the picture-perfect product of such a union could only be female, because the reverse scenario, in which French women would be invited to desire colonial men, would pose too great a threat to the pattern of domination built into gender roles and colonial relations alike.[35] In a context that entails the viewing of the less powerful by the more powerful, the act of looking can only confirm the inequality of the relationship—that is, it can only be objectifying.

It is for this reason that a classic text in feminist film theory, Laura Mulvey's "Visual Pleasure and Narrative Cinema," can be useful here, despite the obvious differences between a "live" visual experience and a film.[36] To the extent that Mulvey's essay can enhance our understanding of the imbalance of power cultivated by certain specular configurations that play on sexual difference, it can certainly provide a framework within which to consider a beauty contest designed to appeal to men. But the essay can also serve to illuminate the domestication of other differences—in this case, racial—at work in the same image.

Mulvey's emphasis on narrative structure foregrounds the effects produced by certain visual expressions of temporality. The spectacle of *métisses* on display would at first glance seem to exist outside of linear time, creating what Mulvey describes as the fetishistic scopophilia that confers gratification in the mere sight of the object.[37] But the contestants vying for recognition as the product of the "best colonial marriage" do, in fact, come equipped with pasts: each bears witness to a tropical romance between a (fearless) French male colonist and an (exotic) indigenous woman. The narrative thus implied, according to Mulvey, would turn the specular relationship into one of voyeurism, whose sadistic aspect she explains by referring to a familiar Freudian landmark: "[For the voyeur], pleasure lies in ascertaining guilt (immediately associated with castration), asserting control and subjugating the guilty person through punishment or forgiveness."[38] Unable to accept the difference he encounters, the voyeur must explain it in terms of a deficient similarity, imagining that the woman he observes has voluntarily put an end to the originary resemblance he ascribes to her. The male spectator who assigns blame for the creation of lack is indeed himself the perpetrator of the crime; the guilt that he "ascertains" in the woman is his own, which he has projected onto her.

In the colonial context, the phantasmagorical conversion of difference into lack takes skin color as its object. Racial complexes function like phallocentrism to the extent that they read the presence of melanin as the absence of whiteness, just as the presence of the female sexual organ is represented negatively as the lack of a male sexual organ. The positing of a French (or an Aryan) race as a norm in relation to which other races are degenerate is analagous to Freud's designation of the feminine as a deviation from the masculine norm. It is at the juncture of these racist and masculinist discourses that the Miss France d'Outre-mer contest must be situated.

As one scholar so eloquently puts it, the world's fairs "sucked the world into patterns of dependence, dominance and subjection on one great site."[39] The relationship cultivated between observers and observed at the Best Colonial Marriage Contest was not unlike that between France and its colonies: the closer they got to each other, the more apparent it became that there was an insurmountable barrier between them. The act of bringing them together did not create the barrier; it just made it visible, as if in anticipation of the question with which Aimé Césaire begins his *Discours sur le colonialisme,* "J'admets que mettre les civilisations différentes en contact les unes avec les autres est bien; que marier des mondes différents est excellent. . . . [m]ais alors, je pose la question suivante: la colonisation a-t-elle vraiment *mis en contact?* [I acknowledge that putting different cultures into contact with each other is a good thing, that to unite different worlds is an excellent thing. . . . but I ask the following question: has colonization really *established contact?*]."[40] Because the colonies were yoked to France in a relationship of domination, there was no way they could be either fully assimilated or free to associate with France—neither fully included in French political life nor entirely autonomous.

The spectacle of the Best Colonial Marriage Contest contained both an irreducibly nonmetaphorical significance—that of the position of *métisses* in the political and social structures of colonialism—and an allegorical one: that of the nationalist fear of emasculation by Germany that had been invoked in order to justify France's emasculation of its colonial possessions. By definition, imperialist assertions of superiority entail the conversion of difference into lack. Like the voyeurism elicited by one of the most celebrated national icons, Marianne in her ill-fitting bodice, the Miss France d'Outre-mer contest repeated in microcosm the projection of guilt onto the object(s) whose subjection was desired.

The ideological conversion of difference into lack made possible the collaboration between expansion and exclusion that characterized French imperialism at its "apogee." Discussions of French national identity that fail to take this collaboration into account are therefore necessarily inadequate. Recently, for example, Rogers Brubaker has opposed what he calls France's "concentric" and "assimilationist" conception of nationhood to a "bounded," "differentialist," and "ethnocultural" ideal based on essentialist notions of group identity—which he attributes to Germany.[41] Brubaker does acknowledge that both discourses have at certain moments coexisted in France: "At the time of the Dreyfus Affair, during the Vichy regime, and again in recent years, the prevailing French idiom of nationhood—state-centered and assimilationist—has been challenged by a more ethnocultural counteridiom, represented today by Jean-Marie Le Pen."[42] To these three historical moments, Brubaker also adds the interwar period.[43] According to this model, the 1937 Exposition would bear witness to a confrontation between two idioms, the "ethnocultural" one represented by the eugenicists, and the "assimilationist" one represented at the Miss France d'Outre-mer contest. In this view, the fair would mark a moment in which France struggled for self-definition, caught between the assimilationist legacy of the Revolution and the rising star of a new and divisive world order. However, this reading of the Dreyfus affair and the interwar period as anomalous blips in an otherwise uniform national landscape creates a simplistic binary between ethnocultural and assimilationist conceptions of nationhood. To relegate exclusionary discourses in France to the status of a "challenge" posed to a "dominant" assimilationist discourse is to overlook the fact that these have always coexisted in what Maxim Silverman calls "a single anthropological project in the modern era," a project he calls alternatively "modernity" and "the enlightenment concept of 'Man' (*sic*) and the community."[44] This project is located at the intersection of imperialism and nationalism, a site upon which a eugenics conference and a Best Colonial Marriage Contest could both exist, not in confrontation or contradiction, but as complementary expressions of a single conception of nationhood.

In 1936 the prominent geneticist Lucien Cuénot, who was among those urging the French government to upscale its efforts to redress the declining birthrate, warned prophetically: "France, headed towards ruin by its absence of a family policy, would make a very nice German colony."[45] Indeed, his prophecy was to be borne out sooner than he might have thought possible, as the merits of assimilation and association were debated at the border between Occupied France and Vichy.

Notes

I wish to thank Terry Rowden, Talia Schaffer, Rebecca Spang, and Steven Ungar for their helpful comments on an earlier draft of this essay.

1. Paul Dupays, *Voyages autour du monde: Pavillons étrangers et pavillons coloniaux à l'Exposition de 1937* (Paris: Henri Didier, 1938), 271. Unless otherwise noted, all translations in this essay are my own.

2. Ibid., 272.

3. According to Lois W. Banner, the first modern beauty contest was held in New York in 1854, the brainchild of P. T. Barnum. See Lois W. Banner, *American Beauty* (Chicago: University of Chicago Press, 1984), 255.

4. These figures are from Raoul Girardet, *L'Idée coloniale en France de 1871 à 1962* (Paris: Hachette, 1972), 80.

5. Pierre Montagnon, *La France coloniale* (Paris: Pygmalion/Gérard Watelet, 1988), 458.

6. See, for example, Girardet, *L'Idée coloniale.*

7. "Concours du Meilleur Mariage Colonial, Exposé du projet," dated 15 April 1936, in A.N. (Archives Nationales, Paris) F12 12258, n.p. Although the proposal is not attributed, it can be assumed that its author is Maurice de Waleffe, who conceived and organized the event.

8. Citing David Lloyd George, Hannah Arendt writes that "Clemenceau insisted at the peace table in 1918 that he cared about nothing but 'an unlimited right of levying black troops to assist in the defense of French territory in Europe if France were attacked in the future by Germany.'" *Imperialism* (San Diego, Calif.: Harcourt Brace Jovanovich, 1968), 9.

9. See Françoise Thébaud, "Maternité et famille entre les deux guerres: Idéologies et politique familiale" in *Femmes et fascismes,* ed. Rita Thalmann (n.p.: Tierce, [1987]).

10. "Concours du Meilleur Mariage," n.p.

11. Alice Yaeger Kaplan, *Reproductions of Banality: Fascism, Literature, and French Intellectual Life* (Minneapolis: University of Minnesota Press, 1986), 101–6.

12. See Susan Groag Bell and Karen M. Offen, *Women, the Family, and Freedom,* vol. 2 (Stanford, Calif.: Stanford University Press, 1983), 306–10.

13. *Eve,* 27 June 1937, 3.

14. See *Le Livre d'or officiel de l'Exposition Internationale des arts et techniques dans la vie moderne* (Paris: SPEC, 1938), 151.

15. From the "Extrait certifié conforme du Procès verbal de la Séance du 22 mai 1936, de la Commission Permanente," in the "Dossier relatif aux comptes du Comité du Meilleur Mariage Colonial" in packet 3 of A.N. F12 12258, n.p.

16. Quotation from the journal *Eugénique,* cited by William H. Schneider, "The Eugenics Movement in France 1890–1940," in *The Wellborn Science,* ed. Mark B. Adams (New York: Oxford University Press, 1990), 69–109. For a more detailed history of French eugenics, see Schneider's *Quality and Quantity: The Quest for Biological Regeneration in Twentieth-Century France* (Cambridge: Cambridge University Press, 1990).

17. Schneider, "The Eugenics Movement," 72.

18. Ibid., 75.

19. Cited in Schneider, *Quality and Quantity,* 248. Schneider also cites a 1938 pamphlet written by Jean-Marie Baron that calls type B blood "the source of all social ills" (254).

20. Founded in 1935, the International Latin Federation of Eugenics Societies had

been conceived as an alternative to the International Eugenics Federation, which in the 1930s was dominated by the Nazis and the Americans. See Schneider, "The Eugenics Movement," 97.

21. *Rapport du Premier Congrès Latin d'Eugénique* (Paris: Masson et Cie, 1937), 99.

22. Ibid., 25.

23. Ibid., 30.

24. See Michael R. Marrus and Robert O. Paxton, *Vichy France and the Jews* (New York: Basic Books, [1981]).

25. *Rapport du Premier Congrès,* 30.

26. For further discussion of the assimilation myth in colonial (and postcolonial) discourse, see Maxim Silverman, *Deconstructing the Nation: Immigration, Racism and Citizenship in Modern France* (London: Routledge, 1992), 31, 95–125.

27. Michael Crowder, "The Administration of West Africa," *Tarikh* 2, no. 4 (1969): 62.

28. Albert Memmi, *Portrait du colonisé* (Paris: Gallimard, 1985), 91. First published in 1957.

29. Martin Deming Lewis, "One Hundred Million Frenchmen: The 'Assimilation' Theory in French Colonial Policy," *Comparative Studies in Society and History* 4 (January 1962): 150.

30. Georges Balandier, "Preface," *L'Histoire* 69 (1984): 3.

31. Quoted by Jean Suret-Canale, *French Colonialism in Tropical Africa 1900–1945,* trans. Till Gottheiner (New York: Pica, 1971), 85.

32. Of assimilation, Lewis writes: "What was wrong with 'assimilation' was not that it was illogical, unrealistic, or impossible, but rather that no serious effort was ever made to carry it out"; "One Hundred Million Frenchmen," 153. Association he characterizes as a retreat from the pretense of democracy, an attempt "to reassure Frenchmen that they were not about to be inundated by the votes of millions of natives in the French colonies" (151).

33. Henry Béranger, "Avant-propos," in *L'Empire Colonial Français à l'Ile des Cygnes* (Marseille: G. Saroul, 1937), 5.

34. Ibid.

35. In *Black Skin, White Masks* (New York: Grove Press, 1967), Frantz Fanon writes of the imbalance of power that cuts across personal and political lines: "Since he is the master and more simply the male, the white man can allow himself the luxury of sleeping with many women. This is true in every country and especially in the colonies. But when a white woman accepts a black man there is automatically a romantic aspect. It is a giving, not a seizing" (46 n).

36. Laura Mulvey, "Visual Pleasure and Narrative Cinema," in *Narrative, Apparatus, Ideology,* ed. Philip Rosen (New York: Columbia University Press, 1986), 198–209. Since Mulvey's article first appeared in 1975, much has been written to problematize it. See, for example, Jackie Stacey, "Desperately Seeking Difference," in *The Sexual Subject* (London: Routledge, 1992), 244–47; David Rodowick, "The Difficulty of Difference," *Wide Angle* 5, no. 1 (1982): 4–15. See also Mulvey's "Afterthoughts on 'Visual Pleasure and Narrative Cinema' Inspired by *Duel in the Sun*," in her book *Visual and Other Pleasures* (London: Macmillan, 1989): 29–39. It is not within the scope of this essay to com-

ment on the adequacy or implications of Mulvey's arguments for the discipline of film theory.

37. Mulvey, "Visual Pleasure," 205.

38. Ibid.

39. John M. MacKenzie, quoted in Paul Greenhalgh, *Ephemeral Vistas: The Expositions Universelles, Great Exhibitions, and World's Fairs, 1851–1939* (Manchester: Manchester University Press, 1988), x.

40. Aimé Césaire, *Discours sur le colonialisme* (Paris: Présence Africaine, 1955), 9.

41. Rogers Brubaker, *Citizenship and Nationhood in France and Germany* (Cambridge: Harvard University Press, 1992), 5, 6, and passim.

42. Ibid., 13–14.

43. Ibid., 111.

44. Silverman, *Deconstructing the Nation,* 25 (Silverman's *sic*).

45. Quoted in Schneider, "The Eugenics Movement," 97.

3 / Céline on the 1937 Paris Exposition Universelle as Jewish Conspiracy

Philip H. Solomon

In March 1934, the Municipal Council of Paris decided to hold an *exposition universelle* (in the United States such an event is designated a world's fair—I will keep one of the French terms and refer to it as an exposition) in Paris that would open in May 1937. Three months later, the French government approved the project and the funds for its realization. The exposition would take place in the center of Paris—principally, the area around the Eiffel Tower on the Left Bank of the Seine and the Palais de Chaillot, built for the 1937 Exposition, on the Right Bank, with construction extending along both banks of the river. Ultimately, the exposition would cover some 250 acres—a large site by French standards but less than one-fifth the area occupied by the 1939 New York World's Fair.

Following the hugely successful 1900 Exposition, Paris had been the location of two other expositions: the 1925 Exposition des arts décoratifs et industries modernes, which occupied an area of Paris slightly to the east of the 1937 site, and the 1931 Exposition coloniale internationale, held in the Bois de Vincennes, a far more marginal site, in the southwestern part of the city. The first of these functioned primarily as a showcase for the luxury goods that France, and particularly Paris, produced—glass, furniture, tapestries, clothing, and so on. As Jean-Jacques Bloch and Marianne Delort note, "Elitism was everywhere"; that is to say, only the wealthy could properly appreciate and, of course, afford to purchase such items.[1]

As for the Colonial Exposition, it was the last display of unalloyed imperial-

66

ism in which the various colonial powers (England was not a participant, but the United States was) could exhibit the products and peoples of the lands they had conquered. Unlike the 1925 Exposition, the 1937 Exposition would be addressed to middle- and working-class audiences. It too would display colonialism, in the individual national pavilions and in the separate structures erected on pontoons in the Seine that were devoted to particular French colonies. Comparing the colonial exhibits at the 1937 Exposition with those of the one in 1925, Paul Greenhalgh comments that the floating French pavilions seemed by their very construction to reflect an attitude that was "non-committal and ephemeral" and thus were a sign of the "decline" of the imperialist enterprise for France and the other colonial powers.[2] As we shall see, colonialism would be a major theme in Céline's description of the 1937 Exposition, but it would be so-called Jewish imperialism that he would portray.

Although the project for the 1937 Exposition was approved by a centrist government under Gaston Doumergue, it was to be completed by and indissociably identified with a very differently oriented government, that of the Popular Front, under the leadership of Léon Blum—a short-lived experiment that lasted barely a year, 5 June 1936–22 June 1937 (Blum attempted, in vain, to form a new Popular Front government in March-April 1938). Hence, ironically, by the time the exposition was fully open, the government with which it had been so closely associated was no longer in power. For its detractors as well as its supporters, the Popular Front government was not judged solely on its ideology or political accomplishments but also with regard to the historical circumstances that brought it into existence.

The event that precipitated the emergence of the Popular Front began on the evening of 6 February 1934. Right-wing demonstrators started to gather at the Place de la Concorde, a short distance from the Palais Bourbon, the seat of the French Chamber of Deputies. Many of them were members of extremist organizations, such as the Jeunesses Patriotes, Camelots du Roi, Croix-de-Feu; others belonged to various veterans' groups.[3] Whatever their particular political grievances might have been, most believed that the democratic political institutions of the Third Republic had become corrupt and inefficient. A number of factors had generated that sentiment, among them the constant shuffling of ministers (five different governments within the past twenty months), the effects of a worldwide economic recession that were belatedly reaching France, an admiration for the conservative values and efficiency of the fascist regimes in Italy and Germany, and a growing polarization between Left and Right.

Right-wing antiparliamentarianism had been further exacerbated by the Stavisky affair, which had exploded that past December. Alexandre Stavisky, a

Russian-born Jew and naturalized French citizen, had been involved in a number of swindles but had always escaped prosecution, ostensibly with the help of political connections. After being implicated in yet another fraud, this time involving bonds issued by the city of Bayonne, he fled to Chamonix, Switzerland. When the police arrived, they found him dying—a suicide according to the official reports, but there was widespread belief that he had been murdered so as not to expose the political friends who had supposedly protected him and profited from his activities. "In the eyes of the right," Philippe Bernard and Henri Dubief comment, "Stavisky was a typical foreign Jewish financier mixed up with crooked parliamentarians."[4]

The demonstration of 6 February became increasingly violent over the course of the evening, eventually causing the police to open fire on the mob. The riot left fifteen dead and nearly fifteen hundred wounded, and caused the resignation of Edouard Daladier's Radical government (the Radicals, i.e., the Radical Socialists, were, despite their name, more centrist than leftist). This violence from the Right succeeded in galvanizing the Left to take action against what was perceived as a fascist threat to the Republic. Over the course of the next fifteen months, a coalition was forged among Radicals, Socialists, and Communists that would be victorious in the elections of May 1936. A crucial factor in the forming of that coalition was a change of ideology by the French Communist Party, following new directives from Moscow, that sanctioned cooperation between Communist parties and other parties on the Left in the name of opposition to fascism. Although the Communist Party would play a crucial role in the implementation of the cultural and economic policies of the Popular Front, it did not accept any ministerial positions, preferring not to alarm the electorate by participating directly in the new government and to maintain its political independence as the loyal opposition.

Most of the major social legislation of the Popular Front was passed during the first few months after it assumed power. It put an end to widespread labor unrest by means of the Matignon accords, which raised salaries and established collective bargaining agreements. Workers were granted a forty-hour workweek and a two-week paid vacation. The government also nationalized war-related industries and restructured the Bank of France.

One of the major concerns of the Popular Front was to restore a sense of republicanism to the nation by bringing French culture to the masses. Its broad-based efforts in that direction ranged from organizing museum tours to funding films and popular theater. In so doing, the Popular Front was able to draw upon a preexisting infrastructure, such as the Maisons de Culture (meeting places for cultural activities) established by the French Communist Party. As

Julian Jackson writes, "To the extent that we can talk of a Popular Front cultural doctrine, it was largely the creation of the Communist Party."[5] The displays of French literature, art, and technology at the 1937 Exposition, set up to appeal to and educate the masses, were further steps in the movement to eliminate the social distinctions that had kept the lower classes from being involved and taking pride in the accomplishments of the nation.

The Popular Front quickly succumbed to a deteriorating economic and political climate: a worsening economic situation wiped out many of the gains made by the workers and brought about renewed labor unrest; a continuing flight of capital helped undermine the value of the franc; a growing disaffection by the Communist Party, whose own domestic and foreign agendas became increasingly incompatible with those of the Blum government, eroded the Front's parliamentary support; a hesitant foreign policy that failed to sustain the Republican side in the Spanish Civil War and to respond to fascism in general further alienated the Left ; and the unrelenting opposition from the Right left the government little room to maneuver.[6]

Although the Right objected to the overall ideology of the Popular Front and particularly to its Communist support, it was, above all, the identity of Blum as a Jew that drew its wrath. Blum had been a target for anti-Semitic attacks ever since he became the leader of the French Socialist Party (officially in French the SFIO, the Section française de l'internationale ouvrière) in 1920. His ascendancy to the premiership of the Popular Front government unleashed a barrage of anti-Semitic vituperation, particularly from the extensive right-wing press, against Blum personally and against the so-called Jewish government he headed, that had not been seen since the Dreyfus affair.[7] In his *Anti-Semitism in France,* Pierre Birnbaum examines the attacks against Blum and offers a liberal sampling of their language. The epithets in question typically tend to emphasize the Otherness of the Jew in terms of geographic origin (e.g., "oriental invader"), anti-Christianity (e.g., "Socialist Satan"), animal nature (e.g., "lizard"), sexual menace (e.g., "a complete sexual pervert"), and political subversion (e.g., "Marxist agent of Communism").[8] The historian Pierre Gaxotte saw in Blum the embodiment of "evil" and "death."[9]

At the investiture of Blum as Prime Minister on 6 June in the Chamber of Deputies, Xavier Vallat, a conservative Catholic deputy, later commissioner-general for Jewish affairs under the Pétain government, calmly declared, "For the first time, gentlemen, this old Gallo-Roman country will be governed by a Jew." The obvious message of Vallat's declaration was that Blum (whose parents and grandparents had been born in France) was irrevocably an alien, a person who, by virtue of being a Jew, could not be French, and, by extension, the Popular Front government he led was no less of a foreign presence. The 1937 Exposition, so closely linked with the Blum government, was similarly stigmatized. Thierry Maulnier, a right-wing journalist, expressed his hope that the Blum regime would collapse (given its Jewish connection) and gleefully greeted the delays that had arisen in finishing the construction of the buildings for the exposition: "The exposition they have announced with such great fanfare as the triumph of the Popular Front government will not be ready. Good News."[10] The exposition was depicted in an anti-Semitic periodical called *L'Antijuif* (The anti-Jew) as a "Kikeville [Youpinville]," filled with Jews described as a "mercantile population, sticky, gluey, jabbering a native Yiddish mixed with broken French, dashing about, squealing, shouting, howling."[11] The *Cahiers céliniens* reproduce a letter written on 5 April 1937 to a friend and former lover, the Danish ballerina Karen Jensen, in which Céline complains, in an obvious reference to the Popular Front, that "the Jews and the Communists are becoming more and more insolent—the time is not far away when one will have to flee or die."[12]

Sometime in early June, shortly after the official opening of the exposition (May 24)—which would eventually attract three million visitors—Céline, vacationing in Saint Malo, on the coast of Brittany, decided to take an active role in the ideological struggles that were dividing France and began work on the first of the three anti-Semitic pamphlets he would publish over the next four years, *Bagatelles pour un massacre* (Trifles for a massacre) (none of the pamphlets has been translated into English).[13] Although these works are usually referred to as "pamphlets," they merit that appellation by virtue of their polemical tone, not their length—they all run to between three hundred and four hundred pages. The work was completed probably in November and published on 18 December 1937. Although in *Bagatelles* Céline alleges more personal reasons, it is likely that the writing of the pamphlets was precipitated by the opening of the exposition and all that such an event symbolized.

But Céline was not one of the legion of hack writers generating the flood of anti-Semitic literature that was sweeping across France during the 1930s in response to such factors as the rise of anti-Semitism abroad, notably in Nazi Germany, the increased immigration of Jews to France from Germany and from Eastern Europe, the stridency of the Right in France, and, of course, the presence of an important Jewish political leader like Léon Blum. Céline was the celebrated author of *Voyage au bout de la nuit* (Journey to the end of the night) (1932), though a second novel, *Mort à crédit* (Death on the installment plan) (1936), had not met with the same critical success.

Céline had also published a play, *L'Eglise* (The church) (as yet untranslated into English), written before *Voyage*, but not published until 1933, following the latter's favorable reception. The third act of the play—the traditional farce of medieval theater (*farce* is the word for stuffing in French—a comic interlude "stuffed" into the middle of an otherwise serious play)—is a heavy-handed anti-Semitic satire of the League of Nations, for which Céline had worked as a health officer. Céline depicts the League of Nations as being run by Jews for their own enrichment and aggrandizement, encouraging wars as a means of profiting from the sale of arms to all sides. A trip to the Soviet Union in July 1936 had led to the publication that same year of a brief text, *Mea Culpa*, in which Céline denounces the Bolshevik Revolution as having led to a new form of oppression of the proletariat.[14]

The anti-Semitic content of *Bagatelles* is no different, as Alice Yaeger Kaplan and Paul Kingston have demonstrated, from that of other anti-Jewish writings of the period.[15] Indeed, what enabled Céline to turn out *Bagatelles* so quickly is that it borrows so abundantly from those writings, as Céline himself acknowledged in listing some of his sources in his second pamphlet, *L'Ecole des cadavres* (School for corpses) (1938) (34). Anti-Semitic literature is by its very nature egregiously intertextual, for it assumes, true to its propagandistic intentions, that the more frequently an accusation is repeated, the more likely it will be accepted as true, as a "fact of nature," having lost in that process of reiteration any trace of fabrication.

Céline was a lifelong anti-Semite. In his biography of the writer, François Gibault relates that Céline's father, a lower-level employee in an insurance company, would rant against the Jews at the dinner table and buttress his vituperations with quotations from the "bible" of French anti-Semitic literature, Edouard Drumont's *La France juive*, first published in 1886.[16] Later, after being condemned as a traitor for his anti-Semitic writings (his pamphlets as well as his articles in the anti-Semitic press),[17] Céline would claim that the pamphlets were pacifist in intent, written only against "certain Semitic clans who were pushing us into war."[18] It should be noted that until the passage of the Marchandeau decree in April 1939, making it illegal to defame or insult in print a particular ethnic or religious group (with the intent to incite hostility against its members), there were no restrictions on the publication, distribution, or sale of anti-Semitic writings. The latter were readily available in bookstores, at newsstands, and, particularly, at the various "Centers for Documentation and Propaganda" that served as clearinghouses for and publishers of anti-Semitic documents of all kinds (some of these centers received support from the German propaganda services). We know that Céline consulted some of the anti-Semitic literature available at one of these centers when he wrote

Bagatelles, the center located at 18, rue Laugier, directed by one of the most vociferous anti-Semites of the period, Darquier de Pellepoix (who would later succeed Xavier Vallat, as commissioner for Jewish affairs under the Pétain government). In short, there existed an anti-Semitic infrastructure to assist those who wished to engage in the struggle to rid France of Jewish influence.

A history of anti-Semitism is, of course, beyond the scope of this study. Having already stated that Céline's anti-Semitism does not differ conceptually from that of the already existing literature, I would like to define very briefly the nature of that attitude. Céline's anti-Semitism is founded essentially upon what Gavin Langmuir terms "chimerical assertions," "chimerical" because such assertions are unproved and/or unprovable.[19] They emerge, in Céline's writings, from a conflation of medieval religious anti-Semitism with post-Enlightenment, racial anti-Semitism. For the former, Jews, as Léon Poliakov has shown, are viewed as the murderers of Christ and as the sworn enemies of the church he and his apostles founded; as allied with the forces of darkness, the Devil and the Antichrist; as engaging in occult, diabolical practices; as inherently deceitful and deceptive; as malodorous, diseased, misshapen, and priapic.[20] However, given that Jewishness was a religious determination, once the Jew converted to Christianity, all such opprobrium was lifted. Insofar as latter-day anti-Semitism is concerned, Jewishness is a biological—racial—rather than merely a religious designation, and the Jews are held responsible for the political, economic, and aesthetic modernism that has brought about the decline of Western civilization by destroying the old, "natural" order. Moreover, the Jews, supposedly attempting to control every field of endeavor in the various countries in which they have settled, are seen as engaged in an international conspiracy to subjugate the gentile populations and establish a Jewish world government.

As Céline indicates in *Bagatelles*, his mission in writing the pamphlet is to enlighten his readers as to the Jewish menace to France, to "uncover in everyday existence . . . the implacable, conquering Jewish megalomania" (124). To accomplish that goal, he offers a reading of what one might call the "social text," one that deciphers its otherwise deceptive writing so as to reveal the occulted presence of the Jews and thus permit the reader to perceive clearly the ways in which they have penetrated and corrupted French society for their own insidious purposes. Hence the Jew, and all that the term will come to connote, will constitute the transcendental signified of that social text, that which explains and structures it. Moreover, such a reading will, as Céline attempts to demonstrate, reveal that the social text is ultimately a palimpsest, for it is founded upon, written over, another text—the elaboration of a worldwide Jewish conspiracy as depicted in a supposedly authentic Jewish document *The Protocols of the Elders of Zion.*

For Céline, the 1937 Exposition must be read and interpreted within the framework of that larger social context, as analyzed in *Bagatelles,* within which it is embedded and for which it serves as a focal point. Given his reputation as the author of *Voyage au bout de la nuit,* with its probing, uncompromising dissection of the human condition, who, the readers of *Bagatelles* might ask, would be better qualified to uncover the hidden truths of the social text than Louis-Ferdinand Céline? It was no doubt the author's reputation that led to the pamphlet becoming a best-seller of sorts, some seventy-five thousand copies sold by the end of the war as opposed to sales of one hundred thousand for *Voyage au bout de la nuit.*

The exposition is held directly responsible for the generation of *Bagatelles.* Céline relates that he had submitted the scenario for a ballet, titled *Voyou Paul. Brave Virginie* (Hoodlum Paul. Brave Virginia)—included in *Bagatelles*—to the arts committee of the exposition with the hope that, with the appropriate choreography and music added, it would be one of the many cultural entertainments presented to the fairgoers. It was turned down ostensibly because the author was not one of the favored Jewish or pro-Jewish artists. As Céline informs his readers, this rejection followed on the heels of another, that of an earlier ballet scenario, *Naissance d'une fée* (Birth of a fairy), which the Paris Opera refused to accept, supposedly because Céline was unable to enlist the services of a Jewish musician to compose a score for it. For Céline, the committee's refusal to accept his ballet was not merely a personal affront, for which he as victim would justifiably counterattack by writing the pamphlet ("Now you'll see anti-Semitism," he tells a friend as he prepares to go on the offensive [41]); it was an assault on the French nation by people who are irrevocably foreigners. "Nothing for the French. Nothing for the children of the native soil" (40). It should be noted in passing that there is no hard evidence to substantiate any submission by Céline to the exposition arts committee.

Although Céline holds the exposition responsible for the writing of *Bagatelles,* he devotes only two pages to its actual description. Its importance lies, as I have already indicated, in what it represents in terms of the larger social text. Céline states that the exposition will indeed close, as it must, but it will nonetheless endure as a "souvenir" of "the official capture of all of France and the French people by the great temporal and spiritual power of the kikes" (232).

Céline's reference to the exposition as a demonstration of the "colonizing fury" (232) of the Jews is supported by his frequent recourse to the lexicon of colonialism throughout the pamphlet. Blum is portrayed as leading an army of Jews whose objective is the "submission of the natives." "This is the way," he adds, "things happen in Africa. Only over here, in France, we are the wogs" (96). According to Céline, the conjoined irony and shame of France's present situation is that the colonizer has become the colonized. France, the conqueror of so much of black Africa, has itself been conquered by "nigger-Jews." "The Jew is a nigger," Céline reiterates tirelessly throughout the pamphlet, "the product of the interbreeding of niggers and Asian barbarians" (191-92). The unquestioned assumption in this hybridization is that black Africans are "obviously" primitive: that is to say, subhuman, sexually animalistic, devoid of any culture of their own.

Conflating the Jews with Negroes, with all that such an association connotes, had become a commonplace of racial anthropology. As Sander Gilman notes, it marked the Jew, of supposed African origin, as "inferior," "diseased," and "ugly."[21] The blackness of the Jew can also be linked with the Jew's association with the Devil as the force of darkness. But, despite such associations, and despite the supposedly typical Jewish physiognomy so widely displayed in anti-Semitic caricatures—large hooked nose, heavy brows, thick lips, and so on—the Jews, unlike Negroes, cannot be identified so readily by physical appearance. They are, Céline notes, "camouflaged, disguised, chameleons" (127). Hence, their colonization of France has not been perceived as such, for it has taken place surreptitiously from within, abetted by the ignorance of the general population. "Colonization 'from within' is the most infamous, the most ignoble of colonizations. Colonization by Negrito-Jews represents the height of moral and physical degradation" (96). Although Céline does not hesitate to castigate the French people for a variety of flaws, ranging from their provincialism to their failure to read books, faults not necessarily attributable to the Jews, he nonetheless asserts, as indicated in the above quotation, that this otherwise healthy Aryan body has become diseased from within by the presence of Jews as "parasites" (170).

Céline's comments on the Jewish colonization of France within the context of a condemnation of the 1937 Exposition become that much more trenchant given the exposition's display of France—albeit less than enthusiastic—as a great imperial power. Such comments are also meant to remind Céline's readers of the Colonial Exposition of 1931. He suggests in recalling the latter how quickly France has succumbed to Jewish domination, for only six years separate the two expositions, and thus how urgent is the need to recapture France from the Jews before more time has passed. Céline also suggests that such rapid "progress" could not have taken place haphazardly, but must be the result of a concerted effort.

The "Negro-Jew" as colonizer of France is further linked to the 1937 Exposition in aesthetic terms, a link that brings us back to the rejection of Céline's ballet, the point of departure for the writing of *Bagatelles*. Céline decries the exhibiting of the works of the half-Jewish (on his mother's side) Marcel Proust at the exposition and thereby giving the "irresolute, buggering, weak in the chest [references to Proust's homosexuality and asthma] Prout-Proust" (126) the same classical status as the genuinely French Balzac, further proof, he indicates, of the Jewishness of the exposition. The conferring of such an honor on a Jew permits Céline to link the exposition with both the French educational system and literary criticism, notably the reception of Céline's own works. The problem with the educational system, and Céline devotes several pages to an analysis of its failures, is the sort of French language it promulgates. As soon as French students enter the *lycée* they are, Céline argues, "anesthetized" to life, namely, to the emotions that give it substance, and are thus taught to live by "fraud" and "imposture" (164). They learn to read and express themselves in a neoclassical-style language that, having been refined over the centuries, is no longer capable of expressing feelings. They acquire and are conditioned by an "ideal French for robots" (167).

Such a system has been shaped, at least in part, according to Céline, by the models established by such "Jewish" writers as Montaigne (also half Jewish), and Proust and by various Judaized writers ranging from Racine to Anatole France. Such a style serves Jewish interests in terms of what Céline calls elsewhere the "international robotization of the minds [of the Aryan populations]" (183). He sees this process of dehumanization at work not only in language and literature, but also in painting, music, and cinema. It serves, Céline argues, to subjugate more easily those whom the Jews wish to control, transforming them into "ass-lickers, slaves, suckers of Jewish despotism" (186) by destroying in them what the Jews fear most—"genuine, spontaneous emotion, set to the music of natural rhythms" (183). The Jews fear such emotion, and thus seek to eliminate it, because they are constitutionally incapable of feeling it. For Céline, this inability is not the result of some sort of cultural deprivation, but is, perforce, like the very definition of the Jew, biological—that is to say, racial. The racial makeup of the Jew contains, according to Céline, a Negro component, stemming from a shared African origin. In defining the Jew's natural lack of sensibility, Céline emphasizes the latter in terms of a geographic determinism that results in a subhuman nervous system: "The Jew, whose African nerves are always made up more or less of 'zinc,' is endowed with only a crude [nervous] system, one that falls below the human scale . . . the nervous system of a nigger" (192).[22]

One final implication of the Jew's robotlike insensitivity and its imposition on the Aryan population as part of the process of colonization from within, an implication that brings us back to the 1937 Exposition and its "responsibility" for the anti-Semitism of *Bagatelles,* concerns, as I have already noted, the reaction of the critics to Céline's own writings. If literary criticism, as well as criticism in the other arts, is controlled by the Jews—the critics, Céline claims, are all "filthy bastards, Jews" (15)—then any criticism of Céline's writings, including the hostile reception of *Mort à crédit,* condemned for its so-called obscenity, and the rejection of Céline's ballet scenarios, is necessarily invalid, because the critics, Jewish or Judaized, are incapable of appreciating one of the very qualities that Céline perceives as essential to his style, his "métro émotif." In his description of that style in *Entretiens avec le Professeur Y* (Conversations with Professor Y), Céline describes himself as a literary inventor. His invention is "having returned emotion to the written language . . . the emotion of the spoken language to the written language."[23] Hence, to display Proust is to reject Céline, not merely on aesthetic grounds but also because his novels and ballet scenarios are an extension of his pamphlet in that they threaten Jewish linguistic and literary hegemony.

Céline's overview of the architecture of the exposition is, as one might expect, negative. Paying what could be considered a backhanded compliment to the Jews, he states that for a people that is usually so "oracular" (234), they could have created something more spectacular to present the "grandeur of . . . the Jewish Empire" (234). Instead, they constructed a "crappy, grotesque collection of drab, crumbling, overblown hovels" (235), an assemblage that, he notes, merely adds to the filth and asphyxiating atmosphere of Paris, "the world's most unhealthy city" (237). Although Céline does not hold them responsible for conditions in Paris, he suggests that the Jews, typically associated with cities, are not the ones who would think of "dismantling" (240) Paris, opening it up by means of a system of major highways leading to more salubrious areas of the country or enlarging the Seine. For Céline, Paris, its particular geographic circumstances notwithstanding, suffers from the same unhealthiness that afflicts the Jews, the conjoined corruption of overurbanization and excessive civilization.

The only foreign pavilion at the exposition that Céline mentions is that of the Soviet Union. Although he refers to Hitler several times in the pamphlet, saying at one point that he would like to form an "alliance" with Hitler because "Hitler doesn't like the Jews . . . and neither do I" (317), he says nothing about the German pavilion designed by Hitler's favorite architect, Albert Speer. The Soviet Union's and Germany's pavilions, the exposition's most massive and most blatantly propagandistic national structures, faced each other, forming a strategic gateway leading toward the Palais de Chaillot on the Right Bank, opposite the Eiffel Tower. This confrontation of radically opposed ideologies, which were already at war in Spain, was apparently an accident of site planning. For Céline, what is important is the connection between the Soviet Union as a state run by a Communist Party directed by the Jews and the exposition as a representation of the Jewish colonization of France. Céline states that the exposition was "kikified [enyoutré]" in part through the agency of the "nice Soviet pavilion" and the "directives of the C.G.T. [the Confédération Générale du Travail, a Communist-led confederation of labor unions]" (232). As for the C.G.T., the Confédération did support the programs of the Blum government and provided crucial assistance when construction on the exposition was delayed and additional labor needed to be hired. However, Céline is not so much interested in the particulars of the C.G.T.'s support of the Popular Front as he is in demonstrating that the Jews are involved in preparing a Bolshevik-style revolution in France, analogous to the one that overthrew the czar in Russia, and that the exposition is an example of the Popular Front's involvement in that revolution.

In *Mea Culpa*, Céline had denounced the Russian Revolution as having instituted a new form of tyranny, that of the Communist apparatus over the working masses. As for the Jews and their role in the revolution, Céline mentions them only in passing, suggesting obliquely that being Jewish or being allied with Jewish interests gives one a decided advantage. "To be looked on favorably by the people these days," he comments, is to "ensure that you'll have a cushy existence." "Provided you're ready to feel somewhat Jewish, you're set for life" (18). The labor situation at what Céline calls the "great kikefest of 1937" reveals, such as he describes it, a perfect example of the exploitation of the working class by the Jews. He declares that "everything that counts . . . everyone who commands [is Jewish]" (29). Those who perform the manual labor are all Aryans, tyrannized by their Jewish bosses. Such a situation makes clear not only Jewish plans for dominating the Aryan population but also that the Jewish colonization of France and the Communist revolution in Russia are, ultimately, part of the same scheme to achieve worldwide Jewish domination.

"Jews and Communists are for me synonymous" (51), Céline declaims, and he notes that Maurice Thorez, head of the French Communist Party, is but an agent of the Jews, the "ideal Aryan for Jewish sleight of hand" (302). Hence, the Communist support of the Popular Front government can be seen as yet another example of the Jewish colonization of France from within, but, more important perhaps, also as the first step in the coming Jewish-Bolshevik revolution in France, the link between the government of Stalin and that of Blum. Throughout *Bagatelles*, Céline repeats the accusations, first circulated by the opponents of the Bolsheviks, that the Russian Revolution was directed and paid for by Jews. Drawing on the well-known Jewish origins of such revolutionary leaders as Trotsky and Kamenev, reactionary propagandists in Russia, as Léon Poliakov has demonstrated, transformed Lenin into a Jew and fabricated documents purporting to show how Max Warburg, Jacob Schiff, and other Jewish financiers provided the Bolsheviks with their funds.[24] Such accusations were meant to rally the Russian people against the revolution and, initially at least, were favorably received by Western governments. They rapidly became grist for the mills of anti-Semites throughout Europe, as well as in the United States. Céline tirelessly repeats such accusations and goes so far as to quote a report supposedly made by the British Secret Service that described Lenin and his family as "typically Jewish" (283), even speaking Yiddish among themselves.

As part of the process of convincing his readers that the Jews used the Russian Revolution to seize power and thus ultimately persuade them that France risks a similar danger, Céline devotes several pages to describing his experiences in the Soviet Union (Leningrad). The inclusion of such material in *Bagatelles* constitutes, as Nicholas Hewitt has noted, the "confessional side" of *Mea Culpa*, replacing its abstractions with firsthand observations.[25] Wherever Céline goes, he discovers Jewish officials commanding Aryan workers while attempting to maintain the official party line, "Judeo-Mongol wind" (118), of social progress under Communism. His experience at the celebrated Marinksi theater directly links his observations of a Soviet Union under the heel of the Jewish Bolsheviks with the 1937 Exposition as the sign of a similar fate awaiting France. The Marinski, as Céline depicts it, puts on splendid performances of the classical ballet repertoire, but the best seats are reserved for Jews and it is run by a Jewish director. It should not be surprising, then, that when Céline submits a ballet scenario to the director it is turned down, ostensibly for ideological reasons, because it is not sufficiently socialist. But the association of the Marinski with the Jews and his previous rejections by the Jews associated with the Paris Opera and the 1937 Exposition leave his readers to draw the obvious conclusion—that he has once more been a victim of Jewish power.

Céline's supposed personal victimization by the Jews, the Russian Revolution, the coming to power of the Popular Front, what passes for social progress in general—all these phenomena are viewed by Céline as part of a larger pattern, a historical text that incorporates a variety of social texts. As is the case with the latter, that historical text must be deciphered. That is to say, such events, properly interpreted, yield a scientific view of history. And the link between apparently disparate events is a Jewish world conspiracy. "The triumph of the Bolshevik revolution," Céline writes, can be conceived only with regard to its long-term implications as "with the Jews, for the Jews, and by the Jews" (50). The Popular Front is but an "advance on the Jewish future" (78). All forms of what Céline refers to as "social progress" become nothing more than a means to an end, which is the "coming to power of the Jew" (50). Céline finds the proof for such a conspiracy in a text supposedly elaborated by the Jews themselves—the notorious *Protocols of the Elders of Zion.*

From Céline's perspective, historical events validate the *Protocols,* which, in turn, can then serve to explain the events in question. An initial reading of the *Protocols* would, according to Céline, give the reader the impression of a "fraud," a "fantasy," an "insanity" (277); in short, a fiction and not a historical document. But if one accepts the premises that Céline has established with regard to the nature and activities of the Jews, then the *Protocols* become "reasonable" with respect to the "evolution of things" (277). They become the ur-text of the palimpsest constituted by the social and historical texts that overwrite it.

By the time Céline wrote *Bagatelles,* the *Protocols* had become the standard reference work for the anti-Semitic writer. According to Norman Cohn, whose *Warrant for Genocide: The Myth of Jewish World-Conspiracy and the Protocols of the Elders of Zion* is the definitive study of the document, the *Protocols* was concocted in Paris by agents of the Russian Secret Police and intended for the use of Russian anti-Semites.[26] The document was first published in a St. Petersburg newspaper in 1903 (Céline gives 1902) and appeared in book form in 1905. During the period of the Russian Revolution it was widely circulated as a means of discrediting the Bolsheviks as instruments of a larger Jewish conspiracy. The *Protocols* consists of a series of twenty-four lectures (the number varies according to the edition) supposedly taken from the minutes of a secret meeting that took place during the first World Zionist Conference held in Basel, Switzerland, in 1897. At that meeting, an Elder of Zion, a member of the supersecret international Jewish government, told a delegation of representatives to the conference about a long-term conspiracy by various Jewish groups throughout the world to undermine Aryan societies through such strategies as democratization, the manipulation of finances, control of the masses through the media and systems of education, and subversion of morality. The ultimate result of this plot will be the enslavement of the non-Jewish populations and the establishment of a Jewish global tyranny. By implication, the 1937 Exposition, as Céline has described it, becomes an instrument to undermine Aryan society, an aspect of the larger conspiracy, and a demonstration of the progress of that conspiracy.

Although Céline quotes from the *Protocols* in *Bagatelles*, it is likely that he took the material from other anti-Semitic writings. In 1920, Roger Lambelin, a well-known anti-Semitic writer, made the first translation of the *Protocols* into French. A year later, the *Protocols* was shown to be a forgery, pieced together for the most part from a little-known novel by Maurice Joly. The novel, titled *The Dialogues in Hell between Montesquieu and Machiavelli*, published in 1870, was written to denounce the autocratic policies of Napoleon III (represented by the figure of Machiavelli). The revelation that the *Protocols* was a forgery did not, of course, deter the anti-Semites from continuing to cite the document. They simply assumed that the evidence presented was an effort to conceal the conspiracy it describes. "There exists," Céline states, "but one reality as the basis of all politics: the Jewish worldwide conspiracy" (242–43).

One of the signature monuments of the 1937 Exposition was the Colonne de la Paix (Column of peace), a column built up in sections and topped by a free-form, bushlike metallic sculpture. In Céline's eyes, the sculpture becomes a "Star of David, the Star of the synagogues" (125), an emblem of the Jewishness of the exposition. But Céline also refers to the monument with a variety of phallic images, notably "Blum's Dick [la Bite-Blum]" (236). Céline's transformation of the Colonne de la Paix into a gigantic Jewish phallus is consonant with the equation he establishes through the pamphlet between Jewish political and social dominance and Jewish sexual power. As Thomas C. Spear notes, *Bagatelles* presents the Jew as both "emasculated . . . and emasculating."[27] The inability of the Jews to appreciate the new virility—spontaneous emotion—that Céline's writings have injected into a French literature and language robotized and sterilized by such "Jewish" writers as Montaigne and Proust is a sign of their aesthetic castration. The latter is, however, counterbalanced by their inherent priapism. The notion of Jewish hypervirility has its roots in the medieval association of the Jew with the Devil in terms of animalistic and inverted sexuality. In modern anti-Semitic iconography, the stereotypical Jewish nose, oversized and hooked, has been associated with the phallus.

Céline emphasizes the sexual prowess of the Jew by drawing upon the association between the Jew and the Negro—with the latter assumed to exhibit a primitive, and thus excessive, sexual capacity. "Women, particularly French women," Céline writes, "are crazy about kinky hair, Abyssinians, their astonishing dicks" (89). "The Jews," he later notes, "are like all the niggers, cocks in the form of men" (327). However, Céline emphasizes not so much the threat of the hypervirile Jew seducing Aryan women but, in keeping with the notion of the Jew's otherness, the Jew as sodomite. Sodomy, specifically anal intercourse, buggering, is the sign of Jewish power and of Aryan submission to that power.[28]

In describing the Colonne de la Paix as the "Bite-Blum," Céline was certainly aware of the derogatory sexual epithets that had been directed against the leader of the Popular Front. These remarks constitute one of the contexts in which the text of Céline's attack must be read. Pierre Birnbaum has examined the variety and what is often the contradictory nature of such epithets, all of which are meant to differentiate the Jew as diseased and degenerate Other. Some of the attacks against Blum were generated by (mis)readings of his *Du Mariage*, which was first published in 1907, in which he advocated a more liberal sexual education for young girls. Birnbaum cites an article from 1907 in a regional Catholic newspaper castigating Blum's book; it is representative of the sort of comments about the book and about Blum as a typical Jew bent on undermining French morality that would continue into the 1940s. The writer of the piece states that "the Jew [Blum] can be content with his work," that "work" being the "breakdown of the family and society."[29] Blum, a meticulous dresser, was viewed by his anti-Semitic contemporaries as an effeminate dandy, the embodiment, in their eyes, of the Jewish decadence that was undermining the "virility" of authentic French values. A writer for the anti-Semitic newspaper *Je suis partout* described Blum as "in the habit of dressing up as a mad virgin in a low-cut, sleeveless gown . . . made up and perfumed" (155).

Despite being described as effeminate, Blum was also portrayed as a Don Juan who, like his coreligionaries, was always seeking to seduce innocent Aryan women. Léon Daudet, perhaps the most brilliant of the anti-Semitic publicists of the time, wrote of Blum's heterosexual proclivities: "The Blum tribe, in the person of its leader, has come amongst us to satisfy its needs, in the manner of burglars who come to plunder a private dwelling" (161). Lastly, Blum was also portrayed as a homosexual with a fondness for buggery, another degenerate trait associated with the Jews, and accused of having affairs with a variety of male political figures. Birnbaum cites a scurrilous poem of the 1930s that describes Blum as having acquired his sexual inversion while a student at the "abnormal school" (a play on the name of the prestigious Ecole Normale Supérieure that Blum attended), and that reads in part: "Blum is always lying low in order to play the . . . Rear end game" (164).

In a passage that portrays Blum as having the outsize feet—also suggesting the phallus—and short legs of the typical Jew, both traits differentiating the Jew from the Aryan and indicating physical (and thus mental) degeneracy, Céline refers to Blum as "Mr. Blum Karfulkenstein, the Bulgarian" (323). Blum, a third-generation Frenchman, apparently received a new name and a new country of origin, thanks to a Bulgarian newspaper, shortly after becoming the prime minister of the Popular Front government, a development that was enthusiastically received by his anti-Semitic detractors. The name, which literally means "carbuncle stone" in German, was meant to sound ponderously German-Jewish to the French ear and thus to mark Blum more clearly as a foreign Jew. The Bulgarian origin attributed to Blum differentiates him no less clearly as a foreign invader from a part of Europe that borders on Turkey, as one of the Asian Jewish hordes invading France. Bulgarian has another resonance as well, one surely not lost on Céline as well as others alert to etymologies. In the Middle Ages, the designation Bulgarian—*bougre* in Old French—marked a nationality that was both heretical (the Bulgarians were Eastern Orthodox) and, by extension, sodomitic. *Bulgare* is the origin of the English *buggery/bugger* as well as of the modern French *bougre*, which simply means "guy" or "fellow."

The Jews, exemplified by their "leader" Léon Blum, are, for Céline, sodomites in that as a result of their power, of their worldwide conspiracy, they have transformed France into a Jewish colony, into an abject and humiliated subject. "France is a female nation," Céline writes, a nation that, like aging prostitutes, is "ending up in the hands of the niggers, very happy, very drunk, very entertained, properly screwed up the ass, properly beaten." And then he adds, extending the comparison: "France is now naked! It's time for the nigger. The Jew up her ass, that's what makes her happy, he'll split her apart, that's his role" (243). The Colonne de la Paix, the "Bite-Blum," thus becomes the sign that the Jews have socially, politically, economically, and aesthetically sodomized France. Céline concludes that this "long erection consecrates their triumph," that "the Jews from now on will screw all of you [French people] up the ass, as they wish, when they wish, where they wish" (125).

Céline's portrayal of the 1937 Exposition as part of an all-embracing Jewish conspiracy is meant to transform it into a rallying point for his readers, to have them see its presence as a call to rise up against their colonizers and take France out of the hands of the foreigners responsible for the corruption and degeneration that have eroded everything that is authentically French before a Russian-style revolution consolidates the Jewish hold over the country and makes such a restoration impossible.

But Céline offers no solution for the "Jewish problem," such as he defines it in *Bagatelles*. At one point he states, "Send them back to Hitler, to Palestine, to Poland" (165). He also calls for a limitation of Jews in the professions in proportion to the number of Jews killed in World War I. Given the false statistics on which he bases that limitation—stereotypically, the Jews were considered shirkers during the war—Jewish participation in the professions would become virtually nonexistent. In a similar vein, should France find itself again at war, it would be the result of Jewish machinations, and thus the Jews should, Céline insists, be placed in the front lines with no possibility of exemption from service. As for sending the Jews back to Hitler, a reference no doubt to the German Jews who had taken refuge in France, Céline could not have been totally ignorant of what sort of treatment they would receive. He had visited Nazi Germany in 1935 and would maintain contact with and receive assistance from the medical establishment of the Third Reich during the war.[30] When Céline states, "I would like to make an alliance with Hitler. He doesn't like the Jews and neither do I" (317–18), it is difficult not to believe that he is, at least indirectly, suggesting that all Jews be subject to the kind of restrictions the Nazis had begun to place on German Jews after the passage of the first Nuremberg Laws in September 1935—and we are less than one year away from *Kristallnacht* (9–10 November 1938) and the institution of open violence against the Jews. My purpose in noting Céline's remarks concerning Hitler and in recalling these dates is to remind the reader that however delirious Céline's anti-Semitic vituperations might appear, or whatever personal psychological function they might serve, they were not generated in a historical vacuum. There is a historical reality to anti-Semitism, with which all anti-Semites are perforce somewhat familiar, that predates the publication of *Bagatelles* and accompanies its appearance, and it relates a sordid tale of deprivation, expulsion, torture, and murder. As for the Holocaust to follow, one would be naive to think that the systematic extermination of millions of Jews was not sanctioned by writings such as *Bagatelles*, whatever the claims of ignorance or assertions of nonviolence on the part of their authors.

This is not the first time I have made such remarks regarding the accountability to history of the anti-Semite in general and of Céline in particular. In response to similar comments in my *Understanding Céline*, one of the book's reviewers (who will remain nameless) noted that my "attitude" was "old-fashioned," reminiscent of the sort of attack against Céline one might have made in the 1950s.[31] I would like to conclude my examination of Céline's reading of the 1937 Exposition by responding to the above-noted critique, for it touches on a variety of issues relevant to my demonstration and to this volume.

It is obvious that the sort of anti-Semitism characteristic of *Bagatelles* has not become a mere historical curiosity, as, for example, its revival in Russia and in its former satellites amply demonstrates (ironically, the Jews having once been blamed for the Russian Revolution are now being held responsible for the demise of Communism). As we have seen, the anti-Semitism of *Bagatelles* can be linked to particular social and political circumstances in the France of the

1930s, among them the absence, until the Marchandeau decree of 1939, of legal restrictions regarding the publication and dissemination of materials defaming a particular ethnic or religious group; the public acceptability of anti-Semitic discourse, both spoken and written; the polarization between Left and Right, with the latter, abetted by a strong, vociferous press, espousing anti-Semitism as an "answer" to what it perceived as a decline of Western civilization in general and of the institutions of the Third Republic in particular; the example offered by Nazi Germany, in the context of fascist ideology, of state-sponsored anti-Semitism; and the perception of the Popular Front as a Jewish government under the leadership of Léon Blum and, coextensively, with the participation of the Communists, as a potential instrument of revolution that would permit a "Jewish-Bolshevik" seizure of power analogous to what had supposedly occurred in Russia.

However specific these phenomena may be to the France of the 1930s, and one might also include a collective memory of the Dreyfus affair (which was never juridically resolved—Dreyfus had to be given a presidential pardon), they can be placed in the larger European context of a continuing malaise with regard to modernism, in the broadest sense of the term, a modernism accentuated and accelerated by the ravages of the First World War. Céline, we may recall, was a combatant in that war, wounded and decorated. One could argue that the pacifism Céline acquired from his wartime experience had by the 1930s become inseparable from the trauma of modernism—associated with the war—and thus from a public, political display of the anti-Semitism he had harbored since his youth. One might speak of modernism here in terms of multinational capitalism; increased industrialization, the evolution of supranational ideologies (notably communism and fascism), secularism; the emergence of the "masses" in terms of the anonymity of the individual and the threat of proletarianization experienced by the petty bourgeoisie (the class into which Céline was born); as well as new modes of representation in the arts.

For Céline, the Jews, implicated historically in such developments, and still bearing the stigma of traditional religious anti-Semitism, become the instigators and perpetuators of this new order. They become indissociable from the state that has granted them all the rights and benefits of citizenship, and thus, particularly given that France is under a government led by a Jew, the anti-Semite becomes by definition opposed to the institutions that have, however legally, permitted such a phenomenon to occur.

Céline, as we have seen, also attacks the Jews in aesthetic terms, from a populist, vitalist perspective. One of the most salient signs of the Jews' irrevocable alterity is their insensitivity to the emotion that Céline wishes to restore to

French literature by his use of popular language in written form. In this opposition between nature and culture, emotion and reason, lies a means of separating the authentic French person from the Jewish foreigner on the basis of race. One might think in this context of the Nazi concept of "blood," the life force that unites the *Volk* and necessarily excludes those who are not born German or Germanic.

In using the term "old-fashioned," my critic was no doubt also referring to my failure to conform to more contemporary modes of criticism in which Céline's anti-Semitism is not a relevant issue—structuralism and deconstruction. Each of these, in its own way, has viewed the literary text as self-regulating, autonomous, and self-reflective. They have, moreover, tended to break down the category of literature by considering the latter to be just another form of cultural production or social practice. It is one thing to consider the pamphlets—as do so many of Céline's critics—as an aberration worthy of at least a perfunctory condemnation; it is quite another to view them strictly in terms of their style and thus no differently from Céline's works of fiction. This latter perspective permits Céline the pamphleteer to be recuperated as stylist, his anti-Semitism bracketed, mythologized, or psychologized.

That recuperation was accomplished in the 1970s and 1980s largely through the agency of the prestigious French journal *Tel Quel,* preoccupied with subversive modes of *écriture,* and particularly through the publications of one of its luminaries, Julia Kristeva. In her influential *Pouvoirs de l'horreur,* she describes the pamphlets as constituting the "phantasmatic substratum on which [Céline's] entire work is built" and as the "prolongation of the savage beauty of his style" (205). Thus, they become in her analyses both a reflection on the genesis of his style and a continuation of it. Although she states that Céline's anti-Semitism is an "untenable political position" (157), she readily depoliticizes that position to portray Céline's hatred of the Jew as a "rage against the Symbolic Order instituted by Jewish monotheism" (209). Hence, Céline's style, his appeal to emotion and musicality—which Kristeva perceives in terms of syntactical dislocations that permit the expression of otherwise repressed affective pulsations that shatter or render ambivalent the boundaries that separate self and other, life and death, inside and outside—becomes an oedipal revolt against, among other constraints, traditional literary and linguistic structures, a "liberating truth" (211). The anti-Semitism of the pamphlets is occulted in the name of stylistic innovation.

In light of Kristeva's comments or the more general perception that the literary value of Céline's novels justifies his anti-Semitic diatribes, one can ask, as does Leo Bersani, "whether art has the task of repairing and redeeming" the "catastrophes" of history.[32] The more historically oriented approaches to literature that have recently emerged, of which this volume is a reflection, may not adequately answer the question Bersani poses. But I believe they will, at least with respect to Céline's writings, renew what Donald Preziosi has termed the "problematic of contextual reintegration" and thus reformulate the conditions of their intelligibility.[33]

Notes

1. Jean-Jacques Block and Marianne Delort, *Quand Paris allait "à l'Expo"* (Paris: Fayard, 1980), 140. Unless otherwise noted, all translations in this chapter are my own.
2. Paul Greenhalgh, *Ephemeral Vistas: The Expositions Universelles, Great Exhibitions, and World's Fairs, 1851–1939* (Manchester: Manchester University Press, 1988), 69.
3. The various right-wing extremist groups, the so-called Ligues, were abolished by the Popular Front government on 18 June 1936.
4. Philippe Bernard and Henri Dubief, *The Decline of the Third Republic,* trans. Anthony Forsteer, vol. 5 of *The Cambridge History of France* (Cambridge: Cambridge University Press, 1985), 225.
5. Julian Jackson, *The Popular Front in France: Defending Democracy, 1934–38* (Cambridge: Cambridge University Press, 1988), 118.
6. For the history of the Popular Front government, see ibid. and Bernard and Dubief, *The Decline of the Third Republic.*
7. The right-wing press falsely accused Jean Salengro, Blum's minister of the interior, of desertion during World War I. Its attacks were a principal factor in pushing him to commit suicide on 18 November 1936.
8. Pierre Birnbaum, *Anti-Semitism in France: A Political History from Léon Blum to the Present,* trans. Miriam Kochan (Oxford: Basil Blackwell, 1992), 104, 152, 151, 156, 271.
9. Cited in ibid., 102.
10. Quoted in Block and Delort, *Quand Paris,* 169.
11. Quoted in Alice Yaeger Kaplan, *Relevé des sources et citations dans Bagatelles pour un massacre* (Tusson: Du Lerot, 1983), 102.
12. *Cahiers céliniens,* no. 5, *Lettres à des amies,* ed. C. W. Nettlebrock (Paris: Gallimard, 1979), 233–34.
13. Louis-Ferdinand Céline, *Bagatelles pour un massacre* (Paris: Denoël, 1937). Page numbers for further references to this work appear in text in parentheses.
14. Louis-Ferdinand Céline, *Mea Culpa* (Paris: Carpe Diem, 1984 [1936]).
15. See Kaplan, *Relevé des sources*; Paul Kingston, *Anti-Semitism in France during the 1930s: Organizations, Personalities and Propaganda* (Hull: University of Hull Press, 1983).
16. François Gibault, *Céline, 1: Le Temps des espérances (1894–1932)* (Paris: Mercure, 1977), 57.
17. See Philippe Alméras, *Les Idées de Céline* (Paris: Bibliothèque de la Littérature Française Contemporaine, 1987).

18. *Cahiers céliniens,* 319–23. In his *La Vie de Céline* (Paris: Grasset, 1988), Frédéric Vitoux relates that Céline was warned by his wife, the dancer Lucette Almansor, about the difficulties he would suffer as a result of writing *Bagatelles* (308). Similar warnings are expressed by Céline's friend Gen Paul, the painter, in the pamphlet (57–58).

19. Gavin Langmuir, *Toward a Definition of Anti-Semitism* (Berkeley: University of California Press, 1990), 327–28.

20. Léon Poliakov, *From the Time of Christ to the Court Jews,* trans. Richard Howard, vol. 1 of *The History of Anti-Semitism* (New York: Vanguard, 1965), 163–69.

21. Sander Gilman, *The Jew's Body* (New York: Routledge, 1991), 172–73.

22. Throughout Céline's works there is a North/South polarity. The South is a place of disease and corruption, the North a place of health and virility. That polarity is, of course, reflected in the title of the second volume of the trilogy, *Nord* (North), that traces Céline's flight from France (the South, where he is threatened by the Resistance) to Denmark (the North, where the political climate is more favorable and where Céline has hidden money from his royalties). For the history of geographical determinism, see Clarence J. Glacken, *Traces on the Rhodian Shore: Nature and Culture in Western Thought from Ancient Times to the End of the Eighteenth Century* (Berkeley: University of California Press, 1973).

23. Louis-Ferdinand Céline, *Entretiens avec le Professeur Y* (Paris: Gallimard, 1981), 21.

24. Léon Poliakov, *Suicidal Europe: 1870–1933,* trans. George Klim, vol. 3 of *The History of Anti-Semitism* (New York: Vanguard, 1985), 181–86.

25. Nicholas Hewitt, *The Golden Age of Louis-Ferdinand Céline* (Leamington Spa, U.K.: Berg, 1987), 142.

26. Norman Cohn, *Warrant for Genocide: The Myth of Jewish World-Conspiracy and the Protocols of the Elders of Zion* (London: Eyre & Spottiswoode, 1967).

27. Thomas C. Spear, "Sodom and the Jew: A Reading of Céline's Pamphlets," in *Céline and the Politics of Difference,* ed. Rosemarie Scullion, Philip H. Solomon, and Thomas C. Spear (Hanover, N.H.: University Press of New England, 1994), 109–10.

28. See Julia Kristeva's comments on Céline's anal eroticism in her *Pouvoirs de l'horreur* (Paris: Seuil, 1980), 216. Page numbers for further references to this work appear in text in parentheses.

29. Quoted in Birnbaum, *Anti-Semitism in France,* 159. Birnbaum quotes several other authors as well; page numbers for those quotes appear in text in parentheses.

30. For an examination of some of Céline's German connections, see the recent article by Albrecht Betz, "Céline im Dritten Reich," *Merkur* 8 (August 1993): 721–29.

31. Philip H. Solomon, *Understanding Céline* (Columbia: University of South Carolina Press, 1992).

32. Leo Bersani, *The Culture of Redemption* (Cambridge: Harvard University Press), 108.

33. Donald Preziosi, *Rethinking Art History: Meditations on a Coy Science* (New Haven, Conn.: Yale University Press, 1989), 37.

Part II

Colonial Projections

4 / Pagnol and the Paradoxes of Frenchness

Lynn A. Higgins

They say you can never step in the same river twice. A story, too, is always in flux, as individual and collective consciousness evolves, producing new meanings for new cultural contexts and historical moments. There is in the fiction of Marcel Pagnol an anecdote that returns with variations throughout his career, metamorphosing from the theater through films and finally to prose fiction, retaining the following narrative outline. A man and woman fall in love. After the man's departure (usually for Africa), the woman discovers she is pregnant. Attempting and failing to inform her lover by letter of her situation, she marries someone else to legitimate her son (the child is always a boy) and salvage her reputation. The first lover returns, and the baby's paternity is disputed and finally resolved among the mother, the father, and the grandfather.

This core fable makes its first appearance in the trilogy of films adapted from Pagnol's plays. In *Marius* (1931, directed by Alexander Korda) the eponymous hero leaves Fanny, who will shortly discover she is pregnant, with his gruff but loving father César, choosing instead to follow his seafaring wanderlust: "I long for elsewhere [J'ai envie d'ailleurs]," he says. The sequel unfolds in *Fanny* (1932, directed by Marc Allegret) and *César*, which Pagnol himself adapted to the screen in 1936. Then in 1940, Pagnol directed his own scenario of *La Fille du puisatier* (The well-digger's daughter), in which a young aviator once again leaves for Africa, this time having been swept up in the *mobilisation générale* of 1940. Otherwise the anecdote is familiar, as it was again in 1953, in Pagnol's film of *Manon des sources*, in which his wife Jacqueline Bouvier (Pagnol, not

91

Kennedy) appeared in the title role. Finally in 1963, the fable reached its most complete elaboration in the novel *L'Eau des collines* (The water of the hills),[1] consisting of *Manon des sources* amplified by what one critic calls its long "prologue," the tale of Manon's hunchbacked father, *Jean de Florette*.[2] Following closely the film of a decade earlier (where the father's tale was revealed in flashbacks), *L'Eau des collines* is no doubt among the earliest cinematic novelizations. Today, Pagnol is enjoying renewed popularity thanks in large part to Claude Berri's 1986 films of the two novels.

The story of Manon and her father is most superficially a tale of avarice and revenge. Jean Cadoret inherits from his mother, Florette, a run-down estate in the hills of Les Bastides, outside Marseilles. He renounces his comfortable living as an urban *fonctionnaire* and returns with wife Aimée and daughter Manon to the locale of his mother's birth, with idealistic and extravagant plans to raise rabbits and vegetables. The neighbors, César Soubeyran and his nephew Ugolin, covet Jean's tract of spring-fed land, as Ugolin dreams of cultivating carnations for profit. The two conspire to seal off the estate's water supply at its source and then look on with feigned concern while the new owner ruins his health hand-carrying water in heavy jars, until he is finally killed by the dynamite with which he had hoped to blast a well. The first novel ends as the Soubeyran plotters, having finally purchased the tract of drought-ruined land at a risible price, gleefully unplug the spring.

Manon des sources picks up the story some years later as Jean's grown daughter, now a reclusive goatherd, begins to piece together evidence of the Soubeyran crime and to suspect the passive guilt of the villagers, who hid their knowledge of the source's location rather than come to the aid of outsiders. The rest of the novel recounts Manon's revenge. In her turn, she blocks the underground spring that supplies water to the village. Eventually induced to restore the fountain water, she marries the village schoolteacher and gives birth to a son. Pagnol's narrative template becomes visible when César Soubeyran—a Marius grown old—discovers, too late, that Florette, his adolescent love, was the mother of Jean, and that she had tried to reach him by letter after his departure for Africa to inform him of her pregnancy. He is thus forced to recognize on his deathbed that he is a sort of reverse Oedipus, having killed his own son without knowing who he was.

We might well ask: What is the place of this fable in Pagnol's imagination? What impulse can account for its persistent reappearance? How can we explain its continuing appeal, even today? And what can it possibly have to do with this volume of essays on "contested nationhood"? Springing from no known autobiographical source, the anecdote seems to have the status of a personal myth. By concentrating on the two-volume novel *L'Eau des collines*, I intend to show as well that it can be understood as a national mythos, adaptable through its varying narrativizations to express successive crises in modern French collective identity.

By no means considered a political writer, Pagnol produced an oeuvre virtually devoid of allusions to specific historical events. The reference to the debacle of 1940 in *La Fille du puisatier* stands out as the only significant exception, without counting a few forays into social satire that depict, in very general terms, corruption in education (*Topaze*, the play of 1928 adapted to film in 1932) and boxing (*Un Direct au coeur*, 1932). His political commitment—if it was that at all—took the form of involvement in the cultural politics of his native region. He spoke fluent Provençal in its synthetic form as it had been "revived" during the nineteenth century by Frédéric Mistral and his followers, the "Félibrige,"[3] and his efforts in fiction and journalism—he founded a literary journal called *Fortunio*, which much later became the *Cahiers du Sud*—served the movement dedicated to preserving local language and customs. Although Pagnol left the South to make a career in Paris first as a schoolteacher and then as a playwright, he returned frequently to Marseilles (most notably to create a film studio there during the Occupation), and he is now reputed primarily as a supporter of the *esprit méridional*, painting with witty realism the local landscapes, mores, and dialect of Marseilles and its environs. His idiom is considered (somewhat paradoxically, as I will show) to be "truly French" because regional, indigenous. An *académicien*, he has been portrayed as a canonical but minor writer, an important filmmaker, and a generous spirit, especially when teamed with his favorite actors, Raimu, Charpin, and Fernandel, and the three actresses who were all, in sequence, the leading ladies of his life as well: Orane Demazis, Josephine Day, and Jacqueline Pagnol. He is less known as a proponent of controversial theories about the cinema. Having been among the first to proclaim the end of the silent era and to celebrate the ascendancy of the talkies, he also assigned to the cinema a subordinate role of *théâtre en conserve*. Perhaps for these reasons, Pagnol enjoyed during his lifetime and still enjoys today the status of national treasure or monument, and criticism of his work remains in large part condescendingly hagiographic.

Read as a single though scattered corpus, Pagnol's matrix-fable, most fully developed in *L'Eau des collines*, is structured by a series of contradictions, of which I will enumerate four, that are at the same time characteristic Pagnolian narrative procedures and the markers or semes in a myth of national identity.

Centralized versus Local Traditions

In 1882, shortly before the marriage of Joseph and Augustine Pagnol and thirteen years before the birth of their eldest son, Marcel, the Third Republic had
centralized primary education and made it by law free and universal. One effect (and among the purposes) of these reforms was to subsume regional language and traditions under a unified national standard. Parallel in strategy to
the assimilationist educational policy pursued in French territories overseas,
the new law can be seen as a kind of domestic colonization aiming to instill in
a new generation a common national lore and a homogeneous culture. If, as
Theodore Zeldin argues, Frenchness can be defined in large part in terms of the
possession of French culture and language, centralized education was a key tool
for consolidating identification of individuals with the nation. The new policies thus represented a "cultural revolution" that quickly had the corollary effect of "an organized onslaught on regional and local eccentricity."[4]

Pagnol's four-volume autobiography reveals a tension in this family of *instituteurs* between ardent nationalism and equally strong regional loyalties,
formed at Marcel's birthplace outside Marseilles and reinforced at the family's
country cottage in nearby La Treille. By the time Joseph Pagnol joined their
ranks in the 1890s, the professional culture among schoolteachers, when it was
not overtly hostile to the church, was less religious than the population at large.
Pagnol portrays friendly disputes between his father and his uncle, who was as
royalist and Catholic as Joseph was republican and anticlerical. As official dis-
seminators of republican values, the teaching corps had as its official mission to
act as agents of centralization, in order to build national consciousness throughout a disparate collection of regions. Teachers were routinely assigned to posts
that were not necessarily in their home districts, and Pagnol, following in his
father's profession, himself taught in Marseilles, then in Aix-en-Provence, and
finally at the Lycée Condorcet in Paris, before resigning to devote himself full
time to a career writing for the theater.

Yet Pagnol writes both from and about a regional perspective. The tension in
his work between Provençal peasant pride on the one hand and cosmopolitan,
urban, and middle-class republicanism on the other makes Pagnol representative of his time and of his family's profession.[5] The three films of the Marseilles
trilogy (*Marius, Fanny, César*) give a detailed portrait of local consciousness and
its flip side, xenophobia. Even a Lyonnais is a foreigner—not exotic enough to
trigger Marius's wanderlust, to be sure, but not familiar enough to be fully assimilated. When Fanny's son returns to Marseilles after attending school in
Paris, his grandfather reproaches him for his "foreign" ways, and jokes that he

needs an interpreter to understand what his grandson is trying to tell him. Jean de Florette's mother, Florette Camoins, was considered as good as dead when she married a blacksmith from the neighboring enemy town Crespin. Jean's deformity is even attributed to his mother's having sought a husband beyond the confines of the village: "Florette, she was a tart!" rages Le Papet (César Soubeyran). "If she had stayed with us she would have had straight children like the rest of us" (381). And when César asks Ugolin if Jean is a peasant (understood: "like us"), Ugolin succinctly establishes Jean's status as outsider, irretrievably Other, both physically and socially: "He's a typical town hunchback," he replies. (And the narrator adds: ". . . as if he were speaking of a well-known species"; 78.)

Oral versus Written Authority

L'Eau des collines also stages a conflict between oral and written authority, most often pitting the predominantly oral Provençal tradition against the written language made dominant by the education system.[6] André Bazin suggests how this second opposition devolves from the first when he points out the continuity between Pagnol's regional identity and his attachment to sound films. In contradistinction to Pagnol's own self-description, Bazin sees the writer as not a dramatic author converted to cinema, but as "one of the greatest authors of the talkies." Contrasting theatrical and cinematic speech (and thereby refuting in passing Pagnol's claims about the superiority of the first over the second), Bazin argues that theatrical speech is abstract and conventional. Subordinate to the dramatic action, it can be incarnated by any voice. In the cinema, in contrast, speech is primary: "It exists concretely . . . by and for itself." He attributes the relative failure of *Topaze* to its nonmeridional setting. "The [regional] accent in Pagnol's films," he argues, "does not in fact constitute a picturesque accessory, a note of local color; it is *consubstantial with the text* and therefore with the characters. His heroes possess it as another might have black skin. The accent is the very material of their language, its realism."[7]

The doctrine of *théâtre en conserve* attributed to Pagnol is thus more complex than it seems, because film not only functions as a simple theatrical archive, it also serves to preserve the human voice, with all its materiality and contextual (including cultural) specificity. This task is all the more urgent because for Pagnol, locale is most readily to be found in speech patterns. In his films, verbal always takes precedence over visual in defining character and articulating setting. Contrasting his 1952 filmed *Manon des sources* with Claude Berri's, for example, one notices in the former many more close or medium shots of individuals and groups engaged in conversation and verbal jousting. Pagnol's characters derive their social standing and their comic charm from devices associated with speech. For instance, Belloiseau's partial deafness permits his drinking buddies to exploit him by playing word games while he is holding forth, a good-natured insult of which Belloiseau is perfectly aware and in which he eventually participates. At one point Belloiseau even exclaims, "What a marvel is the human voice!" The mayor owes his authority to his status as the only villager who has access to a telephone. Manon thanks a neighbor for a favor by singing. (All these examples are absent from the Berri version.) Still other characters display verbal tics or communication impediments, such as stuttering, deaf-muteness, or grotesquely thick accents, sometimes accompanied by grimaces.

Bazin's descriptions of theatrical and cinematic speech in fact add up to a distinction between written and spoken discourse, regardless of format. Many episodes in Pagnol's filmed *Manon* demonstrate the distance between what amount to two separate languages, erudite (or official) and popular. During the town's anniversary celebration, for example, Belloiseau pronounces a fervent peroration peppered with pretentious uses of the *passé simple* and imperfect subjunctive. His own and Pagnol's awareness of the ease and the comic potential of passing from one language to another is demonstrated when, at one point in his oration, Belloiseau waxes grandiloquent about the virtues of water and other liquids: "the meager serum, that life-giving liquid that overflows from the mellow mammaries of the capricorn animal (in a word, I mean goat's milk)." The rural engineer called in (by telephone) to rescue the town when its fountain mysteriously runs dry is respectfully considered "un vrai savant" because he is incomprehensible. Meanwhile, the film's viewers can enjoy his verbose but silly description of all the reasons the fountain *might* have stopped and where the water *doesn't* come from. That these episodes go beyond dramatic irony to an alignment of official discourse with a centralized authority that makes light of local needs is driven home by one villager who declares that he doesn't care why the water stopped, but only that he paid for water, and he wants water. Unsatisfied, he storms out, but not before dramatizing his frustration by smashing a statuette that stands in the communal meeting place: the regulation plaster bust of "Marianne" that represents the Republic.

Even in the novel, authenticity resides in the spoken word, and oral supersedes written authority. What the novelized *Manon des sources* lacks in palpable *grain de la voix*, it provides through a rich thematics of spoken language as it differs from the more suspect written discourse. After her husband's death, Manon's mother falls into a form of madness, the principal symptom of which is that she writes letters. Like the Lyonnais in *Marius* or the city-educated grandson in *César*, Jean (that "town hunchback") is ridiculed because his knowledge derives from books. When he announces ecstatically that he has come to Les Bastides in order to "cultivate the Authentic," Ugolin misinterprets the unfamiliar word and reports to Le Papet that the "Orthentic" must be "a plant that grows in books" (79). As in the film, after Manon has punished the village by blocking off its fountain at its underground source, the engineer sent by the government speaks a pseudoscientific babble the gist of which is that he hasn't a clue as to the source (so to speak) of their difficulties. The engineer's style is highlighted through its contrast with the curate's sermon, pronounced in ordinary language accessible to the entire populace, in which he attributes the drought to some secret and unexpiated sin and calls on his flock to repent. In all these instances, the local Marseillais (spoken) patois is the norm, the standard against which other speech stands out as marked, even suspect, particularly if it is learned, urban, or foreign. History, too, as it appears in the written record, is repeatedly discredited by oral tradition. César and Ugolin are able to carry out their plot precisely because the location of the source does not appear on maps or other documents—its existence has been transmitted by word of mouth (*de bouche à oreille*) among insiders. (Clearly this is why they are able to plug [*boucher*] the source.) When one villager, motivated by guilt, decides to direct Jean to the source's location, his wife forbids him to say a word. He therefore devises the compromise of inscribing on rocks several arrows indicating lines that would converge at the spot. But even Jean is unable to read the written signs, and the message is not transmitted. Finally, however, Manon learns the truth by overhearing a conversation between two villagers. In short, written language lies and misleads, is unreadable and suspect, even (as in the case of the rural engineer) when it is spoken.

Nevertheless, letters are so crucial to the development of the story that *L'Eau des collines* is almost an epistolary novel. The Soubeyran pair write to Florette's friend, asking about the future of the land. The first disadvantage of letters being their delay, the friend replies that the query arrived just as Florette was being laid out for burial. Ugolin writes a suicide note confessing his guilt and his love for Manon. At his death, Le Papet leaves a letter for Manon, granting her all his goods and land. Most catastrophic of all is the original and fated letter from Florette that never arrived in Africa. Writing from somewhere between oral tradition and historiography, Ugolin and Le Papet/César compose their letters, confessions, and testaments in an oral discourse, with a phonetic spelling (and extensively described mental and physical exertion) that preserves their *grain de la voix* and their authority as truth. "Accent is consubstantial with the text."

The message's virtue is nonetheless diluted by writing, and the entire novel, running to some 625 pages in the original, is the saga of a written missive that is suppressed and finally returns in purified (i.e., physical or oral) form. Oracle form, in fact, given that it is Florette's friend Delphine who unravels the tragedy of the letter that never arrived in Africa and solves the mystery of Jean's identity. Delphine is now ancient and blind, so that her words arrive as pure voice, pure oral revelation, unmediated by letters or any but inner vision. Destiny is played out with the considerable delay of several generations, before its logic is revealed. Recognizing the sacred quality of the interchange, César—that crusty old unbeliever—invokes the church steeple, giving his (spoken) word of honor to Delphine that he never received Florette's letter.

The ultimate defeat of the written is to be found in the fact that if letters are not delivered, babies are. Paternal genealogy, like the water source, remains unrevealed in writing, but babies constitute in themselves more reliable signs. Manon gives birth on the very day of César's death. The proud papa expresses his relief that the baby is not a hunchback. The infant slipped out without impediment, he announces, "like a letter in a postbox, but in the opposite direction, of course" (436). Obstructed messages—in the form of letters, the location of the source, genetic information—can finally be transmitted. The missive sent by the grandfather is thus delivered by the granddaughter, and the sins of one generation can be rectified in the next. The curse can be reversed. The infant's patrimony (both his paternal genealogy and his land) is restored. The deformity supposedly caused by exogamy is repaired by another exogamy: because Manon's husband is none other than the schoolteacher assigned by the government to the village, the child represents an ideal offspring in a marriage that joins the native soil ("Manon of the Sources" and of the grotto) with the centralized and emergent national consciousness.

Maternal versus Paternal

As can be understood from the discussion so far, the split between oral and written traditions also correlates closely with divergent maternal and paternal sources of identity. So strong is the fantasmatic (and oh-so-Lacanian or Kristevan) identification of the oral with the maternal and the written with the paternal that in order to begin the first volume of his memoirs—titled *La Gloire de mon père*—Pagnol felt compelled to explain: "Here, for the first time—not counting a few modest essays—I am writing in prose. It seems to me that there are three distinctly different literary genres: poetry, which is sung, theater [include cinema], which is spoken, and prose, which is written."[8] Thus, after so many stories of the *fille-mère*, to speak directly of the father required a major generic shift. On the other hand, whereas Jean (like Pagnol's schoolteacher father) gleans his knowledge from books, his wife names their daughter after Manon Lescaut, not from the book by L'Abbé Prévost, but rather from Aimée's favorite operatic role in her former career as a singer.[9]

Moreover, a conflict between matriliny and patrilinear descent (and its perilous interaction with exogamy—the father is always from "ailleurs") is played out in the characters' names. Jean's official patronymic of record is Jean Cadoret, after Florette's blacksmith husband from Crespin. But again, official written authority hides the truth: Jean turns out not to be a Cadoret after all, a fact inscribed in his nickname, Jean de Florette, following the (oral) tradition in a locale populated by so few families that individuals are more reliably recognized matronymically. In fact, matrilineal legitimacy effectively overrides the written law of the father. Jean receives his inheritance through his mother, and he returns to the maternal home. Paternal lineage becomes the secret, the source of both the curse and identity. The key, however, is often hidden in the nickname. Even after he has discovered that Jean was Florette's son (and remembering his own love for Florette and "what happened one evening when we came back from a dance" (431), old César Soubeyran stubbornly turns a deaf ear to the local oral traditions and remains convinced that "it's a father that makes a son! And the proof is that the son bears his name" (381), and so he forecloses the possibility of recognizing his son.

César could perhaps have deciphered his own secret and prevented both his crime and his tragedy, however, by listening to the voice of his own nickname: he is called Le Papet (grandfather), although he never married.[10] Similarly, Manon's mythical (sacred) status as both saint and sorceress is contained in her matrilinear appellation, Manon des Sources, and in the fact that she is frequently called "La fille des Sources [the girl, but also the daughter, of the Sources]." Indeed, the village's springwater source itself is maternal: the novel opens on a description of the parish of Les Bastides, including an introduction of the fountain as "the origin of the village" (3) (in the French, "la mère de l'agglomération"). Within the novel form, Manon is also the mother or source of her own father in a kind of reverse textual genealogy, her story having generated his, as flashback or "prologue."

Indigenous versus Foreign Sources of Identity

Jean comes home to his mother's castle (as Pagnol himself did, in a later volume of his autobiography),[11] but once there, he wants to cultivate *Chinese* pumpkins and *Australian* rabbits (in addition to the exotic "Orthentic"). Similarly, Pagnol's mythos contains competing strata of literary sources, both indigenous and far-reaching. Manon is apparently based on a Provençal legend, and her character, as an extension of the landscape, embodies that filiation. Her identification with the geography is so complete that she often disappears into it; she enjoys natural conversation with animals and trees. Most important, of course, she is the daughter of the Source. There are, in addition, many biblical motifs: Manon's friend Baptistine, who recognizes Jean, transforming him from the outset into a Christ figure; a beautiful chapter in which Jean acts out the revolt of Job, speaking to an unresponsive God; Ugolin plays to Jean's martyr the role of Judas, who betrays his friend for financial gain, experiences regrets, and hangs himself.

Intertexts in the national literary canon are also apparent and numerous. On several occasions, Pagnol adapted the work of Jean Giono to the screen, and many readers have examined similarities between *L'Eau des collines* and Giono's *Colline*.[12] Further suggestive echoes can be traced to Victor Hugo's *Notre Dame de Paris*, whose familiar elements are evoked in Pagnol's work both by allusion and by thematic transposition: both novels recount stories of a beautiful goat keeper with magical powers (Manon is portrayed as both a *sorcière* and a *sourcière*), an ugly and vicious plotter who falls obscenely and fatally in love with her, and, above all, a hunchback of epic scope. Although Hugo's novel is as deeply Parisian as Pagnol's is meridional, the great romantic writer's signature is legible in *L'Eau des collines* behind the juxtaposition of a Victor (Aimée's former singing companion, who resurfaces after Jean's death) and a Hugo (Ugolin). More significantly, *Notre Dame de Paris* itself played a role in renewing awareness of France's own indigenous—that is, medieval, as contrasted with classical—past.

Jean-Marie Apostolidès has shown how *The Iliad* functions as a structuring subtext in Pagnol's film *La Femme du boulanger*, and classical sources are discernible in the story of Manon as well.[13] Pagnol's pastoral lyricism can be traced as far back as his schoolboy passion for Virgil (he translated the *Bucolics*), and in numerous set pieces from classical mythology: Manon/Diana/Aphrodite surprised at her bath by Ugolin, who watches from a hiding place behind the trees; the comely Florette, a village Venus, married to a blacksmith. Several episodes link Jean to Oedipus: his physical deformity, by which he will finally be recognized; the oracle who reveals the truth about his birth (albeit retrospectively); the curate's sermon in which he compares his parish to "a profane book—a Greek tragedy—[about] the history of the unhappy city of Thebes" (359) and goes on to suggest that misfortune has befallen the village because someone among them has committed a grievous sin; and, most important, the Soubeyran family's tragically cursed fate and the story's generic design.

Narrative and Nationhood

I have outlined the story's contradictions in a way that recalls in both content and method Claude Lévi-Strauss's "The Structural Study of Myth," an essay, it will be remembered, in which Lévi-Strauss uses the Oedipus story for demonstration purposes. Having compiled elements common to multiple versions and offshoots of the myth and arranged them in a conceptual grid of rows and columns, he goes on to explain:

> Were we to *tell* the myth, we would disregard the columns and read the rows from left to right and from top to bottom. But if we want to *understand* the myth, then we will have to disregard one half of the diachronic dimension (top to bottom) and read from left to right, column after column.[14]

Next, he isolates for discussion two pairs of columns—two thematic threads or bundles of mythemes—that prove as relevant to *L'Eau des collines* as to the Oedipus story. In the first of these—the representation of kinship—Lévi-Strauss finds either an overrating or an underrating of blood relationships (in Oedipus's murder of his father and marriage to his mother, for example, as well as in related stories of the fratricidal Eteocles and Antigone's insistence on burying her brother). A second, related theme of monsters and monstrosity appears in the guise of the Sphinx and of a dragon that must be killed in order for humanity to inhabit the earth. Lévi-Strauss analyses these narrative elements in terms of a conflict in the primitive mind over the sources of mankind, specifically, the coexistence of incompatible beliefs in autochthonous versus human origins. In other words, the question is whether humans are generated from the earth itself (*autochthonous*, from the Greek *chthon*, earth: "one supposed to have risen or sprung from the ground of the region he inhabits," "indigenous to a region," "in its place of origin")[15] or from an encounter of two human parents. He interprets the victory of men over monsters to represent a rejection of the theory of autochthony and a dawning knowledge of the role and consequent "overrating" of kinship.

Similar anxieties are legible in *L'Eau des collines*. Blood relationships are underrated by the Soubeyran pair and by the villagers, who instead define individuals according to their geographic provenance and identify them with features of the landscape. Those who do not issue from the very local region are not simply foreigners, they might as well belong to a different species. Exogamy consequently becomes so problematic that Jean's hunchback is superstitiously and xenophobically viewed as the monstrous consequence of Florette's unnatural union with the smith from Crespin. Other forms of monstrosity appear in the story's many verbal and biological distortions: a pair of uncanny stuttering twins, deafness, Ugolin's inhuman avarice, his grotesque love for Manon, and finally his suicide, and of course the monstrous act at the story's source, where César and Ugolin murder their own kin.

The self-inflicted death of "the last of the Soubeyrans" and the presumed extinction of the family line follow a logic of crime and (self-) punishment similar to that found in the Oedipus myth. Lévi-Strauss gives the following formulaic description of the dilemma being worked out in the myth:

> The Oedipus myth provides a kind of logical tool which relates the original problem—born from one or born from two?—to the derivative problem: born from different or born from same? By a correlation of this type, the overrating of blood relations is to the underrating of blood relations as the attempt to escape autochthony is to the impossibility to succeed in it.[16]

Similarly, through its successive incarnations, Pagnol's matrix-fable serves as a sort of "logical tool" that might first stage and then mediate contradictions by making them compatible within a new fictional mosaic. Lévi-Strauss's formula also describes the correlations in *L'Eau des collines* among the multiple paired oppositions of maternal versus paternal origin, oral traditions versus the law, and most especially of personal identity as it might be derived from the regional land (*pays*) or from more abstract notions of blood kinship and collective affiliation (*nation*). It is no wonder that the story of Jean and Manon, César and Ugolin is a vendetta of conflicting claims between those born from (or at least on) the land on the one hand and those who own it by law on the other. The villagers instinctively support the "autochthonous" claimants, but are troubled by conscience because at some level of awareness, they recognize the legitimacy of the outsider, the rightful inheritor. When Jean turns out to be César's son, the Soubeyran family line is restored along with the water. In this way, the ultimate claimant to the land—Manon's child—turns out to be both the legitimate inheritor (born from two) and the descendant of the land itself (born from one).

Another such mediating strategy can be seen in the rhythm of departure and return that recurs throughout Pagnol's oeuvre. Most of Pagnol's important characters find a compromise between their "envie d'ailleurs" and their loyalty to local roots: Jean brings his family back to his mother's birthplace; Ugolin and César both return from military service in Africa; Marius comes back to Marseilles to reclaim Fanny and their son. Jacqueline Pagnol made her career as a movie star in Paris, only to become famous playing the role of a heroine from her native region, and Pagnol himself moved to Paris, then returned to the locale of his mother's castle in order to create his film studio. The emblematic example of this shuttle motif is no doubt Escartefigue, in the Marseilles trilogy, who, when he is not ensconced in the neighborhood café, spends his time as captain of a ferryboat in the Marseilles harbor, and can thus regularly depart without really leaving. His chronic seasickness and his basic contentedness complement Marius's restless wanderlust.

A more abstract sort of return can be discerned in Pagnol's nostalgia for the forms and conventions of the traditional novel. Comparing the novel with earlier versions of Pagnol's fable (particularly the filmed *Manon* of a decade earlier) highlights ways in which *L'Eau des collines* strives for resolution: with its recognition scenes, its reconciliations, its loose ends tied, its sources restored, and its deformities explained and overcome, all blocks, plugs, or humps in linearity have been smoothed out. There remain no obscurities or tangles, no unreadable signs. Moreover, a common logic connects the thematic and the formal nostalgias. Patricia Drechsel Tobin has coined the term "genealogical imperative" to conceptualize the dominance of linearity in Western understandings both of the family, and of narrative. "In life and literature," she explains, "a line has become legitimatized because our causal understanding, always for the West the better part of knowledge, has been conditioned by our existential experience of genealogical descent and destiny."[17] Because in traditional ideals of the family, as of narrative, sequence implies consequence, an imposed linearity generates authority for the cause or source (the parent, God) and legitimacy for the effect or child, linking closure to origin. Jean's back can thus be read as the sign of a family, a community, and a narrative twisted out of shape. Like Oedipus's foot or Odysseus's scar, his deformity holds forth from the beginning the promise (like a narrative intuition or "hunch") that his true identity might eventually be disclosed. His back thus serves as a bridge between his erroneous identification as son of an outsider (he is Jean Cadoret, the "town hunchback") and his legitimate genealogical and local origin (Jean de Florette, son of César Soubeyran). When finally Manon is integrated into the community as a bourgeois wife and mother, the novel simultaneously reaffirms conservative values in the society and in narrative. The ultimate birth of a perfectly formed grandson whose claim is legitimated through legal blood inheritance *and* presence on the land—*pays* and *nation*—means that genetic and epistolary messages have finally been transmitted (the baby "slipped out like a letter in a postbox"), establishing closure in relation to origin and signaling a return to social, narrative, and dorsal rectitude.

But nostalgia is just that. That the story recounts an instance of individuals stuck in the past is emblematized by the fact that at the moment of Jean's death, the clock stops. *L'Eau des collines* attempts to restore a sense of stability that was only a memory in 1963; when the novel was published, the boundaries of both narrative and nation (and the concept of nationality) were in flux, torn apart by the Algerian conflict and, on the literary front, by the experiments of the New Novel and New Wave cinema. Although closure is achieved by the end of Pagnol's novel, its fragile coherence self-deconstructs at every point along the way. Ultimately, despite efforts on the part of the fiction to reconcile all its contradictions, the center does not hold, and, when examined closely, all these conflicting layers collapse under the weight of the very contradictions that define the Provençal region. Parents are the narrative consequence (or "prologue"), not the biological origin, of the child; history is rendered unreliable by legend (but the oral tradition is most fully restored in the written genre of the novel); the most locally rooted culture has sources in the Roman occupation, and the imperial past is as insistent in the geography as the classical sources in the language. The very regionalism whose strength was to resist homogenization ends up being foreign. A search for identity yields only difference, because even (or especially) the most indigenous identity meets its crisis if you trace it back far enough or dig deep enough. It is not coincidental that many of Pagnol's characters are diggers: in a manner that recalls Freud's use of archeological metaphors to represent the unconscious or buried self, they make wells, seek buried treasure, reveal or hide sources. The origin of both the individual and national consciousness turns out to be located beyond boundaries of the state or people, or the reverse, as Bazin notes, "Pagnol owes his international popularity above all, paradoxically, to the regionalism of his *oeuvre*."[18] All of this makes Pagnol an excellent case study in the debate about the canon and the boundaries or even the existence of Western civilization. The heart or source of identity, both individual and national, is scattered, *ailleurs*, and turns out to resemble Roland Barthes's description of the text as onion: you peel off its layers until nothing remains, and you weep.

In other words, Pagnol's nostalgia displays the very weaknesses that Jacques Derrida finds in Lévi-Strauss's method of myth analysis. Postulating that "coherence in contradiction expresses the force of a desire," Derrida identifies in Lévi-Strauss's essay (and we can find in Pagnol's fable) efforts to reconcile conflicting versions and elements within myths and to create an imaginary coherence by means of what Derrida calls an "ethic of nostalgia for origins."[19] Derrida thus accuses Lévi-Strauss of repeating the epistemological strategy of the myths themselves. In effect, he agrees with Lévi-Strauss's own assessment that his structuralist method creates "the myth of mythology." In contrast to this mode of interpretation-by-mythmaking, Derrida proposes an approach that would affirm what he calls "freeplay," that is, the formulation of explanations

(or stories) that would abandon the myth of linearity (the genealogical imperative) and closure, acknowledging instead the irretrievability of origins and our
ignorance of the future.

In order to encapsulate the kind of interpretive outlook he seeks to define,
Derrida introduces another metaphor that recirculates the vocabulary of Lévi-
Strauss's analyses and Pagnol's fable:

> Here there is a kind of question, let us still call it historical, whose *conception, for-
> mation, gestation,* and *labor* we are only catching a glimpse of today. I employ
> these words, I admit, with a glance toward the operations of childbearing—but
> also with a glance toward those who, in a society from which I do not exclude my-
> self, turn their eyes away when faced by the as yet unnamable which is proclaim-
> ing itself and which can do so, as is necessary whenever a birth is in the offing,
> only under the species of the nonspecies, in the formless, mute, infant, and terri-
> fying form of monstrosity.[20]

Pagnol's nostalgia for genealogical linearity, generic coherence, reconciliation
of land and law, mother and father, center and province, requires a tale of epic
proportions to rectify, and the legacy of the hunchback—where deformity is
transformed from a sign of lost origin into a possibility of its retrieval—is the
motive force of the narration. *L'Eau des collines* hovers between Derrida's two
modes of explanation, between glorification of monstrosity and attempts to
erase it.

This Pagnol mythos, as embedded in the recurrent story of the *fille-mère*, can
be read to represent by indirection the anxieties (of authority, legitimacy, identity) that have characterized modern French history. Moreover, if we bear in
mind Lévi-Strauss's statement that "the purpose of myth is to provide a logical
model capable of overcoming a contradiction,"[21] and Derrida's discussion of
what is at stake in providing such myths, the playing out of these tensions
might explain Pagnol's continuing appeal. I want to conclude, therefore, by ex-
amining four historical moments or crises that erupt in the text of *L'Eau des
collines,* or are buried under it, like a secret that none of the characters knows
alone.

The 1789 Revolution

Ugolin hoards his fortune in two forms, hiding both under a rock: he plugs the
spring that will feed his carnations and enrich him, and he buries the family
treasure beneath the hearth. Both are the *source* or *foyer* of the Soubeyran family prestige. The buried treasure—five thousand gold louis—was amassed before the Revolution and has been hidden ever since, passed along from generation to generation, while remaining secret. As such, it is readable as a kind of

persistent royalism. That repressed family history expresses itself in Ugolin's body by means of a tic: his compulsive and conspicuous blinking. Volume 1 ends with a resurgence of that pathogenic royalism. With the unblocking of the source, César crowns his nephew: "I baptize you king of the Carnations [le roi des oeillets]," he says (218). Once again, the literal words—*oeillets* and the *oeil* (eye) of Ugolin's tic—establish the secret logic of Pagnol's mythology, and the king is reenthroned (in what we might call a rein-carnation) in parodic guise or, as Marx would put it, as farce.

That problems of legitimacy and identity dating from the *ancien régime* were on Pagnol's agenda as he wrote *L'Eau des collines* is confirmed by his publication in the following year of a curious essay titled *Le Masque de fer*.[22] This was Pagnol's intervention in the tricentennial rumor of the mysterious masked man who allegedly languished for thirty-four years and died in a dungeon during the reign of Louis XIV. Pagnol summarizes the debate and surmises, like others before him, that the masked prisoner was the king's own twin brother, suppressed in order to avoid challenge to the throne. As Pagnol had very little to add to a legend that had already been recounted by many others, such as Voltaire and Dumas, the real mystery is why he bothered to investigate the episode in the first place. Pagnol hesitates self-consciously between essay and novel as the mystery's appropriate narrative expression, but his familiar motifs of hidden identity, recognition, and suppression of genealogical knowledge tie the essay closely to *Jean de Florette* and *Manon des sources*. Furthermore, given his tendency to link biological to social monstrosity (and his symbolic use of kinship and birth images), it is not difficult to understand why Pagnol would opt for the thesis of the hidden twin from among the numerous explanations that have been offered. His republican sentiments come into play as well, especially in the book's longest chapter, where he paints a scathing portrait of King Louis's odious character and repulsive personal habits. In a more recent evaluation of the case, John Noone suggests that such a masked prisoner may never even have existed, but that the legend may owe its persistence to the need, on the part of postrevolutionary France, to impugn the monarchy's genealogical legitimacy and to vilify its most glorious exemplar by attributing to the Sun King a fratricidal cruelty.[23]

Empire

If contemporary France remains stubbornly postrevolutionary, it is also postcolonial, and the search for inner sources of identity is complemented by the quest for its outer borders. Although the regional flavor of the Marseille trilogy is perhaps its most salient feature, the three films in the cycle teem with references to the world beyond, particularly that of the French Empire: an Arab carpet merchant and a Vietnamese client make brief appearances; Orane Demazis, Pagnol's leading lady in life and film, hails (as does her character, Fanny) from Algeria, as her name (Orane) attests; Marius leaves for "ailleurs" in the ship *La Malaysie*. Similarly, it is specified that Manon's mother had sung in Saigon and Dakar. Within regional identity, imperial difference is a disrupting refrain. In *L'Eau des collines*, empire is a source both of prestige and its loss, not surprising given that the novel was published in the year of Algerian independence. Nor is it surprising that Marius's 1931 cry of imperial enthusiasm—"J'ai envie d'ailleurs"—is matched in anguish (although thirty-two years later its message is reversed), when his elderly incarnation, César Soubeyran, wails that his fate has been "all the fault of Africa" (440).

In figuring the loss of collective identity, authority, and unity as a failure of the written language of paternity, Pagnol's narrative template fits nicely into a more generalized mythography of 1963. The lost letter motif recurs that same year in Alain Resnais's film *Muriel*, and the following year in Jacques Demy's *Les Parapluies de Cherbourg*. In *Les Parapluies*, a couple is separated when the man is conscripted to Algeria. When he fails to write, she marries someone else and has a child. In *Muriel*, a letter that never arrived (or was never written, depending on whom you believe) separates Hélène and Alphonse during their idyll on the eve of the Second World War, until his return from Algeria some twenty years later. Like César Soubeyran, Hélène never marries, but takes responsibility for her nephew, who has himself also just returned from Algeria. (Here again the sinister possibilities of generational repetition are suggested.) In the period 1960–64, the loss of Algeria—and the losses in Algeria, in terms of human life and national identity—are encoded within Pagnol's familiar fable.

César himself is an overdetermined figure of imperialism gone sour: narratively, he will go to any lengths to annex his neighbor's land; his name, omnipresent in Pagnol's oeuvre, is both typically Marseillais and the signifier par excellence of empire. Marseilles between the wars (the novel's temporal setting) is both a boomtown of the French Empire and a monument to the Roman one. As a typical Marseillais name, César/Caesar suggests both the origin and the dissolution of regional identity. It is thus poetically appropriate that Daniel Auteuil, in Claude Berri's film from the novel, playing the role of Ugolin, was awarded the French equivalent of the American Academy Award—a César.

The Occupation

The jury is still undecided about whether Pagnol's 1955 play *Judas* is to be seen as an intervention in the discussion of whether Pétain was a hero or a traitor, whether the Roman and German Occupations are to be compared.[24] In any case, the Occupation is explicitly invoked in Pagnol's fable in its version that appears in *La Fille du puisatier*. The first feature-length production released under Vichy (though made in Pagnol's own Marseilles studio in the *zone libre*), the film recounts the familiar story of the *fille-mère*, but this time the young man's departure is occasioned by his mobilization in the *drôle de guerre*. Due to a scene in which the family listens to the Maréchal's Armistice broadcast, and to the characters' loyalty to work, family, and country (traits that characterized Pagnol's work from the beginning), the film was widely considered to be political propaganda in favor of Vichy and Pétain, later landing Pagnol on the Liberation blacklist.[25] It is unlikely that Pagnol was a Nazi sympathizer, but rather that we are dealing as always with his ambiguous blend of disingenuous realism (the Maréchal did in fact make the speech, after all) and deeper mythical representation of the nation. Where de Gaulle and Pétain were both represented by their supporters as the "father" of the nation, for example, Pagnol's disputed paternity motif takes on topical connotations, and Thomas Elsaesser's characterization of German national cinema after World War II works as well for Pagnol's representation of Occupation France: a fatherless society figured as fatherless family.[26] Whatever Pagnol's own political sentiments may have been, my point is that the Pagnol mythos served once again to encode the national sentiment and identity crisis at a time when France went off to fight in the war and lost paternal authority at home.

Pagnol's Continuing Appeal

In the 1980s and 1990s, a resurgence of right-wing extremism in the form of Jean-Marie Le Pen's National Front Party, with its anti-Semitism and anti-immigrant (particularly anti-Arab) xenophobia, has given a newly sinister slant to the idea that "it is all the fault of Africa." This time we are dealing not with the hotheaded enthusiasm of European adventurers and their *mission civilisatrice*, however, but the paranoid fear of foreign "invasion" (particularly by North African immigrants) and its corollary anxiety about national identity. The current furor in France about the status of immigrants and the new laws voted into effect in July 1993—especially reforms of the *code de la nationalité* that impose new restrictions on acquisition of French citizenship—reveal the complexity of the issue and the depth of the sentiments surrounding it. The debate around the definition of what constitutes Frenchness turns on the opposition between the *droit du sol* (citizenship derived from place of birth; right to citizenship by being born and living in France) and the *droit du sang* (citizenship derived from consanguinity; right to citizenship if born anywhere in the world of at least one French parent). A resurgence of the conflict between autochthony and human genealogy, such is the current version of the question, Born from one or born from two? At stake here again is the very meaning of the national "patrimony" as country (*pays*) or kinship (*patrie*).

Lurking behind and coloring economic anxieties, there is no doubt that immigration is the hottest political issue in France today in large part because, as can be readily seen by the discourse circulating to discuss it, its implications intersect with so many previous crises. It pits the revolutionary tradition of universal and equal human rights against another revolutionary legacy of a homogeneous and centralized state.[27] It also evokes the Occupation, as when those opposed to the new laws evoke the anti-Semitic policies of the Vichy government and compare Interior Minister Charles Pasqua to René Bousquet.[28] The new laws place restrictions on the open-door policy put into place just after the Liberation, and, as Ronald Koven points out, "This is the first time since the end of the Second World War that a foreign presence in France has become the leading item on the national agenda."[29] Perhaps most of all, it evokes France's colonial history, because the primary targets of the new restrictions are immigrants from France's former North African territories. It is widely suggested that the virulence of the debate derives in part from unforgotten rancor and a desire for revenge for France's 1962 defeat in Algeria. What all these moments have in common is an anxiety over what constitutes Frenchness. As Bertrand le Gendre of *Le Monde* puts it, "To require the Algerian and the Senegalese to produce, on demand, proof of their identity is to seek reassurance ourselves about who we are." Nor is it surprising that these issues should arise at this particular historical moment, in the midst of worries about the creation of a European Community, a context whose stakes are once again the nature and survival of the national borders and identity. Le Gendre continues: expanded police rights to check identity papers have as their covert rationale to "comfort citizens of long pedigree in their sense of being French at a moment when that distinction seems threatened . . . [by] the fear of seeing French identity dissolve in an unacceptable cosmopolitanism."[30]

Lévi-Strauss defines myth as a model capable of overcoming contradiction. He continues parenthetically that the task is "(an impossible achievement if, as it happens, the contradiction is real)."[31] "As it happens," the contradictions and crises in French national identity since the Revolution have indeed been real. They have also often found expression only through indirection. Marius's remark "j'ai envie d'ailleurs" can therefore be invoked one last time as a theory of allegory applying to Pagnol's art of fiction. It is this indirection and allegory that account for the cyclical applicability of his mythos, and thus to Pagnol's continuous popularity, through upheavals in taste in both cinema and the novel during the postwar years. Claude Berri's recent cinematic adaptations of *Jean de Florette* and *Manon des sources* (1986) and Yves Robert's renditions of the first two volumes of Pagnol's autobiography, *La Gloire de mon père* and *Le Château de ma mère* (1991) confirm that Pagnol's fable retains its relevance today. At the end of *L'Eau des collines*, Manon has lost her father to a senseless death, her mother to madness, and her own past life, but she has learned her origins, she has assimilated into the community, and she is looking toward the future. In these novels, as throughout his oeuvre, Pagnol's mythos expresses, reformulates, and works through the successive crises in the task of being a nation.

Notes

1. Marcel Pagnol, *L'Eau des collines*, vol. 1, *Jean de Florette;* vol. 2, *Manon des sources* (Paris: Editions de Fallois, 1988). The novels were originally published by the Editions Julliard in 1963. Page references for this work appearing in text are drawn from the translation, *The Water of the Hills*, trans. W. E. van Heyningen (Berkeley: North Point, 1988). In all quotations used in this essay, where no translated edition is specified, the translations are my own.

2. M. Sineux, review of Claude Berri's *Jean de Florette, Positif* 308 (October 1986), 73.

3. See Charles Camproux, *Les Langues romanes* (Paris: PUF, 1974), 81–95. I am grateful to David Rollo for an illuminating conversation regarding the differences between the Occitan of the Troubadours and Provençal as it was re-created in the nineteenth century.

4. Theodore Zeldin, *France 1848–1945: Intellect and Pride* (Oxford: Oxford University Press, 1980), 141.

5. See Jean-Marie Apostolidès, "Figures populaires, figures mythiques dans *La Femme du boulanger*," in *Popular Traditions and Learned Culture in France*, ed. Marc Bertrand (Stanford, Calif.: Stanford University Press, 1985), 287–304, for a study of how Pagnol's 1938 film *La Femme du boulanger* dramatizes a small traditional community's entry into capitalist modernity. Many of the features of traditional society and the stages of modernization that Apostolidès analyzes in the film are at work again in *L'Eau des collines*.

6. Zeldin, *France*, 141, 48. The struggle for Provençal survival was internationally acknowledged when Frédéric Mistral was awarded the Nobel Prize for literature in 1905.

7. André Bazin, "Le Cas Pagnol," in *Qu'est-ce que le cinéma II: Le Cinéma et les autres arts* (Paris: Editions du Cerf, 1959), 121.

8. Marcel Pagnol, *Souvenirs d'enfance I: La Gloire de mon père* (Paris: Editions de Fallois, 1988), 7. This book was originally published in 1957.

9. Pagnol's filmed *Manon* of 1952 confirmed this point about her maternal and oral origins by announcing that her full name is Manon Lakmé Dalilah Cadoret.

10. The importance of this detail is reinforced in the novel, where plot construction is tighter and kinship is more fully worked out, and where it is clearly specified that Ugolin is César's nephew. In the 1952 film, family relationships are vague, and Le Papet could be assumed by viewers to be Ugolin's grandfather. In any case, the film lacks the final *coup de théâtre*—the revelation that Jean is César's son.

11. Marcel Pagnol, *Souvenirs d'enfance II: Le Château de ma mère* (Paris: Editions de Fallois, 1988). This book was originally published in 1957.

12. For example, he adapted *Jofroi* from a Giono short story titled "Jofroi de la Maussan," *Angèle* from *Un de Baumugnes, Regain* from Giono's novel by the same name, and *La Femme du Boulanger* from *Jean le Bleu.* For an account of the sometimes stormy collaboration between Giono and Pagnol, see C. E. J. Caldecott, *Marcel Pagnol* (Boston: G. K. Hall, 1977), 98–108. Gérard Depardieu was immediately reminded of Giono's novel when he read Pagnol's in preparation for his role as Jean de Florette in Berri's film. See Jean-Michel Frodon and Jean-Claude Loiseau, *Jean de Florette: La Folle Aventure du film* (Paris: Herscher, 1987). The two writers—who together represent Provençal regionalism in the novel genre—were close friends for a time, and Pagnol had planned a cinematic adaptation of *Colline* until the association turned rancorous.

13. Apostolidès, "Figures populaires."

14. Claude Lévi-Strauss, "The Structural Study of Myth," in *Structural Anthropology,* trans. Claire Jacobson and Brooke Grundfest Schoepf (Garden City, N.Y.: Anchor, 1967), 211.

15. *Webster's Third New International Dictionary.*

16. Lévi-Strauss, "The Structural Study of Myth," 212.

17. Patricia Drechsel Tobin, *Time and the Novel: The Genealogical Imperative* (Princeton, N.J.: Princeton University Press, 1978), 8.

18. Bazin, "Le Cas Pagnol," 121.

19. Jacques Derrida, "Structure, Sign, and Play in the Discourse of the Human Sciences," in *Writing and Difference,* trans. Alan Bass (Chicago: University of Chicago Press, 1978), 279, 492. The essay was originally a paper delivered at the Johns Hopkins University in 1966.

20. Ibid., 292.

21. Lévi-Strauss, "The Structural Study of Myth," 226.

22. Marcel Pagnol, *Le Masque de fer* (Paris: Editions de Provence, 1965).

23. John Noone, *The Man behind the Iron Mask* (New York: St. Martin's, 1988). See also Joan deJean's review of the book, "The Rumor That Will Not Die," *New York Times Book Review,* 25 December 1988, 2.

24. For a discussion of the play and its reception, see Caldecott, *Marcel Pagnol,* 80–82.

25. Evelyn Ehrlich, *Cinema of Paradox: French Filmmaking under the German Occupation* (New York: Columbia University Press, 1985), 34 and 208 n. 41. See also ibid., 113–15.

26. See Henry Rousso, *The Vichy Syndrome: History and Memory in France since 1944,* trans. Arthur Goldhammer (Cambridge: Harvard University Press, 1991), for discus-

sion of popular perceptions of de Gaulle and Pétain. Thomas Elsaesser, *New German Cinema: A History* (New Brunswick, N.J.: Rutgers University Press, 1989), 239–42.

27. Ronald Koven, "Muslim Immigrants and French Nationalists," *Society* 29 (May–June 1992): 25.

28. As reported by Louis Pauwels, "Ils devraient tout de même cesser d'être absurdes," *Le Figaro Magazine*, 3 July 1993, 15.

29. Koven, "Muslim Immigrants," 28. In a public lecture titled "Immigration, Racism, and 'Foreigners' in France Today" (Dartmouth College, 19 November 1993), Ronald Tiersky has rightly pointed out that, despite the presence of numerous illegal visitors, the current frustration is about legal immigrants, that is immigrants who are not in fact "foreign," but rather French citizens of North African descent. That they are still seen as foreign underlines French difficulty in facing the increasing diversification and decentering of its own cultural (now multicultural) identity.

30. Bertrand le Gendre, "Crise d'identité," *Le Monde*, 16 August 1993; reprinted in *Le Monde Hebdomadaire Internationale*, 19 August 1993, 6. On 15 August 1993, the Conseil Constitutionnel declared several of the new restrictions and expanded police rights unconstitutional on the grounds that they violated the individual freedom of immigrants, rights acquired by means of residence on French territory. The debate goes on.

31. Lévi-Strauss, "The Structural Study of Myth," 226.

5 / Heart of Darkness, Heart of Light: The Civilizing Mission in *L'Atlantide*

David H. Slavin

Imperial "mythistory" erases the historical achievements of colonized people and substitutes insulting stereotypes; this is a familiar refrain of contemporary cultural criticism. Some texts carrying out these displacements display a vitality and longevity that indelibly mark the national identity of the imperial power and recast popular attitudes in a culture of dominance.[1] One such text is *L'Atlantide,* a surreal film based on an equally mythomaniacal novel combining a setting in the heart of the vast Sahara, Foreign Legion officers on a mission (that "imperial manna term" as Roland Barthes called it), and the myth of the lost city. Any one of these ingredients was sure to fire the imagination of French audiences; together they mesmerized. Author Pierre Benoit wrote the novel in 1918 and died in 1962, a career spanning half the colonial era, from its zenith to the loss of Algeria. The story retains its appeal. Publisher Albin Michel continues to issue new editions, and in 1992 the film was remade for the fourth time.

Both book and film glorify France's "civilizing mission," rationalize the destructive impact of colonialism, and discount the Islamic past. Yet they contain hints of profound unease about Africa. Typographical fixity roots the book in time; through remakes, the films have evolved. Jacques Feyder directed the first version in 1921, and the producers rereleased it in 1928. When Georg Wilhelm Pabst remade it in 1932, the film reflected his unconscious pessimism about the future of the white "race." The two versions span the silent/sound divide, are stylistically idiosyncratic, and illustrate changing attitudes toward colonialism, race, and gender roles.

Even to cognoscenti of colonialist fiction, this story is not well known outside of France. A summary is in order. The 1932 film opens with a scholar delivering a lecture on Plato's Atlantis and theorizing that it lies buried in the Sahara rather than under the Atlantic.[2] The camera angle widens and the viewer sees that he is talking to a radio microphone instead of a live audience. The scene shifts to two French officers listening to the broadcast at a desert outpost. Lieutenant Ferrières is skeptical, but Captain Saint-Avit makes an astonishing claim. "I have been to Atlantis . . . two years ago with Captain Morhange . . . there I killed him." Sent to explore the routes from Tunis south into the Sahara, Saint-Avit continues, they were actually on a mission to gather intelligence on the Tuareg, the fierce Berber nomads who ruled the desert.

The scene fades to a flashback, and without any further narration Saint-Avit's story unfolds. The two officers and their guide join a caravan heading into the desert. As they ride their camels, they speculate about the Atlantis legend. Saint-Avit reveals his youthful impulsiveness. Morhange, mature and steady, expresses the view that the Tuareg were once Christians. He wears the cross of a Père Blanc priest, and Benoit modeled him on Charles de Foucauld, an intelligence officer who became a missionary to the Tuareg and was killed by them in 1916. Middle- and long-distance shots of the caravan, the rocking camels, and the open desert are interspersed with the dialogue, consciously imitating the 1921 film's use of the undulating dunes and craggy rocks, of which one critic said, "There is one great actor in *Atlantide*, the sand."[3] An austere, virgin wilderness awaits the intrepid French officers, who will penetrate and tame it with their civilizing hand.

Suddenly their guide points; a shield with a cross-shaped design lies in the sand. "Tuareg!" he exclaims. Saint-Avit rushes off and finds a Targui lying among the rocks. He gives the black-clad figure water, and as Morhange and the guide ride up, the caravan leaves them behind. The Targui seems ill, but as they help him to his camel he stealthily pulls up his veil. The guide leads them through a gorge to an oasis, where they camp. Later, the officers find the guide run through with a spear. When they confront the Targui, he says simply, "He was Châamba; Châamba are enemy." Dependent on the assassin to show them the way, the officers are powerless. That night they are attacked and, in the flurry of rifle shots and spears, separated. Overwhelmed, Morhange shouts the Legionnaires' cry for aid, "Saint-Avit! A moi!"[4] The screen goes dark.

Saint-Avit regains consciousness in the deep shadows of an underground room and sees the Targui who lured them into ambush kneeling before a small altar. He introduces himself as Cegheir ben Cheik; he is the only Tuareg man given a name in the movie. Saint-Avit asks whether he wants a ransom. No, replies Cegheir, you would come back with soldiers and machine guns; you will stay. Saint-Avit stumbles outside into a narrow, winding, windowless street typical of precolonial urban design in North Africa and the Middle East. He spies a man in a Legion officer's cape and limps after him, shouting, "Morhange!" But it is a Tuareg, who turns, laughing. Others squat on the ground, chanting; next to them an old-fashioned gramophone plays the movie's theme, Offenbach's "Orpheus in the Underworld." This surreal juxtaposition, the underground room, and the play of sharp angles of light and shadow in the street suggest the Greek myth of Orpheus's descent into Hades. They also bring to mind Plato's metaphor of the cave, his contrast between the illusion of temporal reality and the higher realm of the Forms.[5]

Saint-Avit faints in the street. The queen's servant Tanit-Zerga arrives to help him back to the room and nurse him. He awakens from the fever in a sumptuous room in a palace with a bevy of serving girls who pamper him. A dandified, mustachioed European in formal evening clothes minces into the room. He introduces himself as Count Velosei, hetman of Jitomir, although he hardly looks the part of a Cossack chief. He speaks cryptically of Queen Antinéa as another European appears, a Norwegian ship captain. How he came to the middle of the Sahara, two thousand miles from any coast, is never explained. Heavily drugged from smoking *kif*, the sailor mumbles incoherently about when "she" will call for him and ignores Saint-Avit until the guards summon the Frenchman to the queen. In a jealous rage, the captain leaps at his rival's throat. Saint-Avit fends off the befuddled man, who warns, "You will finish up just like me."

Saint-Avit enters the queen's chamber; diaphanously clad young women dance to the tune of a small orchestra playing cellolike instruments. At the center of the room, Antinéa sits playing chess with Tanit-Zerga, who smiles longingly at Saint-Avit and withdraws. The lieutenant hardly notices her; he is mesmerized by the queen. A pet leopard or cheetah lying near her snarls and she growls in reply: she is a maneater and Circe; the *kif* and hashish give her magical powers over men. Leading Saint-Avit to the chessboard, she bids him play. The music gets wilder as she checks him again and again, losing pieces but in the end checkmating him. Abruptly she leaves, and the scene shifts to the Norwegian's deathbed. The count directs his funeral; Tuareg pallbearers carry the body through the corridors of the palace. They bow like Muslims but seem to worship the monumental stone bust of Antinéa that is the set's centerpiece, an offensive implication of Tuareg idolatry.

After the funeral, Count Velosei gets drunk and shows Saint-Avit a clipping from *Le Figaro* dated nineteen years before. It reads "Tuareg Prince Marries Well-Known Dancer," Clemantinéa. As the Norwegian foretold, Saint-Avit falls under her spell, smokes *kif,* and begins to murmur, "I have a feeling I shall be called to her today." But the queen has fallen in love with Morhange, who has also been brought to this place, unknown to Saint-Avit. After an African fortune-teller throws bones and tells her, "He will come back," Antinéa summons Morhange and tries to seduce him, but, with his priest's cross prominently displayed on his chest, he spurns her. European patriarchy triumphs over gynarchy, despite the "unnatural" ruler's Medusan gaze and Circe-like ways. In a rage, she orders him to leave.

Saint-Avit has witnessed the quarrel from behind a screen without discovering the man's identity, and he emerges as Morhange leaves. Antinéa kisses him seductively, then weeps and says, "If you love me, you will kill the man who has insulted me." As if in a trance, Saint-Avit picks up a mallet, stalks the receding figure and strikes a mortal blow. He turns over the fallen man, and the two men have one moment of anguished recognition before Morhange dies. The young man kills his elder and replaces him in the affections of a deified woman, a reenactment of the Oedipus myth. Thus, the script cleaves to the Greek mythological theme and leavens it with Freudian misogyny.[6] Pabst accents Brigitte Helm's Nordic blonde looks to sustain his classical Greek theme, adding another layer to the "Aryan model" of Greek civilization. One critic has described her presence as "hieratic . . . *onduleuse,* capricious, majestic, with the soul of the Orient and the fine profile of Athens."[7]

In contrast, Tanit-Zerga, loyal and submissive to her European, helps Saint-Avit escape by disguising him in Tuareg robes and enlisting the aid of Cegheir ben Cheikh, who, for reasons of his own, provides them with water and camels. As they leave the palace, Saint-Avit notices a little boy playing with an amulet and a cross; it is Morhange's. Nearby, a body lies wrapped in a shroud. Saint-Avit pulls back the sheet and sees Morhange's face. Again stricken with grief and remorse, he is led into the desert by Tanit-Zerga. They ride until they run out of water and the camels die. On their last legs, they find a water hole, but the well is dry and Tanit-Zerga soon dies. Saint-Avit covers her with sand and stumbles on, hallucinatory mirages of oases and the sea clouding his brain. He collapses in the sand, but as the camera focuses on his prostrate form, the cruciform shadow of a low-flying plane passes over him like a benediction. Like the radio in the first scene, this shadow emblematically links him with the modern world and signals that he has regained contact with an outpost of Western civilization.

Astounded by this tale, Ferrières suggests Saint-Avit lie down and rest. But the troubled narrator wanders into the courtyard of the fort just as the *méhari,* camel cavalry, bring in a captured Targui. It is Cegheir. He greets Saint-Avit with the traditional "Peace be with you." The captain tells the troopers that he knows the man and orders them to release him. As Cegheir rides off, Saint-Avit smiles a secret smile. He turns up missing at the next roll call, prompting Ferrières to lead a search party. The *méhari* patrol follows two sets of camel tracks, but the wind picks up and begins to cover the trail. As it builds to a sandstorm, they are forced to dismount and take shelter behind their camels. His cape whipping in the wind, Ferrières shouts to the desert, "Saint-Avit! Saint-Avit!" The only reply is the howling wind and blowing sand. In the last shot, a stone bas-relief of Antinéa fills the screen.

Benoit's Maghreb: The Berber Myth and Settler Power

The hand that penned this tale, Pierre Benoit, was born in Albi in the Midi in 1886. The son of an army officer, he was six years old when his father left France to serve in North Africa, and he spent his formative years in the *pied-noir* colonial milieu, attending *lycée* in Algiers. The curriculum of such schools erased Arabo-Berber history, glorified the French conquest, exhorted native pupils to love France, and reminded the sons of the *colons* that they bore responsibility for civilizing their lesser brethren. European and Muslim children sat in the same classrooms, and the double messages amplified the synergies of racial rule.[8]

Benoit's childhood was steeped in stories of the French encounter with the Tuareg, the Apaches of the Sahara. In 1880, as Europe began its scramble for Africa, Paris sent Colonel Paul Flatters on a mission to survey a route for a trans-Saharan rail link to its North and West African colonies. The nomadic caravaneers, not surprisingly, saw this expedition as an invasion. Tuareg guides lured Flatters's men deep into the desert, exhausted their supplies, and led them into an ambush in which the colonel was killed and all the camels captured. Eighteen hundred miles from the Mediterranean, the soldiers could find neither food nor water. The remaining Europeans died eating a false Tuareg peace offering of poisoned dates. The survivors who straggled back to Tunis told a grisly tale of fending off starvation by cannibalizing their dead. The next French attempt to breach the Sahara began fourteen years later from the south. Colonel Eugène Bonnier wrested Timbuktu, the historic entrepôt of the caravan trade at the Bend or northernmost point of the Niger River, from the desert dwellers in January 1894. The Tuareg counterattack killed him and half his men. Then a shady anti-Semitic adventurer, the Marquis de Morès, tried to complete Flatters' route in 1896 and shared his fate. As rivalry with Britain in Africa heated up and ended the perennial indifference the French public had shown toward colonial affairs, the colonial lobby in Parliament gained clout and demanded revenge. Paris replaced Bonnier with General Louis Archimbaud, who swore to "kill as many Tuareg as possible" and sent expeditions to seize Lake Chad. Captain Jean Baptiste Marchand left the Congo in 1896 and arrived at Fashoda in July 1898 for the showdown that almost led to war with Britain.[9]

These events entangled the *colons* in their favorite fantasy, the Berber myth, a self-serving array of half-truths concocted to convince the *métropole* that the Berbers' hatred of their former overlords, the Arabs, and affinity for France made them allies of the colonial enterprise. For advocates of indirect rule led by the Resident General of Morocco Maréchal Louis Hubert Lyautey, the myth justified a policy of indirect rule through traditional elites and paternalistic regard for the Islamic culture. The idea of *la plus grande France* inspired Lyautey to domesticate, "housebreak," the colonial elites.[10] Saharan uprisings in 1916, protracted war in the Rif from 1921 to 1926, and Lyautey's forced retirement in 1925 deflated colonial idealism. Yet despite disillusionment, Lyautey remained influential. He presided over the 1931 Colonial Exposition and ordered that no "Bamboulas," belly dancers, or other vulgarities desecrate its pavilions. Decontextualized representations of the "timeless Orient," replicas of Angkor Wat, and a Sudanese village erected in the Bois de Vincennes and easily reached by Paris métro framed the exotic within the familiar. The sophisticated images of the exposition made the colonial world deceptively accessible.[11]

Lyautey ruled Morocco by meticulously researching local customs and dispensing favors to manipulate the rural tribes, tactics that supplemented but never supplanted military occupation. The other faction of the *parti colonial*, Algerian settlers and their allies in the metropole, advocated "white" rule.[12] Their definition of race dispensed with genetic phenotypes, such as the melanin content of skin, hair texture, and facial features, that Anglo-American racists employed to differentiate categories they themselves had invented. Instead, it emphasized an essentialist idea of culture drawn from right-wing ideologues such as Louis Marin, who posited "true France," the *pays réel* rooted in the "soil" of rural life in opposition to the *pays légal* of sordid Third Republic politics.[13] French essentialists in North Africa claimed that the innate cultural superiority of *pied-noir* settlers justified extending privileges to all Europeans, even the poorest, and excluding natives of all classes and status from citizenship. The polyglot *colons* from Spain, Italy, Portugal, Malta, and France thus elevated themselves to a class-transcendent superior status: white. They insisted on treating the natives as an undifferentiated mass even at the cost of hampering the army's ability to control the *bled*, the outback, by manipulation and favoritism.

Early versions of essentialism were anticolonial. Pierre Loti's novel *Roman d'un spahi* (1881), a forerunner of Benoit's work, was made into a film in 1914 and remade in 1936. It tells the story of a sturdy peasant youth, Jean Peyral, who is drafted into the army and sent to serve in West Africa. Far from his kin, fiancée, village, and folk, he takes an African mistress, who bears him a child. To Loti everything African is black in countenance and soul: Peyral's mistress Fatou-gaye is "roughly equivalent to his yellow-haired dog." In the end, his patrol is ambushed in the bush by a Sudanese potentate's army and massacred. He dies far from his ancestral home. Loti describes Peyral as "de pure race blanche" and associates whiteness with inherent moral superiority. He opposes colonialism on the grounds that it contaminates Europeans' rural, soil-rooted purity.[14]

Most Europeans viewed all positive achievements of Africa as the work of "Hamitic" outsiders from Europe or Asia. In Loti's opinion, Persian, Hindu, and Arab imitation of the West signaled decline, given that these groups had achieved high civilization before Europe. But "Kaffir and Hottentot" had no culture, so imitation meant progress.[15] When the French first encountered the Berbers of the central highland littoral south of Algiers, the Kabyles, they had remained aloof from Abd el-Kader's war of resistance (1830–47). Paris thought it had found its "Hamites" and pursued a policy of wooing them to enlist their aid in colonization. Ethnologists noted that many had red hair, freckles, or green eyes and concluded that they were descended from the Celts, arguing that they were cousins of "nos ancêtres les Gaulois." Catholics believed that the Arabs had converted them from Christianity by the sword and that they would return to the fold. The Second Empire shifted to a policy favoring the Arabs, but the settlers gave their support to the Third Republic in return for virtual home rule that cast down both indigenous groups and provoked the al-Mokrani revolt of 1871 in the Kabyle. Père Blanc missionaries there failed to win converts, further discouraging Kabylophiles. During the war of independence, 1954–62, Kabylia became a guerrilla stronghold.[16]

With the consolidation of settler supremacy, the *colon* ideology gradually merged the Hamitic hypothesis and Berber myth. Both Arabs and Berbers were included among the "people without history." Some *colons* and a few pan-Arabists declared that there were no Berbers at all, only successive waves of Arab migration. Berber language was corrupted Arabic, and "a Berber is simply a man who has never been to school." Others saw only Berbers Arabized to varying degrees, an antipodal conclusion sharing essentialist assumptions. Today, linguists categorize speakers of the hybrid superfamily of Afro-Asiatic languages as "non-European caucasoids" who left a common home in Anatolia in Neolithic times. Africanists argue that closely associated Egyptian, Chadic,

Ethiopian, Berber, and more distantly linked Semitic tongues point to the Horn of Africa as the origin of a Berber out-migration that began six thousand years ago. It is agreed that successive waves of invaders since the Punic expansion "de-Berberized" the Maghreb culturally, but not even the Arabs repeopled the region en masse. For two millennia its most intimate contacts were with the African Sudan.[17]

In Africanizing Islam, the *colons* were raising themselves up to pose as heirs to the Roman Empire. In the 1840s, General Bugeaud had relied on "civilized" infantry to defeat Abd el-Kader's "barbarian" cavalry, proving, as his handbook on colonial warfare studied by all French officers argued, the efficacy of his "Roman" campaign. Streets in Algerian cities were renamed after French or Roman generals. Tourist postcards ignored the Islamic past, and the colonial government of Bône (Annaba) restored St. Augustine's church at Hippo, leaving the Muslim quarters to decay. Settlers in Morocco caught the Roman fever, pressed a disastrous agricultural policy promoting wheat production, and used the rationale that Mauritania had been the "grainery of Rome." The Muslims, in reality among history's most proficient dry farmers, had let it go to rack and ruin. Roman likenings and Hamitic erasures of Islamic achievements reinforced French settlers' sense of superiority.[18]

Tuareg and Missionary: Charles de Foucauld

The French encounter with the Tuareg prompted a resurrection of the Berber myth. In black robes and veiled turbans, their gazelle-hide shields decorated with crosses, they evoked French fantasies of medieval Christian knights. *Tuareg* is an Arabic word meaning "abandoned by God," testifying to their protracted resistance to Arab encroachment. They call themselves Kel Tagelmoust, "people of the veil," and men, not women, cover their faces.[19] But the Muslim world system had integrated the Tuareg by the tenth century into a vast trade empire stretching from China's Silk Road to West Africa, including the entire Indian Ocean rim from the Moluccas to the Swahili Coast. It was based on the *dhow*, the Arabs' maneuverable sailing vessel, and camel caravan. The camel saddle invented by the Bedouin in the late Roman era reduced land transport costs to those of shipping, made wheeled vehicles obsolete, transformed urban environments, and altered relations between rulers and the ruled. The Muslim heartland became the crossroads where the highways of commerce and culture of all three Old World continents intersected. Tuareg Berber and Arab Bedouin caravans plied the Sahara and half a dozen desert routes, one of them by way of the Hoggar Moutains, linked the Mediterranean with West and Central Africa.

According to Ibn Khaldun, by 1400 the nomads making these annual crossings were using more than twelve thousand camels on each route.[20]

The transatlantic slave trade disrupted the African termini of the transsaharan commerce, and nineteenth-century European imperialism completed the process of diverting African trade toward the coasts. Impoverished Saharans turned to banditry and raiding. The decline of the Ottoman suzerainty of the Sahara and Barbary coast accelerated the slide toward anarchy, banditry, and piracy. The Tuareg used their inaccessible mountain strongholds and knowledge of the desert to dominate inhabitants of the Sahara's fringes, exacting tribute, raiding or trading depending on which offered the best return. Tuareg clans exacted *ghefara* from travelers for safe passage, but did not honor one another's guarantees. Rather than attacking caravans by frontal assault, raiders infiltrated them, learned their weaknesses and isolated victims, sometimes offering themselves as guides to those low on food and water and leading them into ambush, as Cegheir does in *L'Atlantide*. Since caravans were loosely knit groups, the *kofflé* would often abandon a victim in order to escape.[21]

Ignoring signs that the anarchy of the desert stemmed from secular decline, the French attempted to impose order and worsened the chaos. To conquer the Sahara, the army assigned General Henri Laperrine, who created a camel corps, the *méhari*, and fought for seven years to seize the central Saharan oases from the Tuareg. After several stinging defeats, the Ahaggar clans submitted in 1905, and the French helped the leader of the peace party, Moussa ag Amastane (in Arabic, Musa Wa'q al-Mustah), become king or *amenoukal,* promising to restore trade and prosperity. But the troops they garrisoned strained the oases' resources. They sunk artesian wells after freeing the African slaves and *harratin* serfs who had maintained the watercourses, *foggaras*, but the wells flooded the oases, bred malaria, and lowered the water table. The date palms, whose fruit was the staple food of the oasis dwellers, began to die. Requisitioning thousands of camels to supply their troops and mount patrols, they impoverished the inhabitants still further and thus fomented more banditry.[22]

As the Guns of August sounded in 1914, Egyptian nationalist Mohammed Ali Duse noted in an editorial, "It may be that the non-European races will profit by the European disaster. God's ways are mysterious."[23] Germany smuggled money and supplies to the Riffians, encouraging them to raid French Morocco. Libyan Arabs ambushed an Italian army of four thousand men in March 1915. Native auxiliaries turned on them, and few survived. Captured arms were distributed throughout the desert and fighting spread from the upper Nile to the Atlantic. Ajjer Tuareg, aided by Turkish officers, besieged French forts, and Musa's Ahaggar, fed up with broken French promises, joined the insurgents. French outposts were withdrawn to the oasis garrisons and Laperrine, France's expert in desert warfare, was reassigned from the Western Front to the Sahara. His troops stamped out resistance by 1918, although southern Tunisia did not submit until 1921 and the general died in a plane crash in the Sahara in 1920.[24]

Father Charles de Foucauld, the model for Benoit's Morhange, died in this insurrection. A former cavalry captain and Saint-Cyr classmate of Laperrine, he had secretly reconnoitered the interior of Morocco for the army in 1883–84. Foucauld became a Père Blanc missionary in 1901, and his hermitage at Tamanrasset doubled as a French listening post in the Ahaggar. He refused to repair to the French fort fifty miles to the south. The Saharan troops then fortified his dwelling with a moat and drawbridge and left him well armed. Despite the precautions, a Tuareg *harka* captured him on 1 December 1916, but was surprised by a French patrol. In the ensuing firefight the young Targui guarding him panicked and shot Foucauld dead. Undoubtedly the Tuareg intended to take him hostage, but the imperialist press spared the details and made him a martyr to the civilizing mission.[25]

The story of Foucauld's dissolute youth and call to God in middle age invited hagiography, and the French right canonized him. Benoit's invocation of his legend was only the first of many. Léon Poirier made a film of his life, *L'Appel du silence,* with full access to family papers and 100,000 francs raised through small donations from thousands of French Catholics. It drew the second highest box-office attendance of 1936, the year of the Popular Front victory, when one would have expected left-wing films to do well.[26] The dutifully reverential reviews described Foucauld as "one who understood the soul of the native and became the victim of fanatical murderers." Foucauld had believed that Islam was the enemy of France and that the Berbers were crypto-Catholics, because in their "associational" form of Islam, *m'rabouts,* or saints, interceded for sinners. Foucauld wanted France to focus its Tuareg policy on conversion, and he deplored using the Châamba Arabs to conquer the Tuareg, which inadvertently encouraged the spread of a reformed, "Protestant" Islam. The orthodox urged reading the Qur'an in the original Arabic, and the Châamba presence in Tuareg territory reinforced its use. To preserve the Tuareg language, Tamahaq, and insulate it from Arabic, Foucauld compiled a dictionary.[27]

Foucauld was wrong. Whatever their prior beliefs, the Berbers proved as impervious to Christianity as the Arabs. To Muslims, the Trinity and divinity of Jesus appeared inconsistent with true monotheism. By his own admission, Foucauld converted only three people in his fifteen years in the desert—an elderly woman slave, a dying infant, and a teenaged boy. No doubt his asceticism and abrasive, antisocial personality interfered with his proselytizing, but other Christian missionaries in the Muslim world had as little success. The Pères Blancs among the Kabyles had by 1900 abandoned the goal of conversion in favor of mutual understanding.[28]

Benoit's Eclectic: The Invented Sahara

Pierre Benoit had extracted from the *pied-noir* milieu in which he was raised a concoction of facts, legends, and stereotypes about the Tuareg and mixed them with Greco-Roman mythology. He became an amateur archaeologist, and in 1906, while doing his military service in a regiment of *zouave* colonial infantry, indulged his interest while on leave by inspecting Christian, Roman, and pre-Roman ruins in the Algerian desert. His allegiance to empire and preoccupation with Christian devotional ideals germinated while he was attending the University of Montpellier. He set out for Paris in 1910, fell in with right-wing politico-literary circles and became a protégé of Louis Barthou, Charles Maurras, and Léon Daudet. Although he never joined Action française, he was an ardent sympathizer and dedicated his first book to its leading light, Maurice Barrès. Mobilized and sent to the front in 1914 along with other young writers of this group, many of whom died, he suffered months in the trenches. He fell ill and was forced to spend the spring of 1915 in hospital. While recuperating, he wrote his first novel, *Koenigsmark*, which reflected the Manichaean anti-German views of his circle. Benoit finished *L'Atlantide*, his second novel, just after Armistice Day. It struck a resonant chord with a wide audience, which welcomed escapist fare as a relief from the nightmares of the war. The imagined Sahara and its denizens fascinated the public, and the work soon became a best-seller. Marcel Prévost, editor of the *Revue de Paris*, serialized the book and, with Barrés's support, it won the Académie Française prize for 1919.[29]

Antinéa, the Circe-like queen who captures, seduces, bewitches, and kills European explorers to prevent discovery of her dystopian Shangri-la, then turns them into electroplated statues, certainly is the most striking character of *L'Atlantide*. She so reminded critics of H. Rider Haggard's *She* that several accused Benoit of plagiarism. Benoit claimed as his inspiration the funerary statue and tomb of Cléopâtre Séléné, queen of Numidia and daughter of Marc Antony and Cleopatra VII, the last Ptolemy to rule Egypt, which he had come across on one of his youthful archaeological expeditions. The man-devouring white woman was a familiar male colonial fantasy, and became a fixture of his forty subsequent novels. All have names beginning with the letter A, probably symbolizing the alpha woman, Eve, source of man's mortality and immortality. Here, too, Benoit anticipated social and political stresses of the 1920s, when conservative commentators railed at the bobbed hair and short skirts of *la garçonne*, the French equivalent of the flapper, and accused them of undermining the family and ruining France.[30]

So Benoit's literary fantasies tapped the French desires for escapism and unnamed fears of a deracinated, unmoored gender system. By the sole criterion of screen adaptations, Benoit rates as the most popular writer between the wars. Five of his novels were turned into silent films, three remade in sound during the 1930s, two remade again in the 1950s. He added two more novels and a movie script to his film credits in the 1930s, and although the settings were more exotic than colonial, they expressed the same escapism and sexual anxiety that mark the rest of Benoit's work. Benoit outdistanced even Emile Zola and Pierro Loti. Four of Zola's works, including *L'Argent,* with a brief colonial episode, were filmed. Only three of Loti's were adapted to film, and only *Roman d'un spahi* qualifies as colonial fiction. Another popular novelist, Jean Vignaud, wrote three books that became films in the 1920s, *Maison du Maltais, Sarati le Terrible,* and *Vénus;* the first two were remade in the 1930s.[31]

Benoit had done some cursory research beginning in January 1918, reading Plato's *Critias,* Orientalist scholarship on the Tuareg, and histories of Christian North Africa. He cast aside the Tuareg's own legends of sirenlike women who lured travelers into the mountains, magical peaks that moved and married. Elaborating a synthetic mythology that imagined Plato's Atlantis swallowed by sand, not sea, drew on the Hamitic hypothesis, and depicted the desert-dwelling Tuareg as descendants of the mythical kingdom's inhabitants, he stripped the Tuareg of their historical and cultural identity. They became a mute human backdrop lending exotic reality to his fantastic story line and striking another resonant chord in French popular culture, the Berber myth.[32]

Films Made and Remade

Feyder's 1921 silent film rearoused this fascination. Film reviews raised it to new heights, reinforcing the image of the *indigènes* as "a race who evoke the Tuareg, horsemen of unknown origin, of noble blood, both European and Asiatic." One critic claimed that "the story has become . . . a new myth." Another expressed the hope that the film would create French pioneers, evoke a desire to leave "our narrow horizon, thirst for fresh air, escape toward the *bled.*"[33] Mistinguett, the famous *chanteuse réaliste*, popularized the story in a song.[34] Feyder's pathbreaking work, the first feature film shot on location in North Africa, started a wave of picturemaking there. It cost a million dollars to produce but was such a box office sensation it quickly grossed immense profits.

Colonial themes became so popular that many silent films were remade in the 1930s.[35]

Pabst's film was not strictly a remake. It strayed from the novel, dehistoricized the story, and removed much specifically French and North African context. Pabst created psychological nuances that ascribed the characters' motivations to internal, emotional drives rather than external commmitments to sexual or colonial conquest. While distancing his film from overt French colonial propaganda, Pabst's Freudian interpretation of Greek mythology associated it more closely with broader traits of European racial identity. The fading of Lyautey's presence, the growing influence of *colon* racial rule, and the illusion of intimacy with colonial peoples encouraged by tourism, postcards, expositions, and ethnography also played a role in his directorial decisions.

Pabst eliminated many of the 1921 film's allusions to the Tuareg, Islam, and heroic French events. He offered no motive for Cegheir ben Cheik, the Tuareg guide, helping Saint-Avit escape. Feyder's Targui says, "The Prophet allows once in one's life duty to give way to pity, and I remember that you have saved my life." Feyder's Tanit-Zerga dies with a mirage of her birthplace before her eyes: "Gaô is there . . . I see it! The town of the 100 domes, of the blue gum trees." In Feyder's grand Egyptian-style palace, a Targui librarian tells the officers Antinéa is a descendant of Queen Clito of Atlantis and the Queen of Sheba. Electroplated, gilded mummies of her lovers and victims, all "famously missing" African explorers, line the corridors. Pabst's queen, Brigitte Helm, is given a more accessible past and more psychological power. She seduces rather than drugs the men. Jean Angelo played Morhange in both films, but in the 1932 version he resists Antinéa more out of maturity and a firmer grasp on his European male identity than out of faith and priestly virtue. Pabst's oedipal theme reflects the growing influence exerted by Freud. In 1932, Saint-Avit's cavelike prison, the twisted streets of the Tuareg village, the dark, foreboding palace corridors, the replacement of Tuareg characters with surreal Europeans like the Norwegian, the Russian noble hetman, and Helm's portrayal of Antinéa contribute to Pabst's Freudian vision.[36]

Feyder's three-hour epic faithfully re-created Benoit's novel. Unlike Pabst, he had been a newcomer when he began his project, and his producers at Aubert had blanched at his estimates of what the extravaganza would cost. They kept strict control of his budget and warned him against tampering with Benoit's plot, which was still fresh in the minds of the French public. All the actors had arrived in Algiers with the novel in hand. His Antinéa, Stacia Napierkowska, had given him headaches. A lithe dancer when Feyder hired her, she had arrived on location thirty pounds overweight and had to be filmed under wraps, so to speak. Her sensuality contrasts with Helm's cold remoteness, one way in which Pabst's work lacks "Frenchness." Pabst made his seventy-five-minute film simultaneously in French, English, and German, a common practice during the silent-sound transition period. American subsidiaries had invaded Europe and set the tone of the movies before sound allowed a distinctive national cinema to reemerge. Feyder had been more circumspect than Pabst about one French officer murdering another, soothing ruffled patriotism by blaming the crime on *le kif* or *le cafard*, not Freudian subconscious desires.[37]

In gauging how the two films reflected changing popular tastes and attitudes, where they were made is no less important than their technical and stylistic differences. Although the critics gave high marks to both films for verisimilitude, neither was shot in the central Sahara, where the events were supposed to have taken place. Working in the deep desert was technically feasible but financially prohibitive, so both directors took their crews to Touggourt, an oasis town on the northern rim of the true desert at the end of the Constantine-Biskra rail line. The jumping-off point for the transsaharan "rallye" or "raid" M. Citroën sponsored in 1923 to advertise his cars, the town was included thereafter on the auto touring clubs' regular Algerian circuit. A nearby fort, the French complement of which had been overrun and massacred during the al-Mokrani revolt of 1871, proved ideal for the scenes of Saint Avit's return to civilization.[38]

The film crews thus joined a stream of wealthy tourists who had been swarming over Algeria for several decades in search of the exotic. André Gide, who visited Biskra in 1895 and 1896, was invited into a private home where dozens of African, Arab, and Jewish women danced to exhaustion to exorcize demons. In contrast, the notorious Ouled Nayle, "holy prostitutes" who made their home in Biskra, put on a show for the tourists. Invariably, Gide was the only French witness to many intimacies, and he suspected that "the paid guides show the [tourists] a trashy Africa in order to protect the Arabs, who like calm and secrecy, from intruders. For I have never met a single one of them in the neighborhood of anything interesting. . . . the hotels are full of travelers, but they fall into the trap set by the quack guides and pay dearly for the falsified ceremonies tricked up for them." Thirty years later, a disgusted Wyndham Lewis cursed the "Baedekered blight" descending on the region.[39]

In light of all this tourism, the film principals' comments about the "primitive" natives who played the roles of extras sound laughably ignorant. George Root, Pabst's publicity flack, described them as having the "admirable instincts of primitives who felt no self-consciousness under the eye of the camera." Jean Angelo assumed in 1921 that the locals had never seen a camera. The *qaid* advised that they be shown a movie to give them an idea of what would be expected. Feyder had one flown in specially from Paris, a sad melodrama that provoked laughter all the way through. The film bewildered them, as one might expect as they could not read French, but they tried to show appreciation for the efforts to entertain them. Napierkowska, who grew up in Scutarie near Istanbul and had a more open mind, said passing caravans harassed the camera crews and tried to destroy equipment because the *Roumi,* or infidels, "had no right to steal with images a part of the sky." Their disapproval suggests they understood the function of cameras very well. Abd el Kader ben Ali, who played Cegheir and was an Algiers café owner, shrewdly squeezed Feyder for bonuses by threatening to quit at strategic moments.[40] Even in Morocco, where once Lyautey's native affairs officers might have roundly criticized phony stereotypes of the Berbers, a leftist director, Jean Benoît-Lévy, raised the notion of "natural actors" to the level of a theory after filming *Itto* in 1934. "Primitive peoples" were "like children" in front of the camera, he claimed. Yet the Berber clan he hired as extras had played in six earlier feature films, ten years' acting experience, and they dubbed his crew "les Ait Cinéma," the movie clan.[41]

Le Cafard

Ignorance had a darker side. Europeans routinely turned a blind eye to brutal massacres and outrages in the colonies, and colonial officers conveniently attributed adventurism, defiance of orders, brutality toward enlisted men, and depredations of the civilian population to attacks of *le cafard,* literally "homesickness," but better translated by Kurtz's last words in *Heart of Darkness:* "The horror, the horror." French officers like Laperrine and parliamentary deputies treated *le cafard* as a real illness, caused by too much sun, which "boils the blood and calcinates the brain." The only antidote was *le pinard,* army ration wine.[42]

Two real-life Kurtzes, Captain Paul Voulet and Lieutenant Charles Chanoine, went on a rampage in the western Sudan in 1898. The two unleashed irregular mercenaries, *goumiers,* who plundered and impressed local people, then killed Colonel Jean Klobb, whom Paris had dispatched to investigate their marauding. Voulet declared himself king of an empire around Lake Chad, but when he began shooting his men to restore discipline, they mutinied and killed both officers. The army and the press attributed their acts to a sub-Saharan version of *le cafard, la soudanité. Le Temps* reported Klobb's death on 21 September 1899 and concluded, "The irreparable act was committed in one of those moments of mental aberration which the strenuous life of torrid Africa seems to encourage." Voulet's second in command was the son of General Charles

Chanoine, minister of war in the Brisson cabinet, whose sudden resignation had brought down the ministry in October 1898 in the midst of the Fashoda incident. Klobb's death became entangled in the Dreyfus affair, with the Right claiming the Radicals and Waldeck-Rousseau cabinet were trying to use the murder to impose more civilian control of the army. Trying to heal the wounds of the affair, the government encouraged the press to sweep under the rug the murder, mutiny, and deaths of thousands of Africans.[43]

The colonial system had set the tragedy in motion. Paris abdicated decisions to junior officers on the spot, whose heads were filled with amoral, white supremacist notions and whose one advantage over the Africans was the destructiveness of their firepower. Four thousand troops occupied the Sudan, tsetse fly country where no pack animals could survive. They needed bearers to move everything; transport depended on forced, *corvée* labor, which disrupted economic life in the region. The *tirailleurs* recruited or impressed into the army expected booty as part of their pay, and plundered the rural areas. As in the Sahara, the French invasion brought chaos and economic disruption and provoked resistance, not the other way around. Governments that tried to bring the officers to heel were accused of undermining the army.[44]

Magical notions of the evil effects of place, a hallmark of fairy tales, pervaded literature and film about the colonies. As Chinua Achebe points out, *Heart of Darkness* conveys the message that "Kurtz . . . foolishly exposed himself to the wild irresistible allure of the jungle."[45] André Gide, no friend of French colonialism, concludes *The Immoralist* with Michel transfixed by the peculiar, translucent North African light and the boy whom he had taken as lover, drawing into his paralysis the four friends who have come to rescue him. Antinéa draws her occult powers from her mysterious kingdom. *Le Grand Jeu*, Feyder's 1934 film about the Foreign Legion, depicts *le cafard* in Nicolas's drunken outbursts about forgetting the past, Pierre's furniture smashing, and street scenes of Legionnaires, Spahis, and *goums* drinking, fighting, and carrying off screaming women. In *La Bandera*, Julien Duvivier's 1935 film about the Spanish Legion, Gilieth is drawn inexorably to the Maghreb after stabbing a man in Paris. The inversion of place suggests that a murderer like him belongs there. His lover, Aicha, tells him she has seen French soldiers go into fits of rage and smash everything in a room. He assures her that he is calm. Another scene shows a soldier having his face elaborately tattooed, like a Maori warrior. "Ah, I want to see the civilian dunghill [*fumier*] again," he explains, "this will take away the longing to go home if *le cafard* strikes me." "What a world!" muses Gilieth's friend Mulot.[46] *Indigènes*, however, specialized in random, senseless violence. *La Bandera* and *Le Grand Jeu* both use the device of an invisible sniper picking off one legionnaire among many building a road, a symbol of civilization proper. Neither film considers how roads threatened the way of life of caravaneers, or that the snipers were resisting an army of occupation.

Popular culture, particularly film, retreated from the grand colonial myth of *mission civilisatrice* and took refuge in the myth of individual redemption. Men who committed crimes at home and fled to North Africa regained their place in white European society by sacrificing themselves on the altar of the *mission civilisatrice*. In the Popular Front era, 1934–39, these sagas of individual heroisms gave way to intimate love stories in exotic settings. The growing accessibility and familiarity of North Africa may explain the scaling down of cinematic themes. Millions visited the 1931 Exposition and several hundred thousand a year became tourists in the Maghreb. Algerian migrant workers crossed and recrossed the Mediterranean. Picture postcards were photographed in North Africa, printed in France, sold in North Africa to tourists, and mailed back to France to decorate French mantels. These comings and goings created illusions of familiarity, with French responsibility for conditions in the colonies rationalized by assumptions of African backwardness and *le cafard.*[47]

Despite repeatedly illustrating European benevolence and power, film conveyed a profound pessimism about the colonial venture, a sense that the European presence in Africa was tentative and fleeting. In the Foreign Legion films made in France, the ride to the rescue, a standard device of Hollywood westerns, arrives too late.[48] In seven of the twelve classic colonial films, the death of the hero and the European woman's return home to the *métropole* resolve the plot. In the films discussed above, including the biography of Foucauld, the man embarks on a hero's quest and invites martyrdom. Drawn inexorably south, he breaks all ties to home, as represented by its women, to accomplish his journeys.[49]

Cinéma colonial reflected French fascination with the non-European, colonial Other and fears of the polluting, corrosive effects of contact on European racial, national, and personal identity. Chinua Achebe remarks that "the West seems to suffer deep anxieties about the precariousness of its civilization and to have a need for constant reassurance by comparison with Africa."[50] This insight applies to French relations with North Africa. Conrad located the heart of darkness in the European soul drawn into black Africa. So, too, the imaginary Maghreb's Orientalist exoticism drew French painters, writers, filmmakers, and tourists to a heart of light: the peculiar, shimmering, ultraclear light of the Mediterranean littoral; the unrelenting, merciless glare of the Sahara sun.

Notes

This essay was written with the financial support of the American Council of Learned Societies. I would like to express my appreciation to the ACLS; to Professors Steven Ungar and Dudley Andrew of the University of Iowa, who led the NEH Summer Seminar that inspired this research; and to fellow seminar participants and Professors Herman Lebovics and David Prochaska, who read earlier drafts of this essay. The usual disclaimers apply.

1. See William H. McNeill, "Mythistory, or Truth, Myth, History and Historians," *American Historical Review* 91 (February 1985); Herman Lebovics, *True France: The Wars over French Cultural Identity, 1900–1945* (Ithaca, N.Y.: Cornell University Press, 1992); Fernand Braudel, *The Identity of France*, vol. 1, *History and Environment*, trans. Siân Reynolds (New York: Harper Perennial, 1990); Edward Said, *Orientalism* (New York: Pantheon, 1978); Rana Kabbani, *Europe's Myths of Orient* (Bloomington: Indiana University Press, 1986).

2. A note on my sources for *L'Atlantide*: Boulanger, Megherbi, Abel, and Loutfi all focus on the 1921 film but are often unclear about whether they are referring to the silent film, the talkie, or the novel. Pierre Boulanger, *Le Cinéma colonial* (Paris: Seghers, 1975); Abdelghani Megherbi, *Les Algériens au miroir du cinéma colonial* (Algiers: SNED, 1982); Richard Abel, *French Cinema: The First Wave 1915–1929* (Princeton, N.J.: Princeton University Press, 1984); Martine A. Loutfi, "North Africa in the French Movies," in *Proceedings of the Fourth Meeting of the French Colonial History Society*, ed. Alf Heggoy and James J. Cooke (Washington, D.C.: University Press of America, 1979). Pabst's film compounds the confusion because he actually made three different films, in French, German, and English. *Pour Vous*, the French film magazine, discusses Pabst's French version. I watched a videotape of the English-language version, *The Mistress of Atlantis*, held by the UCLA Film Archive. The sound quality is poor. Sierek saw *Die Herrin von Atlantis*, and there are some discrepancies between English and German versions. Karl Sierek, "The Primal Scene of the Cinema: Four Fragments from *The Mistress of Atlantis* (1932)," in *The Films of G. W. Pabst: An Extraterritorial Cinema*, ed. Eric Rentschler (New Brunswick, N.J.: Rutgers University Press, 1990). To maintain narrative flow, I will refer to the specific version of the film only when it affects my argument.

3. Louis Delluc, "Notes," *Cinéa*, 10 June 1921, 9, and "Quelques films français" *Cinéa*, 9 September 1921, 5, cited in Abel, *French Cinema*, 154–56; Boulanger, *Le Cinéma colonial*, 42; Megherbi, *Les Algériens*, 85; George Root, "Sur la piste du Hoggar" (interview with Pabst), *Pour Vous*, 12 May 1932, 3.

4. John H. Galey, "Bridegrooms of Death," *Journal of Contemporary History* (April 1969).

5. Sierek, "The Primal Scene," 126, 128, 133.

6. Ibid., 128–29, 134, 139, 144–45; Pierre Sorlin, Michèle Lagny, and Marie-Claire Ropars, eds., *Générique des Années Trente* (Paris: PUV, 1986), 169, 172–73; Loutfi, "North Africa," 136.

7. This quote is from René Lehmann's summary of *L'Atlantide*, "Atlantide," *Pour Vous*, 9 June 1932, 9. *Pour Vous*, 4 July 1932, 12, described her character as the daughter of the prince, but Brigitte Helm, the actress who plays the part, neither looks nor

acts as if she were nineteen. On the "Aryan model," see Martin Bernal, *Black Athena: The Afroasiatic Roots of Classical Civilization* vol. 1, *The Fabrication of Ancient Greece, 1785–1985* (New Brunswick, N.J.: Rutgers University Press, 1987); see also Molly M. Levine and Robert Pounder's review of Bernal's book in *American Historical Review* (April 1992): 440–64.

8. Charles-Robert Jouvé, *Leçons d'histoire et de civilisation: Cours élémentaire des écoles indigènes et cours préparatoire des écoles françaises de l'Algérie et de l'Orient,* 12th ed. (Paris: Belin frères, 1894), 8–10; Emanuel Sivan, "Colonialism and Popular Culture in Algeria," *Journal of Contemporary History* (January 1979): 26. See also research on report cards in Fanny Colonna, *Instituteurs Algériens 1883–1939* (Paris: PFNSP, 1975), 163–65, 172; Albert Memmi, *The Colonizer and the Colonized* (New York: Orion, 1965), 104–5; John Ruedy, *Modern Algeria: The Origins and Development of a Nation* (Bloomington: Indiana University Press, 1992), 119–21.

9. Douglas Porch, *The Conquest of the Sahara* (New York: Knopf, 1984), 115–24, 136–46, 156–57, 211.

10. The term "housebreak" was used by Maréchal Lyautey to describe his strategy for controlling Moroccan clients. He was specifically referring to his attempts to bring to heel Mohammed Abd el-Krim, leader of the Rif Republic in 1924. Lyautey to Poincaré 19 fevrier 1924, in Pierre Lyautey, ed., *Lyautey l'Africain: Textes et lettres,* 4 vols. (Paris: Plon, 1953–57), 4:245–50; David H. Slavin, "Anticolonialism and the French Left: Opposition to the Rif War, 1924–1926," Ph.D. dissertation, University of Virginia, 1982.

11. See Lebovics, *True France,* 52–97, esp. 52, 81 (chap. 2, "The Seductions of the Picturesque"), for insightful analysis of the Colonial Exposition. My thanks to Professor Lebovics, State University of New York, Stony Brook, for allowing me to read the prepublication manuscript of his book. See also Michèle Salinas, *Voyages et voyageurs en Algérie 1830/1930* (Toulouse: Privat, 1989), 69–71, 77, 79, 99; and the French government's *Annuaire statistique,* 1930, 313; 1935, 298; 1936, 303. "Mouvement des voyageurs entre l'Algérie et l'extérieur" averaged about 180,000 per year. On postcards, see David Prochaska, "The Archive of *Algérie Imaginaire,*" *History and Anthropology* 4 (1990): 373–420, esp. 414–16; Malek Alloula, *The Colonial Harem* (Minneapolis: University of Minnesota Press, 1986), 3–7.

12. Edmund Burke III, "The Image of the Moroccan State in French Ethnological Literature: New Light on the Origins of Lyautey's Berber Policy," in *Arabs and Berbers: Ethnicity and Nation-Building in North Africa,* ed. Charles Micaud and Ernest Gellner (Lexington, Mass.: Heath, 1972); Charles-Robert Ageron, *Les Algériens Musulmans et la France, 1871–1919,* 2 vols. (Paris: PUF, 1968), 1: 268–83, 2: 873–90.

13. Lebovics, *True France,* 135–49.

14. Pierre Loti, *Le Roman d'un Spahi* (Paris: Calmann-Lévy, 1979 [1881]), 115, 117, 179, 253, cited in Alec Hargreaves, *The Colonial Experience in French Fiction* (London: Macmillan, 1981), 41–45; Martine Astier Loutfi *Littérature et colonialisme* (Paris: Mouton, 1971), 24–26; Léon Fanoudh-Siefer, *Le Mythe du nègre et de l'Afrique noire dans la littérature française* (Paris: Klincksieck, 1968), 13, 107, 187; Ada Martinkus-Zemp, *Le Blanc et le Noir, essai d'une description de la vision du Noir par le Blanc dans la littérature française de l'entre-deux-guerres* (Paris: A.-G. Nizet, 1975).

15. Pierre Loti, *Vers Ispahan* (Paris: Calmann-Lévy, 1904), 294; cited in Hargreaves,

The Colonial Experience, 37; Basil Davidson, *Lost Cities of Africa,* rev. ed. (Boston: Little, Brown, 1970), 9–14. See J. H. Greenberg, *Studies in African Linguistic Classification* (New Haven, Conn.: Yale University Press, 1955), the first counter-Hamitic study of African language origins.

16. Burke, "The Image of the Moroccan State"; Ageron, *Les Algériens Musulmans,* 1: 268–83, 2:873.

17. Ruedy, *Modern Algeria,* 9; Robin Bidwell, *Morocco under Colonial Rule* (London: Frank Cass, 1973), 48–49, quoting General Brémond, Professor Bernard, Mostafa Bechir, Mehdi Ben Barka; Philip E. Ross, "Hard Words: Trends in Linguistics," *Scientific American,* April 1991, 136–47; Luigi Luca Cavalli-Sforza, "Genes, Peoples and Languages," *Scientific American,* November 1991, 107–8; Basil Davidson, "The Ancient World and Africa: Whose Roots?" *Race and Class* 29 (Fall 1987): 1–15, esp. 8–11; see also works by Cheik Anta Diop and Molefi K. Asante's *Kemet* (Philadelphia: Temple University Press, 1989).

18. V. G. Kiernan, *From Conquest to Collapse: European Empires 1815–1960* (New York: Pantheon, 1982), 71–76; B. H. Liddell-Hart, "Armies," in *New Cambridge Modern History,* vol. 10 (Cambridge: Cambridge University Press, 1960), 320–21; Dennis Mack Smith, *Mussolini's Roman Empire* (New York: Penguin, 1976), viii, 32, 42–43, 84; David Prochaska, *Making Algeria French: Colonialism in Bône 1870–1920* (New York: Cambridge University Press, 1990); Will Swearingen, *Moroccan Mirages: Agrarian Dreams and Deceptions 1912–1986* (Princeton, N.J.: Princeton University Press, 1987), 28–35.

19. My thanks to Thomas Penchoen, professor of Middle East languages and literature, for his elucidations. See Alal al-Fasi, *The Independence Movements of Arab North Africa* (Washington, D.C.: American Council of Learned Societies, 1954; rpt. New York: Octagon, 1970), 118–19; Porch, *The Conquest of the Sahara,* 65.

20. Cited in Davidson, *Lost Cities of Africa,* 97. See also Richard W. Bulliet, *The Camel and the Wheel* (Cambridge: Harvard University Press, 1975), esp. chap. 8, "A Society without Wheels"; William H. McNeill, "The Eccentricity of Wheels: Eurasian Transportation in Historical Perspective," *American Historical Review* (December 1987): 111–26.

21. Eric Wolf, *Europe and the People without History* (Berkeley: University of California Press, 1982), chapter on slave trade; Alan K. Smith, *Creating a World Economy: Merchant Capital, Colonialism and World Trade 1400–1825* (Boulder, Colo.: Westview, 1991), 142–50; J. E. Inikori, ed., *Forced Migration: The Impact of the Export Slave Trade on African Societies* (New York: Africana, 1982); Philip Curtin, *Economic Change in Pre-Colonial Africa* (Madison: University of Wisconsin Press, 1975); Roger Anstey, *The Atlantic Slave Trade and the British Abolition* (London: Macmillan, 1975); Frederick Cooper, "The Problem of Slavery in African Societies," *Journal of African History* 20, no. 1 (1979); Porch, *The Conquest of the Sahara,* 67–75. Eric Hobsbawm's *Primitive Rebels* (New York: Norton, 1965), provides a comparative, peri-Mediterranean perspective.

22. Porch, *The Conquest of the Sahara,* 236–39, 259, 262, 271–72.

23. In Duse's *African Times and Orient Review,* quoted in Immanuel Geiss, *The Pan African Movement* (New York: Africana, 1974), 229–30, 222–28, on Duse, colleague to W. E. B. Du Bois and mentor to Marcus Garvey; Immanuel Geiss, *War and Empire in the 20th Century* (Aberdeen, U.K.: Aberdeen University Press, 1983), 43.

24. Edmund Burke III, "Moroccan Resistance, Pan-Islam and German War Strategy, 1914 to 1918," *Francia* 3 (1975): 434–64; Charles de Foucauld, *Reconnaissance au Maroc* (Paris: Challamel, 1887); Porch, *The Conquest of the Sahara,* 299–301; al-Fasi, *The Independence Movements,* 50–51, 118. Porch understates the extent of this rebellion, whereas al-Fasi, a founder of the Moroccan nationalist movement and its historian, may overstate it.

25. Porch, *The Conquest of the Sahara,* 278–86; al-Fasi, *The Independence Movements,* 118.

26. Ginette Vincendeau, "French Cinema of the 1930s: Social Text and Context of a Popular Entertainment Medium," Ph.D. dissertation, University of East Anglia, 1985, 173. The other three top films were *César* (Marcel Pagnol), an oedipal drama set in a Marseilles café; *Le Roi* (Pierre Colombier), about the love affairs of a Ruritanian king; and *Mayerling* (Anatole Litvak). Perhaps it should not be surprising that escapism and Catholic edification filled the screen. In 1938 the most popular film in France was Disney's *Snow White and the Seven Dwarfs!*

27. Lucien Wahl, "L'Appel du silence," *Pour Vous,* 30 April 1936, 6; J.-M. Huard, "Léon Poirier nous parle de Charles de Foucauld," *Pour Vous,* 7 May 1936, 6; review of *L'Appel du Silence* in *l'Ami du Peuple,* 11 October 1936. *L'Appel du silence* has become a cult classic for contemporary France's racist right; see Raymond Chirat, ed., *Catalogue des films français, 1929–1939* (1975). See also Ernest Gellner, *Muslim Society* (Cambridge: Cambridge University Press, 1981), 155–65; Fanny Colonna, "Cultural Resistance and Religious Legitimacy in Colonial Algeria," *Economy and Society* 3 (1974): 233–52; Porch, *The Conquest of the Sahara,* 284–86.

28. Porch, *The Conquest of the Sahara,* 287–89. The Algerians trusted the Pères Blancs enough to allow them to stay after independence in 1962, and Pères Blancs scholarship remains of the highest quality, aimed at understanding rather than social control, but confined to ancient history and other subjects with few political implications. See, for example, François Dessommes, P.B., *Notes sur l'histoire des Kabyles* (Fort National, Algeria: SEND, 1964).

29. Louis-Marie Clénet, "Benoit et le mouvement intellectuel français de l'entre-deux-guerres," in *Pierre Benoit, témoin de son temps,* ed. Edmond Jouve, Gilbert Pilleul, and Charles Saint-Prot (Paris: Albin Michel, 1991), 178, 185.

30. Louis Chaigne, *Vies et oeuvres d'écrivains* (Paris: Bossuet, 1933), 237–40, 249–52; Edmond Jouve et al., *Pierre Benoit,* 19, 54–57, 64, 127, 135–37; Sanford Elwitt, *The Third Republic Defended* (Baton Rouge, La.: LSU Press, 1986), 293; Benjamin Martin, *Hypocrisy of Justice in the Belle Epoque* (Baton Rouge, La.: LSU Press, 1984); Mary Louise Roberts, "Samson and Delilah Revisited: The Politics of Women's Fashion in 1920s France," *American Historical Review* (June 1993): 657–84, esp. 668–74, on conservative, Catholic, and natalist criticism of the *femme moderne;* see also Victor Margueritte, *La Garçonne* (Paris: Flammarion, 1922).

31. Raymond Chirat, ed., *Catalogue des films français, 1919–1929* (1984) and *1929–1939* (1975). See Pierre Sorlin, "The Fanciful Empire," *French Cultural Studies* (June 1991): 143–44, for a brief description of *L'Argent.* This article should be viewed with caution, as it contains many factual errors, particularly about the film *Itto.*

Films from works by Emile Zola are as follows (directors' names in parentheses): *Le*

Rêve (1930, Jacques de Baroncelli), *L'Assommoir* (1933, Gaston Roudès), *L'Argent* (1936, Pierre Billon), and *La Bête humaine* (1938, Jean Renoir).

Films from works by Pierre Loti include three versions of *Pêcheur d'Islande* (1915, Henri Pouctal; 1924, J. de Baroncelli; 1933, Pierre Guerlais), two versions of *Le Roman d'un spahi* (1914, H. Pouctal; 1936, Michel Bernheim), and two versions of *Ramuntcho* (1918 and 1937, J. de Baroncelli). *Le Roman d'un spahi* is set in the Basque region and West Africa, *Pêcheur* on the Côtes-du-Nord, and *Ramuntcho* on the Basque coast.

Films from works by Pierre Benoit include two versions of *L'Atlantide* (1921, J. Feyder; 1932, G.W. Pabst), three versions of *Koenigsmark* (1923, Léonce Perret; 1935 and 1952, Maurice Tourneur), *La Ronde de nuit* (1925, Marcel Silver; screenplay by Benoit), *Le Puits de Jacob* (1925, Edward José), three versions of *Châtelaine du Liban* (1926, Marco de Gastyne; 1933, Jean Epstein; 1956, Richard Pottier), *Princesse Mandane* (Benoit's *l'Oublié*) (1928, Germaine Dulac), *Les Nuits moscovites* (1934, Alexandre Grandowsky), *Boissière* (1937, Fernand Rivers; screenplay by Benoit), and *Angelica* (1939, Jean Choux).

32. Pierre Benoit, *L'Atlantide* (Paris: Albin Michel, 1921); Louis Chaigne, *Vies et oeuvres d'écrivains,* 240.

33. René Lehmann, "L'Atlantide," *Pour Vous,* 9 June 1932, 9; *Cinémagazine,* 17 June 1921.

34. The song begins, "In the mountains of the Hoggar / A queen with an evil gaze / Reigns, it is said / Antinéa is her name"; quoted in Boulanger, *Le Cinéma Colonial,* 132; Megherbi *Les Algériens,* 85–87.

35. "Extraits du carnet d'un filmeur par Jacques Feyder," Dossier L'Atlantide (1921), Cinémathèque française, 1st folder, no. 664 A-B-C, Bibliothèque de l'IDHEC, Palais de Chaillot, Av. Albert de Mun, Paris; Jacques Feyder, letter to the editor, *Pour Vous,* 20 June 1929, on the 1929 rerelease of *L'Atlantide*; see also Boulanger *Le Cinéma colonial,* 38, 131–41, on Feyder's 1921 version. Besides *L'Atlantide*, eight major films were remade: *Les Cinq Gentlemen Maudits* (1919, Luitz-Morat; 1931, J. Duvivier), *Sarati le Terrible* (1922, L. Mercanton; 1937, A. Hugon), *Les Hommes nouveaux* (1922, L. Donatien; 1936, M. l'Herbier), *Le Prince Jean* (1927, R. Hervil; 1934, J. de Marguenat), *La Maison du Maltais* (1927, H. Fescourt; 1938, P. Chenal), *Feu!* (1927, J. de Baroncelli; 1937, J. de Baroncelli), *L'Occident* (1928 and 1938, H. Fescourt), *Le Roman d'un Spahi* (1914, H. Pouctal; 1936, M. Bernheim). Frédérique Moreau, "Le Cinéma colonial: Un sous-genre, le film légionnaire dans les années 30," *L'Avant-scène,* 1–15 April 1982, 27.

36. *Ciné-Miroir,* 1 May 1922. This issue, the premier issue of this magazine, sixteen tabloid pages, is devoted entirely to text and photos from Feyder's film. *L'Atlantide* script and eight-page program, Cinémathèque français, no. 664 A–B–C, Bibliothèque de l'IDHEC, Palais de Chaillot, Av. Albert de Mun, Paris.

37. Jean Angelo, "Au Hasard de mes souvenirs," *Ciné-Miroir,* 16 November 1928, 742; Stacia Napierkowska, "Mes Souvenirs," *Ciné-Miroir,* 15 April 1923, 125; Jacques Feyder and Françoise Rosay, *Le Cinéma, notre métier* (Geneva: Skira, 1944), 14, 21–22, 50; Yves Dartois and Marcel Carné, "Les Deux Atlantide," *Pour Vous,* 23 June 1932; George Root, "Sur la piste du Hoggar avec Pabst," *Pour Vous,* 12 May 1932, 3; Lehmann, "Atlantide"; Megherbi, *Les Algériens,* 85–87; Victoria deGrazia, "Mass Culture and Sovereignty: The American Challenge to European Cinemas, 1920–1960," *Journal of Modern History* 61 (March 1989): 53–87, esp. 57–58, 61–65, 70; deGrazia

cites Douglas Gomery's "Europe Converts to Sound" and Dudley Andrew's "Sound in France: The Origins of a Native School," both in *Yale French Studies* 60 (Winter 1980): 80–93, 94–114.

38. Salinas, *Voyages et voyageurs,* 54–56, 70, 82.

39. André Gide, *The Journals,* 4 vols. (New York: Random House, 1955), 1:36; Gareth Stanton, in "The Oriental City: A North African Itinerary," *Third Text* (Spring/ Summer 1988): 25, quotes Wyndham Lewis's *Journey into Barbary* (London: 1987).

40. Napierkowska, "Mes Souvenirs," 157; Angelo, "Au Hasard de mes souvenirs," 742; Root, "Sur la piste du Hoggar avec Pabst," 3.

41. Jean Benoît-Lévy, *The Art of the Motion Picture* (New York: Coward-McCann, 1946; rpt. New York: Arno, 1970), 167, 214–16; Boulanger, *Le Cinéma colonial,* 117–18. On similar "Baudrillard moments," see Timothy Mitchell, *Colonizing Egypt* (New York: Cambridge University Press, 1988), 4–5.

42. Kiernan, *From Conquest to Collapse,* 127, 130.

43. Porch, *The Conquest of the Sahara,* 181–97, esp. 195–97.

44. Ibid., 183; A. S. Kanya–Forstner, *The Conquest of the Western Sudan* (Cambridge: Cambridge University Press, 1969), 263–74; Douglas Porch, *The French Foreign Legion* (New York: HarperCollins, 1991), 249–50; Kiernan, *From Conquest to Collapse,* 127, 130.

45. Chinua Achebe, "An Image of Africa: Racism in Conrad's *Heart of Darkness," Heart of Darkness, Joseph Conrad,* ed. Robert Kimbrough (New York: Norton, 1988), 261.

46. *L'Avant-scène,* 15 April 1982, 56, 57.

47. See Lebovics, *True France,* 51–97 (chap. 2, "The Seductions of the Picturesque"), on the Colonial Exposition. See also Salinas, *Voyages et voyageurs,* 69–71, 77, 79, 99; and *Annuaire Statistique,* 1930, 313; 1935, 298; 1936, 303. On postcards, see Prochaska, "The Archive of *Algérie Imaginaire*"; Alloula, *The Colonial Harem,* 3–7.

48. On D. W. Griffith's use of the "ride to the rescue" device, see Michael Rogin, "The Sword Became a Flashing Vision: D. W. Griffith's *Birth of a Nation," Representations* 9 (Winter 1985): 157, 164, 178–79, 187.

49. See Joseph Campbell, *The Hero with a Thousand Faces* (Princeton, N.J.: Princeton University Press, 1968); as well as Robin Morgan's critique, *The Demon Lover: On the Sexuality of Terrorism* (New York: Norton, 1989), 54–68, esp. 58–63. See also Sorlin et al., *Générique des Années Trente,* 154.

50. Achebe, "An Image of Africa," 251–52, 261.

Part III

Screening Vichy

6 / Collaboration and Context: *Lacombe Lucien,* the *Mode Rétro,* and the Vichy Syndrome

Richard J. Golsan

Le Cinéma, c'est le spectateur qui le fait, beaucoup plus encore qu'un livre le lecteur. Le cinéaste, c'est le spectateur.　　　　*Marguerite Duras*

Of the major films dealing with the Occupation produced in post-Gaullist France, none has proven more controversial than Louis Malle's *Lacombe Lucien.* Hailed by both the Right and the Left after its initial release in January 1974—prominent leftist critics like Jean-Louis Bory praised it as "the first true film . . . about the Occupation," and *Le Figaro* and *Rivarol* lauded it, respectively, as "a beautiful film of high moral standing" and as "a work of great quality"[1]— *Lacombe Lucien* soon fell on harder critical times. Beginning around February of the same year, a series of lengthier assessments of the film began to appear in newspapers and reviews reflecting a broad range of political and ideological perspectives. These reviews were uniformly negative. In the extreme right-wing periodicals *Minute* and *Aspects de la France,* the film's young peasant protagonist was condemned for his lack of political idealism—an idealism, these reviews contended, that typified those Frenchmen who joined the *milice* or chose to serve Hitler and the Nazi cause. Assessments on the left were equally hostile, if more subtle and wide-ranging in their criticisms. These commentaries, in fact, deserve closer scrutiny, because they reflect significantly on the *mode rétro,* the wave of nostalgia for the 1940s and the Occupation in particular that swept France in the mid-1970s and of which Malle's film is considered a prime example.[2] They also raise troubling questions concerning the accuracy and legitimacy

139

of aesthetic judgments of the film. Finally, when considered in conjunction with more recent commentary, these assessments suggest two hypotheses: first, that *Lacombe Lucien* and its critical reception can teach us more about postwar views of the Occupation and French self-perceptions since the war than about the history of the period itself, and second, that the film is less a symptom of what Henry Rousso has labeled the "Vichy syndrome" than its victim.[3]

In several articles and interviews dealing with *Lacombe Lucien* that appeared in the summer of 1974 in the pages of prestigious leftist reviews, including *Les Temps modernes* and the *Cahiers du cinéma*, criticisms of Malle's film were inseparable from more ubiquitous condemnations of the *mode rétro*. Critics including Christian Zimmer and Pascal Bonitzer as well as leading intellectuals such as Michel Foucault attacked Malle's film as symptomatic of a broader and dangerous malaise sweeping the nation in the wake of the recent election of Valéry Giscard d'Estaing as president. For these critics, the *mode rétro* represented not only a "snobbish fetishism of old things" but a "derision" or "false archeology of history."[4] What the *mode rétro* sought to accomplish, they believed, was a sinister rewriting of history, and specifically the history of the Occupation, in order to challenge and indeed to undermine the image of heroic and widespread resistance against Nazism, an image nurtured by the recently defeated Gaullists: "Gone the *grand designs*: the Resistance was one, and so was Gaullism. . . . Gone also virtuous indignation, intransigence, fidelity."[5] In the place of this Gaullist myth of resistance was substituted a more "realistic" image of the period in which the roles of ideology and political commitment were downplayed and the choices and actions of individuals were attributed to the vagaries of chance or "fate" and "human nature" itself. A more accommodating attitude toward former collaborators and even the Nazis themselves was in the air. Writing in the July 1974 issue of *Les Temps modernes*, Christian Zimmer asserted,

> The hour has come to familiarize oneself, in the most affective sense of the term, with the ex-enemy, and books appear on Hitler—the man, not the politics, and the bookstores are now selling collections of *Signal*, the Nazi weekly for French readers.[6]

The moral of the tale, according to Zimmer, was that there were ultimately no heroes or villains, only everyday human beings who were the victims of circumstances, which is to say, of History itself. In this scenario, little if anything separated *résistant* from *collabo* in historical terms and, in any event, if the truth were really known about the period, one would be forced to admit that "the French people didn't give a damn about fascism."[7]

Whitewashed in this fashion, fascism, and Nazism in particular, could assume an erotic charge in that it constituted the expression of "obscure forces" and "buried 'instincts'" that slept in the souls of all human beings, criminals, "honest people" and victims alike.[8] The inevitable result of this line of reasoning, according to Pascal Bonitzer, was that fascism and human nature were conflated, and to deny the connection would be to deny falsely the existence of some of humankind's most basic (if darkest) impulses.

For Michel Foucault, the *mode rétro* eroticized power not only in works such as *Lacombe Lucien*, but in Liliana Cavani's *Night Porter*, where an ex-Nazi officer reasserts his sexual dominance over a former victim who is all too willing to go along with her tormentor. For Foucault, what was most disturbing about these representations of the eroticism of (fascist) power was that they found an echo in contemporary politics as practiced by Giscard: "It is certain that Giscard built his campaign in part not only on his physical presence but also on a certain eroticization of his person, of his elegance."[9]

By linking representations of Nazi eroticization of power in the cinema to Giscardian politics of the mid-1970s, Foucault underscored the degree to which the *mode rétro* derived from important changes in the French political landscape after the fall of Gaullism. French critics at the time, including Foucault, Bonitzer, and Zimmer, and more recently British critics such as Alan Morris, have all viewed the *mode rétro* as embodying the bourgeoisie's effort to rid itself and the nation of a heroic image of resistance with which it felt uncomfortable and that failed to coincide with its own historic role during the Occupation.[10] At the same time, it supposedly represented the Pétainist, collaborationist right's effort to come "out of the closet" and vindicate itself in the eyes of History, or more precisely, to rewrite its own history, after hiding behind Gaullism during the postwar period.[11] According to Foucault, the recent events of May 1968 lent a real urgency to this revisionism, because the student uprisings had brought home the fact that popular revolutionary upheaval was not something that took place only in other countries but something that could occur under the noses of the French ruling classes. In order to disarm the potential for popular struggle in advance, it became necessary to empty even the most controversial moments in the nation's history of their conflictual content:

> The struggles became not part of the present but part of the eventual future of our system. It was thus necessary to place them at a distance. How? Not by interpreting them directly, because this would expose them to all sorts of denials, but in proposing a historical interpretation of old popular struggles that took place among us, to show that in fact they [these struggles] never existed! Before 1968, it

was "That won't come here because that kind of thing takes place elsewhere": now, it's "That won't come here because it never took place! And look, even something like the Resistance, about which many people have thought so much, look a little closer. . . . Nothing. Empty, it rings hollow!"[12]

Thus, the Occupation, rather than being a period of grand ideological confrontations, popular struggles, and heroic endeavors, was transformed into a time when a few troublemakers caused ripples on the surface of the nation's well-being but failed to affect its depths.

Given the critique of the *mode rétro* sketched out here, it is easy to see how discussions of *Lacombe Lucien* became inscribed and indeed subsumed in a broader polemic against Giscardism and its implications for French political and cultural practice. Malle's hero was considered the perfect example of an essentially apolitical, insignificant, and indeed mediocre individual who happens by chance to join up with the French Gestapo because he gets a flat tire on his bicycle and is caught after curfew by his future cohorts. The fact that the young Lucien could just as easily have joined up with the Resistance is confirmed by the fact that, earlier in the film, he had already been turned away by the local Resistance leader and schoolteacher, Peyssac (whom he later betrays to the Gestapo), before setting out on his ill-fated bicycle trip. Ideological distinctions between the two camps are lost on Lucien, who, at various points in the film, naively asks who the Jews and the Freemasons are, implying that he has no idea why they are persecuted and why they are "France's enemies." Lacking a core of political beliefs that would bind him to his fellow *gestapistes*, Lucien remains with them because he enjoys an almost unlimited power, a power that allows him to impose himself on the Horn family, wealthy Parisian Jews attempting to flee persecution and reach the Spanish border and safety. He enters the Horn household, treats the father disrespectfully and, on occasion, abusively, and seduces the daughter, France, who is unquestionably drawn to a man she should absolutely loathe. Lucien's animal magnetism apparently confirms his status as a prime example of the *mode rétro*'s disturbing emphasis on the link between (fascist) power and eroticism. Indeed, France Horn, Lucien's sexual partner, is also entirely at his mercy throughout the film.

Condemned as a work fitting the broad parameters of the *mode rétro* as elaborated by Foucault and others, *Lacombe Lucien* became the target of related criticisms that also sought to tie the film to a reactionary politics and aesthetics. In the leftist *Charlie Hebdo*, Delfeil de Ton blasted the film as an attempt "to make innocent those who furnished the victims of the Nazi organization" in presenting the young peasant as a fundamentally sympathetic and "normal" adolescent.[13] In an exchange with Malle in the pages of *L'Humanité dimanche*, the former Resistance leader René Andrieu argued that the film's lack of verisimilitude was confirmation of a reactionary apologetics. According to Andrieu, it was highly unlikely in historical terms that someone frustrated in his effort to join the Resistance would immediately swing to the other extreme and sign on with the Gestapo, or that a Jewish girl would voluntarily sleep with "a torturer for the *milice* [sic]."[14] Andrieu also protested what he perceived to be a condescending portrait of peasants in the film, presented as "crude, weak, greedy, incapable of generosity."[15]

Rather than criticize *Lacombe Lucien*'s supposed lack of historical verisimilitude or its hostile characterization of the lower classes, Christian Zimmer dismissed the film in its entirety as a reactionary *chef-d'oeuvre* structured on the duality of formal perfection and a cynically pessimistic vision of human imperfection and corruptibility. The film's negative worldview, Zimmer continued, affirmed "the impossibility of changing man and the world," while its seamless purity of form made such a vision seem ineluctable.[16] In other words, the perfection of art confirmed the imperfection of humanity, and history itself, as a force of change, was once again stripped of all meaning and significance.

In his own commentaries on *Lacombe Lucien* at the time of the film's *succès de scandale*, Malle generally failed to counter many of the charges of reaction against his film, and in several instances he in fact confirmed, perhaps inadvertently, the bases upon which these charges were made. Speaking of the role of chance in Lucien's *engagement* during his exchange with Andrieu in *L'Humanité dimanche*, Malle stated that "without the flat tire nothing would have happened to him, he would have remained at the hospice." He also described Lucien as "extremely normal," thus, in a certain sense, legitimating the latter's actions, no matter how repugnant, by making them appear part of the "normal" order of things.

Malle did challenge claims that *Lacombe Lucien* was riddled with historical inaccuracies and distortions, basing his responses in part on his and cowriter Patrick Modiano's knowledge of the period as well his own personal experience of the Occupation.[17] Responding to Andrieu's charge of the improbability of Lucien's political trajectory, Malle noted that "there is a part of the population which does not possess a political conscience."[18] For such individuals, presumably, a radical shift of this sort would not seem particularly incongruous or inconsistent.[19] In an interview with Gilles Jacob in *Positif*, Malle also emphasized the fact that, given the hardships and privations of the period, "[a lot of] people found themselves in the *milice* because they simply had nothing to eat." It was completely understandable, therefore, that "there was a little of everything in the *milice*, people on the lam as well as minor provincial noblemen, workers as well as former members of fascist leagues."[20] Malle went on to insist on the authenticity of Hippolyte, the black member of the Gestapo group with which Lucien becomes involved, noting that other "non-Aryans" such as Arabs were recruited into the French Gestapo by the infamous Bony\Laffont gang near Limoges. Finally, in response to Andrieu's charge that the France-Lucien liaison seemed highly improbable, Malle asserted that in Toulouse, Jewish girls were known to have slept with their enemies in order to save their families.[21]

Malle's comments in interviews given around the time of the release of *Lacombe Lucien* certainly help vindicate the film where charges of historical inaccuracy are concerned. Conversely, his more recent remarks, and especially recollections of his childhood and family life during the Occupation, lend themselves to serious misinterpretation, especially when the supposed "ideological underpinnings" of *Lacombe Lucien* are at issue. In *Louis Malle par Louis Malle*, a collection of reflections on his life and films published in 1978, Malle describes the bad faith and hypocrisy of his own wealthy bourgeois family in dealing with the history and memory of the Occupation:

> My family, like many French people, had confidence in Pétain at least until 1942. Pétain was the great warrior, the hero of 1914, a person the bourgeoisie respected. When I was with the Jesuits in Paris in 1941, they made us sell in the streets, from shop to shop, portraits of the Marshal. . . . When I recall this episode, I anger my family! Like everybody, they have a selective memory. But at the time, they needed to reassure themselves.[22]

In effect, Malle's commentary on his own family confirms a crucial motivation attributed to the *mode rétro* as defined by its critics in that it depicts a reactionary bourgeoisie eager to ignore its own dubious past, a bourgeoisie that would be receptive to and indeed likely to promote the deheroicized version of the Occupation presented in *Lacombe Lucien*, a film made, not coincidentally, by one of its own. Moreover, Malle's reflections on his own attitudes at the time are suggestive of the degree to which the family's conservatism had tainted his own views. Speaking of a local Resistance member with whom he and his schoolmates became familiar, Malle notes that "given our social origins, this resistance fighter was on the other side of the fence."[23]

Louis Malle par Louis Malle also deals at length with the director's rather amoral and apolitical adolescence, an adolescence concerned more with rebelling against parents and other authority figures than with coming to grips with the political realities of the day. It is this adolescence, in fact, upon which Malle sought to draw in developing the character of Lucien: "In working on

Lacombe Lucien, I tried to recall what I felt at the time."[24] The wily Quercy peasant, it would appear, is also the alter ego of the coddled bourgeois, Malle himself. To the degree that Lucien is presented in a sympathetic light in the film, therefore, it could be argued that through its central character *Lacombe Lucien* constitutes an apology for the decadence of the bourgeoisie.

My intent here is not to suggest that *Lacombe Lucien* does indeed embody the reactionary ideology attributed to the *mode rétro,* or that in making the film, Malle was complicitous with the historical revisionism attributed to his class. On the other hand, it could be argued, I believe, that Malle's comments on *Lacombe Lucien,* at least in *Louis Malle par Louis Malle,* suggest an inability on the filmmaker's part to separate his "family romance" from his conceptualization of the Occupation and his representation of it on film. For this reason, he remains blind (or perhaps indifferent) to charges that *Lacombe Lucien* embodies a reactionary and revisionist bourgeois ideology because the issues these charges raise are for him linked less to broad, impersonal ideological issues than to intensely personal and familial concerns. In fact, Malle did not exorcise his personal ghosts where the Occupation is concerned until 1987, with the making of *Au Revoir les enfants.* In this film, which has proven much less controversial than its predecessor, Malle at last deals directly with his most significant memory of the war, the arrest by the Gestapo and deportation of a Jewish boy being hidden by priests in the Jesuit school Malle had attended. At the same time, he confronts the decadence and indifference of the bourgeoisie in the representation of the film's young protagonist's spoiled, superficial, and politically naive mother and her son's quasi-incestuous attachment to her. Indeed, the introduction of the theme of incest personalizes *Au Revoir les enfants* not only in relation to Malle's biography but in relation to his career as a filmmaker as well, as it recalls the principal theme of the 1971 film *Le Souffle au coeur.* In this sense *Le Souffle au coeur, Lacombe Lucien,* and *Au Revoir les enfants* form a trilogy in which the troubled and conflated memory of family relations and childhood experiences during the Occupation are worked through and resolved over a period of almost twenty years. It is not surprising, therefore, that many of Malle's most astute and impersonal observations about *Lacombe Lucien* have been made since the completion of *Au Revoir les enfants.*[25]

The convergence of the film's critical reception and Malle's reading of his own experiences and background into the work do suggest that during the 1970s, *Lacombe Lucien* became trapped in a cultural, historical, and political context that created a scandal around the film and ultimately distorted and foreclosed discussion of its qualities as a work of art. In his study of the *mode rétro,* Alan Morris notes that any number of works prior to Malle's film and to

the fall of Gaullism had blurred the distinction between collaboration and resistance and emphasized the role of chance or opportunism implicit in the
choice of one over the other. These works include Marcel Aymé's *Uranus* and
Le Chemin des écoliers, Jean Genet's *Pompes funèbres*, and Pierre de Boisdeffre's
Les Fins dernières. In Genet's work, the central character, like Lucien, joins one
side simply because the other side turned him down. Even Lucien's oppor-
tunistic and juvenile amorality, or moral "idiocy," as one critic described it, had
long since been on display in the maudlin, simpleminded, and real-life memoirs of the collaborationist actress Corinne Luchaire.[26] None of these works,
however, has proven as controversial as Malle's film, in some cases because they
simply lacked artistic merit, but for the most part, because the climate of the
times, dominated as they were by the myth of resistance, simply made the revisionist message of these works fall on deaf ears.

If *Lacombe Lucien* has in fact been "freeze-framed" by the historical context
in which it first appeared, it is important both to examine what has been
"edited out," so to speak, and to examine the film's subsequent reception to determine if changing historical and political contexts have allowed the film to re-
cuperate a certain autonomy as a work of art. Artistic autonomy is of course a
dangerous and debatable proposition. In the case of *Lacombe Lucien*, however,
it is an important and indeed crucial consideration because the evaluation of
the film as a work of art has always been tied to its supposed ideological bent or
how well or "correctly" it treats the historical period it purports to represent.[27]
In other words, judgments of *Lacombe Lucien* have always been precisely that.
Assessments of the film have either been "for" or "against," with no middle
ground possible. The critic must either attack or defend it, and the film itself
must be shown to reflect a specific ideology that determines plot as well as
characterization.[28] There can be no room for *ambiguity*. The critic who accepts
the film's ambiguities and willingly suspends judgment is guilty of a cowardly
critical blindness and paralysis, and probably revisionist politics as well.[29] For
example, to acknowledge the ambiguities of Lucien's character, to allow for
both his cold brutality and his apparent capacity for love is to permit "the recuperation . . . of a bastard,"[30] whereas to embrace "the duality of human ambivalence" that, some argue, characterizes the vision of *Lacombe Lucien* is to be
seduced by the work's reactionary ideology.

And yet, to even the most casual observer, the film is nothing if not ambiguous, both when important insights into the central characters are provided and
during crucial moments in plot development. For example, Lucien's brutality,
his potential for sadism, is strongly suggested in a number of scenes early in the
film. In the opening segment, Lucien kills a bird with his slingshot, apparently

for the sheer pleasure of it. Later, he massacres rabbits with the cold precision of an executioner and kills chickens with the same dispassion. In a scene carefully placed just before the massacre of the rabbits, however, Lucien helps remove the carcass of a dead horse from the family barn. When the others leave to have a drink without so much as a second look at the horse, Lucien stays behind with the animal, clearly affected by its death. Which is the real Lucien? The issue, of course, becomes much more important later in the film, when Lucien's dealings with other human beings are at stake. Is the real Lucien the sadistic killer, the *collabo* who betrays, tortures, and, in a scene remarkable for its exquisite cruelty, destroys the model ship of the Resistance doctor's son just to witness the latter's anguished incredulity, or is he the concerned but ineffectual adolescent who tries to lead Horn away when Horn, no longer able to tolerate a life of fear and degradation, essentially signs his own death warrant by showing up at the Hôtel des Grottes, the Gestapo headquarters? Finally, is the real Lucien the crude and thoughtless adolescent who foists himself on the Horn family, or is he the savior of France and the grandmother, whom he rescues from a German soldier and leads to a rustic and almost idyllic country retreat at the end of the film? Even this choice is not clear, because the film leaves the spectator in doubt as to whether Lucien intentionally decides to save France and the grandmother in killing the German soldier or kills the latter to get a gold watch Lucien wanted.[31]

Any number of similar ambiguities and ambivalences can be cited in relation to other major characters and scenes. Despite the *mode rétro* critics' assumptions concerning a clear connection between eroticism and power in the film, the attraction between France and Lucien cannot be reduced to such abstract, totalizing concepts. Not only are Lucien's own feelings where France is concerned too complex, but so, too, are hers vis-à-vis Lucien. Nowhere is this more evident than near the end of the film, when France holds a rock over the head of the sleeping Lucien but cannot make up her mind to kill him. This episode occurs, moreover, when France and Lucien appear to be happily and unproblematically in love with each other during the "country idyll" at the end of the film, when political power, at least, is no longer an issue.

Ironically, *Lacombe Lucien* is *least* ambiguous in its portrayals of secondary characters, whose function in the film is precisely to represent particular political groups or viewpoints. Lucien's fellow *gestapistes* are unequivocally corrupt and malicious, from the fanatical fascist and anti-Semite Faure to the sleazy aristocrat Jean-Bernard de Voisins and his cruel, superficial, and stupid actress girlfriend Betty Beaulieu, to the alcoholic leader of the group, Tonin.[32] By contrast, the characters who represent the Resistance, the *instituteur* Peyssac and

Professor Vaugeois, who is tricked into revealing his Resistance sympathies when Jean-Bernard pretends to be a wounded Resistance fighter in need of medical attention, are notable for their courage and dignity. To the degree the film takes a political stance, then, it would appear to be *pro-Resistance*, but this has been ignored by critics whose readings of the film's politics are predicated on reductive interpretations of the film's more ambiguous central characters.[33]

In a recent interview with Melinda Camber Porter, Malle has stressed the degree to which his art is centered on the representation of the irrational, the illogical in human behavior. This interests Malle not out of a sense of perversity, but because "each time I come to a turning point in my life, either in work or personally, I make irrational decisions."[34] Such illogic, such irrationality, certainly lends itself to inconsistency and therefore to ambiguity, but to renounce his commitment to these tropes would be to betray his art. Discussing *Lacombe Lucien* in another recent interview, Malle notes that, as in all his films, "I did not want to simplify, I did not want simply to paint a portrait of a traitor. Rather I was looking to analyze an individual in all his contradictions."[35]

Malle realizes, nevertheless, that it is precisely the renunciation of the irrational, the ambiguous, that the public wants: "People want fiction to be more 'real' than life which means they want to eliminate the illogical."[36] During the 1970s, this was especially true, of course, of *Lacombe Lucien*, where political and ideological inconsistency and "irrationality" were simply unacceptable. For Malle, the result was not only a willful ignorance of the subtleties of his art but a necessary foreclosure of discussion of the film's most profound political insights. According to Malle, such insights are not to be gained in unambiguous and heavy-handed *films engagés*, because these films "drive their nail in so heavily that they permit no serious political reflection."[37] Although Malle does not elaborate on what "serious political reflection" inspired by *Lacombe Lucien* might reveal, one possibility is suggested in his interview with Porter, where Malle notes that, in beginning a film, "I take my starting point as an unacceptable, impossible, and shocking idea and try to render it acceptable."[38] At the time of the making of *Lacombe Lucien*, this would entail not the creation of a countermyth to the Gaullist myth of Resistance, which itself had already been seriously undermined by Marcel Ophuls's 1971 documentary *Le Chagrin et la pitié*, but by challenging the mythmaking process itself by offering ambiguities to reflect upon rather than dubious certainties and another version of "the truth" about the Occupation.

If Malle's intention in making *Lacombe Lucien* was to demythify the Occupation rather than to create a countermyth to Gaullist resistancialism, few if any commentators in the post-*rétro* era are willing to consider the film in this light. In fact, in a recent essay on Vichy's legacy, "Cinquante ans après," Stanley Hoffmann specifically refers to what he labels "the *Lacombe Lucien* myth," successor to the Gaullist myth, which paints the portrait of "a weak and complicitous France, where there would only have been a handful of resistance fighters, where the regime could not only further the desires and pressures of the occupier, but could count on the support of a debased people."[39] That the "*Lacombe Lucien* myth" embraces social, political, and historical issues well beyond the scope of Malle's film is only the most obvious of the ways in which it misrepresents it. But then the context of Hoffmann's remarks confirms that the movie *Lacombe Lucien* has long since surpassed its role as a work of art about the Occupation to become part of the historical discourse of the memory of the period itself. In this case, fiction has replaced fact as a source of *knowledge* about the period, and any effort to judge the film must first extricate it from its own myth and the discourse of history itself.

One wonders, in fact, whether current assessments of *Lacombe Lucien* are judgments of the film or of the myth it has inspired. To be sure, these assessments are uniformly negative. In a recent interview, Marcel Ophuls dismisses *Lacombe Lucien* as "rather ludicrous," without further comment.[40] In his preface to a recent special issue of *Esprit* titled "Que faire de Vichy?" Eric Conan refers to the "nihilism" of *Lacombe Lucien* while condemning it for presenting a "simplistic account" and ignoring the complexities of the period. Such a description is certainly more in keeping with straightforward claims of the myth than the ambiguities of the film.

But if these assessments are to be taken seriously as commentary on Malle's film itself, it is important to determine the context in which they were made. Almost twenty years after the release of *Lacombe Lucien*, interpretations of the Occupation have indeed changed, but they have become no less controversial. The demise of the Gaullist myth of resistance and the end of the *mode rétro* have ushered in, among other things, the reawakening of Jewish memory, and with it, public and judicial debates on crimes against humanity and Vichy's, and indeed France's, role in these crimes. As Henry Rousso has noted recently, after the death of de Gaulle "the closet was opened and things quickly became uncontrollable." The trial of Klaus Barbie in the mid-1980s, and the controversies surrounding judicial proceedings involving charges of crimes against humanity against the *milicien* Paul Touvier, the former secretary general of Vichy police René Bousquet, and Vichy officials Jean Leguay and Maurice Papon have produced any number of revisionist *re*readings of the Occupation. The potential for political mythmaking where the Occupation is concerned seems endless, as both the context for the debate and the discourses that attempt to contain it become increasingly confused and contradictory. For example, in *Remembering in Vain: The Klaus Barbie Trial and Crimes against Humanity*, Alain Finkielkraut notes that during the trial of Klaus Barbie, Barbie's lawyer, Jacques Vergès, sought to recontextualize the Occupation and strip the notion of crimes against humanity of historical specificity and meaning by comparing Nazi atrocities to those committed by the French in their former colonies.[41] At the same time, Vergès sought to invert the notion of good and evil in its most basic configuration by painting Barbie not as a torturer but as the victim of a white European-Israeli conspiracy. Within this context, Vergès also sought to effect another spectacular reversal by allying his Nazi client to the peoples of the Third World who were victims as well of European and Jewish hegemony. Cocounsel for the defense pointedly included an Arab and a Congolese lawyer.

Controversy surrounding the Touvier and Bousquet affairs has involved revisionism of equal magnitude, but in a more specifically national context. The protracted debate surrounding the former *milicien* Touvier, once pardoned by President Georges Pompidou in an effort to *end* the controversy surrounding *les années noires*, has dredged up the role of the Catholic Church in harboring war criminals and raised serious questions as to how willing the French really are to try one of their own for crimes against humanity.[42] This last point is especially crucial because, according to French law, condemnation of Touvier on these grounds would require condemning the Vichy regime itself for mandating state policies involving "ideological hegemony." When in April 1992 a French court exonerated Touvier on the grounds that Vichy did not practice "ideological hegemony" despite the anti-Jewish decree signed by Pétain in October 1940, it cast itself in the role of historian and, in effect, rewrote the history of the Occupation.[43] In violating its institutional function in this fashion, the court revealed once again the extent to which efforts to deal with the period and put its troubling memory to rest end up confusing fact and fiction and compromising institutional discourses that seek to come to terms with its intricacies. Is it any wonder that in a context such as this *Lacombe Lucien* is perhaps more important as a historical myth, a version of history, than as a work of art?

If the Touvier affair has raised serious concerns about the role and efficacy of the legal system in reconciling the nation to its troubled past, the Bousquet affair unsettled the political valencies whose stability is certainly crucial to ending the nation's obsession with the Occupation.[44] Bousquet's Radical Socialist pedigree, his long-standing friendship with and political support for Mitterrand after the war,[45] and the latter's apparent effort to quash proceedings against Bousquet in October 1990 provided fodder for the extreme Right's effort to dredge up Mitterrand's dubious past during the Occupation and suggest that collaboration with the Nazis was actually more widespread and significant on the Left than the Right.[46] Delays in the trial of Bousquet in 1990 as well as Mitterrand's apparent reluctance since to discredit Vichy totally as part of the nation's past prevent such claims from being definitively dismissed.

According to Henry Rousso, the Vichy syndrome has since 1974 been in its "obsession" phase, and a look at recent scandals and controversies suggests that the term is entirely appropriate. In fact, to the degree to which these scandals suggest that there is no end in sight, that *les années noires* are becoming more and more undecidable, the term *desperation* might be an even more appropriate label. This is certainly implicit in the title of the recent *Esprit* special issue, "Que faire de Vichy?" No amount of research on the period, no amount of discussion or debate in the media, appears to resolve the issues raised or reconcile the nation to its past. Is it any wonder, then, that a film as ambiguous, as "undecidable" as *Lacombe Lucien* should inspire curt and impatient dismissals? In a cultural and historical climate seeking closure on the entire period, ambiguity, irrationality, and illogic become "ludicrous" or "nihilistic." Or do they? The recent release of two controversial and troubling films, Claude Chabrol's *L'Oeil de Vichy* and Jean Marboeuf's *Pétain*, as well as the shocking murder of René Bousquet on 7 June 1993 suggest that no doors on the period have really been closed; no definitive interpretation, no "master narrative," has managed to impose itself.[47] If this is so, *Lacombe Lucien* will in all probability get another day in court.

Notes

This essay is dedicated to the memory of Edouard Morot-Sir, scholar, mentor, and friend. I would like to thank Krista May for her help in preparing the final version of this essay.

1. Quoted in F. Garçon, "La Fin d'un mythe," *Vertigo* 2 (April 1989): 111. Unless otherwise noted, all translations in this chapter are my own.

2. A number of commentators have argued recently that the *mode rétro* continues today, a claim not at all unreasonable given the continuing obsession with the Occupation and the number of literary and cinematic works dealing with the period. For this perspective on the *mode rétro*, see the conclusion of Lynn Higgins's *New Novel, New Wave, New Politics* (Lincoln: University of Nebraska Press, 1996); and Alan Morris, *Collaboration and Resistance Reviewed: Writers and the "Mode Retro" in Post-Gaullist France* (New York: Berg, 1992). For my purposes here, I shall use the term in the more restrictive context of the period incorporating the fall of Gaullism and the rise of Gis-

cardism in the mid-1970s, because this period produced a specific response to *Lacombe Lucien* that would be modified by subsequent events.

3. Rousso describes the Vichy syndrome as a "neurosis" affecting the entire nation, a neurosis born of France's inability to reconcile itself to what are commonly referred to as *les années noires.* The neurosis manifests itself in repression and distortion where the memory as well as the history of the period are concerned, and the "return of the repressed," especially in artistic works dealing with the period, often results in scandal, controversy, and denial. See especially the introduction to Rousso's *The Vichy Syndrome: History and Memory in France since 1944,* trans. Arthur Goldhammer (Cambridge: Harvard University Press, 1991).

4. Pascal Bonitzer and Serge Toubiana, "Anti-Rétro: Entretien avec Michel Foucault," *Cahiers du cinéma* 251–52 (July–August 1974): 5.

5. Christian Zimmer, "La Paille dans le discours de l'ordre," *Les Temps modernes* 336 (July 1974): 2495.

6. Ibid.

7. Bonitzer and Toubiana, "Anti-Rétro," 5.

8. Pascal Bonitzer, "Histoire de Sparadrap," *Cahier du cinéma* 250 (May 1974): 47.

9. Bonitzer and Toubiana, "Anti-Rétro," 10.

10. See Morris, *Collaboration and Resistance Reviewed,* chap. 2.

11. It is of interest to note that the "depoliticization" of the Occupation associated with the *mode rétro* does not jibe with the right-wing critiques of *Lacombe Lucien* mentioned above. These critiques note their displeasure at Lucien's *lack* of political idealism and commitment when he joins the Gestapo.

12. Bonitzer and Toubiana, "Anti-Rétro," 13.

13. Quoted in Garçon, "La Fin d'un mythe," 116.

14. "*Lacombe Lucien* et l'Occupation: Louis Malle s'explique, René Andrieu conteste," *L'Humanité dimanche,* 3 April 1974, 20–21.

15. Ibid., 20.

16. Zimmer, "La Paille," 2493.

17. For Malle's comments on Patrick Modiano's contributions to the film, see Colin Nettelbeck and P. A. Huston, *Patrick Modiano: pièces d'identité, écrire l'entretemps* (Paris: Lettres Modernes, 1986), 55; and especially Phillip French, *Conversations avec Louis Malle* (Paris: Denöel, 1993), 118.

18. "*Lacombe Lucien* et l'Occupation," 22.

19. In Phillip French's recent *Conversations avec Louis Malle,* 126–27, Malle recounts an anecdote that encouraged him to make *Lacombe Lucien* and that supports the view that extreme and rapid shifts in political allegiance were not uncommon during the Occupation, especially among young and impressionable boys. Malle's friend Jean-Pierre Melville, a former resistance fighter, was traveling from Bordeaux to Paris on the train in 1943 with a fellow member of the Resistance. In their compartment was a young man who announced he was off to join the Waffen SS to "fight for his country." By the time the train arrived in Paris, the two *résistants* had completely changed the young man's mind. He had decided to join them in the Resistance.

A number of historically documented instances also support the notion that radical swings from one political extreme to the other were not at all unusual in France during this period. The most obvious example is Jacques Doriot, who went from leader of the

Parti communiste in the early 1930s to leader of the fascist Parti populaire français in the late 1930s and the 1940s. Paul Jankowski documents fairly large numbers of similar conversions among the masses in his study of the PPF in Marseille, *Communism and Collaboration: Serge Sabiani and Politics in Marseille* (New Haven, Conn.: Yale University Press, 1989).

20. Gilles Jacob, "Entretien avec Louis Malle (à propos de *Lacombe Lucien*)," *Positif* 157 (March 1974): 29.

21. "*Lacombe Lucien* et l'Occupation," 20.

22. Louis Malle, *Louis Malle par Louis Malle* (Paris: l'Athanor, 1978), 9.

23. Ibid.

24. Ibid., 13.

25. Malle's two films about the Occupation have often been compared, most recently by Lynn Higgins in "If Looks Could Kill: Louis Malle's Portraits of Collaboration," in *Fascism, Aesthetics, and Culture,* ed. Richard J. Golsan (Hanover, N.H.: University Press of New England, 1992), 198–211. In an earlier review of *Au Revoir les enfants* in the *New York Review of Books,* 12 May 1988, Stanley Hoffmann discusses the two films and strongly expresses his preference for *Au Revoir les enfants*, which, based on his personal experience of the Occupation, he considers far more convincing and authentic than the earlier film. Hoffmann also remarks on the theme of incest in *Au Revoir les enfants* and the connection with *Le Souffle au coeur,* but he does not show how the link between familial themes and the Occupation slant Malle's early views on *Lacombe Lucien,* as I have argued here.

As these remarks suggest, a more detailed comparison here of *Lacombe Lucien* and *Au Revoir les enfants* would be superfluous. Nevertheless, I should like to state my own preference for *Lacombe Lucien,* if for no other reason than the fact that the history of its reception reveals so much about the troubled memory of the Occupation. I shall also argue that the film's ambiguity makes it in many ways one of Malle's most representative works.

26. See Corinne Luchaire, *Ma Drôle de vie* (Paris: Sun, 1949). It is of interest to note that Luchaire's memoirs had long fascinated Patrick Modiano and influenced his own views on the Occupation. It is therefore not unlikely that they influenced the initial conception of the character of Lucien.

27. In French, *Conversations avec Louis Malle,* 126, Malle notes that at the time of the making of the film he was aware of the fact that certain aspects of the film were not "politically correct" and were bound to stir controversy. The example he cites is the inclusion of the black Gestapo member, Hippolyte. Malle was, however, totally unprepared for the general assault on the film's supposedly reactionary ideology.

28. Or, as Christian Zimmer argues, determines its "formal perfection." "La Paille."

29. Bonitzer's comment along these lines is worth quoting in full: "The blindness or paralysis . . . of the critics in dealing with the meaning of this film (a paralysis that one often finds expressed in the use of the word 'ambiguity,' this term, notably applied to the film by revisionist critics) always in reality reflects the position of the critic himself, who doesn't know if a negative judgment is in order or not: this serves to suspend the critical act." "Histoire de Sparadrap," 43.

30. Jean Delmas, "Sur les écrans," *Jeune Cinéma* 77 (March 1974): 34.

31. It is interesting to note that even those critics who are not particularly concerned

with the film's politics or underlying ideology tend to strip the film of its ambiguities in developing their interpretations. For example, François Garçon sees the film as primarily a love story involving a "young *milicien*" and a "persecuted Jewess." In keeping with this reading of the film, he describes the scene involving Lucien's shooting of the German soldier and the flight of Lucien, France, and the grandmother in the following terms: "In Lucien's presence, a German officer decides to take France and the grandmother as hostages. Without hesitating, Lucien shoots the man with a burst of machine-gun fire and rushes out with the young girl." "La Fin d'un mythe," 112. Needless to say, this is not what happens on-screen.

32. All of these characters are borrowed from the early novels of Patrick Modiano. For a discussion of the impact of these works on the scenario of *Lacombe Lucien*, see my essay "Collaboration, Alienation, and the Crisis of Identity in the Film and Fiction of Patrick Modiano," in *Film and Literature: A Comparative Approach to Adaptation,* ed. Wendell Aycock and Michael Schoenecke (Lubbock: Texas Tech University Press, 1988), 107–22.

33. Although Malle himself is not interested in heroes and villains in the film, he does acknowledge that if there is a "personnage positif," it is Horn, who, despite his contradictions, is notable for his "dignity" and "integrity." See French, *Conversations avec Louis Malle,* 122.

34. Melinda Camber Porter, *Through Parisian Eyes: Reflections on Contemporary French Arts and Culture* (Oxford: Oxford University Press, 1986), 86.

35. French, *Conversations avec Louis Malle,* 122. These artistic concerns also apparently figured in the choice of Pierre Blaise to play the role of Lucien. Malle notes that "there was in him [Blaise] something very strong and very ambiguous. He could pass for the worst of traitors and at the same time he was very touching. Blaise was so good that he caused me a lot of trouble. *Many people almost thought the film was an apology for collaboration because Blaise was so moving and so troubling that it was impossible to hate him completely*" (122; emphasis added).

36. In Porter, *Through Parisian Eyes,* 86.

37. Malle, *Louis Malle,* 31.

38. Porter, *Through Parisian Eyes,* 84.

39. Stanley Hoffmann, "Cinquante ans après," in "Que faire de Vichy?" (special issue) *Esprit* 181 (May 1992): 39. I will return to the significance of this title as it concerns *Lacombe Lucien* at the end of this essay.

40. In Porter, *Through Parisian Eyes,* 11. In French, *Conversations avec Louis Malle,* Malle notes that he was aware that Ophuls had been "shocked" by precisely the film's ambiguity. Malle goes on to suggest that Ophuls's discomfort with *Lacombe Lucien* stems from divergent ambitions on the part of the two directors in making their respective films, *Lacombe Lucien* and *Le Chagrin et la pitié*: "*Le Chagrin et la pitié* is an ideological film. Ophuls wanted to make a demonstration, show what had happened in a provincial town, Clermont-Ferrand. He wanted to expose things that had been covered up. He was trying to prove something and denounce collaboration. He was making a moral judgment. For me, the demonstration had been made. I wanted to move beyond it. Rather than judge, I wanted to study a type of comportment that is despicable and without doubt difficult to understand. After all, if people are shocked by ambiguity,

they shouldn't go to see my films. Ophuls's films and *Lacombe Lucien* function on entirely different levels" (129–30).

41. Alain Finkielkraut, *La Memoire vaine: Du crime contre l'humanité* (Paris: Gallimard, 1989) has recently been published in English as *Remembering in Vain: The Klaus Barbie Trial and Crimes against Humanity,* trans. Roxanne Lapidus (New York: Columbia University Press, 1992).

42. For the role played by the Catholic Church in harboring Touvier, see René Rémond et al., *Paul Touvier et l'Eglise* (Paris: Fayard, 1992).

43. This decision was overturned in June 1993 by an appellate court, and it now appears that Touvier will stand trial for crimes against humanity, should his health hold up (Touvier is suffering from prostate cancer). The fact remains, however, that the reversal of the original verdict may well not have occurred had there not been public outcry.

44. Since this essay was written, Paul Touvier has been tried and convicted of crimes against humanity in a trial that took place in Versailles during March–April 1994. The April 1992 decision acquitting Touvier had been partially overturned, and the former *milicien* stood trial for ordering the murders of seven Jews at Rillieux-la-Pape in June 1944. The trial as well as the historical implications of the verdict were vexed from the outset, however, because in order to secure a conviction, the prosecution had to show that Touvier's crimes had been committed at the behest of the Nazis and not of the Vichy authorities. This was so because the part of the April 1992 decision that exonerated Vichy itself had not been overturned. In effect, if Touvier's crimes could be shown by the defense to have been committed at the behest of Vichy, he could not be convicted of crimes against humanity. For an excellent discussion of Touvier's trial, what it accomplished and failed to accomplish, see Eric Conan and Henry Rousso, *Vichy, un passé qui ne passe pas* (Paris: Fayard, 1994), 109–72.

45. Mitterrand's friendship with Bousquet has recently caused a scandal of its own. Following the publication of Pierre Péan's *Une Jeunesse française: François Mitterrand 1934–1947* (Paris: Fayard, 1994), which chronicles Mitterrand's extreme right-wing activities before the war, his career at Vichy during the Occupation, and especially his friendship with Bousquet, public outrage was so intense that Mitterrand went on television on 12 September 1994 to defend his actions and try to save his reputation. He was only partially successful, and the controversy continues at this writing, although Mitterrand's rapidly failing health has generated a good deal of sympathy.

46. In this connection see the neofascist *Le Choc du Mois* exposé on Bousquet (December 1990) as well as the special issue on Mitterrand's right-wing past (July–August 1991).

47. Bousquet was murdered by a man known by the police for his emotional instability who previously had been imprisoned for plotting to kill Klaus Barbie. The man entered Bousquet's apartment by claiming to carry legal documents, and was not interfered with by Bousquet's bodyguard. The fact that Bousquet was murdered some five days after the Touvier decision made it possible for Bousquet to stand trial for crimes against humanity has created, understandably enough, suspicions in certain quarters.

7 / Family Fictions and Reproductive Realities in Vichy France: Claude Chabrol's *Une Affaire de femmes*

Rosemarie Scullion

Contemporary feminist thought from Simone de Beauvoir on holds that women have been relegated to footnote status in conventional historiography and their experience thus effaced from the historical record. The validity of this claim is appreciable even in very recent rewritings of modern French history, a prime example of which can be found in Jean-Pierre Azéma's 1979 contribution to the multivolume series *La Nouvelle Histoire de la France contemporaine*. In *De Munich à la libération*, Azéma details the turbulence and trauma of the immediate prewar and Occupation years in France, acknowledging only in condensed, subtextual form the crucial contributions made by French women to the Resistance.[1] The same footnote format is also adopted for an account of the Vichy regime's repressive gender and reproductive policies, which, the author tersely notes, ushered at least one female abortionist (or "maker of angels" [*faiseuse d'anges*] as it is known in the vernacular) to the guillotine during the war.[2] A similar indifference to the sexual politics of the Vichy regime can also be found in other major accounts of the Occupation period.[3] Such historical minimizing of this prominent feature of the Occupation legacy is all the more conspicuous in light of Claude Chabrol's more recent effort in *Une Affaire de femmes* (1988) to underscore the centrality of sexual politics in the Vichy regime's collaborationist rule. Chabrol's film not only brings into relief the Vichy regime's ruthless hypocrisy with respect to women, but also elucidates some of the subtle cultural tensions and gender dynamics that have been eclipsed in more linear, event-focused histories of the period.

In the discussion that follows, I propose to explore the historical and ideological implications of Chabrol's filmic representation of the case of Marie-Louise Giraud, the last woman in France to be executed by guillotine following her 1943 conviction for performing illegal abortions. In addition to highlighting the specific ways in which women suffered from the enactment of Vichy's population policies, a historical reality that Chabrol captures with great poignancy in *Une Affaire de femmes*, I shall contrast the regime's pronatalist posturing with the genocidal zeal with which it administratively initiated and orchestrated the deportation of thousands of Jewish children to death camps in Poland beginning in 1942.[4] Countering the widely held notion that the sexist and racist policies energetically pursued by Vichy conservatives after the fall of France in June 1940 were dictated by or emulated those of the fascist occupier and are therefore specific only to the Occupation era, I shall argue that the ostensibly contradictory gender and racial politics of the period in fact cohered perfectly within the collaborationist regime's own reactionary logic and adhered closely to its central political aims.

Chabrol borrows the title *Une Affaire de femmes* from a 1986 narrative by attorney Francis Szpiner, which, the opening credits inform viewers, "freely inspired" the film's screenplay.[5] Szpiner's title aptly characterizes the gender distinctions at work with respect not only to the burdens of human reproduction typically placed on women, but also to those of ensuring the survival of the family unit in an economy of scarcity produced by the rigors of war and foreign occupation. Historian Henri Michel has shown that under the Occupation, the difficulties of procuring food, clothing, and other vital necessities—a direct consequence of the rapacious terms of the Franco-German armistice of 25 June 1940—presented daily tribulations particularly for women, who are customarily charged with maintaining the domestic unit.[6] In addition, nearly 100,000 fatalities from the brief war, the absence of two million male breadwinners held prisoners of war in Germany, widespread unemployment, and, after February 1943, the institution of the STO (Service de travail obligatoire [Compulsory Labor Conscription]) further conspired to eradicate or drastically diminish the incomes of many French households, privation that in the daily scheme of things became the chief preoccupation of women.

Miranda Pollard notes that Vichy's efforts to reinvigorate the French family, whose prewar demographic decline had, or so the childless Marshal Pétain reasoned, contributed directly to the military defeat of June 1940, also significantly increased the economic vulnerability of working women.[7] Seeking to reverse what was deemed the disturbing prewar trend toward greater female employment, a development that had begun to afford a modicum of economic autonomy to women working outside of the home, Vichy conservatives began in 1940 to mount a vigorous ideological and institutional campaign designed to return "la femme au foyer [woman to the hearth]," an initiative that was to become the centerpiece of Pétain's familial and pronatalist social agenda. Such measures secured for the male working population the meager employment opportunities that the destruction of war and the devastating terms of the armistice afforded the French economy. They also effectively divested women as a whole of the modest economic and educational gains achieved in the immediate prewar years, and this in spite of the alarmist discourses already circulating, especially on the Right but also in more moderate political circles, that decried, particularly following World War I, the increasing depopulation of the French nation.

But the notions of egalitarianism, individualism, and meritocracy shaping republican education policies were quickly expunged from Vichy's gender-distinct curriculum, which was redesigned with the aim of keeping young girls' academic endeavors confined to the arena of "home economics," studies centered primarily on matters of health, housekeeping, cooking, laundry, and lessons in "family psychology and morals."[8] The newly differentiated educational programs would, it was hoped, successfully alleviate competition in the labor market by reducing female employment, which, as one 1943 report by the commissioner general for the family contends, only encouraged "the egotistical escapism of young girls wishing to obtain positions permitting them to be independent and to buy expensive clothes."[9] Along with its sweeping educational reforms, Vichy policy makers also moved to curtail the availability of divorce, to stiffen the penalties for abortion, and to reward fathers of large families with a variety of legislative, administrative, and fiscal perks.[10] But while it touted the virtues of paternalistic family values and formulated an ideology aimed at promoting the vitality and fecundity of the French family, Vichy's institutional practices actually saw that the bulk of the nation's material resources were destined to feed the Nazi war machine rather than to nurture the vast numbers of French children its policies sought to produce.[11]

In *Une Affaire de femmes,* Chabrol foregrounds the privation and hardship women encountered in their daily wartime routines, portraying in the film's opening sequences the daunting challenges women faced in securing basic necessities for their families' survival. He introduces his protagonist, here named Marie Latour, as she scours the countryside saddled with two small children in search of rudimentary foodstuffs. Situated in a provincial urban setting in 1942, the story of Marie Latour is that of a woman whose husband has been held prisoner of war in Germany, presumably since the defeat two years earlier.

The actual events portrayed in the film took place in Cherbourg, Normandy, a port city in the occupied zone whose strategic significance in the continuing German war effort against England made it an outpost of intensive military surveillance and activity. As a poorly educated, unskilled working-class woman, Latour finds herself in a situation mirroring that of millions of women struggling to sustain the family unit in the absence of a family wage earner, circumstances that produce in this young, spirited woman a deep sense of frustration and rancor running conspicuously counter to the images of maternal contentment cultivated and celebrated in Vichy's fantasies of familial bliss.

Although she freely vents the feelings of frustration that accrue in her bleak, joyless existence as sole provider and caretaker of two young children, Marie Latour clearly prefers this situation, one that affords her a measure of personal autonomy, to that of having a third dependent, her husband Paul, placing even greater demands on her already strained emotional and financial resources. He returns in the early portions of the film, and the icy greeting she accords him indicates that she has few expectations that the family reunion and her husband's return from Germany will alleviate the family burdens she has shouldered in his absence. A lackadaisical individual with more interest in amusing himself with cutouts than in procuring a living wage, his presence in the family only heightens interpersonal tensions and actually diminishes the relative freedom Marie enjoyed during his captivity. Her seething resentment toward male authority, animosity that Chabrol repeatedly shows her displacing and projecting onto her young son Pierrot, is clearly contained within the bounds of the family and appears to derive from an intuitive understanding of the institutional constraints of marriage and the relentless demands that marital and maternal obligations have placed disproportionately on her. Highly conscious of the onus of child rearing, this young wife and mother guards against further accruing responsibility for any more dependents by steadfastly spurning her husband's sexual advances. When he erupts in rage after she has once again rebuffed him, Marie calmly but firmly remarks, "Men who lose wars become as mean as wounded bulls," recognizing in some sense that "la femme au foyer" was bound to bear the emotional brunt of the French military defeat, a very astute observation when one considers the deeply sexist implications of the Vichy regime's natalist crusade.

While his choice of subject matter raises issues related perforce to women's reproductive rights and their subordinate socioeconomic and cultural status, oppression of which he at times appears fully cognizant, on numerous occasions, Chabrol's "freely" adapted account of Szpiner's case study (a text that in and of itself poses a variety of narratological and historiographic problems) displays its own gender bias.[12] The sexism of Chabrol's interpretation of the case and of its historical significance is subtle though palpable throughout the film. It becomes more apparent in a comparative analysis of the film and the text upon which it was based. Chabrol's own comments on the film and the historical circumstances it portrays are even more startling in their demeaning treatment of female sexuality and his gross exaggeration of the power women wielded during this period. In an interview given shortly after the film's American release, for instance, Chabrol explained:

> I was between 10 and 15 during the war. . . . Most of the people were zombies. People were poor—the idea of putting papers on your breast to keep warm in winter was true. The men were nothing, prisoners beaten by the Germans. Young men were sent to Germany to work. That's why many abortions were done at that time. The women were masters of the situation. And they had "accidents" not only with Germans but with whatever men were available.[13]

He goes on in a smugly bemused tone to compare the historical figure Giraud to his leading lady, Isabelle Huppert, whose glamor and erotic appeal, although clearly attenuated by the asceticism of the times, contrast sharply with the rather dowdy character she portrays, one whom Chabrol wryly describes as "fat, a little ugly, drinking very much and not very much older. Not an angel."

Marie Latour's deficiencies as a mother are indeed signaled very early in the film. In the opening scene, she impulsively strikes her son Pierrot out of sheer exasperation with the task at hand when he does not scrupulously follow her directives as they struggle to gather food. She is also particularly curt and dismissive in her attitude toward her male child while, conversely, she lavishes attention and affection on her daughter, Mouche. This favoring of the female child over a male sibling is noteworthy for, as de Beauvoir remarks in *Le Deux-ième Sexe* (The second sex), in the patriarchal order of things, the male child is most often the mother's reproductive pride and joy, through whose prospective achievements and freedoms in the privileged male world she vicariously lives.[14] Obviously aggrieved by such flagrant favoritism and disregard for his emotional well-being, Latour's son silently and stoically withstands her mistreatment, the same martyr posture in which his father Paul is presented throughout much of the film. Casting two of the film's most prominent male characters as victims of unchecked female domination, manipulation, and spite conforms less to the historical evidence, however, than it does to the peculiar view of the period Chabrol himself expressed when he claimed that under the Occupation "women were masters of the situation." Court documents indeed convey the extent to which investigators and prosecutors in the case were scandalized by the temerity with which Giraud had purportedly kept her husband dazed with the steady supply of alcohol she funneled into the household and had shamelessly paraded her lover before him. However, excepting the testimony of one outraged neighbor who declared that Giraud had allowed her children to go barefoot while playing outdoors (testimony that was later refuted), abuse and neglect of her children were not among the charges against her that could be substantiated.[15] But from the outset, Chabrol's unflattering portrait of Latour's conduct and temperament does little to endear this character to the spectating audience and mobilizes considerable negative affect toward her that detracts significantly from an awareness of and empathy for the very real constraints and duress of her plight as a working-class mother.

Yet paradoxically, if one brackets the surface meanings and tensions present in this account of family life under the Occupation, along with consideration of the director's authorial intention, it is clear that, perhaps in spite of himself, Chabrol's adaptation of Szpiner's *Une Affaire de femmes* enunciates truths and meanings with respect to women's lives that extend beyond the Giraud case and even its historical specificity. His patently sexist directorial and interpretive slant notwithstanding, in many respects, the portrait of mother and housewife-turned-abortionist Chabrol sketches in his film is quite remarkable in that it resists facile constructions of female victimization as well as stereotypic notions of the seedy, back-alley profiteer. That is, rather than casting his protagonist as an admirable example of self-conscious resistance to the Vichy regime's repressive conservatism and reproductive tyranny or, conversely, as a streetwise opportunist in pursuit of personal gain on the margins of the law, Chabrol depicts Marie Latour in a highly complex and variegated form. Choosing, for instance, to make no mention in the film of Giraud's past criminal record and to portray her filmic corollary as a rather ordinary, respectable housewife, Chabrol effectively divests abortion of the moralizing discourse of criminality and delinquency that was central to the 1943 case.[16] He treats it instead as a common concern of sexually active women, activity for which the culture apparently gave male partners little responsibility. Latour's outward conformity to the proscriptions of married life as well as the banality of her daily existence in the early portions of the film also make her often irascible demeanor an uncommonly frank expression of and commentary on the resentments and animosity circulating within the bounds of an institutional structure that so greatly constricts women's identities and aspirations. Again, it is de Beauvoir who underscores the nefarious effects for society as a whole of the repressed rage and frustration produced by the debilitating, all-consuming demands of motherhood.

> The great danger our mores have children run is that the mother to whom we hand them over, hands and feet bound, is almost always a dissatisfied woman: sexually she is frigid or unfulfilled; socially she feels inferior to men; she has no control of the world, nor of her future; through the child, she will strive to compensate for all these frustrations; understanding the extent to which the current situation of women prevents them from thriving and how many desires, revolts, pretentions, demands [women] secretly harbor, it is frightening [to think] that defenseless children are abandoned to them.[17]

Indeed, Marie Latour's often castigating tone and rare displays of emotional warmth stand in stark contrast to the boundless affection and self-effacing devotion our culture configures in its idealized imagery of motherhood. And yet it is also apparent that this woman cares deeply for her children's welfare, capitalizing on all of the resources available to her in efforts to provide a modicum of material comfort, pleasure, and joy in her children's lives as well as her own. Although he clearly renders Latour unsympathetic in displaying her outbursts of anger and her forbidding, at times haughty character, in allowing her to express negative feelings that the culture has vigilantly repressed in its mythologizing of motherhood, Chabrol in effect opens a textual space in which to critique the disempowerment of women and children in the patriarchal family and to fathom such overt expression of a full range and variety of human feelings as a counterforce to the institution's monologic authoritarianism.

The circumstances that lead Marie Latour to the dangerous practice of performing illegal abortions in wartime France evolve quite by happenstance. In a gesture of friendship and female camaraderie, she comes to the aid of a distraught neighbor, who, at the insistence of her partner, is attempting to induce an abortion by immersing herself in a concoction of what she hopes are toxic household substances. Yet again, the circumstances sketched here bear a striking resemblance to those described in *Le Deuxième Sexe*, where, in a discussion of abortion rights—or rather, in 1949, the lack thereof—de Beauvoir chides bourgeois patriarchy for hypocritically asserting the universal sanctity of all human life at conception, while in the realm of the contingent producing privileged male subjects who readily urge women to avail themselves of all means necessary to rid themselves of the burden of parenthood. In this illegal undertaking, however, women were generally left to their own devices, transforming the dilemma into a matter solely for women, that is, "une affaire de femmes."[18]

Latour first comes to understand the value of her knowledge regarding abortion techniques when, following the success of the procedure for her neighbor Ginette, she receives, as a gesture of thanks, a phonograph and collection of records. Luxury items she accepts with euphoria, the phonograph mitigates the tedium of the mother's life by allowing her to enact her lifelong fantasy of becoming a professional singer. Undereducated, unskilled, and unemployed, she must, in the conventional legal scheme of things, rely on her husband's meager earnings to alleviate the dreariness in her life. She is thus understandably elated when her own paramedical expertise takes on significant exchange value in the feminine domain to which she has been consigned. The actual source of her knowledge regarding the abortion technique remains unstated, and her non-responsiveness to Ginette's direct questions concerning whether she herself had ever availed herself of the procedure commits this information to the realm of the unspoken and the shameful. Given the otherwise circumspect life she appears to have led prior to this event, however, it is clear that this know-how has been acquired in the rather normal course of her existence as a woman, that is, conveyed by word of mouth as part of an unwritten code of knowledge with which women have historically adapted to and countered the repression and control of their sexual and reproductive lives.[19]

It is in the aftermath of the successful "favor done for a friend" that Marie Latour experiences the thrill of the free market and a measure of economic autonomy that allows her to fathom a future unconstrained by the limits of her husband's paltry earnings. With remarkable entrepreneurial savvy, she gradually, even unwittingly, begins to develop her markets and to diversify her commercial interests in illicit conduct through a friendship she brazenly forges with Lulu the prostitute, a woman whose warmth, humor, and good-natured impudence provide respite from the drudgery and solitude of Latour's daily existence as a housewife. The sphere of female friendship and emotional intimacy is indeed an important structural configuration in this film, functioning, I would argue, as a site of resistance to the patriarchal norms of sexual and familial conduct that the Vichy regime so vigorously sought to enforce. For instance, early in the film, Marie informs her young son of her plans for the evening, declaring: "You know, my Pierrot, I'm going to the café tonight, I need to have some fun. I'm young, after all." In the father's absence, she clearly views her young son as an instance of male authority before whom she must justify her actions. In the delightful evening of dance, song, and drink to which she treats herself, Marie revels in her friendship with Rachel, a young Jewish woman who is deported soon after and whose loss causes her far more grief than had her husband's prolonged captivity in Germany. Her subsequent bond with Lulu is originally solidified, it would appear, not only out of a desire to experience a sense of adventure and daring but also out of a need to fill the affective void that Rachel's deportation left in her life. In the stairwells of apartment buildings, in wartime cafés largely emptied of their male presence, in beauty parlors where ordinary housewives mingle with tawdry prostitutes, and in the spaces of family living to which they have been relegated, women cavort and collaborate in their efforts to withstand the hardships of the war, Occupation, and numerous forms of gender-bound oppression that Vichy's National Revolution only exacerbated. This form of female bonding in the face of male-generated military violence and economic dislocation is a prime defense mechanism for women confronting political, economic, and historical circumstances over which, contrary to Chabrol's assertion, they had little control. The realm of female friendship offers great solace and comfort in which Latour occasionally abandons her defensive posture and allows "a kinder, gentler" self to emerge, traits that in Chabrol's adaptation greatly nuance the image of the spiteful wife and self-centered, neglectful mother he also unmistakably projects. Interestingly, a comparative reading of the Szpiner text and Chabrol's interpretation underscores the significance of a specifically female domain of knowledge and cultural practices that mitigated the stresses of daily life, provided women with a sense of mastery over their destiny, and most important, as we shall see, also functioned as a network for the circulation of information regarding the procurement of illegal abortions. Chabrol deletes this latter function from the feminine sphere he describes and, in so doing, elides what, from a cultural and historical perspective, is one of the most intriguing aspects of the Giraud case.

Following the success of her operation on Ginette, a makeshift procedure conducted with soap, water, and rubber tubing, Latour informs her husband that her fortune-teller has predicted she will become fabulously wealthy, adding that the seer envisioned her surrounded by a coterie of women. Although Chabrol chooses to make of this tidbit but a passing reference, in reality, Cherbourg's circle of female fortune-tellers, specialists in the occult who were largely consulted by other women in the community, functioned as a conduit for the clandestine exchange of information regarding the availability of abortions. In fact, several of Giraud's codefendants in the case were described (and denounced) in court proceedings as "cartomanciennes [tarot card readers]" who, along with having treacherously undermined the solidity of the French family in their complicity with Giraud, had used their so-called visionary powers to swindle unsuspecting women with their ungodly traffic in superstition.[20] One of the defendants claimed to have taken up clairvoyance only as a means of supplementing her income in her husband's absence. But the practice itself suggests the persistence of traditional cosmological beliefs in the supernatural that church officials and societal elites alike had for three centuries been struggling to eradicate.[21] A prime example of what *Annales* historians termed the historical *longue durée* of mental structures (or *mentalités*), the non-

Christianized, nonmedicalized, and nonrationalized beliefs in what the modern era has pejoratively termed old wives' tales were seen as heretically opposed to the political and religious norms imposed on popular culture from above from the early modern period on.

Robert Muchembled has argued that this terrain of premodern cultural beliefs, rituals, and practices was in fact one over which women had held considerable sway for more than a millennium. It was also a corpus of knowledge and rites that had come under violent attack during the infamous witch hunts from the mid-sixteenth to the mid-seventeenth century, in which an estimated eighty thousand Europeans, the vast majority of whom were women, were burned at the stake. In Muchembled's view, the witch hunts in France were primarily a rural phenomenon stemming from dramatic social, cultural, and economic transformations that saw a centralizing state and ecclesiastical apparatus bent on extending its hegemony into the country's outerlying regions.[22] Brutally repressed in the early modern era, mutant forms of the traditional popular cosmology resurfaced in modern cities in the guise of fortune-tellers and tarot card readers, who, Eloïse Mozzani has noted, are distant urban cousins of the premodern era's traditional wise women of the countryside.[23] Viewed from the vantage point of the Giraud case, their survival well into the twentieth century points to what might be construed as a thriving feminine counterculture operating on the margins of the triumphant, male-dominated rational order. Feminist critics have also noted that throughout the West, traditional beliefs in the supernatural were closely allied with women's knowledge of and predominance in matters of reproductive health and childbirth, self-help practices whose functions were gradually usurped by the male medical corps beginning in the early modern era and extending through the late nineteenth and early twentieth centuries.[24] Seen in the *longue durée,* then, while Vichy's energetic prosecution of the Giraud case diverged significantly from the more enlightened and progressive stances of the republican regime it supplanted, it can also be seen in the long purview as a continuation of modern patriarchy's attempted erasure of women's spheres of influence, authority, and autonomy.

Perhaps as a result of his own phallogocentrism (a term that Jacques Derrida defines as the assertion of rationality-bound "male firstness"),[25] Chabrol occults the numerous traces of the popular cosmology that are evinced in the Giraud case and makes the feminine network into which his protagonist taps in order to obtain clients a purely eroticized one that exists chiefly to serve male sexual desires and interests. Rather than consorting spiritually and, of course, commercially with female deviners, as did Marie-Louise Giraud, Chabrol's Marie Latour cultivates the network permitting her to market her illicit trade through her friendship with the prostitute, Lulu. Consonant with Chabrol's claim that French women romped while their men were away slaving in Germany or suffering as prisoners of war, most of Latour's clients in *Une Affaire de femmes* are those who have had pre- or extramarital "accidents" with German soldiers and, Chabrol suggests, with any other Tom, Dick, or Harry roaming the Occupation landscape. Although married women seeking to limit family size also figured among Giraud's clients, Chabrol focuses far greater attention on the erotic escapades and deceit in which women were supposed to have massively engaged while the Germans were plundering the country and pummeling the male population. In so doing, he activates much the same misogynist impulse at work during the postwar purges, in the early stages of which countless women were stripped naked, shorn, and then paraded before a taunting public for their "horizontal collaboration" with the occupying forces.

Marie Latour's initial acquisition of Ginette's phonograph and the relative ease with which her skills increase her cash earnings unfetters a craving for material possessions and exposes an insatiable lack that compels this woman to take ever greater risks, about the legal consequences of which she remains remarkably insouciant. Much like Louis Malle's protagonist in *Lacombe Lucien* (1974), the young peasant upstart who is blinded by the spectacular fruits of his collaborationist labors and remains entirely oblivious to the political implications of these deeds, Latour is also singularly naive about matters related to the political sphere, most particularly the relationship between her family-planning activities and their subversion of the ideological imperatives of the moment. As a female counterpart to Malle's parvenu, however, Marie Latour is decidedly less sympathetic, because in her avarice and *arrivisme* she not only strives to transgress the bounds of social class but, more important, defies the abnegation of self that in our culture, Julia Kristeva argues, is a central feature of the experience of motherhood but also an essential component of the reproduction of human culture.[26] Yet Marie Latour's selfhood is one that obstinately refuses to be forgotten, and it is this resolute refusal to allow her self and her desires to be effaced by the paternalism of her society and her times that makes this ordinary, not particularly likable, woman such an intriguing personage in the history of struggle for reproductive rights.

As long as her practices are confined within the space of the feminine—in this context, the kitchen in which she performs abortions when her husband is away—Marie's legal risks are in fact minimal, for in the end, such activities on the margins of the law actually serve a useful purpose, providing a space in the interstices for extrainstitutional male sexual gratification (rooms she rents by the hour to Lulu and other prostitutes) and offering her services for eliminating the by-products of such illicit sexual activity (abortion).[27] It is when her ambitions and desires overextend those bounds, however, that she runs an ever-increasing risk of meeting her demise. Although he is clearly emasculated, not only by his wife's callous disregard for his sexual needs but also by her stunning success in providing creature comforts for the family, Latour's husband Paul is perfectly content to benefit from his wife's entrepreneurial talents as long as he retains sexual control of her body, albeit in a decidedly impotent form. That is, as long as he retains a degree of mastery over her sexual conduct, which he closely monitors in his absence through the gaze of his son, from whom he pries the details of his mother's daily activities, he is loath to forsake the riches deriving from her illicit exploits. His childlike ineptitude is underscored not only by his lack of steady employment and pajama-clad days spent dillydallying in the house, but also by the endless hours he spends playing cutouts, a hobby whose trenchant features recurrently invoke his own emasculation at the hands of his very determined and resourceful wife but also presage her final fate at the hands of the state: death by guillotine.

The metaphor of castration is, as I have now amply suggested, an important rhetorical feature in this film. It figures in the husband's incessant scissors play, his indolent passivity as it is contrasted with his wife's industrious bustling about, in her singularly undeferential attitude toward his male being and authority, and, of course, in the severance of uterus and fetus occurring in the abortions themselves. The imagery of castration is also a key element in one of the film's most important segments, in which the community is gathered for a highly ritualized game of slaughter in which the winner is to be awarded a sumptuous goose, a rarified foodstuff that is clearly intended by the Occupation authorities overseeing the spectacle to anesthetize the sense of generalized privation wrought by their wholesale pillaging of French resources. The sport consists of arming participants with a saber and fitting them with an oversized papier-mâché headdress depicting Mother Goose. With their vision obstructed by the towering mask, a series of contestants attempt in one fell swoop to behead the fowl, with the successful party winning the prized object. This scene presents a semiotically dense visual metaphor connoting at once the humiliation and threat to his masculinity Latour's husband has experienced in the family, the gelding of French national honor and independence by the victorious Nazi Huns, and, once again, Latour's own decapitation at the close of the film. The scene also plays significantly on the unconscious anxieties of the culture at large, for the spectacle staged here presents male characters donning the guise of a presumably benevolent maternal figure of childhood lore, who, in terrifying phallic fashion, skillfully brandishes a deadly, dismembering weapon.

Replete with castration and oedipal angst as well as sacrificial catharsis, the ceremony effectively confounds a multiplicity of gender traits and parental identifications in a manner that, at least on the unconscious level, is apt to strike terror in the heart of spectators reduced by the Occupation forces to the status of helpless children. At the same time, however, the ritual also allows for a release or purging of that affect through the collective beholding of a creature of delicacy's masterful slaughter. Most important, the scene doubly occults the source of the political violence to which the society itself was being systematically subjected by masking the Germans as benevolent, generous caretakers of the population and by, quite literally, disguising their French lackeys, for the individual who exhibits the greatest skill and savage finesse in slaying the goose turns out to be a suave but sadistic collaborationist rogue. The scene concludes with all participants applauding his dexterous performance and promptly returning to normal routines wherein the spectacle's latent political content remains effectively repressed.

Amazingly, overt manifestations of the systemic political violence practiced by the occupying forces and the collaborationist French regime rarely impinge upon the consciousness and daily lives of Chabrol's characters. The two notable exceptions to this are the café owner's reference to Rachel's deportation by the "Fritz" and one very disturbing scene in which a young man desperately attempts to escape arrest by flinging himself from a second-story window, only to be shot dead by authorities before a crowd of petrified onlookers. The intrusion of such violence into Marie Latour's seemingly carefree, and by this time thoroughly hedonistic, daily existence momentarily shatters the illusion of normalcy she has, as an ordinary French citizen, been precariously able to maintain. In historical terms, such insouciance is entirely conceivable prior to 1942, the year of "La Relève" and the institution in France of the Final Solution, which began the mass, and highly visible, gathering and deportation of the country's Jewish population.[28] Shielding one's consciousness from the brute realities and rapidly worsening political conditions was no doubt also hindered by Germany's November 1942 military invasion of what had previously been the unoccupied zone and by its move the following February to begin forced labor conscription in the form of the STO. By November 1943, 1,400,000 French men *and women* (a historical fact that Chabrol conveniently overlooks in his statement about the period) had been coerced into laboring in German armament factories, circumstances that undoubtedly altered the daily routines in many French communities and that, in some cases, spurred recalcitrant youths to join the underground resistance gathering momentum in the countryside.

Chabrol signifies the brutal repression unleashed by German and French authorities by including in his narrative a dramatic scene in which an individual courageously catapults himself from architectural heights in order to attempt escape, a choice that, when compared once again with the Szpiner text, is quite revealing of subtle gender dynamics at work in his text. This scene in fact closely resembles an episode in Szpiner's account in which a young woman who had sought an abortion from Giraud committed suicide by throwing herself from a window when she was about to be arrested by Vichy authorities, preferring self-inflicted death to the humiliation of having an adulterous liaison and subsequent abortion publicly exposed and condemned. But the desperation of women subjected to such police coercion is given no expression in the film, except as it relates to Latour's individual and seemingly unique circumstances. Yet Chabrol appropriates this textual material and transforms it into the death-defying gesture of a freedom-seeking individual whose identity goes unnamed and the circumstances of whose arrest remain unspecified, thereby representing a generic, and predictably male, victim of the regime's terror.

Evidence of Chabrol's male-centered pathos in a text presumably foregrounding the plight of women (i.e., "une affaire *de femmes*") is also discernible in another factual detail in the Szpiner narrative that the director distorts in what is plainly an effort to implicate men in the victimization suffered as a result of Vichy's reactionary family policies. In one of the film's most eloquent and moving scenes, Chabrol gives voice to the deep sorrow and trauma of a young impoverished married woman who is overwhelmed by the reproductive chaos in her life, a voice that would surely have gone unheard and unheeded in the male-dominated institutions shaping her destiny. After unsuccessfully attempting to induce an abortion herself by ingesting a host of noxious substances, she comes to Latour seeking assistance in terminating a seventh pregnancy. Riveting in its anguished tone and substance, the woman's brief soliloquy speaks volumes on the physical, psychological, and emotional torment women have tacitly suffered in the solitary confines of the *famille nombreuse*. Falling seriously ill following Latour's procedure, the woman subsequently dies as a result either of Latour's intervention or of her own frantic, self-mutilating attempts to terminate the pregnancy, a cause that is never determined. Several weeks later, Latour receives an unannounced visit from the woman's sister-in-law, who informs her of the woman's death and, even more tragically, of her husband's grief-stricken frenzy, which compelled him to commit suicide by hurling himself before an oncoming train. In standard female self-abnegation, the woman righteously adds that she herself will be taking on

the responsibility of raising her orphaned nieces and nephews, clearly recognizing the burden as the will of God ("It is the Lord who has sent me this hardship"). Representing Vichy's feminine and maternal ideal, the sister-in-law's
moralizing discourse introduces a crack into Latour's armor of defenses and
denial, for the words of this model of Vichy womanhood haunt her for the
remainder of the film, leading her to begin secretly questioning if "babies in
their mother's womb have a soul."

While the high drama and pathos of this scene drive home the very salient
point that children, women, and men all suffer in varying degrees from the
rigid and oppressive codes of conduct patriarchy imposes on its subjects, the
historical fact remains that this woman's death was actually the result of
makeshift practices necessitated by the criminalization of abortion. What is
more, the suicide of the husband who was so traumatized by the loss of his
loved one was, in reality, a pure figment of Chabrol's imagination. As Szpiner
notes, the spouse of "Louise M.," the woman on whom the film's character was
based, served as a prime prosecution witness in Giraud's trial. That Chabrol
gratuitously martyrs yet another man in his film is, cumulatively speaking, unquestionably meaningful, especially when one considers the wealth of possibilities Szpiner's text offers for representing the multiplicity of ways in which the
numerous women prosecuted in this case had been victimized through their
structural entanglement in a complex web of paternalistic institutional practices and cultural norms.

Marie Latour's initial motive for practicing abortions seems to have been
that of simply improving the material conditions of everyday life. In her quest
to fill the lack that marriage, motherhood, female friendship, and increasing
material wealth fail to satiate, her desires ultimately compel her beyond the
pale of tolerated female misconduct. Having seriously underestimated her husband's wrath and the legal arsenal he might levy against her in retaliation, she
seeks to placate him sexually by inducing her maid, a prime symbol of her newfound upward mobility, to act as her surrogate while she, in turn, gallivants
with the collaborationist thug of goose-slaying fame whose overt misogyny
does little to inhibit her adulterous passion. Armed with his cutouts and the
impotent rage of a poor cuckold, Latour's husband recognizes that he has lost
all mastery of the situation and proceeds to craft an anonymous letter to local
authorities in which he informs them of his wife's clandestine commerce and of
her whereabouts.[29]

Although Chabrol portrays his protagonist throughout much of the film in
an unbecoming light, both personal and political, when she is drawn into
Vichy's juridical web and ordered to stand trial before a high court in Paris

(a court she naively believed to be reserved for communist subversives), Chabrol swiftly and unambiguously reconfigures Marie Latour as the sacrificial lamb of Vichy's quest to revalorize "Travail, Famille, Patrie [Work, Family, Fatherland]."[30] The novelty of the regime's view of abortion as a capital crime against the French state and the French race is effectively conveyed in the astonishment with which Marie's lawyers and cellmates alike receive the news that she will be tried before the most draconian (and politicized) court in the land rather than treated, as in the normal course of such affairs, as the perpetrator of a relatively minor infraction of the criminal code. The obscene hypocrisy of this new political and juridical posture is not lost on the upscale Parisian lawyers involved in Latour's defense, servants of the state who recognize that the decision to guillotine a woman for a crime as commonplace as abortion, while other branches of the same government were handing Jewish children by the thousands over to the Gestapo, was a matter of pure political expediency, an ideal opportunity to display the rigor of the New Order, which was not, unlike the effeminate Third Republic, loath to execute a woman.

Unlike those who choose to view the Occupation legacy from the perspective of what Robert Paxton calls the "shield theory," the notion that Vichy systematically adopted measures designed to protect French society from the rigors of Nazi rule to which other occupied countries had been subjected, Chabrol very ably identifies in the final portions of the film a far more insidious process at work in the politics of collaboration. In spite of Chabrol's often skewed vision and questionable treatment of the gender problematics in this case, he offers an insightful, truculent assessment of the general thrust of Vichy's aims in which, politically speaking, there are no holds barred. With candor, verve, and considerable dramatic tension, his denouement forcefully reveals a seedy political underside of opportunism and ruthlessness with which the conservative regime seized upon the defeat and the occupier's presence to carry out a vendetta against internal ideological foes who had prevailed in the immediate prewar years and whose egalitarian and universalist ideals it reviled.

It is only following her imprisonment in Paris that Latour, plainly disoriented and overwhelmed by the seriousness of her situation, begins to recognize forms of oppression she has suffered as a consequence of her class status and gender position, an awareness she has been conspicuously lacking up to this point. It is a scene in which, from the tenebrous depths of her prison cell, she lucidly identifies the inequities of a social system that forces women from the lower ranks of the society to produce children while divesting them of the human and material resources required to care for them, muttering, "C'est facile de pas faire de saloperies quand on est riche [It's easy not to get your hands dirty when you're rich]." She also very astutely observes that all of the individuals standing in judgment of her are men ("Il n'y a que des hommes là-dedans! . . . Qu'est-ce que tu veux qu'ils y comprennent, les hommes? [There are only men in there! . . . How can you expect men to comprehend?]," individuals who are, in her mind, constitutionally incapable of comprehending the plight of women faced with such dire life circumstances and severely restricted options for securely raising children while retaining their own human dignity.

This scene is followed by one in which the lawyer arguing her case and the government's prosecutor presenting the charges before the court discuss the possibility of showing this young, uneducated wife and mother a measure of leniency, an eerie exchange in which ideological strands of paternalism, misogyny, racism, and authoritarianism are meticulously woven into a tapestry of cultural and political despotism. Marie Latour, the state's advocate reasons, is but one morsel of the putrefying limbs on the social body that must be mercilessly severed and sacrificed for the greater good of regenerating the health and vigor of the Fatherland. The chilling sadism displayed in this scene by one of the presiding officials in the case appears to have a ripple effect throughout the entire penal system, manifesting itself in the austere disciplinary rigor of the nuns overseeing the prison regime and, after her death sentence, even in the demeanor of Latour's fellow inmates, one of whom gleefully mimes a throat-slitting gesture as Latour is being transferred in shackles through prison corridors. This latter caper is, I would argue, not entirely gratuitous, because it inter- and subtextually introduces into the film's signifying terrain another important dimension of Vichy's project of hygienic social amputation: the deportation of more than seventy-five thousand Jews to death camps in Poland between 1942 and 1944. The inmate's gesture is, in fact, identical to that which Polish peasants performed for the trainloads of unsuspecting Jews from across Europe about to be ushered into the Third Reich's gas chambers. One of the most sinister and haunting images of unadulterated human brutality captured in Claude Lanzmann's 1986 film *Shoah*, its flashing recurrence in the similarly exclusionary context of Chabrol's film two years later is, in all likelihood, no mere coincidence. Read intertextually, the gesture instantaneously invokes the memory of Vichy's numerous "other" sacrificial objects and invites viewers aware of and alert to the reference to establish systemic links between the logic of the execution they are about to witness and the fate of other social "undesirables" sacrificed during the war on the alter of Vichy's ideological trinity: "Travail, Famille, Patrie."

How, one might wonder, did Vichy reconcile its direct complicity in deporting more than ten thousand fully birthed Jewish children to what was widely acknowledged to be certain death and, with the full participation of its head of state, the execution of Marie-Louis Giraud for her twenty-six "crimes" against the human embryo—a mind-boggling contradiction by any standard of political logic?[31] Chiefly, it would seem, by forging a new, racially imbued sense of national identity in which Jewish children, be they of recently immigrated or native-born parents, were henceforth to be considered non-French, aliens who were of little use in bolstering the nation's lagging population statistics, and even less so in reversing the "moral decline" that vile "foreign" influences had introduced into the society in the decadent years of the Popular Front, the era of "Blum et consorts." Moreover, in founding the collaborationist Etat Français and in promoting its National Revolution, Vichy reactionaries sought not only to preserve a thread of national honor in the face of a crushing military defeat; they were equally intent upon surgically removing all agents of the heady democratizing "excesses" of the Popular Front era, during which workers, women, and "foreign" minorities, had, much like Marie Latour, all somehow forgotten the place of their subaltern selves in society.

Most historians would concur that the anti-Semitic and what Miranda Pollard forthrightly describes as the antifeminist policies pursued by the Vichy regime had antecedents in and built upon both the demographic and antiforeign initiatives of its more tolerant, republican predecessor and were aimed at excluding women and minorities from economic life while strictly limiting their forms of cultural expression and participation. It is perhaps in considering closely the case of Marie-Louise Giraud and the desperate circumstances of the women she encountered in her brief paramedical career that we can appreciate in stark historical terms not only the momentous gains women have achieved in the postwar era, but also the significance of incremental losses that should, Giraud's case and its historical setting remind us, be a matter of concern to all and not simply "une affaire de femmes."

Notes

1. Jean-Pierre Azéma, *De Munich à la libération, 1938–44* (Paris: Seuil, 1978), 168. For a more thorough discussion of this topic, see Paula Schwartz, "*Partisanes* and Gender Politics in Vichy France," *French Historical Studies* 16 (Spring 1989): 126–51. Unless otherwise noted, all translations in this chapter are my own.

2. Azémar, *De Munich*, 93.

3. See, for instance, Robert Aron's classic *Histoire de Vichy* (Paris: Fayard, 1954); Henri Amouroux, *Grande Histoire des Français sous l'Occupation,* 8 vols. (Paris: Laffont, 1976-88); Robert O. Paxton, *Vichy France: Old Guard, New Order, 1940–44* (New York: Knopf, 1972).

4. See especially Michael R. Marrus and Robert O. Paxton, "Massacre of the Innocents," in *Vichy France and the Jews* (New York: Schocken, 1983), 263–70. Marrus and Paxton point out that in both the occupied and unoccupied zones, French officials actually took the initiative in seeing that Jewish children were included in convoys headed east, pressing Theodor Dannecker, SS commander of "Final Solution" operations in France, to procure authorization to begin deporting children as soon as possible. Adolf Eichmann granted this request by telephone on 20 July 1942. "Vichy," they explain, "suggested that children be sent along with the adults, even before the the Nazis were ready to accept them. During 1942, according to Serge Klarsfeld's estimate, 1,032 children under six years of age were sent to Auschwitz from France, along with 2,464 between thirteen and seventeen. Over 6,000 children in that year alone" (262). Marrus and Paxton further note that in the occupied zone, beginning in August 1942, "it was the French police who took the initiative in allocating children to specific convoys leaving France for the east," noting that in this early phase, "Germans were little involved in the deportation of children, and there are even signs they disapproved of it" (265).

5. Francis Szpiner, *Une Affaire de femmes: Paris 1943, Exécution d'une avorteuse* (Paris: Balland, 1986).

6. See Henri Michel, "La Grande Misère des Parisiens ou quatre années de vaches squelettiques," in *Paris Allemand* (Paris: Albin Michel, 1981), 208–80.

7. See Miranda Pollard, "Women in the National Revolution," in *Vichy France and Resistance: Ideology and Culture*, ed. R. Kedward and R. Austin (Sydney: Croom Helm, 1985). One should take note here of the specious character of Pétain's oft-iterated assertion that the defeat was attributable to the paucity of "arms and children [trop peu d'enfants, trop peu d'armes]." In terms of both troops and military hardware, the French and Germans were, in fact, on an equal numerical footing at the outbreak of the war. Azéma, *De Munich*, 70.

8. Pollard, "Women in the National Revolution."

9. Quoted in ibid., 42.

10. Robert Paxton points out that Vichy's family policy actually continued and accelerated the reforms initiated by its republican antecedents in Edouard Daladier's 1939 Family Code, which sought by various governmental measures to foster the growth of "large families [familles nombreuses]." Vichy's expansion of these efforts along more traditional, Catholic, and "organicist" lines leads Paxton to conclude that the conservative regime was most eager to see "women barefoot and pregnant in the kitchen." For further discussion of the continuity and changes in Vichy's family policies, see Paxton, *Vichy France*, 165–68.

11. Historians Paxton and Michel both observe that in spite of the material hardships and deprivation faced by the French population, the birthrate actually began to climb under the Occupation. See ibid., 355–56; Michel, *Paris Allemand*, 260–68.

12. Szpiner's text can be considered historically factual in that it is based on a close reading of the court records from the Giraud case. Yet, in its blurring of the conventional distinctions between history and fiction, the narrative strategy the author adopts in reviving the case and its historical setting is as analytically intriguing as the subject matter itself. For instance, Szpiner makes frequent use of free indirect discourse in a clear effort to heighten the legal drama and human pathos of the events described. He also makes ample use of direct and indirect discourse, which effectively obfuscates the

fact that the utterances and thoughts he attributes to his characters are of his own invention and generated from a position of feigned objectivity closely paralleling that of classical nineteenth-century realist fiction. Furthermore, although he has obviously consulted the judicial records from this case, his text has a vexing absence of footnotes or other precise references to the actual documents being cited or upon which his narrative is constructed. The sole indication of the author's historical or methodological rigor is a brief appendage of secondary bibliographic sources relating to the history of Vichy and its legal institutions along with a note of thanks to historians, judicial archivists, and other consultants in the project. The following passage is a good example of the type of narration that pervades Szpiner's text: "In her cell, with irons on her feet, Marie-Louise Giraud comes to. Dazed. The judge's words resounding in her head: she is condemned to death. And she is alive. She has remarked a change in the guards' attitude toward her. In some of the nuns' eyes, she already reads her demise. She thinks of her children. She examines her new cell." Szpiner, *Une Affaire*, 65. The passage makes no mention of documents left by Giraud that might testify to her state of mind or her innermost thoughts following her death sentence, and it is thus clear that the author is engaging here in the production of fiction, again, as a means of dramatizing the historical event. In order to gauge the extent to which Szpiner's account reveals or distorts historical "truth," one would have to consult the primary archival resources to determine what surplus of meaning his narrative strategy brings to the corpus of police records and legal documents.

13. See Stephen Schaefer's review "An Unblinking View," *Chicago Tribune*, 11 February 1990.

14. Simone de Beauvoir, *Le Deuxième Sexe* (Paris: Gallimard, 1949), 377–80.

15. Szpiner, *Une Affaire*, 116–17.

16. As a young adult, Giraud had on several occasions been arrested for theft and had served a prison sentence for one of her convictions.

17. Beauvoir, *Le Deuxième Sexe*, 372–73.

18. Ibid., 330–43.

19. That Marie-Louise Giraud actually spent time in prison prior to her career as an abortionist necessarily qualifies this assertion, as she would presumably have had greater access to such illicit knowledge by virtue of her previous contact with the world of female criminality.

20. Chabrol confines his representation of the Giraud case to the activities of one woman, thus reinforcing the notion that Latour, acting principally out of personal greed, operated alone. Several other women were in fact indicted with Giraud and were given relatively light sentences (twenty years at hard labor) for their complicity in operating the clandestine network. All of the surviving women who had had abortions performed by Giraud were also prosecuted and convicted. See Szpiner, *Une Affaire*, 115–65.

21. See Robert Muchembled, *Culture populaire et culture des élites dans la France moderne* (Paris: Flammarion, 1978). See also Natalie Zemon Davis, *Society and Culture in Early Modern France* (Stanford, Calif.: Stanford University Press, 1975); Peter Burke, *Popular Culture in Early Modern Europe* (New York: Harper & Row, 1978).

22. See Robert Muchembled, *Sorcières, justice et société au 16e et 17e siècles* (Paris: Imago, 1987). For a thorough discussion of the French state's increasingly energetic as-

sertion of control over women's bodies and lives in the early modern period, see Sarah Hanley, "Engendering the State: Family Formation and State Building in Early Modern France," *French Historical Studies* 16 (Spring 1989): 4–27.

23. See Eloïse Mozzani, *Magie et superstition de la fin de l'ancien régime à la restauration* (Paris: Robert Laffont, 1988).

24. See Barbara Ehrenreich and Deirdre English, *Witches, Midwives and Nurses: A History of Women Healers* (Old Westbury, N.Y.: Feminist Press, 1973).

25. See J. Derrida and Christie McDonald, "Choreographies," *Diacritics* 12 (Summer 1982): 69.

26. See Julia Kristeva, "Stabat Mater," in *The Kristeva Reader*, ed. Toril Moi (New York: Basil Blackwell, 1986), 183.

27. For a discussion of the "positive" (i.e., productive) effects of criminality and its function in maintaining the societal status quo, see Michel Foucault, *Discipline and Punish*, trans. Alan Sheridan (New York: Vintage-Random, 1979).

28. "La Relève," an institutionalized relay game of sorts, was a program instituted in early 1942 shortly after Laval returned to power, in which one prisoner of war was to be released for every three French workers who "volunteered" to work in the Reich. The catch, however, was that Vichy officials were able to recruit only 150,000 skilled craftsmen among a total of 400,000 workers who initially volunteered for the program, so that only 50,000 prisoners, eight times fewer than "promised" by the Germans, were actually released. See Paxton, *Vichy France,* 280–98, and Azéma, *De Munich,* 190–297, for an extensive discussion of the numerous changes in the collaborationist pact from 1942 on.

29. The letter denouncing Giraud was, in fact, anonymous, but it appears to have contained detailed knowledge of the household and the whereabouts of the abortion devices, which police immediately located and seized at the time of her arrest. This suggests that it was either Giraud's husband or her maid, both of whom would have had access to such information, who authored the letter. According to Szpiner, the identity of the informant was never determined, and the letter of denunciation later disappeared from the police records and judicial dossier. See Szpiner, *Une Affaire,* 108–11.

30. The judicial body charged with hearing the Giraud case was a newly instituted structure whose legitimacy was highly contested by long-standing members of the French judiciary, many of whom, according to Szpiner, refused appointments to the court. The State Tribunal was the successor to the Special Section of the Court of Appeals, which had dealt with political prisoners and members of the resistance, hence Latour's understanding that the court had been reserved for trying communists. Although itself notoriously draconian, the Special Section was composed of seasoned members of the judiciary who were willing to take loyalty oaths to Marshal Pétain's "Etat français." The Special Section proved, however, to be unwilling to disregard French judicial precedent to the extent Vichy officials desired in their vigorous prosecution of the country's "terrorists." The court was thus disbanded and replaced with the more compliant State Tribunal, which sent countless Jews and members of the Resistance to their swift execution. It was before this court that Giraud was ordered to stand trial in 1943. The new, far more stringent laws governing abortion went into effect in February 1942, just after Louise M. died. Ironically, had she been denounced and prosecuted at that time, Giraud would have escaped the rigors of the new law and the new

Tribunal d'Etat. Subsequent to that date, her activities were considered a crime against the individual (the unborn child), the French race, and the French state. It was this definition that created a symmetry between the resistance activities and sabotage carried out by communists and other "terrorists" challenging the legitimacy of both the German occupiers and their Vichy vassals and those of the abortionist Marie-Louise Giraud, whose family planning activities had struck at the heart of Vichy's paternalistic and hierarchical notions of nationhood and statehood.

31. Pétain declined the defense's appeal for clemency requesting that the head of state commute Giraud's death sentence and himself declined to sign the document granting a stay of execution. Pétain's refusal to commute the sentence cleared the way for Giraud's execution on 30 July 1943.

8 / *L'Histoire ressuscitée:* Jewishness and Scapegoating in Julien Duvivier's *Panique*

Florianne Wild

A number of well-known narrative films released over the past twenty years have as their explicit content depictions of the traumatic events associated with the occupation of France by Nazi Germany, a threatening moment in nationhood that led the French under the Vichy government to attempt to define their identity in terms of whom they could exclude from their population. These films, which often treat the issues of collaboration and the fate of the Jews in the France of 1940–45, began to fill a gap in the French memory that opened immediately following the Liberation, an amnesic lapse that has been, in the near decade since the Klaus Barbie trial, explored almost obsessively. Such films as *Lacombe Lucien* and *Au Revoir les enfants* (Louis Malle), *Le Dernier Métro* (François Truffaut), and *Une Affaire de femmes* (Claude Chabrol) are set during what is recognizably the historical period of the Occupation. If we may transfer to the filmed narrative Michel de Certeau's analysis of the "historiographic project" as it applies to the novel, these films appear both "realistic" and "historical" because their discourse is furnished with a referentiality that makes the discourse "expressive" and legitimizes it by means of the "real."[1] Their credibility is founded in what de Certeau calls a "supposed knowledge" that meticulously links them to "realistic" economic, social, psychological, and ideological structures: their discourse does not appear separate from its referents. They are thus authorized as historical by the events they are believed to explicate or to signify.[2] These, then, are works that carry out the "historiographic project" as it applies to film.

178

Other films less studied by professional scholars may not feature obvious historical settings, but may nonetheless be located at an intersection of anthropology, psychoanalysis, and film history that serves to illuminate the violent human interactions that make history possible. Such a film is Julien Duvivier's *Panique* (1946), which clearly sets forth the mechanisms of violence in its relation to scapegoating. A woman is murdered in a vacant lot of an urban neighborhood. A resident known as Monsieur Hire (Michel Simon), deemed different from others by virtue of his solitary life and distant manner, comes to be suspected of the murder. He is then framed by the real murderer, Alfred (Paul Bertrand), and Alfred's girlfriend, Alice (Viviane Romance), who together contrive to entrap Hire, using Alice as bait. Invited to Hire's room, Alice plants the murdered woman's handbag. With the suspicions of the neighborhood now confirmed, outrage and panic spread until, in the end, Hire is cornered by an angry mob who drive him to a rooftop, where he falls to his death. In the penultimate sequence, a photograph taken by Hire and discovered in his pocket after his fatal plunge reveals the identity of the real murderer.

What is played out in the narrative, then, are the dynamics of mob misrule and the expulsion of a scapegoat in set decors that include the requisite *boucherie, crémerie*, the "Hôtel Au Petit Caporal" with its café bar and terrace, church, and "Lavoir de la Fraternité." What is established mimetically, then, is a generic *Paris populaire* of the 1940s, a setting made familiar to us by the novels of Louis-Ferdinand Céline as well as the films of Marcel Carné and Jacques Prévert: a Parisian *quartier* of petit-bourgeois shopkeepers preoccupied with the discipline of their large families, their surgical operations or the "lymphatic conditions" of their wives, and the selling of veal cutlets and Camembert. The flora and fauna of the café bar, drifters and *piliers de cabaret* alike, have been typfied in the pages of works by Pierre MacOrlan, Francis Carco, and Marcel Aymé.

Situating *Panique* in History

In its diegesis, however, the film is devoid of any points of historical reference: the years of the Occupation (1940–44) are in no way alluded to. Although atemporality and essentialism are two modes we now associate with Vichy ideology, Duvivier's purpose here, rather than seeking a "timeless Frenchness" in which viewers might comfortably situate themselves, seems rather to provoke disquiet and unease. Despite the refusal of historical specificity or of any precise reference to the Jewishness of the main character, it would seem that what is being broached in the film is the disgrace of the French during the Occupation.

Duvivier's considerable reputation as a director allowed him to leave France for Hollywood during the Occupation years, and *Panique* was the first film he made upon his return. The 1946 date of the film, contemporaneous with the liberation of the Nazi concentration camps in Germany and in Central Europe, tempts us to consider what the imprint of history on this story of scapegoating might be, particularly given that the means to any overt or explicit topical historical foothold are withheld. Conspicuous by their absence are any markers of the era by way of calendars, newspapers, or radio broadcasts on the sound track. Shot entirely on studio sets, the film lacks the now-precious documentary value of Renoir films of the interwar years such as *Boudu sauvé des eaux* (*Boudu Saved from Drowning*) and *Le Crime de M. Lange* (*The Crime of M. Lange*), with their glimpses of 1930s Parisians buying newspapers at the kiosks, hailing taxis, and hurrying along the Quai Voltaire. Besides being locked into set decors, *Panique* is constrained by the classical studio practices of a cinematography in which camera follows dialogue, and the film thus seems to forestall the intricacy of playful analysis afforded by Renoir's depth of field and constantly mobile camera. Despite the enclosure of *Panique* in sets and scenario, however, there are moments when sound, image, and graphics collide in fortuitous ways that cause the film to exceed its studio boundaries.

Reasons for the lack of obvious historical references are a matter of conjecture. In 1946, Gaullist policy was attempting to bring about a hasty reunification of the French immediately after the Liberation and its consequent *épuration*, or punishment of French collaborators. This "putting behind" or consignment to oblivion of what amounted to a near civil war necessarily entailed the whitewashing of long-standing French anti-Semitism, which had made possible a French complicity in Nazi ideology and the carrying out of Nazi programs.[3] Given the political climate of the day, it is possible that Duvivier and his screenwriter, Charles Spaak, intended to exclude from their film all references to Jewishness and to the Occupation. *Panique* at first seems to refer to no other world than the one it is producing. However, further scrutiny reveals it to be among the first, after the Liberation, to suggest that the French would have to come to terms with their recent history.

The first shot presents the scene of the murder of Mlle Noblet, capturing a space midway between *terrain vague* and *place publique*, where vagrant graybeards asleep on benches are driven off by a policeman on his beat to make way for a traveling carnival. Trucks and wagons lumber heavily in the background as the space is cleared of its nocturnal human residue. They bear the names of the yet-to-be assembled machinery and decor of the carnival rides and shooting attractions: the TIR DES NATIONS, the TOURBILLON IMPERIAL, and the BOBSLEIGH, promising the populace thrills, chills, and ersatz violence.

Graphics in the Field of Vision

As the sequence continues, M. Hire is seen returning home by bus at the end of the workday. In a medium long shot, the bus driver cranks the handle that changes the destination of the bus from VILLEJUIF to GARE DE L'EST. The only two markers of place in the film, these names, denoting a town in Val-de-Marne near Paris and the railway station that serves as place of departure for points east, demonstrate how the graphics in the film will tend to turn us toward the traumatic historical events of the recent past, namely, the exclusion by deportation of Jews from France. The panning camera next frames Michel Simon in the medium shot that will be crucial for our viewing of him as the moving figure who "rewrites" the film while moving through it. As he passes to the rear of the bus, behind his head is clearly visible, in large block letters, a painted wall advertisement for the *apéritif* SUZE. In the 1940s, as in the present day, financial backing of a film by a firm in exchange for product publicity was common practice; thus, another manufacturer of *vin doux* had paid for Alexander Trauner's sets for Marcel Carné's *Le Jour se lève* (*Daybreak*) (1939) so that Jean Gabin could wander disconsolately across an urban visual field prominently displaying DUBONNET. The letters SUZE are left hanging in the air until we encounter their phonetic duplicate in a later scene.

Hire is framed next in the *boucherie*, buying a cutlet and remarking dryly that the previous one "hadn't enough blood." The butcher fulminates against the arrival of the carnival, a rival enterprise competing for the appetites of his clientele. "They're going to stuff themselves on sweets and cotton candy! *There ought to be a law against that!*" If we refuse the synchrony of dialogue and image that is forcing upon us the verisimilitude of a narrative, and perceive instead the clash and mingle of dialogue, subtitles, and objects in the frame, the butcher's words might just as well refer to the black-bearded figure with broad-brimmed Homburg who occupies the frame to his left. Will Hire indeed be crucified for his refusal to abide by the Christian "farewell to meat" (*carnevale*)? In the *crémerie*, Hire inspects a Camembert as another customer bursts into frame to announce that a corpse has been discovered. Over the brouhaha of the clientele, the sound track voice of the proprietress accompanies and, in a sense, provides a legend for the medium close shot of Hire: "Dans notre quartier! Il n'y a plus de moralité! Plus de religion! Nulle part! [In our neighborhood! There's no more morality! No more religion! Anywhere!]" Hire's response, "Je me demande si le Brie [l'abri = shelter] n'est pas mieux fait [I wonder if the Brie isn't better aged]," becomes understandable as, roughly, "Give me shelter!"

The Sacrificial Crisis Begins

The curiosity seekers who rush to view the prime spectacle of Mlle Noblet's corpse enact the beginning of what René Girard has termed the sacrificial crisis, in which a loss of difference or distinction signals the breakdown of the social order or communitarian harmony.[4] For Girard, differences among individuals establish their identity and their mutual relationships. Difference within a social order is lost with the initial transgressive act of violence, which erases a taboo and makes possible something that was forbidden. As members of the community become aggressively suspicious of one another and subject to unrestrained and undirected violence, difference is further eroded; each becomes the double of all the others. "As all are violent, any one can substitute for any of the others, all the enemy brothers that each member strives to banish from the community."[5] In Girard's well-known and much-discussed account, the "enemy brothers" then seek an immediate cure by hurling themselves blindly into the search for a scapegoat. They convince themselves that a lone individual, who can be disposed of, is at fault. Though a motive for the murder of Mlle Noblet is lacking at this point, the people of the neighborhood begin to imagine one, just as they set about constructing a perpetrator: "Mais qui? Il faut que ce soit un sadique! Un voyou! [But who? It must be a sadist! a hoodlum!]"

The process of the constructing of a suspect in the spectator's mind is both abetted and theorized in a following sequence entirely reminiscent of Fritz Lang's *M* (1931). Hire's shadow climbs the stairs of his building while the mother of a little girl calls to her to come away. Here the filmmaker is building the sense of an unconscious referent through a transfilmic allusion, another element that becomes a ground for the filmic writing of *Panique*. Hire is turned briefly into "M," a scapegoated figure who finds no ideological space in which to exist and is hunted down by an ad hoc confraternity of cops and criminals. Such an intertextual presence serves to flatten narrative "depth" into a surface tension of figures, scenes, and fragments in its eliciting of spectatorial memory. In addition, it constitutes the first play in the cat-and-mouse game by means of which Duvivier will gull the spectator into a state of doubt and unease with respect to the character of Hire, causing the spectatorial position to overlap with the one occupied by the people of the neighborhood.

Image, Dialogue, and Intertextuality

The detective assigned to the case, Michelet, begins his investigation of the murder of Mlle Noblet by interrogating the loners of the neighborhood, in-

cluding M. Hire. Midway through the interrogation of Hire, the camera regis-
ters a moment of hubris and mild humor. Hire, wittier and more grammati-
cally attuned—or literate—than his fellow citizens, is given to displays of linguistic superiority. In response to the police detective's "Où étiez-vous à l'heure
du crime?" he offers, "Pour répondre à votre question, il faudrait que je susse à
quelle heure le crime a été commis." "Que vous sussiez . . ." repeats the detective.[6] This hyperelegant usage, certainly one of the rare instances of an imperfect subjunctive surfacing in cinematic dialogue, detonates doubly on the
sound track. In addition to functioning as a bit of realistic detail in its connotation of linguistic overcorrectness, its homonym, "Süss," also names a murdered Jew, and forces recall of a moment of film history that contemporary
viewers would prefer to forget. *Le Juif Süss*, an infamous "pan-European" production and no doubt the most virulently anti-Semitic film seen on French
screens during the Occupation, is known to present-day audiences mainly because of the clips from it chosen by Marcel Ophuls for *Le Chagrin et la pitié*
(*The Sorrow and the Pity*). The intertitles of *Süss* allege that its events, which include the hanging of a Jew by the Council of Württemberg in 1738, are based
on historical fact.[7] Scarcely a moment of subjective apprehension, then, this
name that floats to the surface of the narrative by means of association and
contingency, actually serves to stage the film's collective unconscious. The
name Süss links up with the letters SUZE, shots of which recur repeatedly
across the image track. A graphic imperative thus emerges from scene to scene,
forming both an unconscious register and a mnemonic command: Süss is what
the viewers must keep remembering.

The uttering of this line of dialogue in the context of an interrogation, the
purpose of which is to determine identity and whereabouts—he is, after all,
Hire, or "here," as well as "higher," connoting the status of the sacred victim—
has the effect of flattening both the linguistic verisimilitude of his declaration, a
locution meaning "I would have to know," and a psychology of character that
would "portray" him as an arrogant speaker given to airy demonstrations of the
imparfait du subjonctif. The difference between sound and image is here conflated to form a rebus, one whose import can be traced through film history in
relation to the modern history of France. It is as if the film were losing conscious
control of its "zero degree" narrative functions in order to betray problems of filiation in film and history. An uncanny irruption of alterity into the scenario,
this sequence effects a sudden blurring of the distinction between fiction and
history. By awakening a memory of genocide at the moment of the liberation of
the concentration camps in the year before *Panique* was produced, it changes
the way we see the film, from fable of scapegoating to allegory of history.

Victimization and Its Historical Recurrence

The force of this moment must be seen in alignment with a founding concept of psychoanalysis, the return of the repressed. If the past is repressed, particularly the events of a past crisis, it returns in the present from which it was excluded, but does so surreptitiously, yet always on the "site" of the original repression. To recognize the return of the repressed, asserts de Certeau, is to see "the past imbricated in the present, one in the place of the other."[8] The historiographic mode, on the other hand, places the past beside the present, with a hierarchical division between them. To adopt a psychoanalytic mode, then, is to recognize the recurrent victimization from which history cannot seem to extricate itself. Thus, the clues fed to a detective named Michelet—itself a compelling historiographical association—lead infallibly to "another" culpability, that of the French nation, in an unexpected evocation of the victimization that made history function in the years between 1940 and 1944.

The carnival that put down its stakes at the beginning of the film is soon in full swing. Early on, Alice (Viviane Romance) and Alfred (Paul Bertrand) are established as partners in crime: Alice, we learn, had taken a rap for her paramour and is recently released from prison. Amid whirling carnival rides, tightrope walkers, and street singers, they consult the fair's *voyante*. When the fortune-teller sees an "older, well-educated man" in Alice's life, one who will meet with a violent end, Alfred suffers an attack of jealousy and is overtaken by the idea of eliminating Hire. Once, on the hotel stairway, Hire had warned Alice about Alfred. Now Alice pays a visit to Hire's office in order to gain his confidence and sound him out. In a library decorated with astrologer's symbols, Hire presents himself as "Dr. Varga," a figure reminiscent of a kabbalistic scholar in possession of hermetic knowledge. In this guise, he composes horoscopes and dispenses advice to those in need. "Is it Dr. Varga or Monsieur Hire you've come to see?" he asks.

Central to the victimary theme elaborated in Girard is the proliferation of doubles, a necessary stage in the selection of a victim. Central too is the essential ambivalence surrounding the victim himself, who is at once sacred and taboo. The crisis of the loss of distinctions (which doubling implies) is symbolized by the names of the two schemers, Alice and Alfred, specularly bound by love eternal and a life of crime. Like the lovers, the two men in this triangle also partake of doubling by virtue of the fact that both are semistrangers, having come from outside the neighborhood. Appearing suddenly in the midst of a tight-knit community, Alfred ingratiates himself by working as a garage mechanic. Hire himself has lived in their midst since he came from "the fourteenth arrondissement" three years previously, but without fully becoming one of them. Although a metonymic relationship exists between him and other members of the community, there is also a distance between them. He is thus the perfect victim, as he is neither too familiar to the community nor too foreign to it. He is close to the *pharmakos* of fifth-century Greece—a fringe being who did not establish or share the social bonds that linked the rest of the participants, and whose status as foreigner or enemy, servile condition, or age prevented him from integrating himself completely in the community.[9] Hire's given name, Désiré, further designates him as victim: a figure held in a mixture of awe and contempt by the neighborhood, he embodies the ambivalence surrounding the victim, who is both a desired and a repugnant object. Finally, he is split into "Dr. Varga" and "Monsieur Hire," and as such emerges as the only character to "realize" the split human subject and its simultaneous potentials for good and evil. Although his behavior, as called for by the role in the film, is consistent and "all of a piece," a recognition of the dark side of the human being is brought to bear in his photographic hobby. His photo collection, which he calls his "gallery of horrors," constitutes a record of social crimes: the laughter of a madwoman ignored and left to fend for herself in the streets, vagrants foraging for food in garbage cans or asleep under the Arc de Triomphe.

When Alfred pays a visit to Hire's office, Hire humiliates him by virtue of his superior strength and presence of mind. Using that transgressive mode of speech, the pun, Hire threatens him with *châtiments capitaux,* or capital punishment, slaps him around, and throws him out. Redoubling his efforts to get rid of Hire, Alfred then attempts to manipulate the people of the neighborhood, who are seen as living between half-truths and superstitions. Among his cronies at the car garage, he contributes to the chaos of suspicions now holding sway in the neighborhood by his account of the "voodoo practices" he divined in Hire's office:

> He has books everywhere. There was a hypnotizing machine and strange gadgets. He hypnotized Mlle Noblet, like the serpent and the rabbit! And what does he do with his camera? He takes photos of people, then pricks the photo. No wonder people are getting sick in the neighborhood!

This kind of playing upon fears of insidious mastery, or mind control, is reminiscent of both the language and the intent of Vichy policy, which, during June–September 1941, established quotas on the number of Jews allowed to practice in various professions. Limits of 2 percent were set for doctors, pharmacists, midwives, architects, and dentists. After his first six months as commissioner-general for Jewish affairs, Xavier Vallat "could boast that 3,000 civil servants were dismissed, along with similar proportions from positions in the press, radio, movies and 'in all the areas where their functions gave them power . . . over minds.'"[10]

Carnival and the Eruption of Sacrificial Violence

Tellingly, both murders in the film take place during the temporary residence of the carnival in the neighborhood. As a social phenomenon, carnival traditionally catches up the everyday world and holds it in a euphoric state, producing, in Girard's words, "a formless and grotesque mixture of things that are normally separate."[11] Such a situation approximates the sacrificial crisis, in which a loss of "normal" differences must be reinstated. The Bakhtinian *carnavalesque* de-emphasizes the darkness of carnival in favor of the idea of salutary transgression consisting in the overturning of traditional values and hierarchies. The "panic" carnival, on the other hand, as it develops in the film, is more akin to that described by Andrew McKenna as "the one that plays on the margins of Ash Wednesday, the Mardi Gras, which is a prelude to the Passion, as Saturnalia was to sacrifice."[12] It is not masks and other simulacra that perform mimesis here; instead, the loss of individualized identity comes about through the spread of a violent desire to single out a victim and immolate him.

The sequence of the bumper cars prefigures the "accidental sacrifice" at the end of the film, for it is here that Hire becomes the cynosure of violence. If the mechanized carnival is a pathetic, seedy, secular descendant of Dionysian rites, weakened because it is a weekend *deixis,* the bumper car sequence shows how group euphoria can quickly turn to the venting of violence. Alice and Alfred clamber into the cars alongside other fairgoers, and, on the pretext of frightening Hire from following them, crash their car into his. The activity becomes a mimetic and generalized one, as couples screaming with glee encircle Hire in order to smash his vehicle, each in turn. "Look at the guy with the beard!" an onlooker remarks to his neighbor. "Have you ever seen a hunt? Je parle de la grande chasse, la chasse à courre! [I'm talking about a big-game hunt, with hounds!]" Hire has suddenly become the sole object of universal obsession and hatred.

The carnival in the film has come from outside, but does not initiate the violence, any more than violence issues from a force exterior to humans. It both serves as metaphor for a state in which aggression can be unleashed and functions as catalyst for its spread and overspilling. Such a mechanized carnival, continually circulating and returning, overlaps with a more systemic play of violence abroad in the land, which itself takes on a mechanical aspect, as it develops in a repetitive, recurring pattern operating beyond personal motive and intent. In his elaboration of the scapegoating pattern, Girard asserts that it is precisely in such a mechanistic functioning of violence that social communities continue to constitute themselves by expelling the enemy other.

Under a huge arch proclaiming LUTTES FEMININES, a carnival barker in long shot introduces an impressive phalanx of women wrestlers. The crowd will eagerly follow this combat while Alfred, watching in its midst, sends out his thugs to assemble a posse. The butcher closes his shutters in order to join in the settling of Hire's account. Streaming past storefronts on their way to Hire's hotel, the "enemy brothers," now a small crowd, traverse a frame at the top of which looms LAVOIR DE LA FRATERNITE, or "Fraternity Laundry." Intent upon what we now perceive as "ethnic cleansing," they demand entry to Hire's room "in the interests of all." When the hotel owner refuses, they force the door, and to the strains of a military march on the sound track, sack the room and fling Hire's belongings into the street. The other tenants applaud. When the prostitute finds the handbag bearing the initials of Mlle Noblet, "A. N.," word quickly spreads that the murderer has been uncovered. A febrile crowd, as if primed by the intensity of the spectacle of female wrestlers writhing in the ring, pours from the arena on the carnival grounds and into the neighborhood.

A telephone call from Alice summons Hire to the neighborhood and delivers him to the mob. Arriving in haste by taxi, he is confronted by a hostile crowd in the public square. At this moment of confrontation, the camera position is diametrically reversed, or placed on the other side of the 180° line, so that the spectator's point of view becomes that of the victim. In front of the PHARMACIE MODERNE, Hire, a modern *pharmakos*, is reviled, knocked from his feet, and sent scurrying for shelter. He makes his way to the top floor of the building as the crowd howls its disappointment, and thence to the roof. Here he loses his footing and slides to the edge, hanging for long minutes by his fingertips. The moment of greatest cinematic suspense turns the figure before our eyes into a rebus once again, the "sus-pendu." The crowd marvels. Firemen arrive and extend a ladder. Just as an arm reaches out to him, he loses his grasp and plunges downward, through the awning of the *pharmacie*, to the pavement.

The Erasure and Reinscription of History

In their 1943 edition of *L'Histoire du cinéma*, Maurice Bardèche and Robert Brasillach, seeking to define a fascist aesthetics of film, assert that the cinema's purpose should be an expression of national sentiment and its epic mission. The ideal film would be for and about groups, a medium by means of which the individual finds meaning and identity in the crowd depicted onscreen.[13] The crowd scene of Duvivier's film, however, revises this notion by forcing its spectators to consider themselves as (past or potential) mob. Although denunciation rather than mob violence was the modus operandi of the anti-Semitic forces that were encouraged to operate during the Occupation, Duvivier's depiction of the crowd arches back to more ancient memories of anti-Semitic rabble-rousing of the Middle Ages, which began an appalling record of popular massacre destined to stain future centuries of European history. At the same time, the crowd scene begins a demolition of Occupation myths that managed to prevail in France for more than two decades, namely, that Vichy had been the responsibility of a small number of men who were well-intentioned but misled, and that the crimes committed against Jews could be attributed to the German occupier and a few collaborators.

The final act of apprehension in *Panique* takes place on the site of the carnival itself. Detective Michelet, about to make his arrest, watches culprits Alice and Alfred take a last turn in the "bobsleigh." But THE END appears over the bobbing and whirling bobsleigh, with the arrest still pending, as if to suggest that the slaying is no more arrested than is the movement in the shot—the mechanized carnival of sacrificial violence, once set in motion, does not wind down, especially in modern settings. Violence will continue, warns Girard, because scapegoating mystifies its origin by assigning it to the victim, thus sheltering it from any understanding that would cause it to wither away. The selection of a *victime émissaire* seems to be an almost ineluctable event, because it is a recurring one. But its instances nonetheless take place in specific and discernible historical situations.[14]

Duvivier made his film in a moment of grisly topicality. The French nation had just witnessed the viciousness of occupier pitted against resistants, the liberation of the concentration camps, and the civil devastation wrought by the purge of French collaborators. These events were followed by the Gaullist injunction to "passer l'éponge," to whitewash the immediate past in order to bring the nation together. In such circumstances, the filmmaker of *Panique* was obliged to find images of high ambivalence to tell his tale, to say things and not say them at the same time, just as dream censorship, through its "considerations of representability," acting to repress what is too violent, too painful, or too full of desire, allows only acceptable representations to blossom in the slumbering psyche. Such a censorship would seem to be bound up with the necessary process of healing, and bears resemblance to what Robert Jay Lifton describes about those who lived in the aftermath of Hiroshima, namely, that "impaired formulation is a central problem for survivors."[15] Although

Duvivier lived outside France during the Occupation, he is nonetheless a survivor who attempts to tell about the unspeakable. Whether the constraints upon him are self-imposed or imposed from without, his "impaired formulation" is related to the general amnesia of the French, which persisted for decades after the Occupation. What is expelled in this story of expulsion is history, yet as Borges says, the "charm of censorship" is that it forces the artist to speak in more highly elaborated codes. It is the contraints themselves that produce a film compelling enough to demand an unraveling, and that distinguish *Panique* from the more journalistic renderings of Occupation stories that were made in later decades.

There seems at first, then, to be an erasure of the historical situation in *Panique,* but just as Monsieur Hire's photographs—in *mise en abyme*—serve to inculpate Alfred, the real murderer, and to indict the state for social crimes against its marginal citizens, so does the cinematography of Duvivier's film manage its own incrimination by writing the history of French culpability back into the record.

The Aura of Simon and the Shadow of Simenon

Duvivier's film adapts *Les Fiançailles de Mr. Hire,* a 1936 novella by Georges Simenon, the plot of which follows, in the main. But the cinematic treatment diverges radically in its depiction of the principal character. Simenon's Hire lives in the shadows, a downtrodden figure who strives only to subsist, a man with a sordid past, dealing on the margins of legality and occasionally slipping to the other side. He is pathologically timid and withdrawn, an escapee from the oppressive poverty of his father's tailor shop. A single instance of Hire's physical prowess—in Simenon, an episode in a bowling alley—is expanded by Duvivier into a version of Hire as *Mensch,* a person superior physically, morally, and mentally to those who surround him, while he jettisons most other attributes of the novelistic character. The one activity shared by both versions of Hire is his voyeurism: when Alice rents a room across the courtyard of Hire's hotel, he can watch her longingly from his window. When the theme of voyeurism is transferred from print to the cinematic regime, however, the film spectator necessarily becomes complicit in this transgressive activity.

Duvivier's character seems to borrow as well from Michel Simon's previous roles from the 1930s. A "pan-ic" quality lingers in the actor's aura, which mingles memories of the uncontained Père Jules in *L'Atalante* with those of the pansexual disrupter of the bourgeois bookseller's household in *Boudu Saved from Drowning.* Renoir's Boudu, a rootless figure not unconnected to the wandering Jew, eclipses himself and disappears back into the landscape of the River

Marne rather than settle into the social order, which continues as before. In *La Chienne*, Simon performs as Legrand, a well-starched civil servant and uppity colleague destined for a fall into the arms of the ruinous Lulu, and thence into bumhood, to the status of one scorned and reviled.

The Disappearance of Community

In 1989, the Simenon story was remade by Patrice Leconte under the title *Monsieur Hire,* with Michel Blanc as Hire. The change of actors for the title role might stand as an emblem of the transmutation Hire undergoes in traversing the decades from the mid-1940s to the late 1980s. Hirsute and bearded has disappeared in favor of bald, and the markers of "Jewishness" have vanished, to be replaced by codings of "perversion." Where Duvivier's Hire keeps a record, exposed on celluloid, of the social contradictions he witnesses, Leconte's Hire, a melancholic who finds solace with prostitutes, *has* a record: a past conviction and six months in prison for indecent exposure.

Cinematographer Denis Lenoir has shot Leconte's carefully controlled stylistic exercise almost entirely in close-ups, reducing the urban landscape to near abstraction and severing the characters from any social environment. They float in a vague and undefined time past, a *mode rétro* without the Occupation. In this film we are conscious not only of the lack of a historical moment, but of the absence of any markers of place, and indeed, of "Frenchness." Without the spoken dialogue, almost nothing in the film distinguishes it as French. There are no place names. The bleak, brick, largely nocturnal locale might be the suburbs of London, were it not for the fact that one can leave for Switzerland from an otherwise unidentified *gare centrale*. Writing in *Positif,* critic Emmanuel Carrère likens the experience of viewing Leconte's film to that of watching fish imprisoned in an aquarium. Not only has history vanished from this version, but also geography.

The release of *Le Chagrin et la pitié* in 1971 marked the beginning of a 1940s revival in French films that deal with the Occupation as event, not merely as background. After the Klaus Barbie trial in 1987, the Occupation as topic came back in vogue. "It is now a 'classic' subject, a regular fixture of the cinema," writes Henry Rousso, "one which may now be treated without manichaeanism and mythologizing."[16] It is clear that, in Leconte's film, at least, there is no need to allude to Jewishness in 1989: although anti-Semitism has surfaced from time to time in the *lepéniste* rhetoric of "national populism," the storm center in the crisis of French identity has moved elsewhere.[17] The Jew is no longer the most readily identifiable "foreigner," and xenophobic hatreds can now be directed toward the immigrant from the Maghreb. But Leconte's cautious mise-en-scène also eliminates the community from this bland and claustrophobic suburb, and thus no scapegoating drama remains, for scapegoating—in the Girardian sense—originates in, and is inseparable from, the defining of a community. The panicky, blood-hungry neighbors of Duviver's film have become spectral, distantly curious phantoms who peer at one another through the cracks of barely opened hallway doors.

Hire's photography hobby, not a feature of the Simenon character, had been Duvivier's addition, and this also disappears. It is the photograph in Désiré Hire's pocket, his record of the crime, that makes the Michel Simon character a lawgiver, the representative of that system of justice that does not succumb to panic, the system emblematized by the detective who sets himself apart from the crowd, the ratiocinative figure of Michelet. Because there are not, in *Monsieur Hire*, two opposing systems of justice, the sacrificial aspect itself has vanished.

Notes

I would like to thank my colleague James Winchell for his helpful commentary during the writing of this essay, and Tom Conley for the use of his photographic equipment. Unless otherwise noted, all translations in this chapter are my own.

1. Michel de Certeau, *Heterologies*, trans. Brian Massumi (Minneapolis: University of Minnesota Press, 1986), 31.

2. Ibid., 32.

3. See Henry Rousso, *The Vichy Syndrome: History and Memory in France since 1944*, trans. Arthur Goldhammer (Cambridge: Harvard University Press, 1991); Robert O. Paxton, *Vichy France* (New York: Columbia University Press, 1972), on French complicity in the denunciation and roundup of Jewish French citizens, as well as on French police initiatives in this regard. Rousso reports that "one-fifth of the Jewish population (including Jews of foreign as well as French birth) vanished into the camps" (133).

4. René Girard, *Violence and the Sacred*, trans. Patrick Gregory (Baltimore: Johns Hopkins University Press, 1977).

5. Ibid., 79.

6. Where were you at the time of the crime?

To answer your question, I would have to know at what time the crime was committed.

7. The film is credited to the "Alliance Cinématographique Européenne" and bears the name of Veit Harlan as director. In the clips used by Ophuls, we see a Jew, identified as "tyrannical and arrogant," on trial and sentenced to death for having carnal relations with a gentile. Pronouncing sentence, the judge declares, "If a Jew commits an act of the flesh with a Christian he will be hanged before the town to serve as an example to others. They will pay with their blood for the stain of their accursed race!" The Jew is seen begging, "I'm innocent! I want to live! Take my money but spare my life!"

8. De Certeau, *Heterologies*, 4.

9. Girard, *Violence and the Sacred*, 94–97.

10. Quoted in Paxton, *Vichy France*, 178–79.

11. Girard, *Violence and the Sacred*, 160.

12. Andrew McKenna, *Violence and Difference* (Urbana: University of Illinois Press, 1992), 31.

13. See Alice Kaplan's discussion in *The Reproduction of Banality* (Minneapolis: University of Minnesota Press, 1986), 155.

14. See Michel Winock, *Nationalisme, anti-sémitisme et fascisme en France* (Paris: Editions du Seuil, 1982). Winock charts a pattern of further "Dreyfus affairs," or the scapegoating of prominent Jews, throughout the political history of the Third Republic, from Dreyfus to Blum to Mendès-France.

15. Quoted in McKenna, *Violence and Difference*, 128.

16. Rousso, *The Vichy Syndrome*, 235.

17. The phrase "national populism" was coined by Pierre André Taguieff; it is quoted in Winock, *Nationalisme*, 41.

Part IV

Memory as Malaise and Subversion

9 / Truffaut's Adèle in the New World: Autobiography as Subversion of History

T. Jefferson Kline

Qu'est-ce qui pourrait rendre ce qui se passe en moi depuis quelque temps?

Adèle Hugo

Il serait temps que je dise enfin la vérité. Mais je ne pourrai la dire que dans une oeuvre de fiction.

Jean-Paul Sartre

Historicity and Camouflage

As the credits fade from the opening moments of Truffaut's film *L'Histoire d'Adèle H.*, a text appears on the screen announcing, "L'Histoire d'Adèle H. est authentique. Elle met en scène des événements qui ont eu lieu et des personnages qui ont existé." An antique map of America fills the screen, and the camera zooms in on Canada. Another more detailed map of Canada now appears. The continuing movement of the camera narrows in on Nova Scotia and Halifax, as we hear the narration, "Nous sommes en 1863. . . ."[1]

Adèle H. is one of only two of Truffaut's films so anchored in a historical intent (the other being *L'Enfant sauvage*). These three extradiegetic signs—the initial notice, the narrative voice, and the "authentic" maps—fill the screen with an intrusive redundancy that focuses the spectator's attention on questions of the film's historical veracity. Indeed, most studies of this film have focused precisely on this "historical" aspect of the film. To bring the "true story" of Adèle H. to the screen would seem at first glance to engage in a critically important process of reevaluation of France's most unassailable cultural figure—

head, Victor Hugo. The revelation of a seamier side of the great poet through the troubled life of his second daughter would place Truffaut more in step with contemporaries such as Jean-Luc Godard, who were experimenting with film as an ideal medium for cultural critique. After all, the battle cry of the New Wave had been against aesthetics as usual and for the little-known independent artist against the well-known captains of the film industry. Truffaut's major essay on this point left little doubt that for him, the New Wave was to be a revolutionary gesture.[2]

And yet, when we take a closer look, a different set of questions becomes imperative. Why of all possible histories, Adèle Hugo—especially when we consider that Truffaut's particular version of Adèle represents a remarkable distortion of her history by occulting three of the four volumes of her journal in order to focus on a particular moment of her story?[3]

Perhaps we can begin to understand the answer to this question if we first ask, What is history? Michel de Certeau has written,

> Est 'historique', l'analyse qui considère ses matériaux comme les effets de systèmes (économiques, sociaux, politiques, idéologiques, etc) et qui vise à élucider les opérations temporelles (causalité, croisement, inversion, coalescence, etc) qui ont pu donner lieu à de tels effets.[4]

But that is only the idealized version. In fact, as de Certeau points out in *Histoire et psychanalyse*:

> Le 'réel' représenté ne correspond pas au réel qui détermine sa production. Il *cache*, derrière la figuration d'un passé le *présent qui l'organise*. . . . L'opération en cause semble assez rusée: le discours se rend crédible au nom de la réalité qu'il est supposé représenter, mais cette apparence autorisée sert précisément à *camoufler* la pratique qui la détermine réellement. La représentation *déguise* la praxis qui l'organise. . . . Il donne un semblant de réel (passé) au lieu de la praxis (présent) qui le produit: l'un est mis à la place de *l'autre*. . . . Le 'documentaire' . . . est . . . le résultat d'un appareil . . . *codificateur*. . . . C'est un *trompe-l'oeil* qui, à la différence du trompe-l'oeil d'autrefois, ne fournit plus ni la visibilité de *son statut de théâtre ni le code de sa fabrication*. . . . Certes, 'faire parler' le réel, ce n'est plus révéler les secrets vouloirs d'un Auteur. . . . Pourtant la structure reste la même.[5]

De Certeau argues here that we must "repoliticize" historiography by historicizing it, that is by revealing the "conditions mentales de sa production," by understanding that "le temps, c'est l'extériorité, c'est l'autre," and by restoring "l'ambiguïté qui saisit le rapport objet-sujet ou passé-présent." He adds, "*Que 'l'autre' soit déjà là dans la place*, c'est le mode sur lequel s'y insinue le temps."[6]

Precisely where traditionally the historiographer operates a "coupure" between the past and the present that would guarantee his objectivity, de Certeau's psychoanalytic historiographer would redistribute "l'espace de la mémoire": where historiographic tradition places the past and present "l'un à côté de l'autre" the psychoanalytic historian would place them "l'un *dans* l'autre" in order to appreciate the *imbrication* of the one in the other. In so doing, the new psychohistorian would

> 'reconnaitre' dans le discours légitimé comme scientifique le refoulé qui a pris forme de 'littérature'. Les ruses du discours avec le pouvoir afin de l'utiliser sans le servir, les apparitions de l'objet comme acteur fantastique dans la place même du 'sujet du savoir', les répétitions et les retours du temps supposé passé, les déguisements de la passion sous le masque d'une raison, etc. tout cela relève de la fiction. . . . c'est-à-dire *là où l'autre s'insinue dans la place.*[7]

Adèle H. as Autobiography

This twice-repeated phrase, "there where the other insinuates itself in its place," has a particularly charged meaning when applied to Truffaut's *Adèle H.,* for it signals almost insistently a series of scenes in the film that, taken together, articulate a structure that is autobiographical rather than biographical. To look at *Adèle H.* from a decertellian perspective is to appreciate the way Truffaut works within her history to allow Adèle's biography to "hide, camouflage, and disguise" (to use de Certeau's terms) Truffaut's own history. In so doing, we may also appreciate the way cinema may take a significant, if subtle, role in the construction of memory itself.

The first of these scenes occurs soon after Adèle has arrived in Halifax. We remember that she visits a notary, a certain Mr. Lenoir.[8] In order to win his sympathy without drawing attention to herself, Adèle tells him, "Eh bien, voilà. . . . J'ai une nièce en France à laquelle je suis très attachée. C'est une fille un peu trop romanesque. Au cours d'un séjour en Angleterre, elle s'est éprise d'un jeune officier britannique, . . . le lieutenant Pinson du 16ème Hussards. Il a même été question de mariage entre eux. . . . Mes parents, enfin ma famille m'a chargée de faire une enquête" (SC, 11). Of course Adèle is telling her own story, hidden (but not quite) behind the persona of a "niece." This is, of course, a familiar technique for persons seeking help who do not want to reveal that the help in question is for themselves. It also plays a role in what Philippe Lejeune has called "le roman autobiographique" (as opposed to what initially he calls "true" autobiography). Lejeune writes:

> Dans le cas du nom fictif (c'est-à-dire différent de celui de l'auteur) donné à un personnage qui raconte sa vie, il arrive que le lecteur ait des raisons de penser que l'histoire vécue par le personnage est exactement celle de 'auteur': soit par recoupement avec d'autres textes, soit en se fondant sur des informations extérieures,

soit même à la lecture du récit dont l'aspect de fiction sonne faux (comme quand quelqu'un vous dit: "J'avais un très bon ami auquel il est arrivé . . ." et se met à vous raconter l'histoire de cet ami avec une conviction toute personnelle).⁹

Lejeune's example fits Adèle's stratagem so perfectly that we cannot help but notice its paradigmatic value for the film as a whole. Adèle's displaced account to the notary Lenoir recapitulates precisely the displacement from François to Adèle in the appropriation of her story.

Several other elements in the film reinforce and recapitulate this structure. For example, about a third of the way through the film there occurs the following unusual scene. Adèle, who has been pursuing Lieutenant Pinson despite his explicit and repeated rejections of her love, follows him in a cab to the home of a young widow. As soon as Pinson has entered the house, Adèle gets out of the cab and runs into the garden, unseen. There she creeps through the bushes, looking at the lighted windows of the house. Through one of the rear windows, we see Pinson take the young woman in his arms and kiss her passionately. A shot of Adèle indicates that, like the film's viewer, she is intruding on this scene as voyeur. As the couple moves upstairs, followed by three pet dogs, Adèle leans to catch sight of them and then moves under a wooden staircase so that she may get a better view. As they leave our and her view, Pinson viciously throws the dogs down the stairs. Adèle is then seen climbing the exterior staircase to gain yet a better vantage point. A shot of the couple shows them now standing in the bedroom embracing. In the scenario, Truffaut notes, "elle pourrait s'en aller, mais on la sent déterminée à alimenter sa jalousie" (SC 20). The couple falls on the bed in passionate embrace. A series of shots alternating between the couple and Adèle follows until the fade-out. Truffaut underscores the intensity of this unusual scene by alternating between the scene viewed and the viewer no less than twelve times and by an acceleration of this technique in the closing seconds.

There can be little doubt that this hyperinsistence on Adèle's position constitutes an allusion to the most famous of cinematic voyeuristic scenes, those found in Hitchcock's *Rear Window*. François Truffaut was, as is well known, an admirer and a disciple of Alfred Hitchcock. In his book *Hitchcock*, the testament to this relationship, Truffaut tells Hitchcock that *Rear Window* is "one of my two favorite Hitchcock pictures."¹⁰ Earlier he had stated:

Rear Window va au-delà du pessimisme, est un film cruel. Stewart, en effet, ne braque ses jumelles sur ses voisins que pour les saisir dans leurs moments de déchéance, lorsqu'ils se trouvent dans des postures ridicules, lorsqu'ils apparaissent grotesques ou même odieux. . . . Pour clarifier *Rear Window*, je propose cette parabole: la cour c'est le monde, le reporter-photographe c'est le cinéaste, les jumelles figurent la caméra et ses objectifs. Et Hitchcock dans tout cela? Il est l'homme dont *on aime se savoir haï*.[11]

Cinema as Masochistic Voyeurism

As a spectator of *Rear Window*, Truffaut makes it quite clear that he would agree with Christian Metz's assertion that "there is no voyeurism which is not at all sadistic."[12] Laura Mulvey's assessment of the function of voyeurism in cinema also privileges the "active power of the erotic look, giving a satisfying sense of omnipotence . . . and representing woman as spectacle."[13]

In *Rear Window*, however, we recall that Jimmy Stewart is filmed as *inside* looking across a courtyard into the opposite apartment to enjoy the obliteration of a woman by her murderous husband. Here, paradoxically, it is Adèle who is *outside* looking in on a scene that has the effect of obliterating *her*, terms that considerably scramble the more common arrangement of voyeurism. Although the content of the scene is no less erotic, the direction of that eroticism is reversed. In Truffaut's version we seem to have the perversion of this perversion. More than the "masochistic misrecognition" that Kaja Silverman describes as classical narrative cinema's lock on its female spectators, this seems to be a scene in which the sadistic look is indissociably joined to a kind of pure masochism.[14] In addition to (possibly) identifying with the woman in the lighted window, Adèle looks at this erotic scene to gain a maximum of pleasure from the pain of her obliteration from Pinson's affective life. Indeed, the most likely point of identification for Adèle from her position on the outside stairs is with the abused dogs, which have been kicked outside onto the stairs. Immediately after this scene, we hear Adèle in a voice-over, "Ne pouvant avoir le sourire de l'amour, je me condamne à sa grimace. A présent, je veux penser à mes soeurs qui souffrent" (SAH 84, SC 20). The use of voice-over as an element of control as well as Adèle's insistent pursuit of Pinson suggest the degree to which she embeds a sadistic component in her hugely masochistic project.

The centrality and intensity of this sequence place it at the heart of Truffaut's enterprise in this film: not only in its autobiographical tendencies (as I shall demonstrate below), but also in its recapitulation of the functions of sadism and masochism implicit in the act of filming and film viewing. The blatant masochism of the scene just described illumines retrospectively Adèle's mad undertaking. She has followed Lieutenant Pinson to Halifax presumably to secure his hand in marriage, and to this presumed end she displays a single-mindedness that is extraordinary. To reach him, she has had to leave her parents, cross the ocean, sneak through customs, and search him out in a city whose geography, customs, and language are unfamiliar to her. And even before she succeeds in meeting her lieutenant, there are numerous indications that her project is predicated as much on its failure as on the determination to track down Pinson. In a touching scene, soon after her arrival at the Saunderses' lodging house, Adèle commissions her landlord to deliver a note to Pinson, "amoureux de moi depuis notre enfance," as she puts it (SAH 46, SC 13). But Saunders returns later that night with the news that "the lieutenant didn't even open that letter. . . . no, he looked at the envelope, shrugged his shoulders, . . . stuffed it into his pocket without reading it. For a man in love, that's a funny way to behave" (SAH 53, SC 14).

Up until Adèle's meeting with Pinson, the spectator can maintain the illusion that there is simply some misunderstanding between the lovers. When she finally does meet with Pinson, however, she is rendered so hysterical by his presence in the house that she very nearly misses the opportunity to speak with him. Instead, as he waits with increasingly evident impatience, we see her circling her room upstairs, attempting to choose between dresses, in any case denying herself *and the viewer* the pleasure of this long-awaited meeting. Once the two are face-to-face, however, Pinson's attitude dispels any illusions on the viewer's part that this is a case of a misunderstanding. Before he can speak, she places her hand on his mouth to silence him, then hugs him passionately, sighing, "Albert, . . . je vous retrouve enfin!" Pinson stands, arms at his sides, his face impassive, clearly embarrassed by this outburst. His first words are, "Adèle, il ne faut pas rester ici. Vous n'avez rien à faire dans ce pays." To each of her passionate entreaties, he responds coldly. When she speaks of marriage, he retorts that her parents would never consent. When she declares that there is another who wants to marry her, he tells her, "Alors, il faut l'épouser." He does admit that he once loved her, but is categorical in placing this love in the past. Finally, he leaves as coldly as he has come (SAH 71-72, SC 18-19).

In every way, this scene violates to the letter the prescription that Adèle has just given herself for her meeting with Pinson. Before seeing him, she had written, "Lorsque je le verrai, je lui dirai: quand un des deux n'aime pas assez pour vouloir avant tout le mariage, ce n'est pas de l'amour. Il m'a reproché si souvent ma violence que je suis déterminée, lorsque la vie nous remettra en présence, à ne rien faire qui pourrait lui faire peur. . . . Je saurai le convaincre par la douceur" (SAH 62, SC 17).

The degree of Adèle's sadomasochistic pleasure is evidenced immediately after this interview, when Adèle writes and monologues:

Mon amour, je suis tellement heureuse que nous nous soyons retrouvés. Le pire sur la terre, c'était ton absence. Nous ne laisserons plus de malentendu s'installer entre nous. Je savais que tu ne pouvais pas m'avoir oubliée. Quand une femme comme moi se donne à un homme, elle est sa femme. Maintenant, je ne pleure plus. Dans la vie, on ne change pas de père, de mère, d'enfants; on ne change pas non plus de femme ni de mari. Je suis ta femme définitivement. Nous resterons ensemble jusqu'à notre mort. (SAH 83, SC, 19)

What is striking in this monologue is the separation between the painful reality of Pinson's behavior that we have just witnessed (and to which she has already attested in her journal) and the perverse pleasure Adèle takes in moving in the face of that evidence with the power of her (unrequited) love. When Adèle says, "I'll weep no more," she betrays the pleasure that occupies the space of pain in her experience. The evidence that Adèle has already provided in the earlier journal entry indicates that she is beyond accepting any refusal from Pinson as an invitation to forget him. Where there is forgetting on Pinson's part, she rather sadistically denies it. Two of the thoughts here betray just how deeply her masochism has distorted the normal logical processes. When one says (as the original French version states it), "You can't change your father or mother," the logical sequence is, "but you *can* change your friends and lovers." Yet when Adèle pronounces this cliché it is to pervert the truth of the logical sequence. In this fixation there can be only continued suffering. And in her final words, "I am your wife forever more till death do us part [Nous resterons ensemble jusqu'à la mort]," she "quite literally writes herself into a death narrative," as Kaja Silverman has noted. Silverman adds:

> Her most important symptom is precisely this activity of writing and both its "form" and its "content" warrant the closest attention. The physical activity or form of writing is terribly important to Adèle—she consumes vast quantities of paper and ink, and while engaged with those items she invariably falls into a trance-like state. Eventually the pathological nature of this activity is confirmed by the emergence of an additional symptom: the radical impairment of Adèle's vision. . . . Thus through a series of displacements, Adèle's compulsive writing and eventual hysterical blindness come to gratify . . . the wish for self-punishment (i.e. death).[15]

The key to understanding this masochistic love is obligingly provided by Truffaut in a series of scenes that link Adèle to her dead sister, Léopoldine. When she is unpacking her things with Mrs. Saunders, the older woman notices a photograph of Léopoldine and cries, "Oh ! . . . le joli portrait! C'est vous?" Whereupon Adèle "brusquely" grabs the page and answers,

> Non, non, c'est ma soeur aînée. . . . Elle est morte, il y a longtemps. . . . Leopoldine s'est noyée quelques mois après que notre mère ait dessiné ce portrait. Elle avait dix-neuf ans; elle venait juste de se marier. C'est arrivé au cours d'une prom-

enade en bateau. Son mari est mort avec elle. Notre père était en voyage très loin quand il apprit la nouvelle, . . . par hasard, dans un journal. . . . Il a failli devenir fou de douleur.

When Mrs. Saunders asks, "Et vous? Vous avez sans doute été très malheureuse?" Adèle's only response is, "Léopoldine était adorée de toute la famille." To Mrs. Saunders's "Comme elle a l'air gracieux!" Adèle muses, "Son mari a tout fait pour la sauver et, quand il s'est rendu compte qu'elle était perdue, il s'est laissé couler au fond de l'eau pour rester avec elle" (SC, 13). That this scenario corresponds more closely to Ken Russell's *Women in Love* (1970) than to the actual events indicates the extent to which Truffaut has Adèle masochistically mythologize Léopoldine's love and popularity. Finally, when Mrs. Saunders notices Léopoldine's jewels and learns that Adèle always has them with her but never wears them, she coos, "Comme je vous comprends, Miss Adèle. Vous savez, j'aurais tellement voulu avoir des frères et des soeurs." Adèle responds angrily, "Non, vous ne me comprenez pas! Vous ne pouvez pas savoir quelle chance vous avez eue d'être enfant unique" (SAH 47-51, SC 13). Adèle will later actually pass herself off as Léopoldine (SAH 102, SC 24). The physical resemblance between these two sisters serves to accentuate the difference Adèle feels in her family's love.

Adèle's Dreamscapes

Because of the intensity of Victor Hugo's love for Léopoldine, Adèle is forever doomed to experience love as oblivion. And when Léopoldine is drowned, Adèle merely reexperiences the depth of her father's preference: "He nearly went mad with grief." Not surprisingly, Adèle begins to have recurring dreams.

> En surimpression, Adèle dans les vagues se noyant: elle crie, se débat, s'essouffle. . . . Photo en noir et blanc; les vagues submergent Adèle qui lève désespérément les bras. Retour couleur: elle pousse un cri, se réveille. (SAH 97, SC 23)

By means of an economy of the type frequently at work in the unconscious, Adèle oneirically identifies with her drowning sister because that identification affords her the position as her father's favorite. Yet the masochism at work here ensures that this identification can only be with her *dead* sister, that she must suffer and die in order to take up her sister's position. (The fact that this is a recurring dream only adds to the connection between the repetition compulsion and the "death instinct" that Freud outlines in *Beyond the Pleasure Principle*.)[16] Moreover, the images of the sea (her sister had drowned in the Seine), contribute to the idea of suffocation by her mother as well. Yet the sea is also the element (so evocatively filmed by Truffaut) of separation between Adèle and her parents—that is, a symbol of isolation.[17]

In a confirmation of these elements of maternal suffocation and isolation, Truffaut shot (but later cut) several versions of another dream that does much to explain the masochism in Adèle's functioning:

> Une petite fille de trois ou quatre ans (Adèle enfant) enfermée dans un placard crie, pleure, frappe à grand coups contre la porte, tandis qu'on entend, venant de l'extérieur, une musique fantastique au piano. (SC 16)

> Dans un salon anonyme, à peine éclairé par une lumière crépusculaire, une vieille dame vêtue de noir, à l'allure un peu fantastique, chuchotte des choses apparemment effrayantes à une petite fille, les soulignant d'accords bruyants au piano. Puis, comme pour protéger Adèle d'un mystérieux danger, elle l'entraîne vers un placard où elle l'enferme. Sa tante se remet au piano où elle joue le même air qu'au cours du rêve précédent. A l'intérieur du placard, la petite Adèle hurle de frayeur. Elle hurle. (SC 23)

In the original scenario this dream (repeated twice more; SC 23, 44) is predominant to the point of an obsession, and allows us to understand Adèle's masochism as linked to early traumatic experiences of suffocating isolation in the face of the indifference of her artistic parents. Taken together, the two dreams link the early loss of her parents' love with the masochistic identification with her dead sister. They also suggest a link with Adèle's version of masochistic scopophilia in the scene discussed at the outset of this essay, for Renato Almansi has linked the etiology of scopophilia to the early child-mother dyad, where "scopophilia was indissolubly linked with early visual sensitization due to feelings of oral deprivation and object loss."[18] I shall return to this aspect of Adèle's voyeurism below.

No wonder that she has chosen Pinson as her "lover," for he allows her to perpetuate her masochism by treating her repeatedly in the same manner as her father (hence his title of lieutenant—literally "place holder") had done: by obliterating her. The genius of Pinson's behavior here is that he never absolutely denies that he has given Adèle reason to love him, he simply refuses to display the love she feels she deserves. In his refusal, his reference to other women sounds very much like the paternal response to the oedipal desires of the female child:

ADÈLE: Albert, je ne t'ai rien demandé! . . . C'est toi qui es venu me chercher. C'est toi qui as voulu de moi. . . . C'est toi qui profitais des soirées de table tournante pour me toucher le bras. C'est toi qui me caressais dans les corridors. Je me suis donnée à toi, il faut me garder. . . . Vous entendez, il faut me garder!

PINSON: Mais qu'est-ce que vous croyez? J'ai connu des femmes avant vous . . . j'en ai connu après vous et j'en connaîtrai encore. (SAH 109-10, SC 26)

What is remarkable in Truffaut's treatment of Adèle is the parallelism between her masochistic scenario and the "masochistic aesthetic" of von Sternberg's films starring Marlene Dietrich. In *In the Realm of Pleasure,* Gaylyn Studlar describes

> the masochistic economy of desire that reverses expected instinctual progress toward post-Oedipal genitality, masquerades its own polymorphous identity, and refuses the unification of sites of textual pleasure under the phallic "efficiency" of Oedipal narratives. Sternberg's films evidence the implausible coincidence, episodic, repetitive scenes, and abrupt elision of decisive events that are as typical of masochistic narrativity as the fetishistic suspension of action in exquisitely painful waiting.[19]

Studlar includes in this masochistic aesthetic the place of dreams and fantasies (RP 24–25), shifting identifications (RP 35), and mixed characterizations (RP 52). Desire, she argues, is repeated, doubled, given mirror reflection in the masochistic dialectic that confuses sex roles and gender identities (RP 64). Indeed, masochistic characters "engage in . . . transformations in fixation, theatrical exhibition in the depths of humiliation, and self-revelation through masquerade" (RP 158). In masochistic art, she adds, the real world is suspended, replaced by an imaginary time and space (RP 91).

All of these elements punctuate Truffaut's *Adèle H.* Certainly the dreams and fantasies that preoccupy Adèle constitute one of the major systems of repetition in this film. In addition, Adèle begins by hiding her true identity, passing herself off as Miss Lewly to the Saunderses and at the bank; as Madame Lenormand to Maître Lenoir, the notary (as already mentioned; SAH 31, 37, SC 11); and later as her sister Léopoldine (SAH 102, SC 24). In her doubling of desire, she not only witnesses Pinson's revelry with the young woman during the scene of voyeurism, but actually sends him a prostitute as a gift of love in a perverse masochistic substitutive gesture, writing, "Albert, mon amour, regardez bien la jeune femme que je vous envoie. Si vous la trouvez jolie, gardez-la près de vous jusqu'à demain matin. Tu es si beau, Albert que tu mérites d'avoir toutes les femmes de la terre. Accepte ce cadeau" (SAH 129, SC 29).

As for the fragmentation of self, Adèle masquerades as a man in order to enter the Military Circle at the Parc de Bellevue, an experience that merely deepens her pleasure of humiliation. The masquerade of the magician comple-ments this scenario in that Adèle, frequently the masquerader, is completely humiliated when she realizes that her complete belief in the magician is but a false hope.

Increasingly, Adèle lives in a fictive world, not only in her "belief" in Pin-son's love but in her actions as well. At the height of this suspension of reality, Adèle writes to her parents, "Mes chers parents. Je viens d'épouser le lieutenant Pinson. La cérémonie a eu lieu samedi dans une église d'Halifax" (SAH 111, SC 27). When this fiction is exposed, Adèle "corrects" her version in another letter: "Mes chers parents, vous avez raison: je n'ai pas réussi à épouser le lieu-tenant Pinson. Il s'est dérobé malgré ses promesses. J'ai reçu de lui maintes let-tres où il me demande en mariage" (SAH 121, SC 28). Later she will tell Pin-son's future father-in-law that she is in fact his wife and expecting his child (SAH 145, SC 36).

Rather than following a linear development, the film "refuses the unification of sites of textual pleasure under the phallic 'efficiency' of Oedipal narratives" (RP 111). Rather than progression, we witness merely a series of repetitive fail-ures, broken by visual ellipses (dissolves, fade-outs, cuts) that never lead toward closure. In a symbolic break with the "phallic efficiency of the Oedipal narra-tive," Adèle chants, "Née de père inconnu. . . . Je suis née de père inconnu. . . . Mais je ne connais pas mon père si je suis née de père inconnu" (SAH 141, SC 34).[20] As she destroys herself, she "destories" herself as well by undoing the pa-ternity that has left her already without a history. The progress of the film, if progress there be, is tied to Adèle's increasing self-neglect, impoverishment, iso-lation, and final madness. Little wonder that the final image of the film is of Adèle standing by the sea, a scene that does not resolve or close her story, but links it firmly with her dreams and with the opening image of the film.[21] To quote François Truffaut:

> Tout le film tourne autour de l'idée de mariage. [Ce film va] au-delà du pes-simisme, est un film *cruel.* . . . La construction du film est très nettement musicale où plusieurs thèmes s'imbriquent et se répondent parfaitement, ceux du mariage, du suicide, de la déchéance et de la mort, baignés dans un érotisme très raffiné. . . . [C'est un] film de l'indiscrétion, de l'intimité violée et surprise dans son caractère le plus infâmant . . . le film du bonheur impossible . . . le film de la solitude morale, une extraordinaire symphonie de la vie quotidienne et des rêves détruits.[22]

But what is truly uncanny is that Truffaut wrote these lines in reference to Hitchcock's *Rear Window.* One can surmise that *L'Histoire d'Adèle H.* has an ar-chaeology that runs very deep for François Truffaut, given that in looking at

Hitchcock he was already anticipating his own film. Indeed, the scene of voyeurism with which we began this meditation can be understood as more than central to the theme of sadomasochism in the film. It also provides an important link in explaining Truffaut's relation to Adèle. After all, we must remember that all of the discussions of masochism to which reference has been made here are discussions of *male* masochism. In insisting on masochism as being "triumphantly bi-sexual" (RP 32) and in noting that "the male assumes the traits associated with the patriarchy's definition of the feminine: submissiveness, passivity—masochism" (RP 62-63), Studlar is proposing the application of the concept of masochism to a masculine model. And if Adèle fits precisely those traits discovered by Studlar in von Sternberg's films, it may have less to do with the fact that she is a woman than that she is but the creation of a man: François Truffaut. This is the very man who wrote of *Rear Window*: "Nous sommes tous voyeurs, dans un sens quand nous regardons un film intime. . . . Pour clarifier *Rear Window*, je propose cette parabole: la cour c'est le monde, le reporter-photographe c'est le cinéaste, les jumelles figurent la caméra et ses objectifs. Et Hitchcock dans tout cela? Il est l'homme dont *on aime se savoir haï*."[23] To love to be hated is thus the psychological structure that uncannily links François to his character, Adèle. Although Truffaut insists at the outset of his film, "The story of Adèle is true. It is about events that really happened and people who really existed," he does not necessarily limit those truths and events to Adèle Hugo.

Considered from this perspective, a number of uncanny coincidences begin to emerge.[24] Truffaut's version of Adèle's journal emphasizes almost obsessionally the following: (a) loss of paternal love, (b) an unauthorized flight from home by a person we may describe as "craintif et révolté, trop vulnérable et à l'écart de la société,"[25] (c) an obsession that turns a casual experience into a flight from reality and eventually a life entirely given to a fictionalized view of the world, (d) an insistence on voyeurism, and (e) the coded account of these themes and an obsession with writing and literature.

The Story of François T.

François Truffaut's own biography reads almost as a coded reinscription of Adèle's: unhappy with his father and family life, François would slip away unauthorized to hole up in his friend Robert Lachenay's apartment and read (notably Victor Hugo and Balzac) and then, as the cinemas opened up, to lose their afternoons in the irreality of the movies. François, like Adèle, ran away from home because of the perceived injustices of his father. Indeed, François had reason to believe that his mother's husband was not his biological father.

After all, François's mother was married eighteen months after his birth, and François once wrote, "Je ne me sens pas cent pour cent français et je ne sais pas toute la vérité sur mes origines."[26] This phrase evokes Adèle, for there has always been a question of her paternity as well: Sainte-Beuve suggested in one of his poems to Adèle that, indeed, he was her father.[27] Yet another uncanny coincidence links the story of Adèle and the *stories* of François: in *Les 400 Coups*, as he and his friend roam the streets of Paris, Antoine Doinel encounters his mother in the arms of a lover. Now, Truffaut wrote twice to Marcel Moussy that "je pense renoncer à l'idée de la révélation de la bâtardise *pour la remplacer par une autre*. . . . Je n'ai pas écrit la suite, mais je l'ai bien en tête" (C 142, 144). Substituting something else evokes Adèle, for the question of her paternity links her to this concern. Behind ANTOINE *DOINELLE* we can thus perceive nearly hidden, like a palimpsest, or the fragments of a screen memory, the letters *ADELE*. The name of Truffaut's alter ego, *Lache*nay suggests an overdetermined meaning for the letter *H*.[28]

What is not so obvious, perhaps, is that, like Adèle's journal writing, facsimilies of Truffaut's own correspondence show it to be remarkably similar to hers—that is, frequently hypergraphic and similarly encoded. As is well known, Adèle used throughout her writing a specific code, which Frances Guille calls a "jargon adélien."[29] Similarly, in the fourth letter we have from François Truffaut to Robert Lachenay, François writes, "Il faut que tu lises cette lettre avec attention. Surtout les passages que je te soulignerais [*sic*]" (C 20). And elsewhere, in another letter to his friend, he writes cryptically, "tout cela a un sens profond qui échappe même aux gradés mais qui a une réelle valeur" (C 55). Truffaut's correspondence with Robert has an unmistakably obsessional quality to it and is characterized by a need to lie to his friend or misrepresent things to others.[30] And, although the vast majority of letters in this volume are from Truffaut, the writer authorized the inclusion of a letter from Robert's grandmother in the midst of the series of his own. The mildly inattentive reader will thus find him- or herself reading, as if it emanated from Truffaut's pen, "Quand j'étais jeune, il fallait trente mille francs pour épouser un officier, si ma mère avait vécu, j'aurais pu en épouser un, cela m'aurait bien plu" (C 44), an echo of Adèle, who tells Pinson desperately, "Marry me and you'll have 40,000 francs!" It is, uncannily, as though Adèle's voice has seeped into the grain of François's through his alter ego's grandmother. This incident is all the more uncanny as Adèle herself wrote that she was "une femme du dix-neuvième siècle qui s'adresse au vingtième."[31]

A further coincidence binds these two stories: "Le cinéma," wrote Truffaut, "est l'art du petit détail qui ne frappe pas" (C 54). In the opening scenes of the film, Adèle emerges from the sea and immediately proceeds to enact the scenario that Freud had envisaged for the dream work in which unconscious processes, in order to pass the censorship of repression, take shape during the night, elect to take a circuitous route around the censor and utilize a series of disguises. As the figure of movement from the latent to the manifest dream work, Adèle sneaks past the *douane* here, is taken for a ride by a man who bears an uncanny resemblance to Sigmund Freud, and spends the first twenty minutes of the film passing herself off as someone she is not.

But then, so does Truffaut, does he not? Every adjective that has been used to describe Adèle's journal and her role in this film can be applied to Truffaut's direction of the film: it is an obsessional, hypergraphic—or what corresponds to this in film work—a hyperimaged style, entirely coded to hide yet reveal the auto-biographical content at the heart of this work. Adèle can easily be seen to be the feminized other of the *metteur-en-scene*. Her status as *dream*, acquired immediately in the opening scenes, suggests the degree to which the particular anecdote is but a manifest level of latent obsessions of her creator, François.

We may judge just how unusual this film was for Truffaut by his comments during the filming: "Ce film est redoutable," he wrote. "Certaines fois, nous chuchotons toute la journée et nous ne retrouvons notre voix normale que le soir" (C 482, 476). "Il y a là quelque chose d'étrange et de boiteux que je m'efforcerai d'analyser un jour," he worried (C 484). Clearly more confessional than explicative, these concerns go hand in hand with another confession made by Truffaut: "C'est en mélangeant la réalité et la fiction que je fais des erreurs graves" (C 147).

If "cinema is the art of the little detail that does not call attention to itself" (C 54), and not "an authentic history," as the extradiegetically positioned opening notice claims, then *Adèle H.* is cinematic by its insistence on such "little details." The attentive spectator of Truffaut's films will notice that the truly obsessional moments of this film do not necessarily figure at the diegetic level of Adèle's hysteria, but instead occupy the realm of the stylistic, the metacinematic, and the intertextual. Perhaps the most telling of these stylistic traits is Truffaut's hyperinsistence on an alternation of shots from the inside looking out and then from the outside looking in. This alternation draws attention to and certainly figuralizes the position of Truffaut vis-à-vis his "historical subject," especially in the central scene of Adèle's voyeurism, which places her exactly in Truffaut's own position both vis-à-vis the actual scenes viewed *and* symbolically.

It is as though Truffaut were forever trying to re-create and overcome the dynamics of a Lacanian mirror stage in which he would endlessly rehearse the discovery of his "self" as "other" by shifting the specular position back and forth in a vain attempt at assimilation. Such "speculation" (on Truffaut's part and mine) would explain the extraordinarily disquieting scene of the encounter between Adèle and François Truffaut that takes place within the diegesis. Here Adèle races after a man she takes to be her lover (an oneiric condensation of her father) and encounters Truffaut himself, the very man who has mobilized her as a veiled image of himself! Truffaut's own expression in this filmed encounter bespeaks such surprise and dismay that we can appreciate the depth of the obsession that leads him from the *outside* to the *inside* of this film.

Because of this projective identification on Truffaut's part, we can understand his own position as voyeur (as he himself put it in referring to *Rear Window*) as a thoroughly masochistic one. To look at Adèle is to reexperience the (un)pleasure of his own unhappy story. He joins his own exhibitionism to hers in a play of outside/inside that attains vertiginous proportions. In their discussion of the narcissistic function of masochism, Robert D. Stolorow and Frank M. Lachmann note:

> In a structurally deficient individual, exhibitionism may be viewed as a primitive means of shoring up a failing self representation through eliciting a mirroring affirmation of the self from one's audience. . . . The presence of a real or imaginary audience to whom his misery can be dramatized seems to be a consistent requirement of the masochistic character. The specific content of the response which the masochist desires from the audience is variable. He may wish to force expressions of love and of his loveworthiness, of appreciation and approval, or of concern and sympathy. He may wish to punish his audience by evoking guilt feelings or remorse. . . . The common theme in all these variations is that he is not being ignored. By exhibiting his desolation he is being noticed, eliciting a response, having an *impact* on his audience. . . . The experience of having the self reflected back and affirmed . . . might add a desperately needed increment to his sense of self-cohesion.[32]

The phrase "the experience of having the self reflected back and affirmed" suggests the degree to which the lessons of the "story" of Adèle/François are lessons for the film's spectators as well. Just as François watches Adèle watching Pinson, so do we, creating an abyssal structure that captures us in its play. We may watch, but, as so many theorists of the cinematic apparatus have suggested, our watching is to some extent an "affirming self-reflection." Gaylyn Studlar concludes her study of von Sternberg with the observation that cinematic pleasure itself may be masochistic:

> As . . . the acting out mechanism for fantasies . . . it is much closer to masochistic than to sadistic structure. . . . Separation is required by masochism's structure of

desire, a desire that seeks to overcome individuation and restore symbiosis but cannot tolerate the danger of closing that gap. . . . The spectator is also the deprived observer who must be satisfied with the pleasure of expectancy and specular-distanced gratification. . . . The intimacy of perversion prevails even in the pleasure of cinema: the spectator must disavow an absence. (RP 180, 184)

The sadomasochistic identification process (Adèle = François = film spectator) would seem, then, to be overdetermined by the relationship between the specifics of the film apparatus and their psychoanalytic symbology. We are always, like Adèle (and like François behind the camera), on the outside looking in at a scene that paradoxically reflects and obliterates us. But there is yet another potential twist.

If we look a final time at Truffaut's "parable" of *Rear Window*, we see that he has placed the filmmaker in *two positions*: "the courtyard is the world, the reporter/photographer is the filmmaker, the binoculars stand for the camera and its lenses. And Hitchcock? He is the man we love to be hated by." Truffaut's position in relation to this "parable" seems to be a constantly oscillating one: he occupies, on the one hand, the position of "the filmmaker" who masochistically films himself in Adèle; on the other hand, there is *also* the position of Hitchcock, the man *we* love to be hated by. It seems that ultimately, in the final analysis, the cinema offers (as only an unconscious or oneiric operation can) the overdetermined possibility of experiencing, in an unending oscillation, depending on the momentary strength of the spectator's identifications, the masochistic and sadistic perversions of the look.

Memory as an Intertextual Construction

To read Truffaut's *Correspondence* is to read a virtually encyclopedic list of cinematic history. In every letter to his friend Robert Lachenay, he cites seemingly endless lists of films he has seen—small wonder that the book that occupies the place of his autobiography is titled, *Les Films de ma vie*. And small wonder that he wrote to Jean Collet:

> Je suis épaté par la justesse de la comparaison entre les photos jetées par Franca (dans *La peau douce*) et les billets jetés par Adèle. Je n'y avais *jamais* pensé et je me rends compte maintenant que *l'instinct m'a dicté* cette réminiscence! Il m'arrive parfois, en filmant un plan, d'éprouver *la fameuse sensation du 'déjà vécu'*, probablement dans les cas de ce genre. (C 525–26)

There is a symptom here: the memories of film actors and directors are often not limited to their experiences on the set, but include films they have seen as well.[33]

These repeated superpositions of *auto* onto the *biography* of the other suggest, by extension to our own experience of the dream-screen of the movies that memory itself is an intertextual construction. The construction of memory, it would seem, is no longer an affair of the bricks and mortar of one's own personal experience. Instead, our lives are elaborate architectures of fantasmagoria integrating at some deeper level the personal with the collective—not in the Jungian sense of collective archetypes, but in this more directly experiential sense of "autobiocinematography." The mirror stage would not then be "merely" (!) a developmental configuration incorporating the other of the mirror into the phantasm of the self, but an oft-repeated structure whose myriad incorporations fashion and refashion not only our sense of self but the whole realm of the unconscious, grafting the "films of our lives" onto the series of family photographs that are so often the effective basis of our earliest memories. If François Truffaut can "convert" the story of Victor Hugo's daughter into his own, utilizing, as de Certeau argues, history as a filtering of past events through present institutions, then so do we all "pass" the images before us in the darkened theater through the filter of our own unconscious desires into a thousand mirrors, whose fragments become pieces in the construction of the collage of our identity.

(F)au(x)tobiography and the Subversion of History

How politically subversive this project is can be measured when we reconfigure Truffaut's place in Victor Hugo's "family." Hugo, as Gide once lamented, was the greatest French poet. His funeral procession on the Champs Elysées constituted without doubt the most important demonstration ever of French national pride and identity.

Indeed, his paternalism is embedded in the French unconscious like no other figure in French history. By inserting himself in the space occupied by Adèle in Hugo's family, Truffaut subtly, but forcefully, rejects—nay, obliterates—Victor Hugo and the authority of his writing. By embodying Adèle, Truffaut manages an ironic substitution of himself for Hugo as well—as the poet in exile. Truffaut's exile is triple: from France (to Halifax), from poetry (to cinema), and from maleness (to female/other). He thus valorizes everything that Father Hugo is not at the very moment he preempts His place. From the equation Victor Hugo = paternity = poetry = French national identity, Truffaut has derived a new formula: Adèle Hugo = François Truffaut = oedipal revolt = dreamlike scribbling = cinema = a rejection of a certain nationalism. Indeed, we should remember that Truffaut conceived of the Adèle project in 1969,[34] during a period in which he claimed to be leading "une double vie de militant et cinéaste."[35] Truffaut's project, then, moves from "authentic history" to auto-biography to subversive politics. As such, it stands as a testament to the way that cinema is constantly rewriting history, not from the margins, but in the unconscious of its everyday (or everynight) viewers.

Notes

1. François Truffaut, "*L'Histoire d'Adèle H.*," *L'Avant scène* 165 (1976): 9; in English, *The Story of Adele H.*, trans. Jan Dawson (New York: Grove, 1976), 19. All further references to this text will be indicated in the body of the chapter and in notes by SAH and page numbers, followed by the indication of the page numbers in the original French scenario, SC. Unless otherwise noted, all other translations in this chapter are my own.

2. François Truffaut, "Une Certaine Tendance du cinéma français," *Cahiers du cinéma* 31 (January 1954); reprinted in François Truffaut, *Le Plaisir des yeux* (Paris: Flammarion, 1987), 210–29.

3. It is worth pointing out that, of his reasons for filming *Adèle H.*, Truffaut stated the following: "The factors that appealed to me most in the story of Adèle Hugo were: 1. Her story is the autopsy of a passion. 2. The girl is alone throughout the whole story. 3. She is the daughter of the most famous man in the whole world. 4. The man is referred to but never seen. 5. Adèle assumes a number of false identities. 6. Obsessed by her *idée fixe*, she pursues an unattainable goal. 7. Every word she utters and every move she makes is related to her fixation. 8. Though she fights a losing battle, Adèle is continually active and inventive" (SAH 8).

4. Michel de Certeau, *Histoire et psychanalyse entre science et fiction* (Paris: Gallimard, Collection Folio, 1987), 125.

5. Ibid., 70–75; emphasis added.

6. Ibid., 90; emphasis added.

7. Ibid., 94; emphasis added.

8. For an insightful interpretation of the name "Lenoir," see Mary Lydon, "*The Story of Adèle H* or The Insistence of the Letter," *Cream City Review* 7, no. 2 (1982): 33–41.

9. Philippe Lejeune, *Le Pacte autobiographique* (Paris: Seuil, 1975), 24–25.

10. François Truffaut, *Hitchcock* (New York: Simon & Schuster, 1983), 213.

11. François Truffaut, *Les Films de ma vie* (Paris: Flammarion, 1975), 105, 107.

12. Christian Metz, "From the Imaginary Signifier," in *Film Theory and Criticism*, ed. Gerald Mast and Marshall Cohen (New York: Oxford University Press, 1985), 800.

13. Laura Mulvey, "Visual Pleasure and Narrative Cinema," in *Film Theory and Criticism*, ed. Gerald Mast and Marshall Cohen (New York: Oxford University Press, 1985), 810.

14. Kaja Silverman, "Dis-Embodying the Female Voice," in *Re-vision*, ed. Mary Ann Doane, Patricia Mellencamp, and Linda Williams (Frederick, Md.: University Publications of America, 1984), 145.

15. Kaja Silverman, *The Subject of Semiotics* (New York: Oxford University Press, 1983), 79.

16. See Sigmund Freud, *Beyond the Pleasure Principle,* in *The Standard Edition of the Complete Psychological Works of Sigmund Freud,* trans. James Strachey, vol. 18 (London: Hogarth, 1955).

17. These are conclusions reached by Kaja Silverman in her discussion of *Adèle H.* in *The Subject of Semiotics,* 79.

18. Renato J. Almansi, "The Face = Breast Equation," *Journal of the American Psychoanalytic Association* 8 (1960): 43–70, cited in Gaylyn Studlar, *In the Realm of Pleasure: Von Sternberg, Dietrich and the Masochistic Aesthetic* (Chicago: University of Illinois Press, 1988), 46.

19. Studlar, *In the Realm of Pleasure,* 111. All further references to this study will be indicated in the body of the essay by RP and page numbers.

20. See ibid., 81: "Father is nothing, deprived of all symbolic function."

21. This also imbricates Truffaut's other films, particularly *Les 400 Coups,* in which Jean-Pierre Leaud stands immobilized at the end, facing the sea.

22. Truffaut, *Les Films de ma vie,* 105–6.

23. Ibid.

24. See Sigmund Freud, "The 'Uncanny,'" in *The Standard Edition of the Complete Psychological Works of Sigmund Freud,* trans. James Strachey, vol. 17 (London: Hogarth, 1955), 217–56.

25. These are words used by Truffaut to describe himself in François Truffaut, *Correspondance* (Paris: Hatier, 1988), 144. Hereafter, references to this text will be indicated in the body of the text by C and page numbers.

26. Quoted in Gilles Cahoreau, *François Truffaut 1932–1984* (Paris: Julliard, 1989), 22.

27. Frances Guille, "Introduction," in *Le Journal d'Adèle Hugo,* vol. 1 (Paris: Minard, 1968), 36.

28. Thanks to Charles Krance of the University of Chicago for this observation.

29. Guille, "Introduction," 31. She notes, "Très compliquée à transcrire, . . . : encre passé, crayon pâli, râtures, mots ou phrases intercalés entre les lignes ou dans les marges, écriture à lignes verticales sur la page, croisant les lignes horizontales. Ajoutez à tout cela que quelquefois Adèle emploie une espèce d'écriture énigmatique, anagrammatique, ou gribouillage comme elle l'appelle . . . un jargon fait par une mutilation systématique de la langue. Ce déguisement n'est pas exactement systématique et cette prétendue cryptographie n'est pas toujours difficile à déchiffrer. . . . La plupart du temps Adèle se sert de son français 'charabia' pour décrire une aventure amoureuse, ou pour faire le brouillon d'une lettre personnelle . . . D'autre part, un mot énigmatique peut glisser dans un passage sans aucune raison évidente" (30–31).

30. Cahoreau, *François Truffaut,* 77.

31. Guille, "Introduction," 33.

32. Robert D. Stolorow and Frank M. Lachmann, "The Narcissistic Function of Masochism," in *Narcissism and Self-Representation* (New York: International Universities Press, 1980), 34.

33. Bernardo Bertolucci, for example, said of *Il Conformista,* "It was based on the memories I had of films of that era. It was like a memory of my memory." "Bernardo Bertolucci Seminar," *Dialogue on Film* 3 (April 1974): 16. See also Enzo Ungari, *Scena madri* (Milan: Ubulibri, 1982), 71. When Marlon Brando gives his biography in *Last*

Tango in Paris, it is not as an actor, but as though the sequence of film roles he had played (boxer, revolutionary in Latin America, and so on) constituted his own biography.

34. Truffaut notes, "My desire to do a film about Adèle Hugo dates back to 1969 when I read her biography." "Foreword" in SAH (7).

35. *Les Lettres françaises* (11 April 1968), cited in Cahoreau, *François Truffaut*, 248. Truffaut's political engagement had included signing the *Manifeste des 121* during the Algerian war and strident participation in the "Affaire Langlois" in 1968, and extended to defending Sartre's *Cause du peuple* in the streets of Paris in May 1970 (266–67).

10 / "Une Certaine Idée de la France": The Algeria Syndrome and Struggles over "French" Identity

Anne Donadey

What is buried in the past of one generation falls to the next to claim.
Susan Griffin, A Chorus of Stones

For reasons both personal and political, almost all contemporary "Francophone" Algerian writers have felt compelled in their writings to come to terms with the 1954–62 War of National Liberation—what the French used to refer to with euphemisms such as *les événements d'Algérie* (the Algerian events), *opérations de police* (police operations), *actions de maintien de l'ordre* (actions to maintain order), *opérations de rétablissement de la paix civile* (operations to restore civilian peace), and *entreprises de pacification* (pacification undertakings), and finally came to call *la guerre d'Algérie* (the Algerian war).[1] In Algeria, that war has been constructed as the great trauma of the birth of an independent nation. Writing about it often functions as a way for writers to have their works legitimated and accepted, especially if they write in French. (A similar phenomenon can be observed in other fields, especially filmmaking.)

For women, this war was to assume a peculiar significance. In a society where space—real and imaginary—was divided along gender lines, women were for the first time called to participate actively in an armed struggle. However, after the war was won, they were sent back to the private space of the home.[2] The gains that could have been expected from their sanctioned appearance in public life never became reality, because their participation in the war was both mythologized and silenced. The *mujahidat* (women who participated

215

directly in the war) were extolled as heroines and symbols at the same time they were hidden in mental hospitals.

Historical Amnesia and the Construction of National Identity

Writer Leïla Sebbar, born and raised in Algeria by an Algerian father and a French mother, has remarked that the Algerian war "est chaque fois, malgré moi, dans les livres que j'écris [is in each book I write, in spite of myself]."[3] In her 1984 novel *Le Chinois vert d'Afrique*, almost all the characters have been involved to some degree with the war.[4] The protagonists of her novels are most often children of Maghrebian immigrants (also called *Beurs*—originally a Parisian slang term for Arab, which these youths then reappropriated). They never experienced the Algerian war as a direct trauma. Rather, through older Algerians' stories (the oral tradition) and through photography, the teenagers learn about the war. They do not live in Algeria, but, like the author herself, in France. She documents their lives at the periphery of large French cities, where the HLM, the housing projects in the suburbs, become a metaphor for a motley immigrant population ghettoized on the margins of French society. Living in France makes it doubly difficult for the protagonists to gain more than a fragmented knowledge of the Algerian war, especially because until a 1983 decree concerning the *Terminale* (last year of high school) curriculum, the history taught in French schools stopped with the end of the Second World War.[5] In her novels, Sebbar repeatedly presents young Maghrebians who do not know anything about the Algerian war.[6]

The war had similar effects in France to those of the Vietnam War in the United States, and the parallels between these two wars (France participated in both) are not lost on Sebbar, whose "green Chinaman from Africa" is a young boy of mixed heritage named Mohamed. His Algerian paternal grandfather and namesake was sent to fight in what was then Indochina, then returned to France with a Vietnamese wife who gave birth to Mohamed's father, Slim.

The Algerian and Vietnam wars were fought mostly in the 1950s and 1960s, and were the last two major Western colonial wars. Both caused acute violence, followed by collective guilt feelings in the French and American psyches. Whereas in the United States the shame is being exorcized (notably through film), in France the Algerian war has been until recently a rather silenced reality. Such silencing has contributed to the collective forgetting of a war that was never officially recognized as such by the French government.[7] *Beur* writers Azouz Begag and Abdellatif Chaouite comment on the French treatment of the war:

> *Guerre d'Algérie*: terminée en 1962. Comme l'élève efface un tableau en classe, on a effacé le souvenir de cette guerre de l'histoire de France. D'ailleurs cet épisode est

désigné comme "événement." Un événement se caractérise comme un "point de détail."[8]

[*Algerian War*: ended in 1962. Just as a pupil erases the classroom blackboard, the memory of that war was erased from French history. Besides, that episode is referred to as an "event." An event can be characterized as a "detail."]

The reference to the classroom is not accidental. Education is a privileged means of creating civic consciousness in young citizens, and the teaching one receives in school, especially where history is concerned, still retains the central purpose of reinforcing a sense of national identity. At the time when Begag and Chaouite were going through the French school system (in the 1960s and 1970s), the Algerian war was not yet being taught in school. If, as the nineteenth-century French philologist, historian, and Orientalist Ernest Renan argues, forgetting specific elements is necessary to the construction of a national identity, then one might surmise that French national identity continues to be very strong:

> L'oubli, et je dirai même l'erreur historique, sont un facteur essentiel de la création d'une nation, et c'est ainsi que le progrès des études historiques est souvent pour la nationalité un danger. L'investigation historique, en effet, remet en lumière les faits de violence qui se sont passés à l'origine de toutes les formations politiques. . . . L'unité se fait toujours brutalement.[9]

> [Forgetting, I would even go so far as to say historical error, is a crucial factor in the creation of a nation, which is why progress in historical studies often constitutes a danger for (the principle of) nationality. Indeed, historical enquiry brings to light deeds of violence which took place at the origin of all political formations. . . . Unity is always effected by means of brutality.]

One can wonder whether the emphasis on the Second World War in French public life, the media, and education, and on the literary scene, in the past twenty years is not due in part to a displacement, a "Freudian slip": what is being silenced (the Algerian war) resurfaces as an excess of speech about a previous war.[10]

Historian Henry Rousso, in his book *Le Syndrome de Vichy*, uses a similar argument regarding the Second World War.[11] He argues that World War II is one of the "crises profondes de l'unité et de l'identité françaises [deep crises in French unity and identity]" (14); it is of the same magnitude as the French Revolution, the Dreyfus affair, and the Algerian war—each of which crises comes to be partially replayed in the subsequent one. He divides what he calls the "Vichy syndrome" into four phases of evolution, charting a movement from amnesia to obsession: the first phase, one of interrupted mourning (1944–54); the second (1954–71), one of repression (forgetting and amnesia), with a replay due to the Algerian war; the third, from 1971 to 1974, a short phase of the return of the repressed and shattering of established myths about the war; and finally, the last phase (in which we are still engaged), one of obsession (20–21).

Borrowing this model to explore the question of the French in the Algerian war, I would like to argue that the phase of mourning for the loss of French Algeria was quickly stifled by the repression of the pain and shame created by that war, as France moved into the second phase of its "Algeria syndrome." The third and fourth phases of the Vichy syndrome may have been facilitated by the desire to cover up the double loss caused by the Algerian trauma: the loss of innocence (which had been regained by the erasure of memories of Vichy and the collaboration) due to the Nazi-like methods employed by the French military in the Algerian conflict and the loss of a land that signified the end of France's status as an imperial power and thus signaled a crisis in French identity. Rousso suggests this when quoting Krystoff Pomian:

> "Une époque révolue . . . se met, quand vient son heure, à fonctionner comme un écran sur lequel les générations qui se suivent peuvent projeter, en les objectivant, leurs contradictions, leurs déchirements, leurs conflits." C'est ce qui semble s'être passé à l'orée des années 1970 avec le souvenir de l'Occupation. (15)

> ["When its time comes, a bygone era . . . can function like a screen on which the next generations can project their contradictions, rifts and conflicts by objectifying them." This is what seems to have happened in the early 1970s with the memory of the Occupation.]

Regarding the Algerian war, France is still immersed in the second phase of the syndrome, that of repression. French efforts to repress that period create, in Rousso's words, "des rejeux de la faille [replays of the rift]" (87). Just as the Algerian war acted as a replay of the earlier trauma and allowed unresolved issues about it to resurface, the subsequent obsession about World War II, in turn, helped cover up the painful scars of the new conflict. In his article "Mémoire d'Algérie," Mustapha Marrouchi remarks that while the Algerian war remains partly taboo and within the realm of the unsaid, debates rage about World War II and the French Revolution. Just as Rousso notes that it took years before historians were allowed access to the Vichy archives, Marrouchi mentions that the repatriated archives on the Algerian war were still off-limits to scholars in 1990.[12]

In keeping with Renan's thesis and as shown by Rousso, certain aspects of World War II are also silenced: the discourse on the Resistance and concentration camps has served to cover up French collaboration with the Germans

(Rousso, 96). The Germans have been constructed by an official historical discourse (taught in schools) as the archenemy (a "colonizer," as Césaire would say) so as to make it easier to forget that allegiance lines cannot be drawn that easily, and that many French people indirectly gained from or participated in the German occupation. The deep internal divisions of French society under Vichy were more threatening to a sense of national identity than the Occupation itself and were therefore occulted during the second phase of the Vichy syndrome (Rousso, 18). Similarly, the Algerian war reopened ideological rifts between the French—splits that came close to turning into a full-blown civil war—around issues such as the use of torture by the French military, de Gaulle's 1959 policy change from supporting French Algeria to favoring Algerian self-determination, and OAS (pro-French Algeria) terrorism in the early 1960s (Stora, 74–91, 113; Rousso, 94–95). As had been the case after Vichy, these internal divisions were covered up and excised from the collective memory during the second phase of the Algeria syndrome. At the end of their magnificent "picture book" *La France en guerre d'Algérie*, historians Laurent Gervereau, Jean-Pierre Rioux, and Benjamin Stora conclude that

> cette guerre, interdite de reconnaissance nationale, ne peut que revivre doublement, ressassée, inlassable, inclassable, dans les mémoires de ceux qui en ont souffert à des titres divers. . . . L'enjeu français, à trente ans de distance du sang et des larmes d'Algérie, est donc sans doute d'avoir à se pardonner d'avoir tourné une page dont on savait trop bien qu'elle n'était pas blanche.[13]

> [this nonclassifiable war which was refused national recognition can only be brought back doubly, incessantly relived in the memories of those who suffered because of it in different ways. . . . What is at stake for the French, thirty years away from the blood and tears of Algeria, is thus, undoubtedly, having to forgive themselves for turning over a page which they knew only too well was not blank.]

The stakes are much higher than these three historians acknowledge. The war, rather than being simply relived through memory, is actually being waged again and again on French territory through racially motivated incidents and racist discourse. Rather than needing to forgive themselves for turning over a new leaf, the French need to face the consequences of the fact that the page was, in fact, never quite turned.

The Algerian War and Anti-Maghrebian Racism in France

A corollary to the cover-up of the Algerian conflict, a war that is now in a "semiotic twilight zone,"[14] could thus be the increase of racist rhetoric and racist sentiment in France. René Gallissot points out that the Algerian war created a shift from anti-Semitic nationalism to colonial racism in France. Colonial racism returned to France from its Algerian setting by being transferred onto immigrants in such a way that "le Nord-Africain devient l'immigré type // [the North African becomes the typical immigrant]."[15] At the end of his book *L'Identité de la France*, historian Fernand Braudel discusses three main reasons for the "immigration problem" in France: economic, racist, and cultural.[16] He rejects the first two: the immigrants do not take jobs from the French, but perform tasks that the French refuse to do; even though they may create some economic difficulties because they receive benefits and social services, they also contribute to French economic growth and to an increase in the standard of living (189). As for the question of race, Braudel points out that this is a false issue, because Maghrebians are white and the French, with the country's history of immigration, are all of mixed ethnic backgrounds (192). Braudel's analysis of the immigration question thus centers on what he calls "cultural" reasons, which appears to be a code word for Islam as not simply a religion, but also a way of life (195). The two main problems Braudel singles out are, predictably, the authority of the father and the status of women (196).

Braudel's considerations, however, are conveniently idealistic. He brushes aside widespread, viscerally negative perceptions of Maghrebian immigrants in France, sidestepping the crucial issue of racism with facile "melting-pot" comments. As Maxim Silverman argues, "Ideologically constructed differences do not vanish simply by being proved to be of minimal scientific value: 'race' might not exist but racism does."[17] Braudel also neglects to account for the human tendency (analyzed by René Girard in *Violence and the Sacred*) to look for a powerless scapegoat to blame for problems befalling a group (in the case of France, economic problems triggering a psychological uncertainty about national identity).[18] Although the cultural reasons for the problematic insertion of Maghrebians into French society are real, blaming Islam as the only obstacle to Maghrebian integration is a reductive gesture that not only puts the blame on the "Other" side, but also conveniently covers up two long-standing French traditions, patriarchy and racism/anti-Semitism. Braudel's analysis thus inscribes itself in a French, Orientalist discursive tradition that has created what Gallissot calls a "préjugé d'incompatibilité des cultures [prejudged incompatibility between cultures]"; in such discourse, Islam often functions as the marker of irreducible difference.[19] Significantly, Braudel never mentions the Algerian war. Beyond the economic, social, and religious causes for the current anti-Maghrebian racism, the anger displayed at Maghrebians for being "different," for not assimilating as easily as other groups into the fabric of French life, takes root at a deeper, unconscious level. The eight years of violence between Algeria and France have been almost completely silenced or erased in France in an attempt at forgetting (in an interesting parallel to their overexploitation in Algeria).[20]

In that light, the explosion of racist violence in France over the past two decades could well be interpreted as a Freudian return of the repressed. According to Freud, what used to be familiar but has been subsequently repressed resurfaces through unconscious acts and dreams, and expresses itself in the compulsion to repeat.[21] The escalation of anti-Arab incidents in the 1980s, together with the generalization of racist rhetoric in the same period, could be linked to the long repression first of the violent reality of the Algerian war, then of the psychological loss experienced by the French after 1962.

Any analysis of anti-Arab racism and the "immigration question" in France must take into account the historical and psychological scars the Algerian war has left on the French collective unconscious. Unfortunately, the war is rarely factored into studies on immigration. Moroccan novelist Tahar Ben Jelloun concurs with this in his remarkable study of racism in France, ironically titled *Hospitalité française*:

> Pour certains, la guerre d'Algérie n'est pas encore terminée. La présence sur le sol français d'un peu moins d'un million d'immigrés algériens excite leur haine nostalgique, et lorsqu'ils agressent un Arabe, cela s'inscrit indirectement dans le deuil impossible et intolérable que l'histoire exige à propos de "l'Algérie française."[22]

> [For some, the Algerian war isn't over yet. The presence on French territory of a little less than one million Algerian immigrants arouses their nostalgic hatred, and when they attack an Arab, this inscribes itself indirectly in the impossible and intolerable mourning which history demands regarding "French Algeria."]

Ben Jelloun's analysis intersects with Rousso's. Both use the concept of mourning as a key notion to understand the situation in France. Ben Jelloun's "impossible and intolerable mourning" corresponds to Rousso's "interrupted mourning." Unresolved and repressed feelings about the Algerian war fester and are carried over into new situations, such as the question of immigration in France, a topic so charged that simply to say the word in France nowadays tends to trigger overwhelmingly negative reactions. At least at the unconscious level, racist acts can be seen as a continuation of the repressed, lost colonial war. The nostalgia for "French Algeria" discussed by Ben Jelloun is a sign of such a repression. In *Women and War*, Jean Bethke Elshtain notes the link between the two poles of "forgetting, on one hand," and "remembering in nostalgic and sentimental ways, on the other."[23] Memory as the organization of forgetting (Rousso, 14) must substitute nostalgic recollections, "screen memories," to the more painful memories.[24]

The 1992 celebration of the thirtieth anniversary of the end of the Algerian war often served to boost such screen memories rather than to create a space in which painful memories could have been allowed to resurface and heal. French magazine *Paris-Match*'s poll on the French and the Algerian war, for instance, reveals that although the war was deemed the second most important event to have occurred since 1945 (after the May 1968 riots), 44 percent of the people answering the question were against the anniversary celebration because it "fait revivre des souvenirs douloureux [brings back painful memories]." A large majority of the people polled (67 percent) indicated that they believe Algeria's independence to have been unavoidable. (This may explain why they would rather avoid thinking about the lengthy and bloody war fought for nothing—unless one sees this as an a posteriori rationalization that helps them to deal with the loss.) Remarkably absent from these pages, which otherwise make references to *pieds-noirs*, *harkis*,[25] and the Algerian people, is any mention of Maghrebians now living in France.[26]

In the survey, many questions were asked about Franco-Algerian relations and the Algerian people; the responses show a lack of knowledge and/or interest in the topic (the majority of answers fall into the categories "neither" or "doesn't know"). Had questions been asked about Maghrebians in France, the answers might have been much more opinionated. Finally, at the bottom of the page, *Paris-Match* offers several old family pictures of famous *pied-noirs* in Algeria, titled "L'Album de la 'Nostalgérie' [The Album of 'Nostalgeria']." The caption accompanying the pictures centers on these *pieds-noirs*' "tender and marvelous memories" of prewar Algeria and on their current achievements in France. The war itself is never mentioned, in a striking illustration of the role nostalgia plays in the constitution of screen memories.

The link that *Paris-Match* refuses to make between the Algerian war and the current anti-Maghrebian racism in France, so well expressed by Ben Jelloun, is also obvious to Begag and Chaouite:

> D'abord, le temps de la "question" de l'immigration maghrébine n'est pas son temps premier, mais un temps second. Un temps qui fait écho à un autre où l'immigré-visiteur et l'hôte-accueillant se tenaient en position inverse: c'était le "temps des colonies." . . . C'est là le véritable temps premier: celui de l'effraction violente, de la mort d'hommes, au cours duquel les imaginaires ont été marqués pour toujours. Ce premier temps a provoqué des effets bouleversants durables dans le système par son intensité. Il a, d'autre part, amené un deuxième temps, celui du souvenir. Il est réactivé par toutes les énergies et les tensions non liquidées au cours du premier temps. Le temps des discours actuels sur les Maghrébins de France revêt l'allure de cet après-coup de souvenir.[27]

[First, the time of the Maghrebian immigration "question" is not a first stage, but a second one. A stage which echoes another in which the visiting immigrant and the welcoming host were inverted: such was the "time of the colonies." . . . That was the true first stage, that of violent breaking into and deaths, which marked the imaginary forever. Because of its intensity, that first stage created long-lasting, overwhelming psychological effects. It also brought about a second stage, that of memory. That stage is reactivated by all the energies and tensions which were not settled during the first stage. The time of current discourses on Maghrebians in France takes on the form of that aftermath of memory.]

Begag and Chaouite and Rousso are indeed discussing the same phenomenon. The current anti-Maghrebian racism in France, with its violent rhetoric and actions, is "an aftermath of memory," "a replay of the rift" caused by the Algerian war.

In his book *Arabicides*, reporter Fausto Giudice goes even further in investigating racially motivated murders in France in the past two decades. He not only claims that such murders restage the Algerian war, but also suggests that contemporary French society may have been founded on the general "arabicide" committed during the Algerian war on both Algerian and French territories.[28] He claims that the memory of that arabicide "a été sciemment effacée de la conscience historique française [was knowingly erased from French historical consciousness]."[29] Similarly, Pervillé talks about "une volonté officielle d'amnésie [an official desire for amnesia]."[30] Giudice notes that several assailants and murderers of Maghrebians in France between 1970 and 1991 were either Algerian war veterans or children of such men, and implies that the pardon granted for crimes committed during the Algerian war encouraged the repetition of similar acts in France in time of peace.[31]

The Fifth Republic's origin lies in the Algerian war and its devastating effects on the *métropole* in the 1950s. This stable regime, of which the French are so proud, was born out of the Algerian-French conflict, a source that the French prefer not to remember.[32] As Benjamin Stora remarks in *La Gangrène et l'oubli*, the Algerian war was a founding event not only of the Algerian nation, but also of the current French Republic (7, 317). Stora suggests that France's deep involvement with the memory of the Second World War in the 1960s served as a way to cover up the Fifth Republic's shameful origin (222). In the French as in the Algerian case, Renan's assessment is confirmed: the war functioned as a "deed of violence which took place at the origin of [these particular] political formations." In what follows, I will chart how Sebbar's novel deals with such complex issues and confirms the existence of the Algeria syndrome.

Literature as a *Lieu de Mémoire*

In *Le Chinois vert d'Afrique*, Sebbar points repeatedly to the link between current French racism and the Algerian (and Vietnam) war(s) by putting the most offensive racist discourse in the mouths of the Frenchmen who fought in these wars.[33] Mohamed, the novel's protagonist, falls in love with Myra, a young *métisse* (part Moroccan, part Italian, part French) who lives with her grandfather Emile in a lower-middle-class neighborhood (*pavillons de banlieue*) not too distant from Mohamed's housing project. One of their neighbors, Tuilier, exemplifies the most violent racist and classist ideology in the novel. As a young man he fought in Indochina, and he wishes he had been sent to Algeria as well. Tuilier vicariously lives his failed military career through dreams of a neighborhood militia. He sets up a room in his house for target practice and owns a trained police dog named Mao.[34] The large young immigrant population living in the projects provides him with a live target for war games. Together with a handful of other older, working-class, conservative men, he attempts to set up a militia in an act that he calls "self-defense" (233). Taking "justice" into his own hands allows him to give himself more importance and power than he actually has, as he bestows upon himself the mission of "faire des rondes matin et soir avec mon chien Mao. Ça rend service à tout le monde [patrolling the area morning and evening with my dog Mao as a service to everyone]" (137).

The proximity of the housing projects and Mohamed's wanderings around Myra's garden are all that is needed to generate racist hysteria: "Tuilier parle de ses armes, de la guerre, du club de tir, de l'insécurité des banlieues, des voyous, des Arabes qui colonisent la France, de la légitime défense [Tuilier speaks of his weapons, war, the shooting club, insecurity in the suburbs, hoodlums, Arabs who are colonizing France, justified self-defense]" (136). Tuilier's racist discourse is rooted in violence, as he projects his own (real) violence and dreams of a glorious military career onto the (fantasized) violence in the projects, which he associates with Maghrebian immigrants and their offspring; for him, the jump from "hoodlums" to "Arabs who are colonizing France" is automatic. The equation of populations of Arab origin with violent and lawless groups brings about the "logical" conclusion, the need for self-protection—in an ironic reversal of reality, for, as we have seen, the 1980s were marked by the rise in racist crime.[35] Sebbar's use of reported speech and of the enumerative device creates an ironic distance between speaker and reader, helping expose the flimsiness of the argument.

In these few lines, Sebbar has perfectly encapsulated racist and demagogic rhetoric à la Jean-Marie Le Pen. That same racist ideology, which is precisely what Braudel sidesteps so easily in his analysis, has been steadily gaining ground in France, where the Front National, Le Pen's extreme right party, nationally received an estimated 14 percent of votes in the first round of the regional elections in May 1992.[36] The percentages are almost double in some regions such as the South, where a very depressed economic situation coupled with the presence of large *pied-noir* and immigrant populations contributes to a stronger anti-Maghrebian sentiment. In the first round of the presidential elections of April 1995, candidate Le Pen gathered 15.7 percent of all votes (4,673,000). The two extreme-right candidates together (Le Pen and Philippe de Villiers) swept one-fifth of all votes (20.44 percent), almost as much as Socialist candidate Lionel Jospin (23.3 percent) and much more than the Communist and Trotskyist candidates, who scored less than 14 percent together (France 2 evening news, April 24 and April 26, 1995). In the municipal elections of June 1995, Front National mayoral candidates were elected in three southern cities (Toulon, Orange, and Marignane). A former Front National member was chosen as mayor of Nice, one of France's largest cities. Although the French political class is currently unanimous in distancing itself from the Front National, Le Pen's rhetoric on immigration has spread to most rightist politicians and is not being countered very strongly by the Left either. For example, the reform of the French Nationality Code initiated by then Minister of the Interior Charles Pasqua was finally passed into law by the National Assembly in May 1993. These changes make it more difficult for children of immigrants born in France and foreign spouses of French nationals to acquire French nationality. Gérard Noiriel defines the racist rhetoric that Sebbar illustrates in her novel:

> La force de cette stratégie politique tient à ce qu'elle ne s'adresse pas à la raison, mais à l'"inconscient" qui sommeille en chacun de nous. . . . le discours xénophobe joue volontiers sur les fantasmes: la peur, l'exotisme. . . . En martelant constamment les mêmes thèmes, le xénophobe tente de susciter des associations d'idées et surtout d'images qui peuvent conduire aux automatismes de pensée qui illustrent fréquemment les propos racistes.[37]

> [The strength of that political strategy resides in the fact that it speaks not to reason, but to the "unconscious" dwelling within each of us. . . . xenophobic discourse readily plays on fantasies such as fear and exoticism. . . . By constantly hammering on the same themes, the xenophobe attempts to provoke associations of ideas and especially of images which can lead to the kind of automatic thinking frequently characteristic of racist remarks.]

It is no wonder that Tuilier's and his friends' rhetoric in *Le Chinois vert d'Afrique* should be so similar to Le Pen's. Gérard Mermet notes that—like Tuilier and his cohorts—the Front National's typical constituents are men (71 percent) from the lower and lower-middle classes living in large cities.[38] In *Le Chinois vert d'Afrique*, Tuilier's men, who claim to be "pas des violents, pas agressifs ni rien [not violent, not aggressive, really]," long for a context of violence legitimated by the colonial wars (233):

> Si on pouvait employer les grands moyens, ils retourneraient tous chez eux, vite fait. Dommage, c'est loin la guerre d'Algérie, parce que alors là, on rigolerait pas, balayés, ratissés. On a déjà un ancien d'Algérie dans notre comité, c'est un dur. . . . Il en a dans le pantalon. (234)

> [If we could resort to drastic measures, they'd all go back home quick. It's too bad the Algerian war was so long ago, because then, there'd be no messing around, they'd all be swept out, cleaned out. We already have an Algeria vet in our group, he's a tough guy. . . . He's got balls.]

The desire for a revenge over the French failure in Algeria, or rather the desire to take up the Algerian war again, this time on French territory, until a French victory, is shown to be one of the driving forces behind anti-Arab racism. In a psychological fantasy that ignores the factor of economic power imbalance, the situation of the Algerian war is reversed, the Arabs being now perceived as the colonizer: "Ils nous colonisent. . . . On est colonisé [They're colonizing us. . . . We're colonized]" (236). This perverse inversion of the historical situation legitimates "drastic measures" (such as the militia) and the racism of the police force (233). For Benjamin Stora, such a discourse, based on revenge, which perceives the former colonized turned immigrant as a colonizer invading "civilized" territory, reactivates colonial racism and facilitates an unproblematic nationalist identification (288–90):

> La guerre d'Algérie continue à travers la lutte contre l'Islam. . . . La liturgie d'une France enracinée dans la pureté d'une identité mythique, sans cesse menacée, voilà ce qui légitime d'avance toutes les mesures de possibles violences, de "guerre" pour se défendre des "envahisseurs". (291)

> [The Algerian War is perpetuated through the struggle against Islam. . . . The liturgy of a France which would be rooted in the purity of a mythical, constantly threatened identity legitimates in advance any measure of possible violence and "war" taken to defend oneself from "invaders."]

Once again, the Manichean structures of Orientalist discourse exposed by Edward Said are summoned to perpetuate the perception of an alien, external enemy against whom an endangered national unity can be re-created.[39]

Conclusion

For Algerian writers living in France, the strategic need to write about the Algerian war appears all the more intense as their works become "a struggle of memory against forgetting."[40] This is a powerful response to Ernest Renan's argument about forgetting and national identity. Remembering is a crucial act to break the cycle of unconscious repetition resulting in the violent return of the repressed. Ben Jelloun disagrees with Renan as to the use of forgetting: even though France likes to forget certain memories, "l'oubli est mauvais conseiller. Quand il s'installe dans l'histoire, il la mutile et la détourne [forgetting is bad advice. When it settles in history, it mutilates and misappropriates it]."[41] Using the same words as American feminist Adrienne Rich, Ben Jelloun advises us to resist enforced amnesia ("refuser l'amnésie").[42] These writers are all criticizing the construction of a national identity predicated on their erasure as minorities and/or as women. The identity that contemporary Algerian women writers on the margins of Algerian and French societies are trying to establish must of necessity transcend national boundaries, and thus forgetting is of little strategic use to them. For them, it is time to orchestrate the multidimensionality of society's *métissage*.

It is precisely this *métissage* that like the Second World War or the Algerian war, is now contributing to the fueling of another crisis of French unity and identity. Because of unresolved issues carried over from previous crises, many French people feel threatened by the notion that national identities are by definition always already in process. This creates what Gérard Mermet calls an "obsession identitaire [obsession with identity]" among the French.[43] For Stora, the repressed "amputation" of Algeria from France is the cause of a French "gangrene" that is revealed by the current crisis of French nationalism (318). Maxim Silverman suggests that "the current obsession with immigration in France itself [is] indicative of a crisis in the structures of the nation-state," as the unification of Europe is beginning to erode the ideology of French sovereignty.[44]

Elshtain summarizes Hannah Arendt's theory that "the nation, one and indivisible, requires an external enemy to come into being."[45] As the national feeling is being threatened, the repressed returns: the population of Arab origin in France is singled out as the scapegoat, the enemy "Other" endangering some essentialist, fixed, and romanticized essence of *francité*. For Ben Jelloun, "les gens ont peur de ne plus ressembler à l'image qu'ils se font d'eux-mêmes [people are afraid of no longer corresponding to the image they have of themselves]."[46] It is precisely at the point at which the static notion of a "true" French identity is no longer valid that so many people feel the need to mobilize around the fight to preserve it. In the words of Herman Lebovics, the discourse of an "authentic" national identity is generally undertaken "at moments of great cultural-political contestation; and it is just at those conjunctures that the interpenetration of cultures is most evident."[47]

According to Renan, the construction of the nation props itself up on an original violence that is then repressed. But the repressed repeatedly returns, endangering the construction it had originally allowed. Such is the paradox of the creation of national identity. Forgetting both enables and destabilizes that creation. In the case of France and the Algerian war, historical amnesia has been contributing to the compulsive repetition of a blocked situation. In this respect, the spring 1993 changes to the French Nationality Code (which had failed to pass in 1986–87) are part of an ongoing process to separate "us" from "them" legally at a time in which the separations are becoming more blurred.[48] In spite of this recent setback, the insights of the writers mentioned above— especially the French historical scholarship of the 1990s—can still be read as hopeful signs that France may finally soon be ready to enter into the third phase of its Algeria syndrome and to face the ghosts of the past in order to meet the challenges of the future. It is my hope that this essay may contribute in some small way to such an overture.

Notes

1. Noted in Benjamin Stora, *La Gangrène et l'oubli: La mémoire de la guerre d'Algérie* (Paris: La Découverte, 1991), 13. Page numbers for further references to this work appear in parentheses in the text. All translations in this chapter are mine unless otherwise referenced. I have modified existing translations whenever necessary to remain as close as possible to the original.

2. This is by no means a unique or anomalous event in world history. Before rushing to make connections between Islamic culture and the repression of women's rights, readers should remember that the same phenomenon occurred in Europe and in the United States after World War II. In *Women and War* (New York: Basic Books, 1987), Jean Bethke Elshtain uses previous studies to demonstrate that European women's participation in the war did not change their economic status or society's essentialist beliefs about women's place; moreover, even the small percentage of women who participated in the war effort considered it a response to an exceptional situation and did not necessarily expect to continue working after the war (7). Djamila Amrane's *Les Femmes algériennes dans la guerre* (Paris: Plon, 1991), esp. 260–72, bears striking parallels to Elshtain's analysis. During both the Second World War and the Algerian War of National Liberation, few women actually bore arms. According to Marnia Lazreg, "The FLN's definition of women's tasks in the war was based on a conventional understanding of the sexual division of labor," although Amrane adds that women's actual tasks went far beyond those sketched out for them by the male leadership (252–53). Marnia Lazreg, "Gender and Politics in Algeria: Unraveling the Religious Paradigm," *Signs* 15 (Summer 1990): 767. Like European women in the 1940s, many Algerian *mujahidat* saw their participation in the war as an extraordinary response to an extraordinary situation and expected life to return to "normal" at the end of the war (Amrane, 294).

3. Quoted in Jean-Marie Salien, "L'Ironie du métissage dans *Le Chinois vert*

d'Afrique de Leïla Sebbar," paper delivered at the Eighth Annual Conference on Foreign Literature, Wichita State University, Wichita, Kans., April 1991, 4.

4. Leïla Sebbar, *Le Chinois vert d'Afrique* (Paris: Stock, 1984). Page numbers for further references to this work appear in parentheses in the text.

5. Henry Rousso, *Le Syndrome de Vichy* (*1944–198 . . .*) (Paris: Seuil, 1987), 285. Page numbers for further references to this work appear in parentheses in the text. Sebbar's novel was published the year following the decree. Stora notes that 1986 was the first year in which students taking the *Baccalauréat* were asked questions on the Algerian war in a few regions (*La Gangrène*, 353).

6. Leïla Sebbar, *Shérazade, 17 ans, brune, frisée, les yeux verts* (Paris: Stock, 1982), 56, 147, 164.

7. See Serge Berstein, "Une Guerre sans nom," in *La France en guerre d'Algérie: Novembre 1954–Juillet 1962*, ed. Laurent Gervereau, Jean-Pierre Rioux, and Benjamin Stora (Paris: Musée d'histoire contemporaine-BDIC, 1992), 34–39; Stora, *La Gangrène*, 13–24. For a discussion of similarities and differences between the Algerian and Vietnam wars, see David Schalk, *War and the Ivory Tower: Algeria and Vietnam* (New York: Oxford University Press, 1991), 16–37. Since the early 1990s, Algeria and its historical past with France have been covered in the news much more frequently because of current events: the success, then repression of the Muslim fundamentalist group Front Islamique de Salut (FIS), the assassination of President Mohammed Boudiaf, the thirtieth anniversary of the end of the Algerian war, and finally, the ongoing murders of many Algerian intellectuals and foreigners by FIS sympathizers. This is not to say that nothing was published on the Algerian war by French people since the end of the conflict. These works, however, do remain quantitatively low, especially when compared with the amount of discourse still being produced about World War II. Guy Pervillé remarks that although there exist many testimonial and journalistic narratives on the war, very few historical books have been published on the subject in France. Guy Pervillé, "Historiographie de la guerre," in *La France en guerre d'Algérie: Novembre 1954–Juillet 1962*, ed. Laurent Gervereau, Jean-Pierre Rioux, and Benjamin Stora (Paris: Musée d'histoire contemporaine-BDIC, 1992), 308.

8. Azouz Begag and Abdellatif Chaouite, *Ecarts d'identité* (Paris: Seuil, 1990), 11–12.

9. Ernest Renan, "Qu'est-ce qu'une nation?" in *Oeuvres complètes*, vol. 1 (Paris: Calmann-Lévy, 1947 [1882]), 891. In English, "What Is a Nation?" trans. Martin Thom, in *Nation and Narration*, ed. Homi K. Bhabha (London: Routledge, 1990), 11.

10. Rousso notes that although the number of French films on World War II was never high, tens of thousands of books of all kinds have been published on the subject (*Le Syndrome de Vichy*, 254). Although Benjamin Stora asserts that the fewer than 1,300 books published on the Algerian war between 1955 and 1988 in France constitute a large corpus, this number is very low when compared with the outpouring of publications on World War II. Moreover, fewer than ten motion pictures have been released that deal directly with the Algerian war. As of 1989, *La Bataille d'Alger*, one of the most famous of these films, had never been shown on French television. Benjamin Stora, "La Guerre d'Algérie en livres," in *La Bibliothèque des deux rives: Sur la Méditerranée occidentale*, ed. Thierry Paquot (Paris: Lieu commun, 1992), 158, 160.

11. I would like to thank Rosemarie Scullion for bringing this remarkable book to my attention and for triggering my thinking on this subject.

12. Mustapha Marrouchi, "Mémoire d'Algérie: Écrire l'histoire," *Contemporary French Civilization* 14 (Summer/Fall 1990): 245–46, 251–52. In 1991, Amrane noted that the archives of both the FLN-ALN and the French army and police were still inaccessible (*Les Femmes,* 272). After 30 years, in July 1992, the French Ministry of Defense finally opened up most of its archival collection on the war to the public (Pervillé, "Historiographie de la guerre," 309).

13. Laurent Gervereau, Jean-Pierre Rioux, and Benjamin Stora, "Conclusion," in *La France en guerre d'Algérie: Novembre 1954–Juillet 1962,* ed. Laurent Gervereau, Jean-Pierre Rioux, and Benjamin Stora (Paris: Musée d'histoire contemporaine-BDIC, 1992), 304.

14. These words are Jean Bethke Elshtain's on the Vietnam War in *Women and War,* 219.

15. René Gallissot, "La Guerre et l'immigration algérienne en France," in *La Guerre d'Algérie et les français,* ed. Jean-Pierre Rioux (Paris: Fayard, 1990), 345.

16. Fernand Braudel, *L'Identité de la France: Les Hommes et les choses* (Paris: Arthaud-Flammarion, 1986), 185–200.

17. Maxim Silverman, *Deconstructing the Nation: Immigration, Racism and Citizenship in Modern France* (London: Routledge, 1992), 165.

18. René Girard, *Violence and the Sacred,* trans. Patrick Gregory (Baltimore: Johns Hopkins University Press, 1977).

19. Gallissot, "La Guerre," 345. For historical and sociological analyses of French identity and immigration, see Herman Lebovics, *True France: The Wars over Cultural Identity, 1900–1945* (Ithaca, N.Y.: Cornell University Press, 1992); Gérard Noiriel, *Le Creuset français: Histoire de l'immigration XIXe–XXe siècle* (Paris: Seuil, 1988); Dominique Schnapper, *L'Europe des immigrés* (Paris: François Bourin, 1992); Silverman, *Deconstructing the Nation.*

20. Pervillé comments that because the war is used in Algeria as the source of any political legitimacy, writing the history of the National War of Liberation is considered a state matter ("Historiographie de la guerre," 309). It is important to note that, as mentioned earlier, one major aspect of the national war of liberation has also been covered up in Algeria: the participation of women on *all* of the war's battlegrounds (Amrane, *Les Femmes,* 13, 293–94). Benjamin Stora sees a parallel between the Algerian and the French treatments of the war. In Algeria as well, "l'histoire officielle a . . . fabriqué de l'oubli [official history fabricated forgetting]" (*La Gangrène,* 304) by setting the FLN as the only nationalist force, erasing the existence of other, older parties in favor of independence and occulting the violent purges and political murders between the different groups during the war (122, 141–44, 151). The names of war leaders have been erased by an official version that celebrates the united Algerian people fighting on the side of the FLN (162). The war between Algeria and France was also, more dangerously, "une double guerre civile, à la fois algéro-algérienne et franco-française [a double civil war, both Algerian–Algerian and French–French]" (187). In both cases, the civil war aspect was occulted in official versions.

21. Sigmund Freud, *Beyond the Pleasure Principle* (New York: Liveright, 1950

[1922]); and "The Uncanny," in *Collected Papers* (London: Hogarth/Institute of Psychoanalysis, 1934), 4:368–407.

22. Tahar Ben Jelloun, *Hospitalité française: Racisme et immigration maghrébine* (Paris: Seuil, 1984), 24.

23. Elshtain, *Women and War,* 223.

24. Rousso identifies the 1945 Liberation as a screen memory used to cover up French wartime collaboration with the Nazis (*Le Syndrome de Vichy,* 25).

25. The *pieds-noirs* are French colonists in Algeria who had to move back to France after the Algerian victory, often losing everything they owned in the process; the *harkis* are Algerians who fought on the side of France during the war. Those who were not killed as traitors in Algeria were repatriated to France, where they were not only ghettoized in camps but are also often ostracized by other Maghrebians.

26. "1962–1992: 30 ans après . . . ," in "L'Album de la 'Nostalgérie,'" *Paris-Match,* 9 July 1992, 92–93.

27. Begag and Chaouite, *Ecarts d'identité,* 29.

28. Fausto Giudice, *Arabicides: Une Chronique française 1970–1991* (Paris: La Découverte, 1992), 106, 12.

29. Ibid., 337.

30. Pervillé, "Historiographie de la guerre," 309.

31. Giudice, *Arabacides,* 347. History, because it has been repressed, does indeed repeat itself. The 1953 pardon of most Occupation collaborators, legally termed an *oubli juridique* (judicial forgetting), was repeated in the pardon of war crimes committed in Algeria (Rousso, *Le Syndrome de Vichy,* 62, 105). As early as 1962, the French government began making provisions for amnesty. A string of amnesties for war crimes in Algeria followed in 1964, 1966, 1968, 1974, and 1982. Stora suggests that the 1982 complete amnesty and reinstatement of civil servants and military personnel involved in the Algerian conflict was directly responsible for the new rise of extreme right groups in political life because it gave them a new legitimacy (the Front National went from 0.8 percent of votes in 1981 to 14.5 percent in 1988—a sad by-product of Mitterrand's first *septennat*). (*La Gangrène,* 215, 281–83, 289).

32. See, for example, Serge Berstein, *La France de l'expansion: I-La République gaullienne 1958–1969* (Paris: Seuil, 1989), 45.

33. At the same time, she is careful to show that not all war veterans react in the same way: Inspector Laruel and Myra's grandfather, Emile Cordier, are much more open to Mohamed and what he represents than are the other veterans, Laruel because of a certain Orientalist fascination, Emile because of his leftist politics of solidarity.

34. The name is ironic in that it is a tribute to a Communist leader from a conservative man for whom Communism is a code word for the loss of law and order. On the other hand, it is significant in that it foregrounds Tuilier's admiration for the kind of strong, totalitarian form of leadership he would like to exercise over his community and against young Maghrebians.

35. See Giudice, *Arabicides;* Ben Jelloun, *Hospitalité française,* 41.

36. Le Pen, as Rousso mentions, was predictably a supporter of French Algeria (*Le Syndrome de Vichy,* 210). In the first years of the war, Le Pen served as a *parachutiste* (paratrooper) in Algeria, an intoxicating experience for him (Jean-Pierre Rioux, *La France de la IVe République,* vol. 2, *L'expansion et l'impuissance, 1952–1958* [Paris: Seuil,

1983], 135), which may have included his participation in torture during the (in)famous Battle of Algiers (Stora, *La Gangrène*, 290). In *Le Chinois*, Tuilier, commenting on the wars in Indochina and Algeria, says that "La France a tout perdu [France has lost it all]," indicating once again the lingering sense of loss about the wars that significantly informs his thoughts and actions twenty years later (135).

37. Noiriel, *Le Creuset français*, 275–76.

38. Gérard Mermet, *Francoscopie 1993* (Paris: Larousse, 1992), 226.

39. See Edward W. Said's landmark book *Orientalism* (New York: Pantheon, 1978). Sebbar shows another driving force behind racism to be machismo and masculinist warrior values. Tuilier himself, the only son of a war widow, "pour échapper à la tyrannie maternelle, sans le dire à sa mère, il avait choisi de partir pour l'Indochine [to escape maternal tyranny, without telling his mother, he had chosen to enlist and go to Indochina]" (135). As for Marcel, the Algeria veteran of the militia mentioned above, his toughness and fearlessness are metaphorically measured through his virility: "He's got balls" (234). This is literally "proved" to the reader on the next page, a flashback to the Algerian war in which, after seeing dead, castrated young French soldiers, Marcel's company raped village women, then gathered them together and blew them up with grenades: "Un massacre, ce jour-là. Les femmes, les enfants, les jeunes, tout avait explosé, un feu d'artifice [A slaughter, that day. Women, children, youths, they had all exploded like fireworks]" (235).

In this novel, Sebbar foregrounds the links connecting war, hypermasculinity, and sexism, from Tuilier's flight from the maternal to Marcel's company's military exploits inscribed on the bodies of women and children. In her book *Sexuality and War: Literary Masks of the Middle East* (New York: New York University Press, 1990), Evelyne Accad explains that "there is a *jouissance*, an intensity of pleasure men reach in war" (140). The veterans' nostalgia for wartime in *Le Chinois vert d'Afrique*, together with their violent sexual use of women, illustrates Accad's claim. Accad asserts that "masculinity involves aggressiveness and violence, which are . . . linked with . . . exploitation of nature and women" (160). I am not arguing that Sebbar condemns *men* as a whole in an essentialist gesture, especially as she depicts men like Emile Cordier in very positive roles, but that she criticizes *masculinist*, racist values that place the white man at the top of a hierarchy of values predicated on violence. The acts of raping, setting fire to places and people, and killing express a desire for ultimate power waged through violence. Others are controlled through the use of a violence that has gone out of control.

40. Quoted by bell hooks, "Choosing the Margin as a Space of Radical Openness," in *Yearning: Race, Gender, and Cultural Politics* (Boston: South End, 1990), 147.

41. Ben Jelloun, *Hospitalité française*, 33.

42. Ibid., 24. See Adrienne Rich, "Resisting Amnesia: History and Personal Life," in *Blood, Bread and Poetry: Selected Prose 1979–1985* (New York: W. W. Norton, 1986), 136–55.

43. Mermet, *Francoscopie 1993*, 211.

44. Silverman, *Deconstructing the Nation*, 33.

45. Elshtain, *Women and War*, 256.

46. Ben Jelloun, *Hospitalité française*, 43.

47. Lebovics, *True France*, 125.

48. See Silverman, *Deconstructing the Nation*, 64–65, 107.

11 / *La Plus Grande France*: French Cultural Identity and Nation Building under Mitterrand

Panivong Norindr

Many cultural forms, from poetry to the plastic arts, have played important roles in the discursive and representational practices that define, legitimate, and valorize specific ideas of nationhood and of the nation-state.[1] Yeats's or Césaire's poetry, for instance, has been read as "heroic narratives" by *écrivains-patriotes*, "national" poets who have articulated the experiences, aspirations, and visions of, respectively, the Irish and the people of Martinique.[2] Their work, while contesting and complicating the idea of the nation as a continuous narrative of national progress, also elaborates a certain view of the nation. Architecture can likewise be seen as an ambivalent discourse that represents the nation as it problematizes the relation between art and politics. The discourse of architecture in France, as the debate on the Bibliothèque de France seems to illustrate, is a privileged aesthetic language that produces a complex cultural image of France and redraws the boundaries of *francité*.[3] Architecture thus allows us to test the concept of nationhood as "nation-space," as an "assemblage" and construction of a cultural space, and to see how it is engaged in reconfiguring a powerful image of Frenchness.

Although indebted to the work of historians such as E. H. Hobsbawm and Benedict Anderson and architectural historians such as François Chaslin, this essay will examine how the idea of a nation in contemporary France continues to be constructed, contested, and defended in relation not simply to contemporary political ideologies but against a broader system of colonialism that preceded it.[4] My focus here is on assessing the impact of various discourses—

233

political, cultural, aesthetic—that have allowed the powerful "idea" of the nation to emerge in this fin de siècle. I shall concentrate specifically on François Mitterrand's *grands travaux* as a conceptual scaffolding from which to question the process of construction of a French "national cultural identity." Although many critics have suggested that Mitterrand continued the historical tradition begun by his predecessors—for instance, he completed the Institut du monde arabe begun by Giscard d'Estaing—he also respected the *axe historique,* which runs from the Carrousel at the Louvre to the Obélisque of the Concorde and from the Arc de Triomphe to the Arche de la Défense. The continuity between Mitterrand's *grands travaux* and the politics of urban design of his predecessors since the Second Empire can be located in the ways these new urban markers delimit, inscribe, and reconfigure in space an image of France as a dominant cultural center. Mitterrand's *grands travaux,* which are the most ambitious manifestations of his *projet de culture,* can be seen as a complex extension of political reality, as cultural capital, and as an imaginary force of social control. They also function as a force of cultural expansionism reminiscent of the practices of colonial France.

To test this hypothesis, I want first to examine briefly an earlier attempt to circumscribe the idea of the nation through architecture, L'Exposition coloniale internationale de Paris, held in 1931, before turning to Mitterrand's *grands travaux* to highlight the cultural and political logic of "nation building" and to illustrate how France constructs a national identity through architecture. I will not proceed by comparison or analogy, but by "elaboration" and "affiliation," concepts borrowed from Antonio Gramsci. Said defines Gramsci's affiliation as "that implicit network of peculiarly cultural associations between forms, statements, and other aesthetic elaborations on the one hand, on the other, institutions, agencies, classes, and amorphous social forces."[5] He adds: "By elaboration Gramsci means two seemingly contradictory but actually complementary things. First, to elaborate means to refine, to work out (*e-labore*) some prior or more powerful idea, to perpetuate a worldview. Second, to elaborate means something more qualitatively positive, the proposition that culture itself or thought or art is a highly complex and quasi-autonomous extension of political reality."[6]

The Exposition coloniale internationale de Paris indeed elaborated a worldview.[7] Spatial reterritorialization of indigenous buildings and monuments produced a particular understanding of the French colonial empire. Native architectural space was altered to make way for a transfigured vision of indigenous buildings that conformed better to French aesthetic and political ideals. In the 1930s, architecture was elevated to the rank of "leader" among all artistic expressions because as *art total* it was said to embrace, and even subsume, all arts.[8] During the 1931 Exposition coloniale, architects were invested with the authority and power to promote *l'idée coloniale*. The *palais d'exposition* was conceived as an architectonic colonial manifesto, a public and official display of French colonial policies, which determined its discourse, circumscribed its space, and revealed its ideology. Significantly, all of the buildings constructed for the exposition were temporary pavilions not designed to last beyond the duration of the fair, with one notable exception, the Musée Permanent des Colonies, which still stands today although it has been renamed the Musée des Arts Africains et Océaniens. Unlike other pavilions, the Musée, built by Albert Laprade, was not erected as a pastiche of native architecture or a mixture of different styles.[9] The building was to be dedicated as the official temple to the glory of the colonies, and Laprade's challenge was to project the permanence of French culture in a distinctly French idiom. Although the Musée is an elaboration on a classical design, Laprade still managed to produce a French modernist edifice that critics considered to be an emblematic expression of the French nation, the "sublimation of the state."[10]

Its monumental design, one of the best examples of French 1930s architecture, reinterpreted classical forms in a modernist perspective. Construction techniques were also resolutely modern. Reinforced cement, first adopted by de Baudot in 1907, was used unsparingly, in the simplified Ionic-order pillars, floors, cornice, and even in the framework.[11] Because Laprade wanted to transcend the 1920s high modernist aesthetics of smooth white surfaces, the main facade was covered with a yellow stone facing, decorated by Alfred Janniot's phantasmatic bas-relief. The Musée Permanent des Colonies can be said to have inaugurated in that decade a new French style, a simplified "modern classicism" designed to reestablish France as a "leader de l'architecture internationale" and a powerful nation.[12]

Architectural practice reconfigures an important history and a fiction of what nationhood represents in seemingly paradoxical ways. Although the 1931 Exposition has been called the "apothéose de la plus grande France,"[13] only a few buildings can be said to have represented Frenchness. If architecture is a signifier of national identity, it was the vernacular architecture of the colonized peoples at the exposition that conveyed spatially the ideal of *la plus grande France,* a slogan conceived to rival the British Empire's "Greater Britain."[14] The reproduction of Ankgor Wat, Sudanese earth buildings, and the North African Casbah were the highlights of the exposition. These native buildings embodied in ambivalent fashion *la plus grande France* in a number of ways that cannot be discussed here at length. It suffices to say that the hegemony of French culture manifested itself in the way very different types of architecture were integrated in the same space to signify a model empire, a well-ordered and contained modern state. The strategic (re)placement of all these native buildings, built around a straight (Cartesian) avenue, was designed to gallicize their "native" appearance, just as French architects and urban planners had made the *quartier indigène* in Saigon, Casablanca, or Antananarivo conform to a French idiom.[15] The demolition/deconstruction of native architectural "monuments" is not only an appropriate metaphor for the sustained desire to erase ethnic identity, it is also a common tactic still used among nationalists in India, Bosnia, and the former Soviet Republics, with brutal and often tragic effects.

Many colonial myths were perpetuated during the exposition, including the myth of "progress," or the moral obligation to civilize and educate "backward" peoples. But most important, the exposition provided a lesson in French nationalism. At the opening ceremonies, Paul Reynaud, the *ministre des colonies,* declared the following: "Everyone must feel they are a citizen of *la plus grande France,* the one made up of the five parts of the world [A travers l'exposition il faut que chacun se sente citoyen de la Plus Grande France, celle des cinq parties du monde]."[16] The role of architectural forms as an incarnation of such lofty ideals did not escape Reynaud, who imagined a new and greater French nation. But this imagined community, one that relied on yet unformed common memories, excluded the colonized people who did not have the status of "citizen." For this utopic idea of *la plus grande France* to take hold in the French imaginary, cultural difference would first have to be erased; French culture was to be disseminated and, in return, cultural allegiance pledged. In the colonial period, this meant implementing France's policy of assimilation, a process carried out primarily through education. For the "Founding Fathers" of colonial education, the primary aim of instruction was to teach Western notions to the indigenous people, to make them believe that they were members "of the same human family, of the same nation [de la même famille humaine, de la même nation.]"[17] The legacy of the colonial policy of assimilation can be found in its contemporary form in the much-lauded policy of "integration," which rejects native customs and ways as incongruous and inconsistent with the idea of Frenchness.

Early in this century, Emile Démaret, an *inspecteur des colonies,* better known as the author of a treatise on a federated form of colonial government, opposed the French colonial policy of assimilation and suggested the following system:

> One must not dissimulate it: considering the point which the struggle among peoples has reached, the federative principle will increasingly be imposed upon all

governments. . . . The federative concept is the highest degree to which political genius has been elevated. . . . Because the empire is not made up of people of the same race, speaking the same language, having the same customs; the federative system is superior to all others since it can be applied to all nations and all periods and can unite very different peoples.

[Il ne faut pas se le dissimuler: au point où est arrivé la lutte entre les peuples, le principe fédératif s'imposera de jour en jour à tous les gouvernements. . . . L'idée fédérative est la plus haute à laquelle se soit élevé le génie politique. . . . Parce que l'empire n'est pas peuplé de gens de même race, parlant la même langue, ayant les mêmes moeurs, le système fédératif est en ceci supérieur à tous les autres systèmes qu'il est applicable à toutes les nations comme à toutes les époques et qu'il peut unir des peuples très différents.][18]

In 1931, Marshall Lyautey had envisaged this type of union when, as commissary general to the Exposition coloniale, he called for a "Charter for European colonial policy [Charte de politique coloniale européenne]," that would establish "the holy alliance of colonizing powers [la sainte alliance des peuples colonisateurs]." This European community *avant la lettre*, based on cooperation among European colonial powers, never materialized. Nevertheless, *le principe fédératif* is put forward today as the most sophisticated and efficient political system, one capable of solidifying and buttressing the new European Union.

The establishment of this type of political system has been the object of much discussion. The French Right does not agree on the structure this "union" should take. Some members of the Rassemblement pour la République (RPR) favor a "Union of European States," whereas others reject the "federal construction" and approve of a "Europe of nations." The Parti Républicain speaks of a "fédéralisme décentralisé" and disagrees with those who imagine Europe as a "Super-Etat." Giscard d'Estaing endorses "un fédéralisme d'un type nouveau." The Parti Socialiste, staunch defender of the federalist ideal, speaks of "les Etats-Unis d'Europe" and of "supranationalité." Chevènement, on the other hand, prefers "a large confederation of Europeen States."[19] Curiously, only members of the French Communist Party and those of the Front National see eye to eye. They both affirm their opposition to the treaties that were signed in Maastricht on the ground that they surrender French autonomy, Charles de Gaulle's revered "souveraineté nationale." A "logique d'abdication," reported *L'Humanité* after the parliamentary debate on the question. Le Pen favors "une confédération de l'Europe des patries" against a Europe "open to all migratory and commercial movements [ouverte à tous les flux migratoires et commerciaux]." He considers the Maastricht summit and all of the treaties that will be signed thereafter to be a monumental mistake that will undermine France's national integrity. For Le Pen, the Maastricht Treaty is nothing less than "a crime against the nation."[20]

But what do these crimes consist of? What is *la nation*? These questions are suggestive precisely because they interrogate unexamined assumptions implicit in Le Pen's conception of nationhood, a self-evident view of the "nation" shared by many other French political figures. Le Pen presents the Front National as the staunchest political proponent of the "idea of nation" and the champion of the "national cultural patrimony." By "patrimoine," we mean "every form of expression left in the care of the state to be rescued, looked after or reclaimed [l'ensemble des formes dont l'Etat a la garde pour leur sauvetage, leur entretien ou leur résurrection]."[21] Le Pen exploits French fears of being culturally and socially displaced by "inassimilable," and therefore undesirable, elements. His alarmist declarations on the state of the nation terrify those who cling to the memories of *la vieille France,* a vague and nostalgic idea of the way the nation once was, that is to say, a vision of France uncontaminated by the presence of (Third World) immigrants.[22] He elaborates a notion of a national identity based on the myth of national cohesiveness and of an "imagined" common cultural legacy. A slogan like "La France pour les Français" translates spatially as "There is room in France only for the French," betraying the National Front's racist logic of space management. By portraying France's cultural heritage and patrimony—in other words, the "nation"—as being under siege, the leaders of the Front National reduce a complex situation to easily graspable binary oppositions: us versus them, a clash between French culture under attack by outsiders, aliens, *les étrangers.* This Manichaeism conflates a number of issues under one large and problematic issue: "immigration." But no mention is ever made of the legacy of French colonialism, of the historical and economic circumstances that have made many immigrants settle in France. Le Pen offers racist views without apology, expressing in public forums what was once uttered only privately. He can be credited with ushering in a new political era of racial intolerance. The Immigration Bill introduced by Charles Pasqua, France's former interior minister, in May 1993 bears witness to this turn in French public life, a swerving symptomatic of the times, altering, in scandalous fashion, mainstream political thought.

Immigration has become a national obsession, as the second most discussed subject after unemployment. The extreme-right party has exploited particularly well the question of "immigration" in an attempt to perpetuate the image of a society under attack, threatened by the "invasion" of political asylum seekers, illegal aliens, undocumented workers, and unemployed youth of the *ban-*

lieue. Racism, Islam, *le code de la nationalité* are other issues that have also been placed in the same category as excision, polygamy, and *regroupement familial.*[23] These are some of the most recent polemical issues that have made the news headlines, in part because they have been subsumed under the volatile issue of "immigration."[24] The most revealing examples of nationalist fervor, xenophobia, and racism appear in the various declarations made by members of the political bureau of the Front National on this question.

On 2 November 1991, Bruno Megret, a general delegate and the number-two man of the National Front, on the occasion of a colloquium on ecology organized by the extreme-right party in Saint-Raphaël, advocated what he called a "racial ecology." Megret resurrected fascist ideals of racial purity when he attacked the Greens, one of the French ecological parties, for wanting to preserve animal species without being concerned with the alleged imminent "extinction of human races by generalized interbreeding." Quoting Maurice Barrès and Charles Maurras, Megret declared: "Real ecology goes hand in hand with the defense of identity. . . . It posits as essential the preservation of the ethnic, cultural and natural milieu of our people [L'écologie véritable va de pair avec la défense de l'identité. . . . Elle pose comme essentielle la préservation du milieu ethnique, culturel et naturel de notre peuple]."[25] Speaking of the "French people" as a "species," Megret added: "We do not want to be the mammoths or pandas of the human species [Nous ne voulons pas être les mammouths ou les pandas de l'espèce humaine]." Denouncing the Greens for having accepted "a mass immigration which is transforming our towns into Arab cities," the leader of the far right concluded: "Why fight for the preservation of animal species and accept, at the same time, the principle of extinction of human races by generalized interbreeding? [Pourquoi se battre pour la préservation des espèces animales et accepter, dans le même temps, le principe de disparition des races humaines par métissage généralisé?]" .

Megret's spurious logic can be easily rebutted. Had this *polytechnicien* also read Renan, he would have been perhaps less inclined to link the idea of nation with the question of race. At a lecture delivered at the Sorbonne more than a century ago, Renan spoke of the conflation of nation with race: "Nowadays, a far greater mistake is made: race is confused with nation and a sovereignty analogous to that of really existing peoples is attributed to ethnographic or, rather linguistic groups."[26] As Gellner observes, Renan goes on to "deny any materialist determinism of the boundaries of nations: these are not dictated by language, geography, race, religion, or anything else. . . . Nations are made by human will."[27] Human agency and, more particularly, political will determine to a great extent the imaginary boundaries of the nation. It is with these issues in mind that I now turn to Mitterrand's conception of national culture and his vision of urbanity.

Architecture and Nation Building

Mies van der Rohe once declared that the destiny of modern architecture was to translate "the will of the epoch into space."[28] Mitterrand, conscious of the role and impact of architecture as image building, set out to finish what Habermas has called the "project of modernity," a project that "aims at a differentiated relinking of modern culture with an everyday praxis that still depends on vital heritages, but would be impoverished through mere traditionalism."[29] This modernist imperative would allow the construction of the city of the future, and hence, *la nation de l'avenir,* a project first envisioned by modernist architectural masters such as Le Corbusier and others more than fifty years ago. Mitterrand pursued an ambitious and aggressive policy, endowing the French capital with great new architectural works costing a total of at least seventeen billion francs: the Opéra de la Bastille, the marble cube at La Défense, L'Institut du monde arabe, the Parc de La Villette, la pyramide du Louvre, and La Bibliothèque de France are some of the *grands travaux* that have elicited many controversies in the past decade.[30]

His political adversaries (Jacques Chirac, Raymond Barre, Valéry Giscard d'Estaing), appalled by the level of public spending, claim that the French president wanted to "leave monumental traces of himself so that his other deeds can be forgotten."[31] The guardians of French culture, the Académie des Beaux-Arts and the National Commission for Historic Monuments, on the other hand, accuse him of wanting to disfigure Paris, the repository of French culture. The latest project, the Bibliothèque de France, or the "scandal on the Seine," as one critic put it, is the object of intense scrutiny and the subject of the most recent controversy: "The building of the new French library (the Bibliothèque de France) that is just about to be constructed in Paris is a threat to French culture. It is hostile to books, hostile to people, hostile to the city of Paris."[32] How can a building's architecture threaten French culture, or Frenchness? What makes it threatening?

Much more is at stake in these *grands travaux* than Mitterrand's place in the pantheon of great French *mécènes.*[33] These architectural works construct a certain image of Frenchness, an image that transcends the *dispute politicienne* that marks the political rivalry between the mayor of Paris and the French president. These *constructions de prestige* do not simply promote a French cultural renaissance based in Paris but determine a "new" French cultural identity. The avant-garde monuments to French greatness reestablish a stable, fixed, and solid notion of Frenchness and of a cohesive nation at a time when Frenchness and the idea of *la nation française* are said to be under attack from within, from the "new French," the *Beur* and other French nationals from the former French colonies, whom the French call *Français par acquisition*.[34] The customs and ways of these unassimilated "immigrants"—particularly those from the Maghreb and other parts of the Arab world—are seen as a threat to French society because they undermine its essence. They are in the process of "disfiguring" or "diluting" French culture, Frenchness.[35]

After the collapse of the French colonial empire in the 1950s and 1960s, France's role in the affairs of the world has steadily declined. "Paris, capital of the nineteenth century," as Walter Benjamin described it so admirably, is a waning memory.[36] The disintegration of the former Soviet Union and the Warsaw Pact countries, the reunification of Germany, the realization that the United States is the only remaining superpower, and economic and social problems at home have contributed to making France rethink its role, both in the new European Union and in the world.

Political analysts have suggested that the profound changes in France's cultural and political fortune are the telltale signs of a nation experiencing "an identity crisis." Mitterrand did not shun these reports, which claim that France is "a victim of a crisis in civilization."[37] He believed that, as president of France, his mandate was to regild the nation's blazon. Committing much of the country's public resources to monumental public works designed to reestablish "France's influence [le rayonnement de la France]" and reasserting France's rightful place among the great nations of the world were part of Mitterrand's presidential prerogatives.[38] Thus, Mitterrand's ambitious "politique nationale pour la culture," of which the architectural *grands travaux* in Paris are the most prominent and distinct signs, must be seen in the larger context of France's political and economic interests in Europe and in the world. Mitterrand's role can be likened to that of "the architect of the future" who has a distinct vision of France's place in the new world order.[39] His unwavering pro-European stance stemmed in part from his faith in France and its European partners as a competitive economic superpower, capable of challenging (and eventually surpassing) on all fronts the United States and Japan. "France will remain a great nation," he declared, "but our future lies in Europe."[40] But how is France going to remain a great nation with a distinct and strong cultural image, especially within the new European community? What are the images that must be propagated and that will represent France and allow it to reemerge and be recognized as a world leader?

In 1931, it was widely believed that architecture provided "the best trace of the civilizations of a country, of a civilization."[41] Architecture was regarded as a gauge of the sophistication of a civilization. Half a century later, Mitterrand reaffirmed the status of architecture as the premier art by linking the prestige of a nation with that of its architecture: "I have the profound conviction that there is a direct correlation between architectural grandeur, its aesthetic qualities and the grandeur of a people." He added: "For me, architecture is first among all arts. Moreover, it is a useful art [Pour moi, c'est le premier des arts. De plus, c'est un art utile]."[42] Thus elevated, the *grands travaux* stand as monuments dedicated to rebuilding France's national prestige; they exist to project Frenchness and to leave its mark on the map of the so-called new world order. What remains to be examined, however, is the ideological and political underpinnings of the idea of architecture as "useful art."

Mitterrand has said that through architecture, "we are laying the basis for a new urban civilization." His architectural ambition was to initiate "a powerful movement which will transform the city's relation to man, and thus will eventually build the structures of urban civilization [un puissant mouvement qui changera la relation entre la ville et l'homme et qui donc, enfin, bâtira les structures de la civilisation urbaine]."[43] In keeping with socialist ideals and goals, consistent with a conception of a "socialist" culture program, Mitterrand's politics of useful art set out to be more inclusive, "to extend the world of culture to those who had no access to it [élargir le monde de la culture à ceux qui ne pouvaient y accéder,]" giving access to the underprivileged for collective use; in short, it is the democratization of French culture: "To make works of art, yesterday's and today's knowledge, more accessible to everyone, that is the first ambition of the *grands projets* [Faciliter l'accès de tous aux oeuvres, aux savoirs, d'hier et d'aujourd'hui, telle est la première ambition des grands projets]," proclaims Mitterrand.[44]

The question of access was at the heart of the polemic surrounding I. M. Pei's pyramid at the Grand Louvre. Michel Guy, a former state culture secretary, criticized Pei's design precisely because he believed that it would limit public access to the Louvre. Comparing the pyramid to "a gigantic interchange" that would transform the Louvre "into a bad Roissy of art," Guy asserted that the pyramid with its "single entrance" was "nonsense": "It is contrary to all logic to make the public enter the Louvre by forcing the people to go down to the cellars situated in the center of a court. One does not enter a palace through its basement [Il est contraire à toute logique de vouloir faire pénétrer le public dans le Louvre en l'obligeant à descendre dans les caves, situées au centre d'une cour. On n'aborde pas un palais par ses sous-sols]." According to Guy, Pei's pyramid strikes a discordant note not simply because "it does not fit into an architecturally finished environment [il s'insère mal dans un lieu architecturalement fini]," but more important, because the Louvre has been treated "*à la hussarde* ignoring its history and its being [à la hussarde en ignorant son histoire et son être]."[45] The formula *à la hussarde* is particularly instructive. It connotes a brutal imposition or forced violation, a crime of *lèse-majesté* committed by a barbarian.

Guy criticized not only Pei's conception of the pyramid as "the head and heart of the Louvre Palace" and its design—"a glass pyramid right in the middle of the cour Napoléon [une pyramide de verre au beau milieu de la cour Napoléon]"—but also the architect's lack of "reason, measure, and modesty." Implied is that a foreign architect cannot possibly have the cultural sophistication (what the French call *le bagage culturel*) to comprehend fully the "history" of the greatest French Palace, how it has come to be ("an immense palace with its present configuration, the result of centuries of transformation [un immense palais, grandi au cours des siècles jusqu'à prendre la configuration qui est la sienne aujourd'hui]"). The pyramid is therefore "out of place" because it imposes its alien presence upon "l'être" of the Louvre. "Cette étrangeté architecturale," as Guy and other critics have dubbed it, violates the architectural integrity of the Grand Louvre ("un lieu architecturalement fini") and the critic's aesthetic (and moral) sense of French rational grandeur, a Cartesian perspective that needs no foreign interference. The pyramid fails to blend ("s'intégrer") with its prestigious surroundings. The focus of criticism is less on Pei's modern and unconventional architectural design than on the pyramid as an object of scorn because of its perceived alienness, its foreignness in the French cultural landscape; hence, it is incongruous with and alien to "le patrimoine culturel français."

Mitterrand disagreed with his eminent critics. When asked which of the *grands travaux* he preferred, Mitterrand answered: "La Défense. . . . Et le Grand Louvre pour être juste." The reasons he put forward are consistent with his modernist ideal: "I believe that, after all, I have rather classical tastes and I find myself drawn to pure geometrical shapes [Je crois que, finalement, j'ai des goûts assez classiques et que les formes géométriques pures m'attirent]."[46] Unlike his conservative detractors, Mitterrand believed in "a true pluralism, in the expression of images as well as in that of thought, because everything jostles together and lives together in the same age [un véritable pluralisme, dans l'expression d'images comme dans celle de la pensée, car tout s'entrechoque et cohabite dans la même époque]."[47] Pei's pyramid, a project commissioned directly by the president, some say rather high-handedly, crystallized perfectly his faith in a plurality of images, a juxtaposition of the classical with the modern, conveying, at the same time, his vision of France in the vanguard of this fin de siècle.[48]

Although Mitterrand encouraged a heterogeneity of images for which his ambitious *politique architecturale* will be remembered, he was reluctant to assign political meanings to a vision of the city he considered personal. This resistance does not reveal a lack of foresight. Rather, it expresses the circumspection of an experienced statesman who realized the inherent contradictions in any of his pronouncements or endorsements: "I have a certain idea, yes, but I will not reveal it because I will contradict myself," he confessed.[49] Mitterrand's politics of "useful art" remains, however, an ambivalent and problematic proposition. The formulation is in itself an oxymoron, not only because it presumes that art has a didactic or political role to play, but because it also assumes that art mimetically reflects cultural reality. But if we consider architecture to be a cultural form that elaborates the imagination of French political reality, we can regard it as the privileged realm where different discourses on the nation converge and intersect. Because of the many facets and complex modalities of "useful art," and their aesthetic resonances and political implications, Mitterrand warned against too narrow a functionalist interpretation of the *grands travaux*:

> No monument, no facility is to be equated with its use alone. All of them inscribe, in space and time, a certain idea of the useful, the beautiful, of city life and the dealings of men and women among themselves. In this way do we derive the different meanings of the verb *édifier* in French: to build, but also to signify, to advocate—by example or discursive reasoning—certain values, certain virtues.[50]

Here Mitterrand rearticulated his objective in much more ambivalent terms. A strictly utilitarian or functional view of his *politique architecturale* fails to convey the "poetic" character of his project, one that is difficult to map or describe other than in terms of an "ideal" that is at the same time anchored in and abstracted from reality; a relation between the concrete and the ideal that transcends its more immediate and tangible objectives. Chaslin reports that Mitterrand's ambition was to "inscribe in space and chisel into stone our cultural project [inscrire dans l'espace et à sculpter dans la matière notre projet de culture]."[51] The aesthetic, the historical, the political, the utilitarian, and so on, are, therefore, all subordinated to the imaginary. They partake in a certain ideal of what the French nation is and how it should be represented. But Mitterrand also asserted that these architectural *grands travaux* signify and advocate certain values, certain virtues. What are these values and/or virtues? What was Mitterrand's *projet de culture*?

When the Socialists won the presidential election in 1981, one of their first priorities was to transform the cultural landscape of the country. Among the concrete measures taken was the doubling of the budget of the Ministry of Culture. The minister of culture, Jack Lang, was also given unprecedented powers to promote areas of French cultural life that previous conservative governments had neglected. These "large-scale operations in architecture and urbanism [les grandes opérations d'architecture et d'urbanisme]" were to lead this "cultural transformation." The presidential communiqué that first made public Mitterrand's intentions shows the scope of his ambitious *projet culturel*: "Music at La Villette, opera at the Bastille, rock and jazz at the Porte de Bagnolet, dance in Marseille, comics in Angoulême, photography in Arles, and sculpture in Montpellier [Musique à La Villette, opéra à la Bastille, rock et jazz à la porte de Bagnolet, danse à Marseille, bandes dessinées à Angoulême, photographie à Arles, sculpture à Montpellier]."[52] No aspect of French cultural activities and productions would be shunned. If Paris was to be endowed with many new cultural centers, the provinces would not be forgotten. Lyons would be the home of the Conservatoire supérieur national de Musique; Angoulême, the Musée national de la bande dessiné; Arles, a national school for photography; Grenoble, a national center for contemporary art. The organization of neglected disciplines into full-fledged "national" institutes or schools, to be located in provincial cities, pointed to the Socialists' will to broaden the French conception of culture to include "mass culture" (e.g., "bandes dessinées"). Two key concepts communicate the Socialists' desire to make culture more accessible to the people: "moderne et populaire," which, incidentally, also describes the motto of the new French opera, to be built on "la Place de la Bastille, the scene of symbolic union [lieu de rassemblement symbolique]."

Early in Mitterrand's first seven-year term, Catherine Clément asked the president if he intended to impose a Socialist program of culture on France. He answered: "Socialist culture . . . exists and does not exist. It exists in a certain way, yes, in a social approach to problems, in a concern for the expression of what we believe to be popular aspirations, in our will to make this culture intelligible to the greatest number, to make it accessible to those other than the privileged [La culture socialiste . . . existe, et elle n'existe pas. Cela existe d'une certaine façon, oui, dans une approche sociale des problèmes, dans un souci d'exprimer ce que nous croyons être les aspirations populaires, dans notre volonté de rendre cette culture intelligible pour le plus grand nombre, accessible à d'autres qu'à des privilégiés]."[53] This populist desire for inclusion and openness, for making French culture more accessible, is extended to the understanding of other cultures, fostering tolerance of difference and otherness. The

Arche was originally dedicated as the International Center for Communication, the primary objectives of which were to "open France to the events and cultures of the entire world, and help speed throughout the universe the messages our nation carries [apporter . . . à la France une ouverture sur les événements et les cultures du monde entier, et diffuser . . . à travers l'univers les messages dont notre pays est porteur]" before budgetary constraints forced its conversion into an office complex.[54] Similarly, L'Institut du monde arabe was hailed as the concrete embodiment of the "dialogue between cultures." The foundation was officially sanctioned ("reconnu d'utilité publique") by the French government. The logic and reasoning behind such state recognition deserve to be scrutinized more closely.

One could begin with an analysis of the terms used to describe the official mission of the foundation: "To develop a deeper knowledge in France of the Arab world, its language and civilization. To improve communication, cooperation and cultural exchange between France and the Arab world, in the scientific and technical fields in particular. To better relations between France and the Arab world and thus contribute to the development of relations with the rest of Europe."[55] This overture or "dialogue between cultures" follows the logic of the marketplace. This "cultural" investment is designed to bolster economic profits and facilitate the opening of markets in the Arab world. By cultivating its image as an open and tolerant nation, France privileges its economic partnership with Arab countries precisely because of the importance of their markets, without which fewer outlets for the export of their "technologie de pointe"—telecommunication and computer networks, nuclear technologies, and sophisticated weaponry—could be found.

Although Mitterrand's public works have been the object of critical scrutiny—the focus has been limited to their aesthetic and ideological impact[56]—very little attention has been paid to their inscription in the global economy, a system that sheds light on an unexamined aspect of the *grands travaux*. Mitterrand himself made it unambiguous. When asked to comment on the meaning and coherence of his "politique de grands travaux," he answered, "an aesthetic sense, a desire for architectural creation, the selection of *grands travaux* to stimulate our economy [un sens esthétique, le goût de la création architecturale, le choix de grands travaux pour servir à la relance de notre économie]."[57] Mitterrand reaffirmed this view in a rare 1984 interview granted to *Le Nouvel observateur* when he corrected one of his interviewers as to the "fonction culturelle précise" of each of the "grands projets: "culturelle *et* économique."[58] For Mitterrand, the worlds of culture and commerce are linked in complex ways: "A thriving culture reinforces the French national heritage, propagates knowledge and a spirit of invention, creates centers of production [Une culture vivante renforce le patrimoine national, diffuse l'invention et le savoir, crée des centres de production]."[59] Because some of the primary objectives of the *grands travaux* are to spur capitalist growth, stimulate the French economy, and create new centers of production, Mitterrand's *projet de culture*—that is to say, the cultural logic of postcolonial France—cannot be understood exclusively in aesthetic terms; it must also be seen as a gargantuan economic enterprise that relies on cultural capital. Motivated by economic imperatives, Mitterrand's *projet de culture* participates directly in the global market economy. The *rayonnement de la France,* the influence France wants to exert on the rest of the world, is therefore both cultural and economic.

Mitterrand's capitalist *projet de culture,* however, generates its own aporia. It leaves little room for the disenfranchised, unemployed workers, or new immigrants. It displaces urgent questions concerning the legal and social status of immigrants living in France—more particularly, of the Maghrebin minority in France. Although L'Institut du monde arabe appears to be committed to realizing the notion of "dialogue between cultures," this dialogue is transnational in nature, devoted almost exclusively to improving France's relations with its international economic partners. Because trade relations masquerade as "cultural relations," problematic domestic questions are not given attention. L'Institut du monde arabe rarely addresses, directly and in more concrete fashion, issues that affect the *Beur,* the French of Maghrebin descent. L'Institut du monde arabe attracts only the specialists and researchers, not the disaffected youth of the outskirts who are alienated from both French and Arab cultures. Mitterrand has said that "to live the present means to be able to situate oneself [vivre le présent, c'est pouvoir se situer]."[60] But it is legitimate to wonder how these youth can situate themselves within this cultural space, a space where difference must be abolished or hidden and French culture embraced as one's own.

For Habermas, "the tasks of passing on a cultural tradition, of social integration and of socialization require adherence" to what he calls "communicative rationality."[61] As suggested earlier, colonial education and the teaching of French as a universal culture are examples of such an efficient system of communicative rationality. The deployment of such educational tactics—the legacy of colonial France—can still be seen at work today. The French fear of national disintegration, of "dissociation de l'unité nationale,"[62] is therefore countered by the teaching and dissemination of a dominant (official) French culture, one that strives to incorporate and integrate while glossing over the painful histories of oppressed groups of "French" citizens. The dramatic stories of the resettlement of the *harkis* on French soil following the Algerian War or of the Southeast Asians after the Indochinese War and of their experience of "integration" in France still need to be told. Mitterrand's *projet de culture* fails to recognize the complexity of their stories, perhaps because it espouses the ideology of cultural modernity:

> We have a more universalist view of culture, and we thus take everything into consideration; and, in this whole, there are real differences in expression which are internal to France, the political entity: minority languages, "langages," traditions, art forms. We integrate them: why reject them?[63]

Although Mitterrand's statement is ostensibly about the inclusion of minority cultures and expressions, it also bears the imprint of a distinctly French universalist ambition. Rey Chow has noted, in a different context, that "culture remains a force but largely of social control."[64] It is worth noting that Mitterrand used the cultures of Languedoc and Britanny as examples of different cultural expressions, as if such French linguistic and regional differences constituted the only and most problematic source of cultural conflicts in France today. Can the Maghrebin locate themselves in the current inscription of urban space? Mitterrand believed that everyone living in France can and has a duty to find his or her proper place:

> To live the present means to be able to situate oneself. To bring the future to life is, mixing dreams and knowledge, to choose imagination, education, adaptation to a future which, while it cannot be predicted, is on its way.
>
> These new cultural instruments, born of the *grands chantiers* inaugurated in Paris as in the provinces, can be compared to the communal homes which choose a certain image of the city, this form of collective life where, for the first time 2500 years ago, the Greeks sketched out what we still call democracy. History and simple experience teach us that it is the same for cities as for the rest: harmony is not natural there. It depends on men, on their choices, to inscribe, in space and in time, the will to live together or the reign of exclusion, the desire to unite or the resignation to that which separates.
>
> [Vivre le présent, c'est pouvoir se situer. Donner vie au futur, c'est, mêlant le rêve et le savoir, faire le choix de l'imagination, de la formation, de l'adaptation à un avenir qui, s'il ne se prédit pas, se prépare.
>
> Ces nouveaux instruments culturels nés des grands chantiers lancés à Paris comme en province sont autant de maisons communes qui prennent parti pour une certaine idée de la cité, cette forme de vie collective où, pour la première fois il y a 2500 ans, les Grecs ébauchèrent ce que nous nommons encore démocratie. L'histoire et la simple expérience nous enseignent qu'il en est des villes comme du reste: l'harmonie n'y est pas naturelle. Il dépend des hommes, de leurs choix, que s'inscrivent, dans l'espace et dans le temps, la volonté de vivre ensemble ou le règne de l'exclusion, le désir de relier ou la résignation à ce qui sépare.][65]

To trace the origins of French democracy to classical antiquity and a Greek conception of the city and "communal homes" is to claim a problematic filiation. If classical forms of democratic government are indeed inspiring models, to evoke Greek city-states as an emblem of collective life is also to disregard the imperialist ambition of an Athens or a Sparta, or to ignore the divide that separates the citizens from the subaltern, the slaves and women who did not benefit from the same privileges or freedom. Mitterrand's cultural project wants to cement and unify (*rassembler*) the peoples of France. But it also means absorbing and neutralizing difference by coercing the immigrants into assuming the identity and values of the French, by forcing them to become fully integrated and productive members of the French community of citizens; in short, by exerting considerable cultural pressure. It is therefore "democratic" only if we believe that immigrants willingly reject their own native customs and traditions in order to become full-fledged citizens, and wait enthusiastically to be incorporated and transformed into acquiescing members of the French body politic.[66] The question of integration as a form of cultural coercion is beyond the scope of this essay, but nonetheless therein lies the power and success of the French cultural project. And indeed, through his *grand travaux,* Mitterrand wanted nothing less than to "mold the gaze, the memory and imagination of generations and generations. . . . This is not my ambition, but France's [modeler le regard, la mémoire, l'imagination des générations et des générations. . . . Ce n'est pas une ambition pour moi, mais pour la France]."[67]

Mitterrand and National Cultural Identity

Mitterrand's public works are the new symbols of Frenchness, new because, unlike Beaubourg, the French paradigm of postmodernist architecture,[68] the Arche de la Défense[69] or the Bibliothèque de France are aesthetic embodiments of a different kind, linked to cultural processes that have displaced important issues with urgent implications for French society at large. To borrow Fredric Jameson's words, "They insert a different, a distinct, an elevated Utopian language," distinctive of monuments of high modernism.[70] This shift or return to a high modernist conception of monumental building in this fin de siècle is a symptom of the cultural logic of postcolonial France. This shift away from ethnocultural accommodation and *la société multi-culturelle* toward *La France pour les Français* may be detected in the architectural modernist design of Mitterrand's Parisian *travaux présidentiels.*

If, as Edward Said has argued, "culture itself or thought or art is a highly complex and quasi-autonomous extension of political reality,"[71] Mitterrand's public works elaborate an aesthetic and cultural shift that aims at reestablishing

Paris as the cultural capital of the world through the construction and circulation of "strong" images, which the French language captures metaphorically very well: these images are said to be *porteuses,* imparting the idea of grandeur and importance, while at the same time conveying both a symbolic and imaginary message to which anyone can assign a certain idea or virtue. Hence, their power to evoke and communicate a "utopian" image of the nation. "Well before Foucault, Gramsci had grasped the idea that culture serves authority, and ultimately the national State, not because it represses and coerces but because it is affirmative, positive, persuasive."[72] Mitterrand's *grands travaux* present an image of a modern, progressive, culturally and technologically dynamic "nation," one that claims to be sensitive to cultural differences. But behind the benevolent and democratic facade hides a disturbing cultural logic, one that contains and oppresses in order to transform into the self-same.

Mitterrand's utopic vision of a national cultural identity echoes, in an uncanny fashion, the definition of a nation first advanced by Renan more than a century ago:

> A nation is a spiritual principle, the outcome of the profound complications of history; . . . a nation is a soul, a spiritual principle. Two things, which in truth are but one, constitute this soul or spiritual principle. One lies in the past, one in the present. One is the possession in common of a rich legacy of memories; the other is present-day consent, the desire to live together, the will to perpetuate the value of the heritage that one has received in an undivided form.[73]

> [Une nation est un principe spirituel, résultant des complications profondes de l'histoire. . . . Une nation est une âme, un principe spirituel. Deux choses qui, à vrai dire, n'en font qu'une, constituent cette âme, ce principe spirituel. L'une est dans le passé, l'autre dans le présent. L'une est la possession en commun d'un riche legs de souvenirs; l'autre est le consentement actuel, le désir de vivre ensemble, la volonté à faire valoir l'héritage qu'on a reçu indivis.]

Like Renan, Mitterrand invokes common memories, the illusion of a shared past, as elements that bind men and help form a nation. But a more original insight is to be found in Renan's view of a shared amnesia, a collective forgetfulness, as an element essential for the emergence and construction of a nation: "Forgetting, I would even go so far as to say historical error, is a crucial factor in the creation of a nation [L'oubli et, je dirais même, l'erreur historique sont un facteur essentiel de la création d'une nation]."[74] In this discussion of the construction of *la plus grande France* and of Frenchness, this collective amnesia means forgetting the problematic legacy of French colonialism and its attempt to erase ethnic identity and difference. It also means forcing the *Français par acquisition,* the *Beur* and Maghrebins who are unwilling to abandon their faith in order to be considered full-fledged citizens of France, to conform to a normative idea of the "French citizen." Today, the precarious legal status of North African immigrants in France, and particularly the French-born *Beur*, point to the paradoxical nature of French nationhood, a cultural space capable of incorporating some immigrants while excluding others.

If the Louvre pyramid, once the paradigmatic emblem of *étrangeté architecturale* and the focal point of many acrimonious debates, has today been completely assimilated as an integral part of the French *patrimoine*, the mosque continues to elicit controversies. That the French block and often succeed in preventing the construction of mosques in France shows that architecture is symbolic of nationhood.[75] The mosque does not stand as a symbol of cultural, social, and religious difference, nor simply as a focal point of French xenophobia. It can be seen as a rupturing presence that could bring down these imaginary fortifications, these "échafaudages imaginaires," as Valéry called them,[76] on which the cultural "assemblage" identified as *la nation* rests and against which it is fortified. Slogans such as "No to mosques, no to tchador [Non aux mosquées, non au tchador]" and "In twenty years, it's certain, France will be an Islamic Republic [Dans vingt ans, c'est sûr, la France sera une république islamique]" illustrate perfectly the logic that compels supporters of the Front National to call for the expulsion of Arab immigrants from France and to cling to an elitist notion of a homogeneous French culture. Mitterrand's vision of urbanity and his architectural *grands travaux* fortify the construction of a national cultural identity and of an imaginary homogeneous community. His *projet de culture* constructs a utopian unity and a coherent space where deeply entrenched traditions and values that are perceived as being quintessentially "French" can be anchored. Until a more pluralistic notion of Frenchness and "nationhood" is elaborated in France—that is to say, one that would recognize the untenability of a return to an essentialist notion of culture and nation and account for the transcultural nature of cultural exchanges and dialogues[77]—the *Français par acquisition* or unassimilated minorities will continue to be considered aliens and will be unable to find a legitimate place in this "nation-space," a complex discursive formation capable of preventing new cultural expressions that constitute *la nouvelle francité, la plus grande France*, from rising in the new French urban landscape.

Notes

An earlier version of this essay was first presented at the Ninth International Colloquium in Twentieth Century French Studies, held at the University of Pennsylvania in

March 1992. I thank the participants of the conference for their suggestions, as well as Marina Pérez de Mendiola, James Mileham, Tom Conley, and Steven Ungar, for their insights on previous drafts of this essay. Unless otherwise noted, all translations in this chapter are my own.

1. For a succinct historical analysis of the conditions of the emergence of the French nation, see Eric Hobsbawm, "Waving Flags: Nations and Nationalism," in *The Age of Imperialism* (*1875–1914*) (New York: Vintage, 1989).

2. Edward Said, "Yeats and Decolonization," in *Remaking History*, ed. Barbara Kruger and Phil Mariani (Seattle: Bay, 1989), 3.

3. "Ce sont finalement cinq cent soixante-six chercheurs et universitaires qui ont signé la lettre ouverte consacrée à la Bibliothèque de France et adressée par George le Rider au président de la République. . . . Certains n'auraient pas manqué d'y voir la manifestation d'un noir complot où universitaire rimerait avec réactionnaire et dont le chef d'orchestre clandestin serait tapi dans l'attique poussiéreux d'une bibliothèque. Un épisode de la lutte des pervers frelons et des studieuses abeilles. . . . Première conséquence: le conseil supérieur des bibliothèques (CBS) est chargé par l'Elysée d'une mission d'expertise." "L'architecte et les frelons," *Le Monde*, 14 November 1991.

Vidler's cogent analysis of Dominique Perrault's neomodernist design for the Bibliothèque de France, which was brought to my attention after this essay was written, seems to reinforce my critique of Mitterrand's *plus grande France*. Vidler argues that "Perrault's apparently barren version of modernism" appealed to Mitterrand's close associates because of its "social if not Socialist Universalism." He adds: "Supporters of this latter form of universalism, identified with the French republican tradition and more generally with the values of the French Enlightenment, have found in the Perrault library a rallying point against a host of contemporary particularisms based in identity politics and given special urgency by the pressures of the post-colonial condition. Its reassuring abstract forms, tied to no specific agenda, provide an implicit solution—or at least an impartial and undifferentiated coverall—to the multiple and violently competing visions of 'France' and 'Europe' currently breaking up the traditional Socialist coalition." Anthony Vidler, "Books in Space: Tradition and Transparency in the Bibliothèque de France," *Representations* 42 (Spring 1993): 130.

4. The colonial legacy and its complicated network of diverse social and cultural relations have been described by critics as the "postcolonial condition," an undertheorized question that has been the topic of a special issue of *PMLA*. The acknowledgment of the importance of this field of inquiry is indeed encouraging, but at the same time it suggests an attempt at containing and "institutionalizing" this area of study. See Linda Hutcheon and Satya P. Mohanty, coordinators, "Colonialism and the Postcolonial Condition" (special issue), *PMLA* 110 (January 1995). In her introduction to this issue, Hutcheon says that she sees certain dangers in "the rapid institutionalization of postcolonial discourses" (8). In all, 117 essays were submitted for the issue—"a record number" (12).

5. Edward Said, "Reflections on American 'Left' Literary Criticism," in *The World, the Text, and the Critic* (Cambridge: Harvard University Press, 1983), 174.

6. Ibid., 170–71.

7. See, for instance, Ernest Gellner, *Nations and Nationalism* (Oxford: Basil Black-

well, 1983). Gellner relies on two provisional definitions of nation to help him circumscribe this elusive concept: "1. Two men are of the same nation if and only if they share the same culture, where culture means a system of ideas and signs and associations and ways of behaving and communication. 2. Two men are of the same nation if and only if they *recognize* each other as belonging to the same nation. In other words, *nations maketh man*; nations are the artifacts of men's convictions and loyalties and solidarities. A mere category of persons (say, occupants of a given territory, or speakers of a given language, for example) becomes a nation if and when the members of the category firmly recognize certain mutual rights and duties to each other in virtue of their shared membership of it. It is their recognition of each other as fellows of this kind which turns them into a nation, and not the other shared attributes, whatever they might be, which separate that category from non-members" (7). "On the other hand, a definition of the state, though not entirely satisfactory, is drawn from Max Weber's celebrated definition of it 'as that agency within society which possesses the monopoly of legitimate violence. . . . in well-ordered society . . . private or section violence is illegitimate. Conflict as such is not illegitimate, but it cannot rightfully be resolved by private or sectional violence. Violence may be applied only by the central political authority, and those to whom it delegates this right. Among the various sanctions of the maintenance of order, the ultimate one—force—may be applied only by one special, clearly identified, and well centralized, disciplined agency within society. That agency or group of agencies *is* the state'" (3).

8. Beatrice de Andia, "Un Classicisme époré," in Bertrand Lemoine and Philippe Rivoirard, *L'Architecture des années trente* (Lyon: La Manufacture, 1987), 11.

9. Bertrand Lemoine and Philippe Rivoirard, *L'Architecture des années trente* (Lyon: La Manufacture, 1987), 159.

10. De Andia, "Un Classicisme époré," 17.

11. Lemoine and Rivoirard, *L'Architecture des années trente*, 159–63.

12. De Andia, "Un Classicisme époré," 15, 17.

13. Raoul Girardet, "L'Apothéose de la plus grande France," in *L'idée coloniale en France de 1871 à 1962* (Paris: La Table Ronde/Hachette Pluriel, 1972), 175–99.

14. See Léon Archimbaud, *La Plus Grande France* (Paris: Hachette, 1928). Archimbaud was an early proponent of *la plus grande France*.

15. See Gwendolyn Wright, *The Politics of Design in French Colonial Urbanism* (Chicago: University of Chicago Press, 1991).

16. *Le Temps,* 7 May 1931; quoted in Jacques Thobie et al., *Histoire de la France coloniale 1914–1990* (Paris: Armand Collin, 1991), 217.

17. "L'instruction des indigènes aura cette efficacité de combler la distance et, en les faisant vivre des mêmes notions, de les habituer à se considérer et à se traiter comme les membres de la même famille humaine, de la même nation." Rapport du Sénateur Combes sur l'instruction primaire des indigènes, annexe no. 50 à la séance du 18 mars 1892; quoted in Thobie et al., *Histoire de la France coloniale,* 17.

18. Emile Démaret, "De l'idée fédérative dans une organisation coloniale," Conférence faite en mai 1907 au Grand Orient de France. In 1899, Démaret published his *Organisation coloniale et fédération: Une fédération de la France et de ses colonies,* with a preface by E. Etienne; quoted in Thobie et al., *Histoire de la France coloniale,* 16. Démaret's foresight materialized recently in the form of the new "European Union," which

replaced the "European Economic Community." By 1999, Europeans will use a single European currency (ECU)—that is, if Great Britain does not drag its feet—and may well have agreed to adopt a common foreign policy, the next stage in the development of the union. The "idea of a nation" is therefore undergoing rapid and radical transformation in Europe and elsewhere. Thus, Frenchness or Germanness can no longer be understood exclusively in terms of an individual's political allegiance to a nation, especially when the peoples of the European Union will be "European citizens."

19. Even France's revolutionary anthem is under attack for its bloodthirsty lyrics. Jean-Pierre Chevènement, a former defense minister, opposes any changes to Rouget de Lisle's lyrics. The anthem, he says, is "a symbol of the nation and the republic, indispensable in the formation of the citizens." Alan Riding, reporting for the *New York Times* (international edition), 5 March 1992.

20. Quoted in Thomas Ferenczi, "Logiques françaises," *Le Monde,* 6 December 1991, 17.

21. Catherine Clément, *Rêver chacun pour l'autre: Sur la politique culturelle* (Paris: Fayard, 1982), 209.

22. French polls show that the view of French society based on race and racial purity appeals to more than 16 percent of the electorate. In certain regions, the proportion exceeds 20 percent. See, for instance, the CSA survey published in *Le Monde* on 26 February 1993, in which two out of three individuals interviewed said that there were "trop d'Arabes." A 1992 survey conducted by the Institut français d'opinion publique revealed that 75 percent of those interviewed were completely or rather in agreement with the statement "The safeguarding of French identity is a priority today." See Alain Kimmel, *Le Français dans le monde* 251 (August–September 1992): 53.

23. The May 1993 bill introduced by the Baladur government will amend the French *code de la nationalité*. Citizenship will no longer be an undeniable right. Children of immigrants born on French soil will no longer be automatically French citizens. They will have to choose their nationality between the ages of 16 and 21. The pledge of allegiance to the French nation is, in the words of de Villier, "une vérification de l'assimilation." This racist law targets in particular the Beur.

24. To condemn Mitterrand and his socialist governments for not having done enough to resolve this question is not only simplistic, it is plainly biased. Critics have attacked, from various fronts, the complex question of immigration. See William Safran, "The Mitterrand Regime and Its Policies of Ethnocultural Accommodation," *Comparative Politics* 18 (October 1985): 41–63. The Ministère des affaires sociales et de l'intégration and a number of commissions, such as the Direction de la population et des migrations (DPM) and the Commission nationale consultative des droits de l'homme, have been created to review and deal with this polemical issue. The DPM wrote its annual report on the questions of "immigration et integration," and the Commission nationale consultative des droits de l'homme presented to the prime minister its report authored by André Lebu, *La lutte contre le racisme et la xénophobie: 1990* (Paris: La Documentation française, 1991). In March 1990, the Haut Conseil à l'intégration was constituted, with M. Marceau Long, vice-président du Conseil d'Etat, as its president. The Haut Conseil made the following recommendations in its report titled "Conditions juridiques et culturelles de l'intégration." France will outlaw the practice of excision and of polygamy to protect women and children, and has decided that military service will

no longer be determined on the basis of the immigrant's country of origin but rather on his "country of residence" (*Le Monde*, 7 November 1991, 14). According to the council's spokesperson, the goals of these propositions are not to make immigrants abandon their values and customs, but "de séparer celles incompatibles avec le droit des autres," which means "renoncer strictement à ce qui est contraire aux valeurs fondamentales de la société française" (*Journal télévisé* A2, February 1991). These recommendations could be interpreted in a number of ways, not simply because these "valeurs fondamentales de la société française" are not etched in stone but fluid and changing, but also because the French measure the degree of integration according to two different criteria, the cultural and the social. Integration means both "la quasi-assimilation avec la suppression graduelle des différences entre immigrés et nationaux" and "l'absence de problèmes sociaux favorisé par une organisation communautaire à l'anglo-saxonne" (*Journal télévisé*, February 1991, A2). The question of "assimilation" reemerges, once again, at the forefront of the debate.

These reports, unfortunately, diagnose the symptoms of these problems (in a somewhat sensationalist fashion), without recognizing the legitimacy of cultural difference. The refusal to recognize different strands of Frenchness that have emerged in France today as a result of French colonialism, and that, I believe, constitute the new *francité*, will not prevent the radical transformation of the French landscape and its society.

25. This and the following quotes from Megret are found in Olivier Biffaud, "Ecologie raciale," *Le Monde*, 5 November 1991. Maurice Barrès, for instance, links "Frenchness" to a return to *la terre*, a powerful concept that he develops in his trilogy *Les Déracinés* (1897), *L'Appel au soldat* (1900), and *Leurs Figures* (1902), which he dubs "romans de l'énergie nationale." How a sense of nationness is evoked and what forms of narrative express the ideology of the modern nation are two of the underlying questions that are raised in recent studies of his work, issues that remain relevant today, particularly in light of the current French debate on immigration. For a subtler discussion of Barrès's political trajectory, see Eugen Weber, *My France* (Cambridge: Harvard University Press, 1992).

26. Ernest Renan, "What Is a Nation?" trans. Martin Thom, in *Nation and Narration*, ed. Homi Bhabha (London: Routledge, 1990), 8. This 1882 lecture was published in French as "Qu'est-ce qu'une nation?" in Renan's *Oeuvres complètes*, vol. 1 (Paris: Calmann-Lévy, 1947).

27. Gellner, *Nations and Nationalism*, 8.

28. Quoted in Mike Davis, "Urban Renaissance and the Spirit of Postmodernism," *New Left Review* 151 (1985): 108.

29. Jürgen Habermas, "Modernity: An Incomplete Project," in *The Anti-aesthetic: Essays on Postmodern Culture*, ed. Hal Foster (Seattle: Bay, 1983), 13.

30. See, for instance, Sabine Fachard, Catherine Board, Brigitte Lebbar, and Beatrice Le Guay, *Architectures capitales: Paris 1979–1989* (bilingual ed.) (Paris: Editions de Moniteur, 1992); Bernard Tschumi, *Cinégramme Folie: Le Parc de la villette* (Princeton, N.J.: Princeton University Press, 1987).

31. John Ardagh, *France Today*, rev. ed. (London: Secker & Warburg, 1987), 270.

32. Patrice Higonnet, "Scandal on the Seine," *New York Review of Books*, 15 August 1991, 32.

33. A discussion in time of Mitterrand's "public works" would have to differentiate among the *grands projets,* the *chantiers présidentiels,* and the *grands travaux.*

34. Manfredo Tafuri, in his discussion of utopia and ideology in architectural design, gives this definition: "[Architecture,] at least as traditionally conceived, is a stable structure which gives form to permanent values and consolidates urban morphology." Manfredo Tafuri, *Architecture and Utopia: Design and Capitalist Development* (Cambridge: MIT Press, 1976), 42. Denis Hollier, reading Bataille's *Documents* dictionary entry, complicates this traditional view of architecture as mimesis. He writes: "Architecture captures society in the trap of the image it offers, fixing it in the spectacular image it reflects back. Its locus is that of the imaginary understood at its most dictatorial. . . . Architecture does not express the soul of societies but rather smothers it"; he adds, "It exists only to control and shape the entire social arena." Denis Hollier, *Against Architecture: The Writings of Georges Bataille,* trans. Betsy Wing (Cambridge: MIT Press, 1989), 47, 51.

35. French political leaders, in their attempt to come to the *défense du patrimoine culturel national* have made very revealing xenophobic remarks. The former French Communist Party secretary general, George Marchais, has called Paris "Hong Kong-sur-Seine," referring to what the French call the *mini-ghetto* in the Treizième Arrondissement, the first French "Chinatown." Le Pen has called for a forced repatriation of immigrants; Chirac has complained of the "odor" and has spoken of a "seuil de tolérance"; Giscard d'Estaing, of French society threatened by an "invasion." *La gauche,* on the other hand, recognizes the potential danger of "concentrations géographiques ou de 'ghettos.'" Unlike the Chinese of the Treizième or of Marne-la-Vallée, who are tolerated because they are "laborieux et tranquilles" (selon l'ineffable formule du maire RPR, Jacques Toubon, who was Balladur's cultural minister), the North African Muslims are perceived to be "unassimilable."

36. Walter Benjamin, "Paris, Capital of the Nineteenth Century," in *Reflections* (New York: Schocken, 1986).

37. *Le Monde,* 10–11 November 1991, 9.

38. Christiane Duparc and Guy Dumur, "Parce que je suis amoureux de Paris" (interview with Françoise Mitterrand), *Le Nouvel observateur,* 14–20 December 1984, 44.

39. Paul Valéry *Oeuvres complètes,* vol. 1 (Paris: Gallimard/Bibliothèque de la Pléiade, 1957), 1403.

40. Quoted in Alan Riding, "France Pins Hopes on European Unity," *New York Times,* 1 December 1991, 1.

41. Emile Bayard, *L'Art de reconnaître les styles coloniaux de la France* (Paris: Librairie Garnier Frères, 1931), 2.

42. Duparc and Dumur, "Parce que je suis amoureux de Paris," 45.

43. Ibid., 44.

44. François Mitterrand, "Preface," in "Grands Travaux" (special issue), *Connaissance des Arts,* August 1989, 5.

45. Michel Guy, "Le Louvre de la raison," *Le Monde,* 7 December 1984, 1.

46. Duparc and Dumur, "Parce que je suis amoureux de Paris," 42.

47. Clément, *Rêver chacun pour l'autre,* 291.

48. The pyramid of the Louvre, like L'Arche de la Défense, a cube of 110 meters on a side, covered by white Carrara marble, appeals to a man with classical penchant. But

unlike the pyramid, the Arche was selected for the Tête de la Défense after an international juried competition that was won by the Danish architect Otto von Spreckelsen.

49. Quoted in Clément, *Rêver chacun pour l'autre*, 284.

50. Quoted in Fachard et al., *Architectures capitales*, 8.

51. François Chaslin, *Les Paris de François Mitterrand* (Paris: Editions Gallimard/ Folio Actuel, 1985), 19.

52. *Le Monde*, 10 March 1982.

53. Quoted in Clément, *Rêver chacun pour l'autre*, 281.

54. *Le Monde*, 10 March 1982.

55. Fachard et al., *Architectures capitales*, 78.

56. See Pierre Vaisse, "Dix ans de grands travaux," *Contemporary French Civilization* 15 (Summer/Fall 1991): 310–28.

57. Quoted in Clément, *Rêver chacun pour l'autre*, 287.

58. Duparc and Dumur, "Parce que je suis amoureux de Paris," 44; emphasis added.

59. Ibid.

60. Mitterrand, "Preface," 5.

61. Habermas, "Modernity," 8.

62. Clément, *Rêver chacun pour l'autre*, 282.

63. Quoted in ibid., 281–82.

64. Rey Chow, *Writing Diaspora: Tactics of Intervention in Contemporary Cultural Studies* (Bloomington: Indiana University Press, 1993), 129.

65. Mitterrand, "Preface," 5.

66. Hall and Held analyze the boundaries of citizenship, the responsibilities of citizens, the social contract, and the rights and duties that bind individuals to the nation. Although they discuss the case of Great Britain in the 1980s, their insights also apply to the French context. Stuart Hall and David Held, "Citizens and Citizenship," in *New Times: The Changing Face of Politics in the 1990s*, ed. Stuart Hall and Martin Jacques (London: Verso, 1989), 173–88.

67. Duparc and Dumur, "Parce que je suis amoureux de Paris," 45.

68. Pierre Vaisse, although never using the word *post-moderne* to describe the Centre Pompidou, writes: "Le Centre George Pompidou [offre] une synthèse très réussie, quoique aussi peu fonctionnelle que possible, d'idées de Le Corbusier, de Mies Van der Rohe et surtout des constructivistes russes après la Révolution d'Octobre." He adds, "Ainsi la modernité se trouve-t-elle plus ou moins réduite, bien souvent, à un ensemble de citations des oeuvres de ses fondateurs, à un historicisme, ou à un éclectisme qui ne le cède en rien à celui, si souvent dénoncé des architectes du XIXe siècle." Vaisse, "Dix ans de grands travaux," 325.

69. "L'Arche de la Défense, qui devait être le centre mondial de la communication, a été transformé en immeuble de bureaux. C'était pourtant un changement de programme radical." *Le Monde*, 14 November 1991. "And in 1986, after years of debate, work finally began on an extraordinary project, designed by a Danish architect, Otto von Spreckelsen: it is a cube-shaped office block in white marble, 105 metres high, with a hollow centre so that the sky is visible through it as you view it from a distance. Some people regard it as a monstrosity, others as the fitting crown to a majestic thoroughfare." Ardagh, *France Today*, 261.

70. Fredric Jameson, "The Cultural Logic of Late Capitalism," *New Left Review* 146 (July/August 1984): 80.

71. Said, "Reflections on American 'Left' Literary Criticism," 170–71.

72. Ibid., 170.

73. Renan, "What Is a Nation?" 18–19; "Qu'est-ce qu'une nation?" 903–4.

74. Ibid., 11; 891.

75. Recent elections in Marseilles and Lyons have been decided by campaigns based on anti-Muslim, anti-immigrant, and often anti-EC platforms. In December 1989, "A Marseille, la législative partielle du week-end se joue sur un projet de mosquée rejeté par 57% des Phocéens. A Lyon, même levée de boucliers contre le futur minaret: samedi 25 novembre, 3000 personnes scandaient avec Jean-Marie Le Pen, 'Arrêtez la mosquée!'" Two other slogans of the National Front reveal the extent of their fears: "Non aux mosquées, non au tchador," and "Dans vingt ans, c'est sûr, la France sera une république islamique." From a special dossier titled "Immigrés: L'heure de vérité," published by *L'Express,* 8 December 1989, 35–40. In the 1995 municipal elections, three candidates of the Front National were elected as mayors of the cities of Marignane, Nice, and Toulon, further demonstrating the intolerance of the French concerning the immigration question and their desire to safeguard a homogeneous "French identity."

76. Valéry, *Oeuvres complètes,* 1189.

77. The concept of transculturation, as Mary Louise Pratt defines it, is useful here: "Ethnographers have used the term transculturation to describe processes whereby members of subordinated or marginal groups select and invent from materials transmitted by a dominant or metropolitan culture. The term, originally coined by Cuban sociologist Fernando Ortiz in the 1940s, aimed to replace overly reductive concepts of acculturation and assimilation used to characterize culture under conquest." Mary Louise Pratt, "Arts of the Contact Zone," in *Profession 91* (New York: Modern Language Association of America, 1991), 36.

12 / The Coluche Effect

Steven Ungar

The question of who is (and who is not) French used to be a simple matter when citizenship served as the necessary and sufficient criterion for determining identity. Until recently, children born in France were automatically granted citizenship even if their parents were not French citizens. But as policies and laws have changed in light of evolving attitudes toward foreigners, terms such as *alien, immigrant,* and *naturalization* have become increasingly charged with connotations that vary according to ideology, class, and even geography. I propose in this essay to examine a specific phase in evolving attitudes toward national identity in post-1968 France related to immigration from the former French colonies and protectorates in Morocco, Algeria, and Tunisia. I will illustrate this phase by referring to two 1974 performance texts by Michel Colucci (a.k.a. Coluche), a comedian, film actor, and onetime presidential candidate who died at the age of 41 in a June 1986 motorcycle accident.

Post-1968 France has been marked by the decline and demise of the Gaullist vision that had dominated France's identity as nation and society since the 1944–45 Liberation that followed four years of Nazi occupation. Twice since the Liberation, the providential figure of Charles de Gaulle had been called on to save a France divided against itself: first in 1944, to establish a stable republican leadership in the wake of the Nazi occupation and the Etat Français regime that it had established at Vichy; and again in 1958, when the elected Fourth Republic government was unable to contain violence related to self-rule in Algeria.

It is important to recall that the fall of de Gaulle's personal vision coincided with the final stage of France's decline as a colonial power. By the time de Gaulle died in 1970, a year after he stepped down as French president, debate surrounding the fate of the former colonies and protectorates within what was sometimes referred to as Greater France (*la plus grande France*) had broadened from politics and economics to include aspects of collective identity and symbolic representation linked to the mix of attitudes, opinions, and feelings analyzed by *Annales* historians in terms of *mentalités*. Nowhere did this broadening of debate remain more consistently a problem than in issues raised by immigration from North and sub-Saharan Africa in the wake of France's ouster from Algeria following the March 1962 Evian accords.

Despite the reality of self-rule among France's former colonies and protectorates in Vietnam, Morocco, Tunisia, and Algeria, it is questionable to ground any stable colonial/postcolonial distinction on explicit occupation when the *post-* prefix seems less and less to coincide with an end to practices of exclusion and violence.[1] To restate the point in somewhat different terms, the transition from colonial to postcolonial is neither clear-cut nor innocent. In this sense, the ways that we—as teachers and scholars presumably sensitive to the use, misuse, and abuse of language—talk and write about matters of race, racism, and national identity are more than a matter of precision and/or eloquence. To assert that talk is nothing more or other than words is to mobilize a trope of understatement—litotes—that skirts the very real consequences of "talk" and "words" among individuals and groups. It is the nature of assumptions related to talk concerning immigration and identity in mid-1970s France that I want to explore by reference to what I have come to see as a dissident strain within the prevailing idiom of nationness during the first decade of post-1968 France. Words and talk, as I refer to them, then, are understood as integral components of cultural belonging. As such, they constitute instances of how considerations of class, gender, nation, ethnicity, religion, and age converge in specific constructions of identity within the nation-state.[2]

Through the late 1960s, economic considerations propelled immigration from North and sub-Saharan Africa to France by drawing on an available source of mobile and inexpensive labor. Moreover, because the wages earned by foreigners working in France were subject to taxation, they were a source of revenue unencumbered by the costs of training and benefits afforded to native workers. Over the first decade following the legitimation of Algerian self-rule in 1962, immigration remained very much a one-way movement by which citizens of former colonies and protectorates—especially those from the North African nations of Morocco, Algeria, and Tunisia—brought otherness "home" to France in unprecedented numbers. In 1970, the number of resident foreigners was listed by the Ministry of the Interior at 3,061,000, or 6 percent of the total population. Four years later, the same ministry recorded a figure of 4,128,312.[3] (The 1975 census listed a lower number, slightly fewer than 3.5 million.) Of these four million, about one-third came from North Africa. Statistics for 1974 listed 846,000 immigrants from Algeria, 270,000 from Morocco, and 150,000 from Tunisia. By comparison, figures in the same year for the three leading groups of European immigrants listed 812,000 from Portugal, 573,000 from Italy, and 571,000 from Spain.

The five-year rise occurred against a backdrop of evolving government policies toward immigration that ranged from tightly controlled entry to free-flow integration. As early as July 1968, France imposed a unilateral limit on Algerian immigration (one thousand per month, soon raised to slightly under three thousand). By contrast, government measures over the next six years facilitated integration by empowering foreign workers with various rights of representation. By the time the post of state secretary for foreign workers was created in the mid-1970s, immigration was no longer a temporary phenomenon tied to labor and economics, but a broad social problem involving the same issues of housing, health care, education, and crime that affected the entire population. The heightened violence toward North Africans that accompanied this rise in immigration resulted at least in part from what Etienne Balibar has called the extended "imprint of colonial racism," which undermined any assumptions that a decolonized France had broken with the paradigm of earlier ("colonial") practices.[4] To refer to France in general terms as *postcolonial* was not merely inaccurate, but misleading in that the adjective suggested a break with a longer history of prejudice grounded in assumptions about and attitudes toward race that had adapted to an evolving national identity.

On the evening of 19 May 1974, Valéry Giscard d'Estaing appeared on French national television to thank voters who had elected him president earlier that day over the Socialist candidate, François Mitterrand. While viewers awaited the broadcast of Mitterrand's concession, the nationalized ORTF (Office de la radiodiffusion et télévision françaises) decided to air a program of variety sketches it had prepared in advance to fill in just in case of such an unexpected delay. From this black hole in program scheduling emerged a round-faced man in wire-rimmed glasses and bib overalls—"Enfin Coluche vint!"

"*Vulgaire ou grossier*? [Vulgar or crude?]" This is the story of a man whose sense of the moment from the mid-1970s until his death in 1986 came to earn him a cult following on the French left as well as among a generation of adolescents, former *soixante-huitards,* and politicians who saw through the persona of the *râleur* (malcontent, grumbler) Michel Colucci—a.k.a. Coluche—culti-vated with a vengeance on stage, screen, radio, and record. Tellingly, Coluche's following also spread toward the conservative and reactionary right, among others, who relished his persona of *râleur* with little or even no irony. "Histoire d'un mec sur le Pont de l'Alma" (Story of a guy on the Pont de l'Alma) was a satirical sketch: a would-be *blague* (funny story) in the guise of a traditional oral tale consonant with Freud's sense of the joke (*Witz*) as playful judgment.[5] For Freud, a prime measure of the joke was the artfulness with which it de-flected hostility through the interplay of wordplay, narrative, and enunciation ("delivery"). The teller of the *blague* began by invoking a term—*mec*—to de-scribe someone else ("c'est l'histoire d'un mec") whose story also reflected back onto him. Exactly who—or where—was Coluche in this sketch and how did this single word—*mec*—mark the interplay of identities between the actor and the persona he portrayed? Although *mec* sometimes replaces the generic *homme* to designate an adult male, it occurs more often demonstratively, in, for exam-ple, the pejorative expression *pauvre mec* (jerk) or in contrast to a female equiv-alent, *nana* or *nénette*. More marked with connotations of virility than the terms *type* and *gars*, *mec* also conveys a sense of criminality (*un mec du milieu*), as a shortened variant of *maquereau*, for pimp.[6]

Coluche enhanced the persona of storyteller-as-jokester by setting the lat-ter's problems of self-expression within a disposition that allowed him to laugh at himself. A desire to make himself understood—cast by inversion as his wish to avoid being misunderstood—also measured the speaker's attempt to estab-lish complicity with his audience by relating an amusing story they might share in common at the expense of a third party. Only in his fifteenth line was this at-tempt to narrate characterized as not simply amusing, but exemplary ("non, c'est un exemple"). But what is an example in this context if not a normalized perception? The speaker took pains to identify the *mec* as normal—that is, white (*blanc*)—in order to explain his opening assertion—"Ah oui! Parce que y a les histoires, y a deux genres de mecs [Oh yeah! 'Cause there are stories, two kinds of guys]" before qualifying this assertion as necessary: "Mais des fois on est obligé [But sometimes you really have to]." Necessity was also linked to the the adjective *rigolo* (funny, amusing), the verbal form of which, *rigoler*, is a stan-dard slang equivalent of *rire*. An assertion of difference ("C'est plus rigolo quand c'est un Juif [It's funnier when it's a Jew]") once again jumped categories from race to an unspecified mixing of ethnicity and religion. The analogy it im-plied—normal is to abnormal as white is to Jew—was so clearly skewed that Coluche followed it immediately with an unexpected reversal ("Si on n'est pas juif! [If you're not a Jew!]") that undermined the previous assertion as well as the complicity that it sought to convey. Even more forcefully, a second assertion—"Ben oui, il faut un minimum! [Well, that's the very least]"—further inscribed the initial assertion within an extended series of qualifications whose reversals recalled the loophole phenomenon by which Mikhail Bakhtin has analyzed the twists and turns in Dostoevsky's "Notes from Underground."[7]

Because the assertion of difference could no longer be set apart from the reversals that showed it to be normalized and tendentious, statements that first appeared simple and direct soon evolved (devolved?) into more complex and unstable entities. The resulting pattern of assertion followed by qualification, reversal, or negation attenuated the pleasure of complicity between the speaker and his audience while it set Coluche (as subject of enunciation) apart from the storyteller (as product of the enunciation) he portrayed in the sketch. As the source of utterance, Coluche used this pattern to destabilize sympathetic identification on the part of the audience with a persona from whom he took ironic distance. Consequently, it became increasingly difficult to posit a consistent perspective or frame of reference for statements whose provocation was no longer directed simply at an external third party, but perhaps also on occasion at the audience. Such ambivalence was sustained through an extended slippage of categories. Accordingly, the "normal" white *mec* was set apart from the "dark" Jew along a line of associations that implicitly feminized the latter. Wanting perhaps to cover this slippage, Coluche moved quickly from the Jew to another target of "normal" French *mecs*: the Belgians. Yet once again, the speaker undermined the assertion of difference by mocking the Belgians and the Swiss as mirror opposites equally unaware that only history and geography separated them. Feigned indifference ("je m'en moque [I laugh it off]") pointed to scorn because if, as the *râleur* asserted with pristine logic, there were more racists in France than foreigners, he preferred to have it out (*engueuler*) with the minority. After all, he concluded, none of this really mattered to him ("je m'en fous, hein! [Ya see, I don't give a fuck about it!]") because he was neither Belgian nor Swiss nor Jewish, but normal.

"Histoire d'un mec" relied on attempts to ground identity in categories of normalized difference that the sketch systematically qualified and undermined so that what remained was an extended jokework emanating from a speaker whose links with the audience tempered complicity with ironic distance. Was the Coluche persona at one with his audience? Or was complicity instead a projection of presumption and solidarity that Coluche's *râleur* tempered with uncertainty? "Je me marre"—which translates into English as "it cracks me up" or "I'm splitting my gut"—was cast as a dissenting response to a minor news item (*fait divers*). Anger and dismissal typified the reaction of this *râleur* whose laughter—"je me marre" as a variant of *rire* (to laugh)—was hard and cynical. After briefly describing the situation—twenty Portuguese, men, women, and children living in a single room, a disgusting slum—he asserted strong denial—"je dis non"—and refused sympathy—"ces gens-là n'ont pas raison de se plain-dre"—before defending his right to exploit "nos Arabes [our Arabs]" according to a ludicrous logic of proprietary that played off one minority against another. Slippage from national group ("vingt Portugais") to race ("nos Arabes") implied that specific identity mattered less than the economic and social exploitation of which both groups were victims. Throughout the sketch, the *râleur*'s com-plaints expressed a crude chauvinism that precluded any possibility that the complaints of foreigners might be validated over and above those of ("normal"?) French. Thus, the *râleur* once again corrected—"des fois on est obligé [Some-times you really have to]"—those who saw the Portuguese as worthy people ("ce sont de braves gens") who had come to France looking for work when he countered that they had—in fact—come looking for unemployment because their native country was so poor that unemployment did not even exist. The so-lution, for the normal *râleur*, was to deport all foreign workers—Portuguese, Africans, North Africans, but (curiously) not the Jews—to their native coun-tries, where they would certainly be better off because, after all, these were the very places where normal—that is, white French—people went to spend their vacations!

The two 1974 sketches portray a "normal" white *râleur* whose attitudes con-cerning race, ethnicity, and identity bear strong affinity with the figure of Pierre Poujade, the provincial shopkeeper who founded a short-lived political movement in the mid-1950s by tapping into resentment among small shop-keepers and businessmen opposed to what he and they perceived in common as excessive taxation on the part of the government.[8] Two decades later, Coluche's *râleur* tapped into a similar politics of disaffection whose object had evolved from taxes to immigrants. Yet because the *râleur* vented his resentment with such exaggeration, it was hard—but certainly not impossible—to imagine that anyone could take his words at face value.

The auspicious 1974 television showing of "Histoire d'un mec" earned Coluche a national visibility throughout the rest of the decade, to the point where an issue of *L'Express* featured a cover story titled "La France de Coluche." A new plateau of visibility occurred in the fall and winter of 1980–81 when Coluche declared his candidacy for the presidential elections, or, as he chose to deform them, "les érections pestilentielles [pestilential erections]." Once again, an ability to satirize the prejudices of the chauvinist *mec* implied that the potential to uphold normalized difference at the expense of others was widespread, if not universal. Moreover, such satire precluded serious identification with these prejudices as embodied in a figure who was as ludicrous as he was recognizable.

By the time director Claude Berri cast him as lead in the 1983 feature *Tchao Pantin*, Coluche had already worked extensively in commercial film, notably with Berri in *Le Maître d'école* and with Bertrand Blier in *La Femme de mon pote*. Yet the role of the alcoholic gas station attendant, Lambert, that Coluche played in the new film was striking because it transposed onto the movie screen a curious variant of the *râleur* he had developed a decade earlier. In fact, Coluche's Lambert was less of a ("normal") *râleur* than the kind of loser (*paumé*) portrayed a half century earlier by Bardamu, the first-person narrator of Louis-Ferdinand Céline's *Voyage au bout de la nuit*. With sets by the venerable Alexandre Trauner, *Tchao Pantin* conveyed the same bleak urban setting that Trauner had designed some fifty years earlier for Marcel Carné's classic *Le Jour se lève*. In this sense, Lambert was not just an updated Bardamu, but also a descendant of the 1930s poetic realist persona played by Jean Gabin in films from Julien Duvivier's *Pépé le Moko* to Jean Renoir's *La Bête humaine*. Something in Lambert exuded a fatalism that linked him to Céline's Bardamu as well as to the tough-and-tender figures played by Gabin. Ambivalence here set a degree of sympathy and caring against a potential for violence that moved inevitably toward self-destruction.

Where Céline directed violence in *Voyage* toward the very young, the very old, and the very sick, Gabin's poetic realist persona of the 1930s preyed especially on his female partners. Lambert's identity in *Tchao Pantin* is so layered and his behavior so repressed that his progressive eruption into violence takes on the qualities of retribution validated in response to provocation. As Police Inspector Bauer (Philippe Léotard) surmises after two members of a drug distribution network are murdered, it seems that the police are contending with a self-styled *justicier* (lawman, vigilante). The French term is curious, especially in its mixing of principled integrity with retribution. When Lambert assassinates the two men directly responsible for the death of a young North African, Bensousson (Richard Anconina), whom he had befriended, he destroys a significant part of the distribution network for which Bensoussan had worked and that the police had been trying to break up. Lambert's dirty work serves the ends of the same police in which, it is later revealed, he had once risen to the rank of inspector.

Whatever their motivation, the murders committed by Lambert are acts of violence committed by a white French *mec* against North Africans, even if the latter are seemingly "the wrong kind of North Africans." (It is worth noting that Berri substituted the North African Rachid for the Croat in the 1982 novel by Alain Page from which the screenplay was adapted.) In this sense, intertextual links to Gabin's poetic realist figure can be set against figures of the *justicier* such as Clint Eastwood's Dirty Harry Callahan, the vigilante-assassin played by Charles Bronson in the *Death Wish* films, and—at an even greater cultural distance—John Wayne as the obsessed tracker in John Ford's classic 1956 western *The Searchers*.

What I have described as the Coluche effect in the 1974 sketches satirized normalized perceptions of gender, race, and ethnicity at a moment when the evolving demographics of a post-de Gaulle France precipitated crises of individual and group identities along the lines of race, ethnicity, and gender. *Tchao Pantin* provided further instances of unstable identity in Lambert, the ex-cop whose "normal" life collapsed after his son died of a drug overdose, and in Richard Anconina's Bensoussan, who claims that he is half Jewish and half Arab and who asserts a personal identity somewhere between his alleged uncle, Bensoussan "le roi du couscous" and Bensoussan the author of a volume in the "Que Sais-je?" series the young man keeps in his room.

The complexity of Coluche's Lambert points likewise to gender and, in particular consonance with the tradition of melodrama, to a gap between appearance and reality staged progressively in the film as Lambert turns out to be something more or other than the *mec* or *paumé* he first appears to be. This is the gap in a line—an intertext—that resurfaces verbatim from the "Je me marre" sketch of 1974: "Et puis qu'est-ce que c'est que ces Portugais qui viennent retirer le pain de la bouche de nos Arabes? [And who do these Portuguese think they are coming in and taking the bread out of the mouths of our Arabs!?]," as though to remind the spectator with a memory that a *mec* is not just a *mec* and that identity in postcolonial France is layered, unstable, and not always what it appears to be.

Appendix

I. Extract from "Histoire d'un mec sur le Pont de l'Alma"[9]

C'est l'histoire d'un mec . . .

Vous la connaissez? Non?

Oui? Non, parce que si . . . Non, parce que des fois y a des mecs . . . Bon. Ah oui! Parce que y a des mecs . . .

Non, dites-le parce que quand les gens y la connaissent, après on a l'air d'un con. Alors là, le mec . . . Ah oui! parce que y a des mecs, des . . . Non, c'est un exemple.

Oui, y a des mecs . . . Alors, euh . . .

Ca dépend des mecs, parce que y a des mecs . . .

Alors, bon, des fois, c'est l'histoire avec des bagnoles, tout ça. Et puis le mec, oui, euh . . .

Mais là, non!

Ah oui! Non, là, c'est l'histoire d'un mec . . .

Mais un mec normal. Un Blanc, quoi.

Ah oui! Parce que y a les histoires, y a deux genres de mecs.

Ah Oui!

Alors t'as le genre de mec . . .

"Oui, euh . . . Moi, euh . . . , oui, euh . . . oui, oui."

Le mec, oui . . .

Et puis t'as le genre de mec: "non, non."

Alors on leur dit, mais des fois on est obligé.

Non, le mec, non . . .

Mais normal, je veux dire, pas, un Juif.

Ah oui! Parce que y a des histoires . . . Y a deux genres d'histoires, ah oui! y a des histoires, c'est plus rigolo quand c'est un Juif . . . Si on n'est pas juif! . . . Ben oui, faut un minimum!

Et puis y a les histoires, c'est plus rigolo quand c'est un Belge . . . Oui, si on est suisse.

Ou le contraire, un Suisse, si on est belge.

Pace que les Belges et les Suisses, c'est les deux seules races qui se rendent pas compte qu'en fait c'est pareil.

Mais ils se gourent!

En fait, j'exagère, c'est à cause de la distance qui les sépare. Elle est pas énorme.

Mais, oui . . . Mettons qu'on rencontre un vrai con en Suisse, euh . . . c'est un Belge.

Mais dans l'ensemble, ça valait pas le coup de faire deux pays rien que pour ça, hein! Ils auraient pu se débrouiller!

Enfin, un Suisse, moi je m'en moque, je veux pas m'engueuler avec les gens, moi, hein!

Non, y a quand même moins d'étrangers que de racistes en France!

Non, je veux dire, si j'ai le choix, je préfère m'engueuler avec les moins nombreux.

Enfin, un Suisse . . . Moi, je m'en fous, hein! Je suis ni belge, ni suisse, ni juif. . . . je suis normal!

Translation of extract from "The Story of a Guy on the Pont de l'Alma"

This is the story about a guy . . .

You know it, right?

Right? No, because if . . . No, because sometimes there are guys . . . Ya know.

Yeah! Because sometimes there are guys . . .

Okay! Oh, yeah! because there are guys . . .

No, say so because when people already know the story, afterwards you look like an jerk.

Well, then, the guy . . . Oh, yeah! because there are guys, no, sometimes . . . it's an example.

Yeah, there are guys, because there are guys . . .

Well, okay sometimes, it a joke about cars and all that stuff. And then, the guy, yeah, uh . . .

But in this case, no!!!

Oh, yeah! No, in this case, it's the story about a guy . . . But a normal guy. A white guy, I mean.

Ah yes!

Oh yeah! Because there are jokes, there are two kinds of guys.

Well there's your kind of guy . . .

"Yeah, uh . . . I, uh . . . yeah, uh . . . yeah, yeah."

And then there's your kind of guy: "no, no."

Then you say to them, but sometimes you have to.

No, the guy, no . . . It would probably be a "no" guy.

But normal, I mean . . . not . . . a Jew.

Oh yeah! 'Cause there are stories . . . Two kinds of stories, oh yeah! There are stories, it's funnier when it's a Jew . . . if you're not Jewish! . . . Well, yeah, that's the minimum.

And then there are other stories, it's funnier when it's a Belgian . . . Yeah, if you're Swiss.

Or the contrary, a Swiss, if you're Belgian.

Because the Belgians and the Swiss, they're the only two races that don't realize that in fact it's all the same.

But they're wrong!

In fact, I'm exaggerating, it's because of the distance that separates them. It's not all that much.

But, hey . . . let's say that you meet a real jerk in Switzerland, uh . . . he's got to be Belgian.

But all in all, it's not worth the trouble to make two countries just for this, huh! They should have worked it out!

In the end, a Swiss, me, I laugh it off, I don't want to argue with people, really I don't!

No, 'cause after all there are fewer foreigners than racists in France!

No, I mean if I can choose, I prefer arguing with the minority.

In the end, a Swiss . . . Me, I don't give a fuck, really, 'cause I'm neither Belgian, nor Swiss, nor Jewish. . . . I'm normal.

II. Extract from "Je me marre"

Je me marre . . .

Tout le monde se plaint, maintenant.

Alors, vous ouvrez le journal pour apprendre que vingt Portugais, hommes, femmes, enfants, vivent dans la même pièce, un taudis dégoûtant. Une photo. C'est horrible!

Je dis non!

Ces gens-là n'ont pas raison de se plaindre.

On n'est pas allé les chercher!

Et puis, qu'est-ce que c'est que ces Portugais qui viennent retirer le pain de la bouche de nos Arabes?

Je me marre . . .

Sans compter que sur vingt Portugais y en a quand même un qui pourrait faire le ménage!

Ah! non mais, le personnel c'est une calamité!

Alors on vous dit:

"Ah! mais ce sont de braves gens. Y sont venus chercher du travail en France."

C'est pas vrai . . . Feignants!

Ils sont venus chercher du chômage en France, tellement que c'est pauvre dans leur pays, y a même pas de chômage!

Je me marre . . .

Parce que pour qu'il y ait du chômage quelque part, il faut déjà qu'il y ait du travail.

En France, il y a les deux.

Seulement quand il y a du travail, les travailleurs se plaignent de travailler.

"Oui, on travaille trop, on n'est pas assez payés, on nous fout à la porte quand on est du syndicat."

Seulement, quand il y a du chômage, les chômeurs se plaignent de chômer.

Voilà.

Et on peut même pas concilier les deux en remplaçant les uns par les autres, c'est les mêmes.

Je me marre . . .

Alors, on vous dit

"On n'a qu'à foutre les chômeurs à la porte."

Mais en fait on pourrait . . . renvoyer chez eux: les Portugais, les Africains, les Nord-Africains, les Juifs.

Non, pas les Juifs.

Mais déjà, rien que ceux-là!

D'autant que la majorité d'entre eux serait bien mieux chez eux. . . . La preuve, c'est qu'on y va en vacances!

Je me marre . . .

Translation of extract from "It Really Cracks Me Up"

It really cracks me up . . .

Everyone complains these days.

So you open the newspaper and learn that twenty Portuguese—men, women, children—are living in the same room, a disgusting slum. A photo. It's horrible.

I say no!

Those people have no reason to complain.

We didn't go out looking to get them!

And then, who do these Portuguese think they are coming in and taking the bread out of the mouths of our Arabs?

It really cracks me up . . .

Without considering that among twenty Portuguese you'd think there's at least one who might be able to do the housework!

Ah! it's really impossible to get hired help these days!

So they tell you:

"Oh! but they are fine people. They've come looking for work in France."

It's not true . . . the lazy bums!

They've come looking for unemployment in France, 'cause things are so poor in their country they don't even have unemployment.

It really cracks me up . . .

Because in order for there to be unemployment somewhere there must already be others who work.

In France, we have both.

Only when there's work, the workers complain about working.

"Yeah, we work too much, we're not paid enough, we're fired right out the door when we're unionized."

Except when there's unemployment the recipients complain about not working.

There you have it!

It cracks me up . . .

And you can't even reconcile the two groups by replacing one for the other, 'cause they're the same.

It really cracks me up . . .

Then they say to you,

"You just need to throw the welfare recipients out the door."

But in fact one could . . . send back the Portuguese, the Africans, the North Africans, the Jews.

No, not the Jews.

But already, with nothing but those!

All the more so since the majority of them would be better off where they came from. . . . The proof is that's where we go on vacation!

It really cracks me up . . .

(My thanks to Alain Gabon for help with translating these two routines.)

Notes

Unless otherwise noted, all translations in this chapter are my own.

1. Maxim Silverman, *Deconstructing the Nation: Immigration, Racism, and Citizenship in Modern France* (New York: Routledge, 1992), 7.

2. Rogers Brubaker, *Citizenship and Nationhood in France and Germany* (Cambridge: Harvard University Press, 1992), 162–63.

3. Silverman, *Deconstructing the Nation*, 52.

4. Etienne Balibar, "Racism and Nationalism," in Etienne Balibar and Immanuel Wallerstein, *Race, Nation, Class: Ambiguous Identities* (New York: Verso, 1991), 41.

5. See Sigmund Freud, *Der Witz und seine Beziehung zum Umbewussten* (Leipzig: Deuticke, 1902); published in English as *Jokes and Their Relation to the Unconscious,* trans. James Strachey (New York: W. W. Norton, 1963).

6. My remarks on vocabulary and slang throughout this essay rely heavily on Jacques Cellard and Alain Rey's magisterial *Dictionnaire du français non-conventionnel* (Paris: Hachette, 1981).

7. See Mikhail Bakhtin, *Problems in Dostoevsky's Poetics,* trans. Caryl Emerson (Minneapolis: University of Minnesota Press, 1984).

8. Poujade has rejected any parallels between his activities and a coluchisme he dismissed as a "show-business." See Jean-Pierre Rioux, "La Révolte de Pierre Poujade," in *Etudes sur la France de 1939 à nos jours* (Paris: Seuil, 1985); Roland Barthes, "Quelques Paroles de M. Poujade," in *Mythologies* (Paris: Seuil, 1957).

9. This excerpt and the next are taken from Coluche, *Les Inoubliables* (Paris: Fixot, 1992).

Afterword / Identity: Never More

Tom Conley

Identity Papers has been designed to compare the artifacts of France in the 1930s and those of the postcolonial aftermath in which we live. In their general composition and relation to each other, the essays aim to show that the construct of French identity in the 1930s has much to teach us about similar dilemmas that face France and all industrialized nations at the end of the twentieth century. What was then and what is now are hardly the same, but many parallel issues invite a reconsideration of the ways the 1930s are understood and nonetheless figure in forces that determine current conditions of French culture. The editors and contributors to this volume surmise that the formerly great constructs of self, nation, and culture that are built upon identity, like Taine's "race, milieu, and moment" of the nineteenth century, no longer hold sway; they must, in fact, be reconsidered as we have inherited them, but they must also be pluralized.

Identity often amounts to a fiction of stable subjectivity defined by a predictable development in a given locale. But at the end of our century we realize that it has a history that becomes extraordinarily complex with the accelerations and compressions of space and time brought about by international capitalism. Today identity becomes an arena of conflict in most spheres of activity, in both prewar and postwar culture alike, in geographic and linguistic spaces that are increasingly muddled. In their own ways, the contributors to this volume treat topics of a new canon of twentieth-century French culture studies— Céline as pamphleteer, the agrarian politics of the 1937 Exposition, the iconography of tragedy in the mug of Jean Gabin, Pagnol's Provence in the dialogue about regional and national identity, I. M. Pei's homage to Descartes in the courtyard of the Louvre, *cinéma colonial* of the 1930s and 1970s, Miss France d'Outre-mer, the French merry-go-round about the Holocaust in Julien Duvivier's postwar cinema—from specific disciplinary biases but also along the lines of spatial and ideological displacement. Included are the politics of things French in postcolonial geography; the appeal to history as a way of maintaining national boundaries effaced by Malthusian growth of world population; scapegoating, an effect synonymous with an acting out of aggression wrought by social contradiction; agrarian utopias constructed to paper over the collapse of urban infrastructures; the death drive, seen as a logical consequence of the disarray of codes of civility and civilization inherited from the classical regime— all touch on delicate issues of linguistic, geographic, and historical identity.

The theme has been chosen to suggest how different modes, styles, and objects of analysis can provide access to issues of high logical category that turn specialized research toward interrogation of some generally unnamed—and frequently ineffable or unnameable—principles of culture. *Identity Papers* has been designed to show how both French *and* culture studies can be meshed in such a way that the sharp focus of disciplinary inquiry in the former (literature, cinema, new historicism) will assure breadth and perspective by appeal to the latter (where many boundaries have yet to be redrawn). In debates that address the efficacity and political stakes of cultural studies, the participants have wondered if one runs the risk of using culture either to reiterate truisms or to preach self-evident facts without, first, determining some origins in ideology or history. Culture, in a word, has often been used to avoid the complications of history. To speak of French culture is tantamount to transcending the complex processes that have conspired, it seems, to identify the pertinent traits of French civilization.

In American circles of French literary scholars, critics and historians often wonder if the continual elucidation or refined stylistic analysis of the masterworks of the French canon can sustain the effectiveness obtained when the tradition of the *explication de texte* was aligned with New Criticism, a mode of inquiry that owed many of its origins to the G.I. Bill in the post-1945 era, at the very moment when Camus, Sartre, French cinema, and "the text itself" migrated back over the Atlantic in the same tidal wave. Surely the allure of close analysis of self-contained and self-identical works of trim elegance—*La Princesse de Clèves, Adolphe, L'Immoraliste, La Nausée,* and *L'Étranger*—formed a stark contrast to the billowing prose of English novels, taught in America, that, in the words of Henri Peyre, habitually "went to bed drunk." The orientation gave French literature a mix of order, incisiveness, rectitude, candor, precision, and even *science* unavailable to students listening to tweedy professors sermonizing over Thackeray and Jane Austen. And the resistance that good spoken and written French offered to Americans who lacked training in grammar and prosody had the effect of producing a new awareness of syntax and usage.

But the same critics and historians of French, weaned on New Criticism, now discover that the cadres of the discipline were severely limited and that, moreover, its practitioners may have been the guinea pigs of the elegant failure of a civilizing project that continues to mark the teaching of French. In that project the standards of "perfect French" require speakers to become so oedipalized in their relation to the idiom that they must realize, first, how French can only be extremely complex in its "delicate simplicity" and, second, that its genius is related to centuries of collaboration among lexicographers, creative writers, and geographers born of French institutions. The oxymoron of the naturally "difficult simplicity" of French is a deeply embedded idea: whoever learns and uses the language continually relives a sort of Lacanian mirror stage in which the gap between a desire to speak and the inadequacy of one's motor and intellectual competence is felt to the quick. Or if it is not, the French Academy will be marshaled in the name of a Gallic Superego to correct the most confident and self-assured speakers of the idiom. There ensues the articulation of a closed, depoliticized, boundless space in which the classroom becomes the hothouse of a family romance that takes pride in insulating itself from world-scale dilemmas that know none of the refinements of received French.

No wonder, then, that many scholars who grew into French in the 1960s, like the editors of this volume, now embrace culture studies as a welcome alternative to the *dictée*, the *explication de texte*, or close reading of preordained literary masterpieces. The new discipline can enact revenge on what the passage of time has rendered intelligible. In 1995 the hegemony of French studies in the United States now seems based less on a great cultural past than on a number of strategic operations inherited from nineteenth-century colonial practices. Things French in America masked a diaspora that followed the miasms of the Second World War that had first been felt in France in the 1930s. After 1945, cultures were built in the New World along the lines of those that had prevailed in prewar France, and the passage of a colonial ideology traveled from the experiences of missionaries of the 1930s to their spiritual children of the 1950s and 1960s. Claude Lévi-Strauss notes how enracinated the tradition was when, in the early 1930s, members of the French delegation who had been sent to Brazil "formed a small group. . . . All of us through our careers were riding on our success or failure in Brazil, so we all attempted to surround ourselves with an exclusive court, more important than our neighbor's. It was very French, very academic."[1] At the edge of suburbs bordering the rain forest, a French society was constituted with its own internal agendas that had nothing to do with the surrounding cultures. Americans trained under a system that imposed a French elite in the classrooms of the wilderness can now smile when recalling how many of our French teachers, like Baudelairean albatrosses, produced the highest standards of linguistic refinement in French lessons but otherwise lived pitifully isolated lives in a mixed and bustling world, a world in which were spoken languages the teachers refused to recognize.[2]

Yet the failed colonial endeavor held up to American students an inviolably strong model of competence. It may have set the stage for an oedipal rebellion that can account for some of the shifts we are witnessing from French and Francophone studies to a new discipline of culture as we are experiencing it in a geopolitical sphere. The spiritual children of the generation trained in the postwar years, many of whom are contributors to this volume, are preparing an exodus from things patently French for reasons that are no longer simply driven by Freudian mechanics. Not having grown into the patrician culture of France, but living at a moment when the demarcations established by nineteenth-century geography no longer exist, they see how the spatial, linguistic, and paternal borders that produce identity appear archaic in view of current world problems.[3] They observe how any national identity is an effect of history. They note correctly how identity has evolved in dialogues of cultural exchange.

Before turning to the politics that concern the erasure of nationhood, we might surmise how the contributors to this volume envisage the ways that self-identity and French culture move from philosophical and technological spheres of activity in the late Renaissance to practices that were mobilized in the colonial era of the nineteenth century. The technology of identity reaches back to Descartes, the founder of the concept of the French democratic subject. Both the *Discours de la méthode* and the *Méditations* assure the self-presence of the subject through ontological and causal arguments marshaled to prove that the self stands as an integral—if decorporealized or desomatized—thinking machine. No less dramatically, the self is *mapped out* according to permanent coordinates that fix the cogito at a vanishing point in the perspective of its own creation. At once a god and a common mortal, a transcending and a democratic subject, the "I" acquires presence and agency by virtue of its relation with environing space. The configuration is drawn by engineers (*in-génieurs*), whose expertise in logistics, trigonometry, ballistics, and estate sur-

veying assure the philosopher that self-identity is a product of technological—
and implicitly military—operations. Descartes in fact constructs a *theater of activity* in which the qualities of identity can be mass-produced for the ends of
national defense. One of these traits is good sense; another, the ocular virtue of
the subject who never loses track of cardinal points on all four sides of the body
and the nation; another still, a Frenchness resulting from the marriage of the
national idiom to the design of the *Discours*.

The French vernacular conveys the scientific material alluded to in the author's spiritual itinerary and spelled out in what follows in the *Dioptrique* and
the *Météores*. Jacques Derrida has recently underscored the *national* quality of
the *Discours* in a careful appraisal of the affected modesty of the sixth chapter.
Where the narrator submits to the humility of a project that is written in
French, the critic sees "aucune invention, donc, seulement une puissante combination de discours puisant dans sa langue et contrainte par une sorte de contrat social pré-établi et engageant d'avance les individus [no invention, then,
but only a powerful discursive combination in his language, constrained by a
sort of pre-established social contract that has already engaged its individuals].[4]
The politics of French usage have such strong thrust in Descartes's philosophy
that the printed idiom "translates" the higher, foreign, siteless language of Latin
into a tongue that speaks both for and of the nation in itself, co-opting and
dominating itself in its own name.

Another virtue insinuates into identity a process of spatial assimilation that
grounds the creation of the "I." Where the *cogito*, a substantive that typifies the
self-identical subject, is located at the origin of the Cartesian formula, *Je pense,
donc je suis*, it is already set in a position that enables it to dominate the extension in its midst. It begins in and about the performance of its self-realization.
Its presence is confirmed by its spatial appropriation of itself and its surroundings. In the *Discours* the components of the theater are apparent at the moment
when the French idiom allows the survey of a city plan to be assimilated into
the use of the vernacular.

The square attribute of the Cartesian name, its quadrature, is mirrored at
the center of the self, conceived and executed as a gridded map that duplicates
the complete and enclosed itinerary of the greater body of the *Discours*. Given
that the name of the author is signed in allegiance with the collective trait of
the French vernacular, it stands to reason that the story of the constitution of the
ego, told in covertly diagrammatical terms, schematizes a design of colonization that makes self-identity as its currency. The author's notation of himself at
the center of his discourse establishes a *quincunx* or diapered form that, as
Samuel Edgerton has observed, "'incorporates the very nature of hierarchy. It is

both a recognition of regional differences defined by boundaries, and a recognition that the regions across boundaries are commonly shared."[5] An outward movement of appropriation is fostered when any of the four corners of the square can be transformed into a new center. An extending net of graticules is laid over the world; centers are marked at intersections whose sum yields a "centuriated" scheme.[6] If the words of David Woodward are applied to the context of the latent colonial impulse in the Cartesian scheme being put forward in the configuration of discourse and mapped coordinates, we witness a shift from a stable order of center and periphery in a medieval cosmos to a more abstract notion in which space might "be referenced to a geometrical net of lines and longitude and latitude and could thus everywhere be accorded the same importance."[7] A common idiom, like an equipollent mode of mapping, would attribute *equal* values to the speakers of the social order commonly defined by the "maternal" tongue. Recourse to a victorious vernacular, as if Descartes or the king "were saying to them: to be subjects of the law—and the monarchy, you're now, finally, able to speak your 'maternal French tongue'; as if they were given to the mother in order better to put them under the yoke of the father."[8] The father, identified as France, retains authority exactly where an illusion of primal sovereignty is fostered within the confines of gridded space.

In terms of national identity, we can say that the name of France and things French would extend itself technologically, through an expansive appropriation of space in which equal value is attributed to all points on a surface determined by perspectival means. The latter are determined by the point of view of the subject. Subjective equality would be confirmed linguistically, through the prevalence of one, always self-same idiom that identifies its speakers as those who share the same value and right of being. Self-contained and expansive orders are meshed; they set forward an intellectual structure, under appearance of democracy, that enables colonization by means that are not merely military. To see how they foreground a colonial model we can now look at more recent manifestations produced in the aftermath of the industrial era.

Jean Comaroff and John Comaroff have shown how British colonization of South Africa could not work by exclusively repressive practices.[9] Contrary to popular belief, the colonial moment in European history does not entail wholesale conquest by the sword or the scourge of syphilis. Imposition of one culture upon another cannot take place without dialogue and negotiation of both space and language *between* the indigenous and arriving cultures. To gain ascendency, the conquerors assured themselves success if they planted *ideas* of nationhood, a common idiom, freedom, and agency among indigenous tribes (Botswana is the example given by Comaroff and Comaroff) in order to produce a consciousness that would harmonize with the ideological tokens circulating elsewhere in the colonizer's kingdom. It was incumbent upon the colonizer to delude the native populations into believing that they indeed did own rights to their land; that they were "free"; that their languages, although different from that of the European intruder, were in fact integral to them (the natives could have reason to pride themselves in "owning" their language); above all, that these peoples possessed identities, of their own, that commanded universal respect. Once the concepts of property, space, freedom, linguistic autonomy, and self-identity could be passed off onto the native populations, the land could be redrawn to demarcate areas belonging both to the natives and to the newcomers. A space of dialogue could be carved out where a so-called exchange might be set in place where otherwise war would have raged. In order to effectuate passage away from conflict, unmediated imposition of language or of self-given values, the idea of "rights," of "property," and, not the least, "identity" would have to be set in place. Once these terms could be given to be believed, conquest could be assured. At that point the native culture heeds its "rights," it tends to its property, it develops its self-consciousness, and it legislates its linguistic programs according to the model of the conquerors.

The colonial mechanism perpetuates itself at the point where a cultural identity shifts from a historical to a seemingly "natural" condition. The colonizer and colonized recognize that each other's character is "different," but also that each has "subjectivity" or "agency" enough to act together on issues of mutual concern. The colonizer can gently impose a condition of national selfhood through a massive production of images—such as identity papers that all colonial subjects are required to bear—that confer upon subjects a sense of autonomy. The latter is designed to conform to the picture of natural life as it is said to be led in a daily drama or theater of life from season to season, from day to day, and from minute to minute. In the reordering of everyday life there must be produced the image of a continuum, outside of history, that sums up local character, custom, habitat, and habitude. Through that image or a staging of activities that make up the routine of everyday existence, the colonizers' vital spheres of investment and of production are maintained.[10]

For this reason the regime of literature and cinema are crucial for the project of creating and disseminating icons that characterize the colonizer and the colonized in fields of "mutually productive" exchange. As the chapters in this collection show in different ways, the gap between the reality of the colonized world and the various representations only perpetuates the regime of control. When colonized subjects step into the identity traps put forward in literature, cinema, national expositions, or other cultural productions, they risk being assimilated "into a cultural identity frozen by the ethnology . . . , isolated from society as a whole, withdrawn from history, and doomed to repeat itself in a quasi mechanical way."[11] To steer clear of the trap, the colonized population must shed the garments of a timeless and classless "identity" before producing tactical means, local "ways of doing things," that cannot be co-opted either as commodifiable products or as oppositional units in a Western—and eminently tedious—narrative of conflict of race, class, and gender.

A question that this volume puts forward concerns how and by what means identity can be a useful historical artifact in the domain of cultural studies. A first response might follow the aftereffects of conquest by appealing to pluralization. Pluralized identities can "avoid being disseminated in the occupiers' power grid."[12] A tactic can be launched through the construction of multiplicities or fictions that fragment structures tending to unify nation and language. Partial or multiple identities would be inassimilable without being conflictual or oppositional. A second tactic, related to the academic business of French in the so-called liberal arts, would involve a close and sustained view of the ideology of "cultural studies" in their relation to literature and civilization. Deviating from the French canon in order to be rid of classical texts or great dates and events in French and Francophone history might run the risk of reproducing the dialogical model of colonization adumbrated above. Local practices of analysis, that move between and across boundaries of literature, colonial studies, political science, and the arts, can create different ways of doing things, map out different spaces (and not just those of French genius or the *tradition de qualité* that the notorious professors of pure French invoked above had imparted to American natives in the remote deserts of postwar America!). As Michel de Certeau had argued, focus needs to be shifted from a microoperation of French studies—a practice of heterology in monolingual American contexts—to a macropolitics by which literatures and social sciences decolonize or de-identify each other. Such is the task the contributors to this volume have undertaken.

The experience of the editors of this volume attests to the need to reconfigure literary and cultural studies away from colonial or patently "postmodern" agendas. The French canon, the bedrock of an institution exported to America in the postwar years, still exists and is viable. It comprises a redoutable tradition of analysis and of technical formation that gives discipline, vigor, and aura to the craft of reading and writing. The force of time has led us to discover the more complicated history of its virtues in the messy but seminal ferment of the *entre deux guerres*. This fairly recent past, which had not been touched on in any decisive way in the famous manuals of French civilization that were intended to turn us into docile French subjects—from Mauger to André Lévêque and Simone Verdun—leads us to call into question the related paradigm of *la civilisation française*. It is paradoxical but true that literature and cultural analysis can work in ways that indicate how many of the truisms inherited from postcolonial visions can be distorted creatively, by the very modes that were formerly used to construct identity. The authors of the chapters in this volume have taken decisive steps in this direction.

Notes

1. In Claude Lévi-Strauss and Didier Eribon, *Conversations with Claude Lévi-Strauss,* trans. Paula Wissing (Chicago: University of Chicago Press, 1991), 23.

2. In a polemical defense of feminism against the proponents of what she calls the "righting of May 1968," Naomi Schor argues that adepts of a new French right occupy positions of power in the American academy. Naomi Schor, "The Righting of French Studies: Homosociality and the Killing of 'La pensée 1968,'" in *Profession 92,* ed. Modern Language Association (New York: Modern Language Association of America, 1992), 22–34. Identified as male, as embodiments of a neo-Lansonian method and canon, personifications of French usage in the tradition of Grévisse, avatars of a resistance to pluralization, they are shown aligned with the colonial heritage of conquest that deploys an ostentatious monolingualism. If Schor is correct, these emblematic figures pertain less to a "new" right than to a colonial tradition and a diaspora that reaches back to the *entre deux guerres.* They emigrate from a nation that has never "worked through" its former affiliations with fascism. They seek employment outside of France because the French educational institution is economically blocked or they reproduce, at an unconscious level, strategies of containment that had marked colonial Europe since the nineteenth century (see the discussion of the work of Comaroff and Comaroff below).

3. André Siegfried might be the best proponent of the symmetrical paradigm of French geohistorical identity. In *L'âme des peuples* (Paris: Hachette, 1950), he describes "les trois versants français" in ways that imply how the emblem of the "hexagon" so easily takes hold in the diagrammatical imagination: "France opens onto three horizons. By virtue of this triple orientation, it is at once occidental, continental, and Mediterranean. An original and perhaps unique equilibrium results. On its Atlantic front France looks outside, with a window opened onto the world at large: it thus welcomes extracontinental forces and the temptation to venture to distant lands. . . . By contrast, as a continental nation, it holds to Europe by a bond of flesh and blood that cannot be broken, and is thus quite unlike the insular nature of England. The whole eastern strip of the country, what is bequeathed to it in the legacy of Charlemagne that fell to Lothar [Charlemagne's grandson], already belongs to central Europe with numerous geographic and moral traits that observers cannot fail to remark. From this standpoint we are no longer Atlantic, but Continental, land dwellers, we are essentially Europeans. All of ancient and modern history imposes the conclusion that there can be no France without Europe, and that surely, too, there can be no Europe without France. France is an indispensable element in the greater continental system. On its Mediterranean face, fi-

nally, France is in immediate contact with Africa, Asia, the Middle East, and the Orient, that is, an exotic and prestigious space while, in respect to time, the most illustrious past of all humanity. The founding unity of the Mediterranean needs no commentary; everywhere it is the same, from Marseille to Beyrut, from Smyrna to Barcelona. We are thus related to age-old societies, with forms of culture that Northern Europe considers foreign, but with which we have a secret affinity. While our peasant in alpine Provence is far from the merchant of mechanized culture in the New World, we can find in his person some resemblance with the farmer who tills the slopes of China." Quoted in Gaston Mauger, ed., *La France et ses écrivains,* vol. 4 (Paris: Hachette, 1957), 6–7 (translation mine). Aimed at a foreign market, this manual was used in many advanced courses on French civilization in the postwar years. Siegfried allows us to consider Fernand Braudel's nagging question, "Was France Invented by its Geography?" in *The Identity of France,* vol. 1, *History and Environment,* trans. Siân Reynolds (New York: Harper Perennial, 1990), 263–65.

4. Jacques Derrida, *Du droit à la philosophie* (Paris: Galilée, 1990), 228.

5. Samuel J. Edgerton, Jr., "From Mental Matrix to 'Mappamundi' to Christian Empire: The Heritage of Ptolemaic Cartography in the Renaissance," in *Art and Cartography: Six Historical Essays,* ed. David Woodward (Chicago: University of Chicago Press, 1987), 16.

6. Ibid., 21.

7. David Woodward, "Maps and the Rationalization of Geographic Space," in *Circa 1492: Art in the Age of Exploration,* ed. J. H. Levenson (New Haven, Conn.: Yale University Press, 1991), 87. Following W. G. I. Randles, Woodward adds that in the era just prior to Descartes the practitioners of *observed* or empirical space lagged behind the intellectual ambitions of the Ptolemaic cosmographer. The latter could use the equipollent system of graticules both to envisage and to contain the world by *virtual* means that exceeded those available to navigators. Descartes's system of self-mapping would thus be based on the Ptolemaic plan all the while it could make mental space a viable area for conquest. The impact of method on experience cannot be underestimated, especially in our world, where pragmatics and empiricism are valorized to call into question the efficacy of theory (which in France is inevitably aligned with the Cartesian vision). W. G. I. Randles, "From the Mediterranean Portulan Chart to the Marine World Chart of Great Discoveries: The Crisis of Cartography in the Sixteenth Century," *Imago mundi* 40 (1988): 115–18.

8. Derrida, *Du droit à la philosophie,* 299.

9. Jean Comaroff and John Comaroff, *Of Revelation and Revolution* (Chicago: University of Chicago Press, 1992), 198–202.

10. Comaroff and Comaroff's remarks bring subtle shading to the ways the colonizer produces complicity by means of the allure of dialogue and communication. In this respect, they describe a view that can serve to modify, for example, what Bruce Trigger states about the conquest of French Canada insofar as even the writing of its history complies with the colonizer: "Historians still tend to study native peoples only in terms of their relations with Europeans during the early periods of European settlement. . . . Historical research thus mirrors the social alienation of native peoples from the society that occupies the land that was once exclusively their own." Bruce G. Trigger, *Natives and Newcomers: Canada's "Heroic Age" Reconsidered* (Kingston, Ont.: McGill-Queen's

University Press, 1985), 48. By contrast, Comaroff and Comaroff argue that the civilizing mission sought to establish new discourses of subjectivity based on radical individualism and primal sovereignty. The colonizers divide and conquer, but they also win over the colonized when they allow them to fight back in the terms of the former (e.g., to buy back their own land).

11. Michel de Certeau, *Heterologies,* trans. Brian Massumi (Minneapolis: University of Minnesota Press, 1986), 228.

12. Ibid., 229.

Contributors

Tom Conley is professor of French at Harvard University. He taught at the University of Minnesota from 1971 until 1995. His books include *Film Hieroglyphs: Ruptures in Classical Cinema* and *The Graphic Unconscious in Early Modern French Writing*. His translations include Michel de Certeau's *The Writing of History*, Gilles Deleuze's *The Fold: Leibniz and the Baroque,* and Réda Bensmaïa's *The Year of Passages*. He recently held a fellowship at the Smith Center for the History of Cartography at the Newberry Library.

Anne Donadey is assistant professor of comparative literature and women's studies at the University of Iowa. She specializes in Francophone literature and works at the intersection of feminist and postcolonial theories. She is currently completing a book-length manuscript titled *Palimpsests: Women's Writing between Algeria and France*. Her articles have appeared in *L'Esprit Créateur* and the *French Review*.

Elizabeth Ezra teaches in the Department of French at the University of Stirling in Scotland. She recently edited a special issue of *Diacritics* on French colonial history and its postcolonial legacy, and is completing a book about cultural representations of colonialism in interwar France.

Richard J. Golsan is professor of French at Texas A&M University and editor of the *South Central Review*. He has published books on Henry de Montherlant and René Girard and has edited collections of essays on the literature and film of the German Occupation of France during World War II and fascism and culture. He is currently at work on a book on the Touvier and Bousquet affairs.

Lynn A. Higgins is professor of French and comparative literature at Dartmouth College. She is the author of *Parables of Theory: Jean Ricardou's Metafiction* and *New Novel, New Wave, New Politics: Fiction and the Representation of History in Postwar France* and coeditor of a volume of essays, *Rape and Representation*.

T. Jefferson Kline is professor of French at Boston University. He has authored *André Malraux and the Metamorphosis of Death, Bertolucci's Dream Loom: A Psychoanalytic Study of Cinema, Screening the Text: Intertexuality in the New Wave French Cinema,* and *I Film di Bertolucci.* He is currently at work on a translation of Robert Merle's eight volumes of *Fortunes de France* and a study of autobiography in French film.

Panivong Norindr teaches in the Department of French and Italian at the University of Wisconsin-Milwaukee. He has published essays in French literature, architecture, and cinema in such journals as *French Cultural Studies* and *differences.* His book *Phantasmatic Indochina: French Colonial Ideology in Architecture, Cinema, and Literature* will be published in 1996.

Shanny Peer teaches interdisciplinary courses in French history and civilization in the Department of French at New York University. She has published several articles on the 1937 Exposition in Paris and is currently finishing a book project on representations of rural France, the provinces, and folklore in the exposition. Her other publications include an article on Euro-Disney in the *Tocqueville Review* and an article titled "French Civilization and Its Discontents" in *French Historical Studies.*

Rosemarie Scullion is associate professor of French at the University of Iowa. She has written articles on Céline, Ponge, Duras, Foucault, French fascism, and contemporary French politics and culture, and is coeditor of *Céline and the Politics of Difference* (1995).

David H. Slavin has taught European and world history at Emory, Villanova, and Temple Universities and Bryn Mawr College. His essay in this volume is part of a larger work titled *France and Its Others: White Blindspots, Male Fantasies and Imperial Myths in Interwar Film and Popular Culture.* He has also

published "The French Left and the Rif War: Racism and the Limits of Prole-
tarien Internationalism," in the *Journal of Contemporary History.*

Philip H. Solomon (1940–94) received his Ph.D. in French literature from the
University of Wisconsin-Madison. He was professor of French and chair of
the Department of Foreign Languages and Literatures at Southern Methodist
University in Dallas, Texas. He published two books on Céline, *Night Voyager:
A Reading of Céline* and *Understanding Céline,* and coedited the forthcoming
Céline and Paris in the Twentieth-Century French Novel.

Steven Ungar is professor of French and chair of comparative literature at the
University of Iowa. He is the author of *Roland Barthes: The Professor of Desire*
and *Scandal and Aftereffect: Blanchot and France since 1930* and coeditor of
Signs in Culture: Roland Barthes Today. He has written extensively on twentieth-
century French literature and thought in *Diacritics, Yale French Review, L'Esprit
Créateur,* and *SubStance.* He is completing a book with Dudley Andrew on interwar France.

Florianne Wild is assistant professor of French in the Department of Foreign
Languages and Literatures at the University of Alabama in Huntsville.

Index

5702

WITHDRAWN